**State Projections
of the Gross
National Product,
1970, 1980**

Volume III of
Multiregional Input-Output Analysis

Edited by
Karen R. Polenske

This is the third volume in a series entitled *Multiregional Input-Output Analysis,* edited by Karen R. Polenske. The first two volumes contained descriptions of the data assembly, as well as state estimates of final demands, outputs, employment, and payrolls for 1947, 1958, and 1963. Other volumes in the series will contain a presentation of the complete multiregional input-output model and additional descriptions of the data assembly, as well as state estimates of technology and regional estimates of interregional trade flows for 1963 and projections of outputs and interregional trade for 1970 and 1980.

State Projections of the Gross National Product, 1970, 1980

Raymond C. Scheppach, Jr.
Jack Faucett Associates, Inc.

Lexington Books
D.C. Heath and Company
Lexington, Massachusetts
Toronto   London

The data contained in this book are the result of federally supported research. They may be freely used with the customary crediting of the source.

Library of Congress Cataloging in Publication Data

· Scheppach, Raymond C.
    State projections of the gross national product, 1970, 1980.

    (Multiregional input-output analysis, v. 2)
    Bibliography: p.
    1. Gross national product- United States- States.
2. Economic forecasting. I. Title II. Series.
HC110.15S48   339.373   72-8038
ISBN 0-669-84996-0

Published simultaneously in Canada.

Printed in the United States of America.

International Standard Book Number: 0-669-84996-0

Library of Congress Catalog Card Number: 72-8038

Table of Contents

List of Tables

Figure

Display

Preface

The state projections of final demands described in this volume were compiled for use in the multiregional input-output model that has been formulated and implemented at the Harvard Economic Research Project. Tabulations of the state projections for 1970 and 1980, which are contained in Appendix B, have been reconciled with the national final demand projections published by the Bureau of Labor Statistics. Although the original state estimates were completed in the spring of 1970, revisions were made to them in the spring of 1972, when the Bureau of Labor Statistics published revised 1970 national final demand projections. Four additional sets of data were compiled for use in the implementation of the multiregional input-output model: base-year final demands for 1947, 1958, and 1963; outputs, employment, and payrolls for 1947, 1958, and 1963; 1963 interindustry flows; and 1963 interregional trade flows. The methodology of constructing these estimates and the theoretical structure of the overall multiregional model are described in other volumes of this series.

Since this is the first time that United States data have been assembled for such a comprehensive, large-scale multiregional model, it seemed important to explain the exact procedures used to estimate the state data, thus providing a basis for analyzing, evaluating, and adjusting the figures. All published and unpublished sources used are cited, unless permission to do so was specifically withheld by the agency from which the information was obtained. To make the reading of this technical writing less tedious, only brief references to the sources are given in the text, followed by numbers in square brackets. The numbers refer to the complete bibliographic listing provided at the back of the book.

Since March 1967, when the overall multiregional research project was officially begun, a major portion of the work has been done at the Harvard Economic Research Project. However, a substantial amount of the data assembly, such as that for the research reported in the present volume, was done by the staff of Jack Faucett Associates under subcontracts with the Harvard Economic Research Project or under separate contracts with the Office of Business Economics for the interregional trade flows and with the Office of Civil Defense and the Institute of Defense Analyses for an initial set of 1963 output estimates. All of the remaining data were originally assembled by the Harvard Economic Research Project under contract #7-35212 with the Office of Economic Research of the Economic Development Administration, U.S. Department of Commerce. Additional government agencies that had become interested in the overall multiregional project supplied part of the funds to complete the contract in 1970. These agencies are the Office of Systems Analysis and Information, Department of Transportation; the Bureau of Labor Statistics, Department of Labor; the Office of Emergency Preparedness, Executive Office of the President;

the Office of Civil Defense, Department of Defense; and the Bureau of Mines, Department of the Interior. During the period 1971–1972, extensive revisions were made to all the data under a contract between the Office of Systems Analysis and Information, Department of Transportation, and the Harvard Economic Research Project.

Carolyn Anderson and Mary Shirley, of the Harvard Economic Research Project, assisted with making final consistency checks of the tabulations presented in Appendix B. As far as possible, all of the material in this volume has been checked for accuracy. Some of the research, however, had been completed by staff members of Jack Faucett Associates who were no longer available to consult concerning final revisions, either to the data or to the descriptions presented. Raymond Scheppach and I therefore take full responsibility for any errors that may have escaped detection.

Karen R. Polenske

Acknowledgments

As with any research effort, a number of individuals contributed to the completion of the state projections of final demand. Major contributions were made by Emily MacFall, Ernest Mosbaek, Ida Pepperman, Joan Pinsky, John Rodgers, and Theophilos Terrovitis. The computer programming was done by Leo J. Mueller and John W. Eden. Secretarial assistance was given by Mary B. Whittaker, Lee Matthews, and Phyllis Twilley.

The research also benefited greatly from the overall guidance of Jack G. Faucett.

Finally, I wish to acknowledge the valuable assistance provided by staff members of various federal government agencies, particularly the Office of Business Economics of the Department of Commerce and the Bureau of Labor Statistics of the Department of Labor.

Raymond C. Scheppach, Jr.
Jack Faucett Associates, Inc.

List of Abbreviations

AEC   Atomic Energy Commission
BLS   Bureau of Labor Statistics, U.S. Department of Labor
CBP   *County Business Patterns*
CCC   Commodity Credit Corporation
Census   Bureau of the Census, U.S. Department of Commerce
CES   1960 Consumer Expenditures Survey of the Bureau of Labor Statistics
CO   Capital Outlay
DOD   Department of Defense
EDA   Economic Development Administration, U.S. Department of Commerce
FCC   Federal Communications Commission
FG   Federal Government
GNP   Gross National Product
GPCF   Gross Private Capital Formation
GPDI   Gross Private Domestic Investment
GPO   Government Printing Office
GSA   General Services Administration
HERP   Harvard Economic Research Project
HEW   Department of Health, Education, and Welfare
IO   Input-Output
IOPCE   Input-Output Personal Consumption Expenditures
JFA   Jack Faucett Associates
MRIO   Multiregional Input-Output
NASA   National Aeronautics and Space Administration
NEXP   Net Foreign Exports
NINV   Net Inventory Change
NPA   National Planning Association
NSF   National Science Foundation
OBE   Office of Business Economics, U.S. Department of Commerce
PCE   Personal Consumption Expenditures
R&D   Research and Development
SIC   Standard Industrial Classification
SLG   State and Local Government
SMSA   Standard Metropolitan Statistical Area
TVA   Tennessee Valley Authority

**State Projections
of the Gross
National Product,
1970, 1980**

1 Introduction

Projections of final demand by state to 1970 and 1980, the subject of this book, were used as input to the multiregional input-output (MRIO) model implemented at the Harvard Economic Research Project [54]. This model provides a framework for systematic analysis of the economic interdependence among industries and regions of the United States. These projections, in combination with the model, will provide analysts their first opportunity to make in-depth analyses of the regional economic impact of proposed or actual changes in, say, state and local and federal government purchases of goods and services. The direct and indirect effects of specified changes can be measured in terms of changes since 1947, 1958, and 1963 output, employment, and payroll estimates are available from another part of the MRIO project; these estimates are described by John M. Rodgers in *State Estimates of Outputs, Employment, and Payrolls, 1947, 1958, 1963* [60]. Additional uses of the MRIO model include transportation planning and analysis of regional needs for such public services as energy, water, and sewerage. Still other uses are certain to be found, especially at this time, when regional imbalances in the full utilization of economic resources are receiving greater recognition in the focus of public policy.

A complete set of projections by region has been estimated for six components of final demand—personal consumption expenditures, gross private capital formation, net inventory change, gross exports, state and local government net purchases of goods and services, and federal government purchases. The projections were made for 51 regions—the 50 states plus the District of Columbia—and 87 input-output industries. The input-output industries are listed in the appendix, Table A-1. Despite the restricted amount of available data and at times limited statistical techniques for making the projections, the total effort was centered on obtaining a complete input-output industry specification of final demand by region.

For each of the six components of final demand, the sum of the purchases of goods and services by input-output industry in each region was reconciled with the national projections of the Bureau of Labor Statistics (BLS). Although all the 1980 projections published by the BLS have an implicit 4.3 percent annual growth rate of gross national product (GNP), the 4 percent unemployment basic model was chosen for use in this project because it most closely parallels the historical performance of the United States economy [158]. The 3 percent unemployment model can be valid only if monetary and fiscal policies are extremely effective—but historical evidence is to the contrary.

1

Table 1-1
1965, 1970, and 1980 Final Demands (millions of 1958 dollars)

	1965 Actual	1970 Projection	1980 Projection
Personal consumption expenditures	$397,700	$478,600	$ 751,909
Gross private capital formation	90,100	101,000	171,410
Net inventory change	9,000	2,500	13,291
Net foreign exports	6,200	2,500	9,500
State and local government net purchases of goods and services	56,800	74,500	124,600
Federal government purchases of goods and services	57,900	68,800	84,300
Total Final Demand	$617,700	$727,900	$1,155,010

NOTE: The net export figures given in the table are dependent on projections of gross imports and exports. These projections are as follows (millions of 1958 dollars): 1970 exports = 52,500; 1970 imports = 50,000; 1980 exports = 77,839; and 1980 imports = 68,339.

The original BLS national projections for 1970, published in 1966 [160], are dated in that they do not represent a good estimate of either the expected actual trend or the long-term trend compatible with the 4 percent unemployment basic model for 1980. Fortunately, a new set of 1970 projections was made available for this study. The new data are from supplementary statistical tables to the BLS report entitled, *Projections of the Post-Vietnam Economy, 1975* [162] [1] Table 1-1 presents the 1970 and 1980 national projections that were used as control totals.

In making projections of final demand by region, the major difficulty encountered was the lack of any reliable data base. This study therefore revealed and identified priorities for data development. Discussions on the limitations of available data and suggestions for improvement are included throughout the book.

Although the projection techniques differ considerably from component to component, a substantial amount of the effort was applied to developing time series and other statistical relationships for individual states. The maximum quantity of historical state and other regional data was employed to assist in specifying regional differences. Only when regional data were not available was there a reliance on national relationships.

Chapters 2 through 6 describe the projection methodologies for the six basic components of final demand. The 1970 and 1980 state projections of final demand are included in Appendix B.

---

1. The original set of 1970 state estimates was determined in the spring of 1970 by using a linear interpolation between the 1965 actual and the 1980 BLS projection for each input-output industry. These projections were calculated by functional category—education and highways, for example. The present set of 1970 estimates was obtained by prorating the new set of BLS control totals over the original set of state estimates.

2 Personal Consumption Expenditures

Personal consumption expenditures (PCE) is the most important of the five components of final demand, representing approximately 65 percent of GNP in 1969. That percentage is expected to remain relatively unchanged during the 1970s, indicating an average annual growth rate of about 4.5 percent.

Because of the extreme volatility of the investment component, relative changes in total final demand are considerably more unstable than those in PCE. The stability of the relative changes in PCE makes it comparatively easy to generate long-term national projections of PCE, even in input-output industry detail. The dearth of historical regional consumption data, however, hampers such projections of PCE at the state level. Although the Regional Economics Division of the Office of Business Economics is currently working in this area, it will be several years before a significant amount of data is available. Independent researchers have produced a limited number of estimates as part of gross state product statistics for the New England states [52] and Ohio [31], but detail and coverage differ to such an extent that the usefulness of these data for this project was limited.

The choice of a projection methodology was severely restricted by this general lack of historical regional data on PCE in input-output detail. Three basic procedures were considered. The first was to use Harvard Economic Research Project (HERP) 1963 estimates to construct predicting equations by a cross-section approach employing as explanatory variables: temperature differences, urban-rural population mix, level of educational attainment, and personal income. This approach was rejected because the HERP estimates were based upon observed data for only four regions.

The second method was to develop per capita forecasting equations from national time-series data and then apply them to projections of population by state. This procedure was unacceptable because important regional differences are neglected.

Lack of data and the need to identify regional differences in the estimating equations directed the choice of a third method—the basic procedure used in the calculations at HERP of estimates for 1947, 1958, and 1963. The methodology was modified, however, in several places, which will be specified later in the chapter.

3

Table 2-1
Eight Income Distribution Groups

Under $1,000	$4,000 - $4,999
$1,000 - $1,999	$5,000 - $5,999
$2,000 - $2,999	$6,000 - $9,999
$3,000 - $3,999	$10,000 and over

General Comments on Methodology

As of 1972, the most comprehensive regional consumption expenditures data available were the 1960–1961 data given in the Consumer Expenditures Survey (CES) published by the U.S. Department of Labor, Bureau of Labor Statistics (BLS). This survey presents considerable industry detail on average consumption by region, residence, type of family, and income class. At HERP, the detail was reduced to facilitate making PCE estimates by state for 1947, 1958, and 1963[1] by converting the 1960–1961 data to 87 input-output categories and aggregating the consumer units to 32 classes for each of the four regions. The 32 categories of consumer units comprise eight income classes for each of four population groups: urban families, urban unrelated individuals, rural families, and rural unrelated individuals. The eight income classes are given in Table 2-1.

Using these 1960–1961 average consumption expenditures data for four regions as converted by HERP, weighting them by the 1970 and 1980 projected population by income class, and aggregating the PCE estimates that resulted for the 32 consumer units, the necessary state PCE projections were obtained in input-output detail. A rather stringent assumption was necessary: that the consumption of a given item by a family type with similar income and residence will be the same in 1970 and 1980 as it was in the 1960–1961 period. For example, it was assumed that the amount spent on IO-14, Food & kindred products, by a family with an income of between $5,000 and $6,000 a year residing in an urban area of a particular region will be the same in 1970 and 1980 as in the base period. Since the CES data were restricted to four regions, this procedure could be used only under the additional assumption that the average consumption expenditures for all states within a given region were identical. The four regions used in the CES and the states within each region are presented in Table 2-2.

Since it was believed that the per capita consumption of certain items by consumers in a given income class would vary substantially from one state to another within a given region, an effort was made to determine the extent of

---

1. For an explanation of this conversion, see the first volume of this series, *State Estimates of the Gross National Product, 1947, 1958, 1963* [58].

Table 2-2

States Listed by Four Consumer Expenditures Survey Regions

Region 1 – Northeast	Region 2 – North Central	Region 3 – South	Region 4 – West
1. Connecticut	10. Illinois	22. Alabama	39. Arizona
2. Maine	11. Indiana	23. Arkansas	40. California
3. Massachusetts	12. Iowa	24. Delaware	41. Colorado
4. New Hampshire	13. Kansas	25. District of Columbia	42. Idaho
5. New Jersey	14. Michigan	26. Florida	43. Montana
6. New York	15. Minnesota	27. Georgia	44. Nevada
7. Pennsylvania	16. Missouri	28. Kentucky	45. New Mexico
8. Rhode Island	17. Nebraska	29. Louisiana	46. Oregon
9. Vermont	18. North Dakota	30. Maryland	47. Utah
	19. Ohio	31. Mississippi	48. Washington
	20. South Dakota	32. North Carolina	49. Wyoming
	21. Wisconsin	33. Oklahoma	50. Alaska
		34. South Carolina	51. Hawaii
		35. Tennessee	
		36. Texas	
		37. Virginia	
		38. West Virginia	

Note: The states, except Alaska and Hawaii, are arranged alphabetically within each region.

these deviations.[2] Of the ten input-output industries analyzed, only five were found to display substantial consumption differences. The five are as follows: IO-31, Petroleum refining & related industries; IO-59, Motor vehicles & equipment; IO-72, Hotels & lodging places; personal & repair services, except automobile repair; IO-73, Business services; and IO-76, Amusements. For these five industries, an adjustment was made to the consumption figures for those states where the differences were large.

The aggregate for each state for each input-output industry was expressed in purchaser prices to conform with the average consumption expenditures data. To make the estimates consistent with the final demand concept developed by the Office of Business Economics (OBE), the purchaser price figures were later converted to producer prices. Conversion was accomplished by subtracting the values of the transportation, trade, and insurance margins from each consumption expenditures item and adding them to the appropriate input-output industry: IO-65, Transportation & warehousing; IO-69, Wholesale & retail trade; or IO-70, Finance & insurance. This adjustment changed the distribution among input-output industries but not the aggregate total. Certain nonmarket imputations, foreign expenditures, and out-of-home-city expenditures were then added to the relevant input-output industry totals before reconciling the aggregate of all states with that of the nation.

Specific Methodology

For the explanation which follows, the nine states of Region 1, Northeast, for 1970 are used, but the same methodology is applicable to the other three regions, which include the remaining 41 states and the District of Columbia, and for the four regions in 1980.

Step 1. The average consumption expenditures in input-output detail for the region, IO_C, were multiplied by the population projection, PE, for the nine states in the region to obtain a vector of personal consumption expenditures in purchaser prices, IO_E, for each state for 1970.

$$
\begin{array}{ccc}
IO_E & = & IO_C & * & PE \\
(87 \times 9) & & (87 \times 32) & (32 \times 9)
\end{array}
\qquad (2.1)
$$

Step 2. Nonmarket imputations, foreign expenditures, and out-of-home-city expenditures, *AD,* were added to the relevant input-output industries by state to obtain adjusted personal consumption expenditures in purchaser prices.

---

2. For example, the average consumption of amusements for a similar type of consumer living in New York and Maine would be expected to differ considerably.

$$IO_A = IO_E + AD$$
$$(87 \times 9) \quad (87 \times 9) \quad (87 \times 9) \tag{2.2}$$

Step 3. The adjusted personal consumption expenditures in purchaser prices, IO_A, were converted to producer prices, IO_P, to be consistent with the final demand definitions. This was accomplished by subtracting the value of the transportation, trade, and insurance margins, *MA*, for each of the 87 industries.

$$IO_P = IO_A - MA$$
$$(87 \times 9) \quad (87 \times 9) \quad (87 \times 9) \tag{2.3}$$

The total for all 87 industries for each of these categories, that is, transportation, trade, and insurance, was then combined into a single entry, *MT*, and added to IO-65, Transportation & warehousing, IO-69, Wholesale & retail trade, and IO-70, Finance & insurance, respectively, by state to give final unreconciled personal consumption expenditures totals in producer prices, IO_N.

$$IO_N = IO_P + MT$$
$$(87 \times 9) \quad (87 \times 9) \quad (87 \times 9) \tag{2.4}$$

Step 4. The discrepancy between the total for all states and the national total as projected by the BLS was distributed to the states by a uniform percentage, *K*. It was assumed that the bias occurred in the same relative magnitude in all states. This gave final state projections of personal consumption expenditures in producer prices, IO_F.

$$IO_F = K * IO_P$$
$$(87 \times 9) \quad (87 \times 87) \, (87 \times 9) \tag{2.5}$$

Population Projection

To be consistent with the CES, the projection of total population for each state was divided into 32 categories. This required a division of both the family and unrelated individual totals into urban and rural residences. Each of the four categories (urban families, urban unrelated individuals, rural families, and rural unrelated individuals) was then distributed to eight after-tax income classes.

Insufficient historical data created the prime difficulty in projecting these population groups. The *Census of Population, 1960* [123] provides the only historical data available for the required population break on a state-by-state basis. Although other data, based on samples of birth- and death-rates and school enrollment, were published by the Bureau of the Census for the period 1965–1969, the categories are not consistent with the CES breakdown, nor are the data sufficiently reliable for use in this study.

The remaining parts of this section will discuss the following procedures: (1) projection of the total number of families and unrelated individuals by state; (2) division of families and unrelated individuals into urban and rural residences; and (3) distribution of the estimates from procedure (2) to the eight after-tax income classes.

Projection of the Total Number of Families and Unrelated Individuals by State

Although the Bureau of the Census (Census) does not project families or unrelated individuals by state, it does project the number of households by state to 1970 and 1975. Since households represent approximately 95 percent of the total of all families and unrelated individuals, the Census projection of households was used as the basis for these projections.

The first step was to extend the Census projections of households to 1980. Since the growth in households, however, is primarily a function of the population in the age class 19 to 25, and the growth rate in this age class has been historically unstable, mere extrapolation of past trends would not be sufficiently accurate. Therefore, the Census method for this extension was chosen. Essentially, the method applies ratios of the number of individuals in a given age class to the number of families by household type from the *Census of Population, 1960* to a projection of the number of individuals in the age class. Households are classified as husband-wife, other male-head, and female-head families, as well as male and female primary individuals. Age classes are: 14–19, 20–24, 25–34, 35–44, 45–54, 55–64, and 65 and over. Consequently, there are 35 ratios for each state, that is, seven age class ratios for each of the five household types. Assuming these ratios to be constant between 1960 and 1980, the 1980 projection of the number of households by state was obtained by applying them to the Census projection of the 1980 population by age class. For example, 7 percent of the population in 1960 in the age class 14–19 in Georgia was husband-wife families. Thus, 7 percent of the total population in 1980 in age class 14–19 in Georgia, as projected by the Census, was assumed to be husband-wife families. A similar procedure was used to obtain estimates for each of the 35 categories for each of the 51 regions.[3] The sum of the total number of households by state was then reconciled with the 1980 national projections.

To derive the total number of families in 1970 and 1980 by state, the growth rate of the sum for the three categories—husband-wife, other male-head, and female-head families—was applied to the base-year number of families by

---

3. The term "51 regions" will be used throughout this book to represent the 50 states plus the District of Columbia. It is not to be confused with the four CES regions previously discussed.

state as reported in the *Census of Population, 1960*.[4] Similarly, the growth rate of male and female primary individuals was used to project the total number of unrelated individuals by state to 1970 and 1980 with the *Census of Population, 1960* estimates providing the base to which the growth rate was applied.

Urban and Rural Distribution of Families and Unrelated Individuals

The projections of the total number of families and unrelated individuals in each state had to be divided into urban and rural residences. As a first approximation, the 1970 and 1980 totals were distributed between residences according to the *Census of Population, 1960*. The first approximations of the two urban categories (families and unrelated individuals) were then adjusted by the following factor:

$$\left(\frac{PM^i_t}{PS^i_t} \right) \div \left(\frac{PM^i_{1960}}{PS^i_{1960}} \right) \qquad \begin{array}{l} i = 1, 2, \ldots, 51 \text{ states} \\[6pt] t = 1970, 1980 \end{array} \qquad (2.6)$$

where

PM^i_t = metropolitan population of state i in year t

PS^i_t = total resident population of state i in year t

The growth in metropolitan areas was taken as an average of the population growth in the Standard Metropolitan Statistical Areas (SMSA) within each state as projected by the National Planning Association [49]. Since SMSA's represent over 90 percent of the total urban population, the growth in metropolitan population was assumed as representative of the growth in urban areas. An additional assumption was that the growth in the metropolitan population was representative of both urban families and urban unrelated individuals. The rural total for both family types was determined as a residual by subtracting the urban estimates from the previously projected totals.

Income Class Distribution

The 1970 and 1980 projections of urban families, rural families, urban unrelated individuals, and rural unrelated individuals by state were then distri-

---

4. Since there is a slight difference between the CES family definition and the sum of husband-wife, other male-head, and female-head families, a more accurate estimate could be obtained by applying the growth rate to the 1960 actual estimates from the *Census of Population, 1960*.

mean income was identical to the change in per capita income for unrelated individuals.

The 1970 and 1980 mean income projections are based on per capita income projections of the National Planning Association [49]. Estimates of urban family size in 1970 and 1980 by state were obtained by adjusting the 1960 family size for each state by the projected national change between 1960 and 1970 (and between 1960 and 1980). The urban and rural family mean incomes were then estimated by multiplying this new family size by metropolitan and nonmetropolitan per capita income by state as projected by the National Planning Association. The metropolitan and nonmetropolitan per capita income for 1970 and 1980 were taken as urban and rural mean incomes for unrelated individuals. Change in mean income between 1960 and each of the two projection years was then determined from the above data.

Technique for Deriving the New Distribution

The technique employed was the one used by the Income Division, Bureau of the Census. Essentially, the original 1960 information was transformed into a cumulative percentage distribution and the distribution was shifted upward, based on the percentage change in the mean income between 1960 and the projection year. By interpolation and extrapolation, the projection year cumulative percentage distribution was then calculated for the original income classes. The percentage of total population that fell within each class was determined by subtraction. The number of families and unrelated individuals by income class were then determined by multiplying total population by the percentage within each income class.[6]

The results from this method are reliable if the distributions are not significantly different from log normal and the class intervals are not large. Since one of the class intervals was somewhat large ($6,000-$9,999), the base-period distribution was adjusted before making the shift in order to reduce the possibility of error. This was achieved by dividing the total population falling in this $6,000-$9,999 class into four smaller classes: $6,000-$6,999, $7,000-$7,999, $8,000-$8,999, and $9,000-$9,999. The subdivision was calculated from generalized tables prepared from Pareto curves that were fitted to frequency distributions having varying degrees of concentration in the upper class intervals.[7] The procedure can be formalized as follows:

---

6. For a complete explanation of this method, see Mitsuo Ono, "A Graphic Technique for Projecting Family Income Size Distribution" [53].

7. For a complete explanation of this method, see Mary F. Henson, "Trends in the Income of Families and Persons in the United States, 1947–1964" [27].

Table 2-3
The Pareto Curve Distributions (percent)

A	$6,000 – $6,999	$7,000 – $7,999	$8,000 – $8,999	$9,000 – $9,999	$6,000 – $9,999
2.0	35	27	21	17	100
2.0–2.9	40	27	19	14	100
3.0–3.9	44	27	17	12	100
4.0	45	27	17	11	100

Source: Mary F. Henson, "Trends in the Income of Families and Persons in the United States, 1947–1964" [27].

$$A = \frac{F6}{F10} \qquad (2.7)$$

where

$F6$ = cumulative percentage above $6,000

$F10$ = cumulative percentage above $10,000

The percentage of population within each class was computed from the distributions given in Table 2-3.

The method used to determine the projection year distribution can now be formalized as follows:

$$S = \frac{\overline{Y}^{70}}{\overline{Y}^{60}} \qquad (2.8)$$

where

$\overline{Y}^{60}$ = mean income in 1960

$\overline{Y}^{70}$ = mean income in 1970

$$F_i^{70} = \left(\frac{Y_i}{R_j}\right) \cdot \left(F_j^{60}\right) \qquad (2.9)$$

where

F_i^{60} = 1960 cumulative percentage distribution at given income levels

F_i^{70} = 1970 cumulative percentage distribution at given income levels

Y_i = income levels

R_i = $S \cdot Y_i$

i, j = income levels $1, 2, \ldots, 8$

The relation of j is such that $\left| \dfrac{Y_i}{R_j} - 1 \right|$ is a minimum.

An example of this calculation is given in Table 2-4, using the urban family classification.

Special Adjustments

Because the CES does not include data on some nonmarket expenditures or foreign expenditures, adjustments had to be made to the aggregate totals to reconcile this inconsistency with the PCE definition. Additional adjustment was necessary to incorporate expenditures by individuals outside their states of residence. All the procedures are described below. In addition, the methodologies used to convert from purchaser to producer prices and to make special regional adjustments are described in the following section.

Nonmarket Imputations

The values of imputations were estimated independently, since nonmarket goods are not included in the CES. National income accountants advocate such imputations to minimize the impact of institutional and cultural changes on economic measures. For example, if there were a marked shift in the number of people growing and consuming their own food to those purchasing it from others, GNP would exhibit an upward bias. In order to compensate for such a shift, the value of consumption in kind for several important categories is added to PCE.

Imputations which were given special treatment are:[8]

---

8. Although there is a fourth imputation—the rental value of owner-occupied housing—a proxy for these average consumption data was available in the CES. Consequently, it was projected by the same method as all other PCE items.

Table 2-4
Example of an Urban Family Projection by Income Class—1970

1	2	3	4	5	6	7	8	9
Income Classes (Under)	Number of Families by Income Class	Cumulative Percentage of Families by Income Class 1960	1970 Income Levels[a]	$\left[\dfrac{Col.\ 1}{Col.\ 4}\right]$	Extrapolation or Interpolation $[Col.\ 5]/[Col.\ 3]$ Class 1970	Cumulative Percentage of Families by Income Class 1970	Noncumulative Percentage Distribution	Number of Families by Income Class 1970[b]
$ 1,000	4160	3.8	$ 1,237	$1,000 / 1,237	(.81) (3.8) = 3.1	3.1	3.1	4005
2,000	3830	7.3	2,474	2,000 / 2,474	(.81) (7.3) = 5.9	5.9	2.8	3617
3,000	6309	13.0	3,711	3,000 / 2,474	(1.21) (7.3) = 8.8	8.8	2.9	3747
4,000	11305	23.2	4,948	4,000 / 3,711	(1.08) (13.0) = 14.0	14.0	5.2	6718
5,000	11948	35.8	6,315	5,000 / 4,948	(1.01) (23.2) = 23.4	23.4	9.4	12144
6,000	14065	48.5	7,422	6,000 / 6,185	(.97) (35.8) = 34.7	34.7	11.3	14599
7,000	⎫	60.1	8,659	7,000 / 7,422	(.94) (48.5) = 45.6	45.6	⎫	⎫
8,000	36601	65.0	9,896	8,000 / 7,422	(1.08) (48.5) = 52.4	52.4	35.0	45217
9,000	⎭	75.9	11,133	9,000 / 8,659	(1.04) (60.1) = 62.5	62.5	⎭	⎭
10,000		81.5	12,370	10,000 / 9,896	(1.01) (69.0) = 69.7	69.7		
>10,000	20623						30.3	39145

(c marks the brace in Column 3; d marks the brace in Column 8)

[a]This is the shift in mean income times the original income levels. The projected mean income shift between 1960 and 1970 = 1.237.
[b]The total number of families in 1970 was independently projected to be 129,192.
[c]This distribution is determined by the Pareto curves as stated in the methodological description.
[d]Since the $6,000–$10,000 category was divided only for computational purposes, it is now collapsed back to the original income classes.

1.   Food, clothing, and housing in kind.
2.   Services furnished without payment by financial intermediaries.
3.   Food and fuel produced and consumed on farms.

Food, Clothing, and Housing in Kind.   The total imputation for this category in both 1970 and 1980, as projected by the BLS, is slightly in excess of two billion dollars. Based on this small dollar value and the fact that over one-third of the total is for military purposes, whose state distribution is expected to be stable over time, it was judged that a reliable base-period state distribution would be representative for both projection years.

In estimating the state distribution for the base period, unpublished 1968 data from the Office of Business Economics, U.S. Department of Commerce, were used to obtain the percentages for seven occupational groups, given in Table 2-5. For each occupational group, a proxy variable was employed to obtain a state distribution. By summing the state values for the seven occupational categories, the total value for nonfarm food, clothing, and housing in kind was estimated for each state. The important proxy variables and their sources are presented in Table 2-6. For each state, the total was then distributed to input-output industries based on the percentages given in Table 2-7.

Services Furnished Without Payment by Financial Intermediaries.[9]   The 1968 national total for this imputation was first broken down by type of institution, as shown in Table 2-8. Each subcategory was then distributed to states, based on the proxy variable presented in Table 2-9. For each state, the total value of the imputation was determined by summing the values for all institutions.

Correlation analysis of cross-section data for base year 1968 strongly supported the hypothesis that a state's personal income and share of financial imputation are positively correlated. The National Planning Association projections of total personal income by state for 1970 and 1980 were therefore used as a proxy to distribute the BLS national totals [49]. For each state the total was added to IO-70, Finance & insurance.

Food and Fuel Produced and Consumed on Farms.   The national total for this imputation, as projected by the BLS, was only 882 million dollars in 1970 and 814 million in 1980. Given this small dollar value, as well as the expectation that no significant future shift will occur in the state distribution of farms, the 1968 distribution was assumed to be valid for 1970 and 1980. The 1968 data are

---

9. This imputation is for the services rendered and interest accrued but not paid to financial accounts. For example, the interest accrued to a demand deposit account is cancelled out by the service charged by the institution, leaving a small residual that must be paid by the depositor. Consequently, an imputation was made for both the interest accrued and the service fee.

Table 2-5

Occupational Detail of Food, Clothing, and Housing Imputation

Occupational Category	Percentage
Military personnel	33.4
Restaurant employees	10.7
Hotel employees	4.6
Domestic help	18.5
Private hospital employees	22.7
Government hospital employees	7.8
Private school employees	2.3
	100.0

Source: Unpublished 1968 data from the U.S. Department of Commerce, Office of Business Economics [131].

Table 2-6

Data Sources for Distribution Proxies for Food, Clothing, and Housing Imputation

Occupational Category	Proxy	Source
Military personnel	U.S. military population as of June 30, 1969	[142; 143]
Restaurant employees	Payrolls for eating establishments, 1963	[70]
Hotel employees	Payrolls for hotels and motels, 1963	[70]
Domestic help	Annual taxable household wages of employees under Old-age, Survivors, Disabled, and Health Insurance, 1964	[151]
Hospital employees	Payroll expense of federal and total hospital employees, 1966	[70]
	Payrolls of state and local government hospital employees, 1966	[70]
Private school employees	Enrollment in nonpublic elementary and secondary boarding and combined schools, 1965–1966. Average pupil-teacher ratio in nonpublic elementary and secondary schools, 1965–1966	[148]
	Average annual salary of instructional staff in full-time public elementary and secondary schools, by state, 1965–1966	[148]

Table 2-7

**Distribution of Food, Clothing, and Housing Imputation
to Input-Output Industries**

Industry Number	Industry	Percentage
1	Livestock & livestock products	1.2
2	Other agricultural products	1.5
3	Forestry & fishery products	.3
14	Food & kindred products	45.5
16	Broad & narrow fabrics, yarn & thread mills	4.3
18	Apparel	2.6
34	Footwear & other leather products	1.0
71	Real estate & rental	42.2
80	Imports	1.4
		100.0

Source: Unpublished 1968 data from the U.S. Department of Commerce, Office of Business Economics [131].

Table 2-8

**Distribution of Financial Intermediary Imputation
by Type of Institution**

Type of Institution	1968 Distribution (millions of dollars)	Percentage
Commercial banks	$5,779	80.3
Mutual savings banks	205	2.9
Savings and loan associations	513	7.1
Credit unions	103	1.4
Other (investment trusts and holding companies)	600	8.3
Total	$7,200	100.0

Source: Unpublished 1968 data from the U.S. Department of Commerce, Office of Business Economics [130].

Table 2-9

**Data Sources for Distribution Proxies for the
Financial Intermediary Imputation**

Type of Institution	Proxy	Source
Commercial banks	Savings deposits as of June 29, 1968	[20]
Mutual savings banks	Savings deposits as of June 29, 1968	[21]
Savings and loan associations	Interest received (on mortgage loans, investment and bank deposits, and all others), 1968	[22]
Credit unions	Dividends and interest to members, 1968	[149]
	Total dividends on 1968 shares and total interest refunds, 1968	[150]

Table 2-10
Distribution of Imputation for Food and Fuel Produced and Consumed on Farms to Input-Output Industries

Industry Number	Industry	Percentage
1	Livestock & livestock products	13.5
2	Other agricultural products	10.2
14	Food & kindred products	41.8
20	Lumber & wood products, except containers	34.5
		100.0

Source: Unpublished 1968 data from the U.S. Department of Commerce, Office of Business Economics [131].

published in *Farm Income Situation* [67]. The allocation to input-output industries is given in Table 2-10 and was assumed to be constant for all states.

Out-of-Home-State Expenditures

Underlying the general methodology is the implicit assumption that all expenditures in a state are actually made by residents of the state. Consequently, an adjustment was made for out-of-state expenditures by residents. The CES contained observations for five types of out-of-home-city expenditures: food, lodging, recreation, transportation, and all-expense tours. Because transportation was assumed in general to be bought in the state of residence, no special adjustment was made for this expenditure. National totals were projected to 1970 and 1980 for the other four categories by weighting projected national population, stratified according to income class and residence, by the average national expenditures from the 1960-1961 CES.

Because the "all-expense tours" category is really an aggregation of food, lodging, recreation, and transportation expenditures, the national total was distributed as follows: 32 percent to food, 38 percent to lodging, and 6 percent to recreation. The remaining 24 percent was separately classified as transportation expenditures. This distribution is shown in Table 2-11.

The transportation values for all-expense tours were first allocated to four regions of the country according to data on the number-of-person trips, other than by automobile, originating in each of the four regions in 1967 [74]. Within each region, the values for this category were distributed to the states on the basis of 1970 and 1980 population projections. The dollar value for each state was then added to IO-65, Transportation & warehousing.

For food, lodging, and recreation, a state distribution of hotel and motel employment was obtained from the *Census of Population, 1960* [123]. A growth rate for each state, based on a projection of employment in lodging places and personal services by production area, was applied to the 1960 data

Table 2–11

Out-of-Home-City Expenditures Projection by Category, 1970 and 1980
(1958 dollars)

Category	Total Dollar Value	+	Part Of All-Expense Tours	=	Grand Total Distributed To States
		1970 Distribution			
Food	$3,371,629	+	$1,125,455	=	$4,497,084
Lodging	4,121,148	+	1,336,477	=	5,457,625
Recreation	507,996	+	211,023	=	719,019
Transportation	–	+	844,091	=	844,091
		1980 Distribution			
Food	$5,848,508	+	$1,833,279	=	$7,681,787
Lodging	7,085,110	+	2,177,019	=	9,262,129
Recreation	800,297	+	343,740	=	1,144,037
Transportation	–	+	1,374,960	=	1,374,960

Table 2–12

Distribution of Out-of-Home-City Expenditures to Input-Output
Industries by Category

Industry Number	Industry	Percentage
	Food	
1	Livestock & livestock products	3.00
2	Other agricultural products	4.90
3	Forestry & fishery products	0.80
10	Chemical & fertilizer mineral mining	0.01
14	Food & kindred products	87.79
65	Transportation & warehousing	0.20
69	Wholesale & retail trade	0.50
80	Imports	2.80
		100.00
	Lodging	
72	Hotels & lodging places; personal & repair services, except automobile repair	94.50
77	Medical, educational services, & nonprofit organizations	5.50
		100.00
	Recreation	
76	Amusements	100.00

Source: Polenske, K.R., and others, State Estimates of the Gross National Product, 1947, 1958, 1963 [58, t. 2–7, p. 38].

Table 2-13
Projection of Foreign Expenditures in the United States
By Type of Visitor (millions of 1958 dollars)

Type of Visitor	1970	1980
Canadians	$ 472	$ 768
Mexicans	339	501
Other visitors	508	924
Total	$1,319	$2,193

base to determine 1970 and 1980 employment by state. Each category, that is, food, lodging, and recreation, was then distributed to input-output industries as shown in Table 2-12.

Personal Consumption Expenditures Made
by Foreigners

Time-series data on expenditures made by Canadians, Mexicans, and other foreign visitors were projected to 1970 and 1980,[10] and the estimates were adjusted to make their total agree with the BLS control totals of all foreign expenditures. This projection is shown in Table 2-13.

According to an article in the *Survey of Current Business,* June 1967 [37], 78 percent of the expenditures by Mexicans were made in border states and 22 percent in the interior of the United States in 1966. The 1970 and 1980 projections of Mexican expenditures were consequently divided into these two categories (border states and interior states), based on the 1966 distribution. Each total was distributed to the relevant states according to the projected distribution of hotel and lodging employees by state for 1970 and 1980.

Data on point of expenditures made by Canadians in 1967 were obtained from *Travel Between Canada and Other Countries,* Dominion Bureau of Statistics, Canada [9]. Approximately 7 percent of Canadian expenditures were made by people leaving and returning on the same day by car. For 1970 and 1980, 7 percent of the estimated Canadian expenditures were distributed to the border states according to the number of hotel employees in these states. The remainder was allocated to the various regions of the country according to 1967 data on the number of Canadian visitors to each region, and within each region according to the number of hotel employees in each state. Similarly, the expenditures of "other visitors" were distributed to the states on the basis of the projections of

---

10. Historical data are from the *Survey of Current Business,* June issues, 1963-1969 [32-38].

Table 2-14

Distribution of Foreign Expenditures to Input-Output Industries

Industry Number	Industry	Percentage
14	Food & kindred products	30.9
16	Broad & narrow fabrics, yarn & thread mills	1.9
18	Apparel	14.0
54	Household appliances	3.9
63	Optical, ophthalmic, & photographic equipment & supplies	2.0
65	Transportation & warehousing	14.7
71	Real estate & rental	2.0
72	Hotels & lodging places; personal & repair services, except automobile repair	21.9
76	Amusements	8.7
		100.0

Source: Unpublished 1968 data from the U.S. Department of Commerce, Office of Business Economics [131].

Table 2-15

Input-Output Industries Analyzed to Determine Whether State Consumption Patterns Deviated from Those of the Region

Industry Number	Industry
14	Food & kindred products
18	Apparel
29	Drugs, cleaning, & toilet preparations
31*	Petroleum refining & related industries
59*	Motor vehicles & equipment
67*	Radio & TV broadcasting
72	Hotels & lodging places; personal & repair services, except automobile repair
73*	Business services
75	Automobile repair & services
76*	Amusements

*Significant deviations were discovered.
Sources: [1; 70]

hotel and lodging employees. The total for each state was then divided among input–output industries using the percentages given in Table 2-14.

Deviation of State Consumption Patterns from Those of the Region

A methodology which assumes that the bill of goods purchased by an individual in a state is identical to that for the region excludes many important geographic differences. To determine whether an adjustment to compensate for these differences was desirable, the ten input-output industries given in Table 2-15 were further analyzed. This evaluation consisted of plotting average consumption by state against average income and comparing them with that of the region. Industries in which expenditures were large or were expected to show significant differences among states were chosen. Only five of the ten evaluated appeared to exhibit state patterns significantly different from those of the region for reasons other than differences in income.

A separate state estimate based on a deviation between the state and regional average consumption expenditures was then determined for each of these input-output industries. Table 2-16 presents the sources used in calculating these deviations. For the five selected input-output industries, total PCE by state was determined by weighting these new averages by the relevant population projection, as explained in the general methodology section.

Transportation, Trade, and Insurance Margins

The projections of consumption are actually in purchaser prices, thereby requiring a conversion to producer prices for consistency with input-output industry definitions. The BLS 1970 and 1980 national transportation, trade, and insurance margins were used for all states. They indicate the cost of transporting the goods from the producer to the consumer, the amount paid to wholesalers and retailers for distributing the goods, and insurance on the goods. The total value of transportation was subtracted from the purchaser value for each industry, summed, and then added to IO-65, Transportation & warehousing. The same procedure was followed for the trade and insurance margins, which were added to IO-69, Wholesale & retail trade, and IO-70, Finance & insurance, respectively. By this procedure, total PCE of a state is not changed—only the distribution to input-output industries. The actual margins used are presented in Table 2-17.

Table 2-16
Data Sources for State Differences from Regional Averages

Industry Number	Industry	Source	Remarks
31	Petroleum refining & related industries	*Petroleum Facts and Figures, 1967 Edition* [1]	Sum of heating oil #2, gasoline, liquid petroleum gas, lubricating oil and lubricating grease. Barrels were converted to gallons and total value was determined by applying national prices.
59	Motor vehicles & equipment	*Census of Business, 1963.* Vol. I [70]	Table 2: lines 380 and 420.
72	Hotels & lodging places; personal & repair services, except automobile repair	*Census of Business, 1963.* Vol. VI [70]	Table 9: sum of hotels, motels, etc. (pp. 1–57); and other repair services (pp. 1–72); minus armature rewinding (pp. 1–73).
73	Business services	*Census of Business, 1963.* Vol. VI [70]	Table 9: sum of armature rewinding (pp. 1–73); and total miscellaneous business services (pp. 1–62).
76	Amusements	*Census of Business, 1963.* Vol. VI [70]	Table 9: sum of motion pictures (pp. 1–75); and other amusements (pp. 1–75).

Table 2-17
1970 and 1980 Transportation and Trade Margins

Industry Number	Industry	Transportation[a]		Wholesale and Retail Trade[a]	
		1970	1980	1970	1980
1	Livestock & livestock products	.01994	.01935	.21197	.20842
2	Other agricultural products	.11600	.10991	.34227	.34322
3	Forestry & fishery products	.03708	.03693	.54343	.54333
7	Coal mining	.21264	.21333	.33333	.33333
9	Stone & clay mining & quarrying	.35714	.36364	.08929	.09091
13	Ordnance & accessories	.00262	.00234	.51376	.51406
14	Food & kindred products	.03100	.03100	.33400	.33400
15	Tobacco manufactures	.02099	.02104	.25698	.25700
16	Broad & narrow fabrics, yarn & thread mills	.00668	.00704	.52445	.53451
17	Miscellaneous textile goods & floor coverings	.01403	.13462	.50224	.50226
18	Apparel	.02396	.02400	.35226	.35265
19	Miscellaneous fabricated textile products	.01098	.01077	.44221	.44314
20	Lumber & wood products, except containers & boxes	.06785	.06653	.30678	.30769
22	Household furniture	.02805	.02805	.38143	.38151
23	Other furniture & fixtures	.01220	.01346	.47967	.48048
24	Paper & allied products, except containers & boxes	.03994	.03992	.38425	.38589

(continued)

Table 2-17, cont.

Industry Number	Industry	Transportation[a] 1970	Transportation[a] 1980	Wholesale and Retail Trade[a] 1970	Wholesale and Retail Trade[a] 1980
25	Paperboard containers & boxes	.02597	.03125	.11688	.10938
26	Printing & publishing	.04256	.04210	.29503	.30119
27	Chemicals & selected chemical products	.05512	.05523	.24016	.24207
28	Plastics & synthetic materials	.03571	.02857	.25000	.22857
29	Drugs, cleaning, & toilet preparations	.02955	.02936	.38478	.01683
30	Paint & allied products	.01515	.01835	.50000	.50459
31	Petroleum refining & related industries	.04740	.04741	.43205	.46533
32	Rubber & miscellaneous plastics products	.01660	.01676	.41785	.41599
.					
34	Footwear & other leather products	.02269	.02263	.38838	.39046
35	Glass & glass products	.02811	.02874	.52008	.52443
36	Stone & clay products	.04026	.04004	.42351	.42158
37	Primary iron & steel manufacturing	.03333	.02439	.45000	.46341
38	Primary nonferrous metal manufacturing	.02564	.01587	.43590	.46032
.					
40	Heating, plumbing, & fabricated structural metal products	.01705	.01712	.27273	.27397
41	Screw machine products, bolts, nuts, etc., & metal stampings	.01830	.01946	.29617	.29562
42	Other fabricated metal products	.01461	.01510	.44400	.44472
43	Engines & turbines	.01000	.01111	.30200	.30333
44	Farm machinery & equipment	.04545	.03030	.22727	.24242
.					
47	Metalworking machinery & equipment	.01493	.02000	.35812	.36000
48	Special industry machinery & equipment	.01667	.01124	.35000	.34831
.					

51	Office, computing, & accounting machines	.01293	.01445	.47414	.47399
52	Service industry machines	.02284	.02289	.42788	.43009
53	Electric transmission & distribution equipment, & electrical industrial apparatus	.02632	.01667	.23684	.23333
54	Household appliances	.02605	.02600	.35403	.35398
55	Electric lighting & wiring equipment	.01869	.01811	.28972	.29136
56	Radio, TV, & communication equipment	.02002	.02002	.37998	.37998
57	Electronic components & accessories	.01313	.01325	.45051	.44992
58	Miscellaneous electrical machinery, equipment, & supplies	—	.01440	—	.29446
59	Motor vehicles & equipment	.02396	.02393	.16477	.16538
60	Aircraft & parts	.00952	.00952	.27619	.28095
61	Other transportation equipment	.01007	.00990	.30133	.30069
62	Professional scientific & controlling instruments & supplies	.01810	.01752	.43824	.43843
63	Optical, ophthalmic, & photographic equipment & supplies	.01281	.01374	.62707	.59717
64	Miscellaneous manufacturing	.02613	.02603	.39180	.39193
⋮					
80	Imports	.03179	.02962	.31777	—
⋮					
83	Scrap, used & secondhand goods	—	—	1.01679	—

aThe ratios were calculated by dividing the margin figure by the value of the personal consumption expenditures figure in *purchaser* prices.

Source: Unpublished data from the U.S. Department of Labor, Bureau of Labor Statistics [159].

Conclusions and Recommendations

Undoubtedly, if additional resources were available, more reliable projections could have been derived by using additional time-series relationships for individual states and industries. Given this restraint, however, the methodology does provide reasonable projections. Computation of an independent estimate of PCE by state from projections of total disposable personal income minus an anticipated national savings rate compared favorably with the total generated in this study. For both 1970 and 1980, the differences between the two independent projections for all states were less than 10 percent. The input-output industry distribution is, of course, open to greater error.

The greatest distortion in the state estimates results from a lack of any really reliable comprehensive data on the differences in consumption patterns between states. Although corrections were made for some of the most obvious industries, there are numerous other industries that remain candidates for further research.

Undoubtedly the consumer expenditures survey should be expanded to provide more state data for regional analysis. This is particularly important at a time when there is a realization that fiscal and even monetary policy should be designed to have differential regional effects. While the projections of this final demand component admittedly pushed the limit of the available data, this is often necessary to specify those areas where additional data are necessary for meaningful analysis.

3 Gross Private Capital Formation and Net Inventory Change

Gross private domestic investment is the second largest component of GNP and probably the one with the greatest year-to-year fluctuation. Although it is the subject of extensive research, very little is known about the determinants of this component at either the regional or the national level.

Estimation of investment expenditures at the state level poses special problems. First, there are few historical state data on investment that can be used for extrapolation. Second, the variables that determine investment—output, expected sales, and changes in technology—are especially difficult to forecast at that level of regional disaggregation. At the present time, the best procedure for estimating investment by state appears to be a combination of projections of specific explanatory variables at the state level and the use of national relationships.

The diverse nature of the investment components makes estimation of total investment particularly difficult. Demand for finished goods from any single industry depends upon the demand generated by final sales of many other industries. In addition, an investment decision is based on the evaluation of a complex set of factors involving future sales, relative prices, and technological change. Nevertheless, if major shifts in final demand among states and over time are to be analyzed, investment must be estimated. The estimates developed in this study should provide a valuable step towards better understanding of investment at both the national and the state levels.

For projection purposes, gross private domestic investment (GPDI) was divided into its four basic components: producers' durable equipment, plant construction, residential construction, and inventory change. The past and projected values of these four categories are shown in Table 3-1.

Of total GPDI, producers' durable equipment investment is the largest component, comprising approximately 50 percent. It has exhibited a historical pattern quite different from GNP and other components of GPDI. For example, about $25 billion was spent on equipment in both 1947 and 1958, but by 1963 the amount had increased 36 percent, to $34 billion. New construction is about equally divided between plant investment and residential construction. The tight money market and recession, which started in the late 1960s, undoubtedly curtailed residential construction in 1970. The nonfarm component of residential construction is shown separately because different estimation procedures were used for the farm- and nonfarm-expenditures categories. However, the farm component has always been small and will be only a negligible part of total residential construction in 1970 and 1980.

29

Table 3-1

Gross Private Domestic Investment by Component (billions of 1958 dollars)

Component	Actual				Estimated	
	1947	1958	1963	1969	1970[b]	1980[b]
Equipment investment	$24.6	$25.0	$34.0	$ 57.4	$ 57.7	$ 97.2
Plant investment	11.6	16.6	17.9	24.0	20.6	33.7
Residential construction	15.4	20.8	24.8	23.4	22.7	40.5
Nonfarm component	(14.5)	(20.1)	(24.2)	(23.0)		
Real estate and rental[a]					1.7	4.1
Net investment in inventories	-0.2	-1.5	5.8	6.9	0.8	9.2
Total private investment	51.5[c]	60.9	82.5	111.8[c]	103.5	184.7

[a]IO-71, Real estate & rental, is included in plant investment and residential construction for 1947, 1958, 1963, and 1969, but is shown separately in the projections for 1970 and 1980.
[b]Preliminary estimates that have not been reconciled with the final projections in Appendix B.
[c]Figures do not add to total due to rounding.
Source: 1947, 1958, and 1963 [134, p. 5]; 1969 - March 1970 [137, p. 8]; 1970 [independent estimate]; 1980 [158].

The general approach used in developing a methodology to make state estimates for each component, together with a discussion of the major data sources and their limitations, is given in the remaining sections of this chapter.

General Methodology

The general methodology is described in the following four steps:

Step 1. Identification of the basic variables that determine investment for each input-output industry.

Step 2. Estimation of state shares for 1970 and 1980, based on relationships developed in Step 1.

Step 3. Calculation of investment by state by applying estimated state shares from Step 2 to the BLS projection of national investment by industry.

Step 4. Conversion from the consuming to the producing industry classification (for producers' durable equipment only).

In Step 2, the estimation of state shares sometimes involved projecting actual investment and then computing state shares to make the projections for states consistent with the BLS projections for the nation.

The basic variables used in projecting investment in equipment, plant, and inventories were independent projections of output by industry for each state and national capital-to-output and replacement-to-output ratios by industry. Projections of output are described in a later section of this chapter. For the residential construction estimates, independent projections of population and personal income by state constituted the basic explanatory variables. Equations for developing projections in Step 2 were obtained from regression analyses of various sets of cross-section and time-series data. The calculations in Step 4 are self-explanatory. Except for the previously stated modification of the 1970 national figures prior to Step 3, the BLS projections were always accepted as given.

Given that the national BLS producers' durable equipment final demand vector is by industry of sale, which is difficult to project, projections were derived by equipment-consuming industry. The distribution of purchases from consuming industry to producing industry (Step 4) was accomplished by using the 1963 capital flow matrix [10]. A capital flow matrix specifies the industrial distribution of durable equipment purchases for each equipment-consuming industry.

Equipment Investment

Equipment investment serves two purposes. It expands the stock of capital to match requirements for desired output, and it changes the stock of capital to benefit from technological advancements. For this study, the effects of technological change were assumed to be uniform across states. Expected output, therefore, was the major variable to be considered in the distribution of the BLS estimates of national investment to the states.

The BLS national totals for equipment investment comprise the sales, rather than purchases, of equipment by industry. Before estimating the state shares that could be applied to the BLS input-output projections, the projected investment by industry for each state had to be converted from the consuming to the producing industry. The detailed procedures are outlined in the following steps:

Step 1. Identification of the basic variables that determine equipment investment:
  a. Estimation of state output by industry for 1970 and 1980.
  b. Selection of the 1970 and 1980 "replacement-to-stock" ratio for each industry.
  c. Selection of the 1970 and 1980 "equipment stock-to-output" ratio for each industry.

Step 2. Estimation of 1970 and 1980 equipment investment by consuming industry by state:

    a.   Calculation of replacement investment based on output in the same
        year.
    b.   Calculation of net investment based on the change in output from the
        previous year.

Step 3.   Distribution of equipment investment purchases from consuming
to producing input-output industries using the capital flow matrix:
    a.   Distribution of equipment investment in each industry to purchases
        from each industry.
    b.   Summation of figures in each row of the matrix to obtain total equip-
        ment investment by industry.

Step 4.   Distribution of the BLS national estimate to states based on the
distribution calculated in Step 3(b).

The projection of output in Step 1(a) consisted of two parts. First, the
1970 and 1980 output by industry for the nation was estimated. Second, the
share of output in each industry for each state was determined, based on the following equation:

$$X_t = a + bt \tag{3.1}$$

where X_t is the share of national output in year t. The coefficients a and b were
estimated by least squares using state output data previously assembled by Jack
Faucett Associates for 1947, 1958, and 1963 [16]. In some cases, the historical
pattern was erratic, and projections for 1980 were outside reasonable limits. The
following two constraints were therefore placed on the 1980 projections: a
decrease from 1963 could not be greater than half of the share in 1963, and an
increase from 1963 could not be greater than the share in 1963 plus half the
difference between the share in 1963 and 100 percent. In cases where the share
in 1980 was constrained by one of the above limits, the value for 1970 was
obtained by linear interpolation between 1963 and 1980.
    The 1966 national values for output, replacement investment, and stock of
capital were used to determine the "equipment stock-to-output" and "replacement-to-stock" ratios for Steps 1(b) and 1(c). These data were aggregated from
SIC categories to input-output industries. Several methods were investigated for
projecting these ratios. Ratios were computed for 1947 and 1958–1966. Because
the historical pattern for many industries was so erratic, projections to 1980 gave
unreasonable values. For example, the least squares fit of linear equations
frequently gave negative values for 1980. There was no apparent way to easily
adjust for the very erratic nature of the ratios in the years for which data were
available; consequently, the ratios calculated from data for 1966, the latest year,
were used.

The estimation of replacement investment for each industry in each state in Step 2(a) was based on the following equation:

$$I(R)_t = k_1 X_t \tag{3.2}$$

where

$I(R)_t$ = replacement investment in year t

k_1 = the product of the stock-to-output ratio and the replacement-to-stock ratio for the specified industry

X_t = output in year t

The values for k_1 and X_t were obtained as described in the preceding paragraph.

The projection of net investment in Step 2(b) for each industry in each state was based on the following equation:

$$I(N)_t = k_2 [X_t - X_{t-1}] \text{ if } X_t - X_{t-1} > 0$$
$$= 0 \qquad\qquad \text{if } X_t - X_{t-1} < 0 \tag{3.3}$$

where k_2 is the stock-to-output ratio. The outputs for 1969 and 1979 were derived by geometric interpolation between estimates for 1963 and 1970 and estimates for 1970 and 1980, respectively.

Total investment by industry by state is the sum of replacement and net investment estimated in the manner described above. Because replacement-to-stock ratios calculated from 1966 data reflect situations with both increasing and decreasing output, replacement investment was assumed to be based on the output level regardless of whether output was increasing or decreasing. There is no net investment if output is decreasing, and the capital stock-to-output ratio does not increase.

In Step 3, the equipment investment by state was distributed to industries, using percentage distributions for each industry developed from the 1963 capital flow matrix [10]. The estimates in Step 3(a) were summed to obtain total equipment investment by industry and were employed to calculate an industry-by-state distribution of equipment sales for use in Step 4. The national BLS projection figures were then distributed to states.

Plant Investment

The plant investment component was estimated using the same general procedure employed for durable equipment. That is, while equipment stocks and replacement ratios were used to compute equipment investment, plant stocks and replacement ratios were used to project plant investment. However, since all plant investment is purchased from one input-output industry, no industrial conversion of purchases was necessary. The specific steps are given below:

Step 1. Identification of the basic variables that determine plant investment:
    a.   Estimation of state output by industry for 1970 and 1980.
    b.   Selection of the 1970 and 1980 replacement-to-stock ratio for each industry.
    c.   Selection of the 1970 and 1980 plant stock-to-output ratio.

Step 2. Estimation of plant investment by industry by state for 1970 and 1980:
    a.   Calculation of replacement investment based on output in the same year.
    b.   Calculation of net investment based on change in output from the previous year.

Step 3. Reconciliation of plant investment in 51 states with the BLS national projections:
    a.   Summation of plant investment in all industries in each state.
    b.   Reconciliation of estimates by state so that the total equals the BLS national projections.

Steps 1 and 2 are identical to Steps 1 and 2 as previously described for equipment investment. The analysis of plant investment indicated that, as in the case of equipment, the replacement-to-stock and plant stock-to-output ratios could not be projected from historical data, requiring that they be based on 1966, the latest year for which data are available.

In Step 3(a) estimates of plant investment for all industries for both replacement and net investment were added to obtain total new plant construction estimates by state. In Step 3(b) the estimate for each state was scaled as shown in the following equation:

$$X_i = X_i^* \left[\frac{\text{BLS national projection}}{\text{JFA projection for 51 states}} \right] \qquad (3.4)$$

where

    X_i = the final estimate of total construction for plant investment in state i
    X_i^* = the independent projection for state i.

This basic equation was used for both 1970 and 1980.

Net Investment in Inventories

Inventories are held by both producing and consuming industries, and changes in inventories result from planned changes in stocks as well as from unforeseen variations in demand and production. In normal years, the total change in inventories constitutes less than 10 percent of GPDI. The BLS projections show inventory investment as 2 and 7 percent of total investment in 1970 and 1980, respectively.

Because the resources available to this study were limited, a detailed analysis of inventory investment could not be undertaken. The most expedient procedure for making inventory projections by state was to distribute the BLS national projections by industry to states on the basis of the rate of change in output in that particular industry. This approach can be used if output in the producing industry is assumed to be a reasonable proxy variable for changes in inventories held by all industries. Since inventories are a small component of GPDI, this approach will not lead to serious errors in the projections of total investment.

Inventory investments by state for 1970 and 1980 for each industry were computed using the following equations:

$$I(I)_i = \frac{[X_{70} - X_{63}]_i}{[X_{70} - X_{63}]_N} \text{ [1970 BLS national projections]} \qquad (3.5)$$

$$I(I)_i = \frac{[X_{80} - X_{70}]_i}{[X_{80} - X_{70}]_N} \text{ [1980 BLS national projections]} \qquad (3.6)$$

where

$$I(I)_i \qquad = \text{ inventory investment in state } i$$
$$[X_{t1} - X_{t2}]_i \quad = \text{ change in output between year } t1 \text{ and year } t2 \text{ in state } i$$
$$[X_{t1} - X_{t2}]_N \quad = \text{ change in national output between year } t1 \text{ and year } t2.$$

Inventory investment was allocated only to those states for which output increased during the period under study. In view of the method used by the BLS in projecting inventory investment at the national level, the procedure described appeared to be the most appropriate.

Residential Construction

Private residential construction represents over 50 percent of private construction and over 30 percent of total construction. During the period 1950–1968, residential construction expenditures followed a more erratic pattern than most of the other components of GNP, making it unusually difficult to derive long-term projections. In addition, the fact that both total and per capita expenditures for residential construction vary considerably among states complicated the projections. Eight states account for over 50 percent of the total, while California alone accounts for 15 percent.

Almost no state data are published on value of construction put in place, but useful secondary series such as building permits and contract awards data are available. Although the latter information is generally sold by the F. W. Dodge Corporation only to private clients, considerable information is available publicly for the year 1958 [15].

Both time-series and cross-section regressions were considered in developing models for predicting construction expenditures by states. The best results were obtained with the following equation:

$$E_i = 3050 \left[P_t - P_{t-1} \right]_i + 0.026 Y_i \qquad (3.7)$$

where

E_i = residential construction expenditures in state i

P_t = population of state i in year t

Y_i = personal income in state i.

By using the least squares regression technique and 1958 contract awards, the above coefficients were obtained. They show that residential construction expenditures increase $3050 for each additional person and 2.6 cents for each dollar increase in personal income. (The R^2 for the sample data was .96.)

Sample time-series and cross-section data on building permits gave much poorer fits for each of several different models. For years other than 1958, contract awards data also gave considerably poorer fits than the .96 obtained for the above equation using 1958 data. The personal income projection for 1970 and 1980 by state came from the National Planning Association [49].

The final estimate of construction by state was then obtained from the following equation:

$$E_i^* = \frac{E_i}{\sum\limits_{i=1}^{51} E_i} \text{ [BLS national projections]} \qquad (3.8)$$

where

$$\frac{E_i}{\sum\limits_{i=1}^{51} E_i} = \text{the percentage of residential construction in state } i, \text{ based on predictions from equation (3.7)}$$

E_i^* = final reconciled estimate of residential construction for state i.

For both 1970 and 1980, the sum of predictions for the 51 states from equation (3.7) was very close to the BLS national projections.

Concluding Remarks

Final projections of the four components of gross private domestic investment are given in Table 3-2. Although the production of the commodities involved could, of course, occur in other states, in each case the estimates represent sales in the state in which investment takes place. For example, the $798 million for equipment investment in Alabama represents the estimated value of investment put in place by all industries in that state for 1970.

The projections of these investment data are among the most speculative of all the GNP projections for two reasons. First, considerable reliance had to be placed on national series because there was a dearth of any state data. Second, the very nature of this component makes it open to significant shifts both in its relative magnitude compared with other components and in its distribution among input-output industries and states.

Improvements to the investment projections would require substantial effort and involve collection of more data on a state basis. Three suggested methods of improving the estimates follow.

1.   In industries where replacement investment and capital-to-output ratios are believed to be changing, the equations for relating investment to output that were used in this study could be modified through special research.
2.   In those states where industrial patterns appear to be changing rapidly, the projections of output of major industries could be improved by more detailed analysis.
3.   A more recent capital flow matrix would be advantageous in converting purchases from consuming to producing industries.

There are many additional ways in which the projections could be improved, but these three suggestions appear to be the most important in view of insights developed during this research.

Table 3-2

Gross Private Domestic Investment by State and Component (millions of 1958 dollars)

State	Equipment 1970	Equipment 1980	Plant 1970	Plant 1980	Inventory* 1970	Inventory* 1980	Residential Construction 1970	Residential Construction 1980
Alabama	798	1350	292	482	111	184	311	559
Arizona	539	1103	210	423	79	129	248	481
Arkansas	433	732	148	251	72	112	166	310
California	6394	12132	2107	3748	789	1648	3160	5979
Colorado	723	1439	331	640	77	114	252	459
Connecticut	700	1042	210	320	97	141	415	757
Delaware	190	314	69	118	35	132	75	134
Washington, D.C.	260	423	68	121	7	9	120	209
Florida	1846	3915	654	1346	204	323	925	1783
Georgia	1242	2271	394	711	205	577	465	852
Idaho	214	364	67	118	22	42	66	112
Illinois	3679	5688	1234	2014	457	580	1320	2289
Indiana	1455	2150	542	819	250	376	544	951
Iowa	823	1233	220	347	171	213	235	401
Kansas	596	958	244	351	76	149	211	374
Kentucky	804	1425	269	459	121	317	248	441
Louisiana	1413	2506	1236	1957	154	161	382	673
Maine	190	254	51	65	27	58	66	121
Maryland	935	1674	339	608	123	309	509	951
Massachusetts	1342	2069	394	602	177	285	593	1025
Michigan	2513	3993	831	1331	313	501	960	1661
Minnesota	1130	1965	357	620	131	276	381	676
Mississippi	452	779	206	342	78	142	185	332
Missouri	1359	2322	434	756	186	436	442	775
Montana	216	354	98	156	24	43	66	107
Nebraska	459	741	152	270	45	85	100	218
Nevada	200	415	84	181	12	18	75	138
New Hampshire	144	237	48	85	24	46	84	148

New Jersey	2061	3298	977	324	533	955	1723
New Mexico	378	705	478	33	36	123	236
New York	5658	9337	2159	466	629	2192	3864
North Carolina	1276	2344	778	231	459	461	813
North Dakota	154	249	120	8	8	48	82
Ohio	3092	4738	1649	414	929	1172	2026
Oklahoma	582	975	494	58	61	211	377
Oregon	619	977	260	55	147	219	383
Pennsylvania	2715	3595	1137	371	493	1039	1793
Rhode Island	188	282	75	28	50	87	150
South Carolina	599	1047	310	96	218	222	401
South Dakota	166	259	76	8	11	50	83
Tennessee	1010	1774	516	181	331	350	610
Texas	3586	6224	2753	498	752	1171	2040
Utah	357	666	332	53	82	185	221
Vermont	85	126	41	10	16	39	70
Virginia	1051	1785	627	130	248	504	909
Washington	817	1296	349	152	229	349	615
West Virginia	542	735	244	67	109	92	165
Wisconsin	1149	1744	523	198	474	448	796
Wyoming	192	327	309	17	15	33	54
Alaska	104	184	64	6	17	37	65
Hawaii	245	549	197	29	38	79	145
Total	57700[a]	97164[b]	33709	2500[c]	13291	22670	40537

NOTE: These 1970 and 1980 projections represent preliminary estimates that have not been reconciled with the final projections given in Appendix B.

*Includes IO-71, Real estate & rental, but not IO-83, Scrap, used & secondhand goods.

[a]This total reflects $25 million for imports not allocated to states.

[b]This total reflects $50 million for imports not allocated to states.

[c]This total reflects a minus $5,000 million for inventory valuation adjustment not allocated to states.

4 Gross Foreign Exports

Gross foreign exports is the most difficult final demand component to project because it is primarily a function of aggregate world demand and the competitive position of domestic producers relative to foreign producers. Both of these underlying factors are obviously very difficult to forecast. It is therefore fortunate that this component of GNP is the least significant in terms of dollar value.

As for the other components of final demand, the region of purchase was specified as the region where the demand originated. The purchase region for exports was specified as the state of exit; that is, the region where the commodity leaves the United States for a foreign country. If a Canadian farmer purchased farm machinery from a producer in Michigan but the machinery was shipped to Minnesota en route to Canada, the export projection would designate Minnesota as the region of purchase. The reason for this specification is that foreign exports are included in the commodity interregional flow estimates and, consequently, must be considered consumption in the exit region. If the commodities shipped to a region for consumption could be differentiated from those exported from the area to a foreign country, exports could be allocated to the region where production originated. Because the interregional trade data included shipments of exports, the conceptual framework of the multiregional model required that exports be designated according to the exit region.

As with the other major final demand components, the sum of exports for all 51 states for both 1970 and 1980 is equal to the national total for each input-output industry as projected by the BLS.

Methodology

Given the rather low percentage of total GNP represented by exports, as well as the belief that the state distribution of exports by exit area is relatively stable over time, a base-period state distribution was assumed representative of the distribution for both projection years. The vast majority of exports are transported by waterborne commerce through a small number of deep-water ports; therefore, this assumption does not seem unrealistic.

Although the development of the base-period distribution differed between service and nonservice input-output industries, the general approach to projections can be easily summarized in the following steps:

41

IO-70, Finance & insurance.   Historically, exports of this industry are restricted to fire and marine insurance. The value of fire and casualty insurance premiums, reported in the *Statistical Abstract of the United States, 1969*, was, therefore, employed as the proxy variable.

IO-71, Real estate & rental.   Exports of this service consist primarily of royalty payments by foreign to domestic firms. Consequently, total value added by manufacturing industry was used since the more desirable proxy—corporate assets by state—was not readily available. Value added data were obtained from the *Annual Survey of Manufactures, 1966* [69].

IO-72, Hotels & lodging places; personal & repair services, except automobile repair.   The proxy series employed to derive the distribution for this industry was an independent JFA output projection by state [16].

IO-73, Business services.   Exports for this industry are primarily for advertising. The employment in SIC 731, Advertising, from *County Business Patterns, 1967* [84] was consequently employed as the proxy series.

IO-76, Amusements.   In general, these exports represent receipts for foreign film rentals. Employment in SIC 781, Motion picture production & distributon, and SIC 782, Motion picture service industries, reported in *County Business Patterns, 1967*, was, therefore, used as the allocating series.

IO-77, Medical, educational services, & nonprofit organizations.   Expenditures by foundations, published in the *Statistical Abstract of the United States, 1969*, were employed to allocate the national total to states.

IO-78, Federal government enterprises.   Exports for this industry consist mainly of postal services. The number of postal employees by state, reported in the *Statistical Abstract of the United States, 1969*, served as the proxy variable.

IO-79, State & local government enterprises.   Export receipts are for electrical power sales from states bordering Canada and Mexico. Electrical generating capacity of publicly owned companies in those states, published in the *Statistical Abstract of the United States, 1969*, was consequently employed as the allocating series.

Conclusions and Recommendations

The factors that underlie the demand for a country's exports are so complex that even national projections in industry detail are highly speculative. It follows, then, that projections of this component in regional detail are open to substantial error. Given this restriction, only a small amount of the total project resources was committed to this projection since it was believed that resources could be utilized to greater advantage in assembling more reliable projections of other final demand components. The methodology described in this chapter allowed the projections to be compiled in a simple but systematic way.

Since commodity export statistics represent some of the most reliable economic data available, lack of data was not a restraint in making projections for those commodity-producing input-output industries. On turning to the service industries, however, the general dearth of state input data necessitated considerable reliance on proxy variables. Government agencies should consider filling this data void.

5 State and Local Government Net Purchases of Goods and Services

The purpose of this chapter is to describe the methodologies used to project state and local government (SLG) net purchases of goods and services by state to 1970 and 1980. Each estimate represents the purchases of the state government and of the local governments within the state, regardless of where the goods and services were produced. As a percentage of GNP, SLG purchases have increased from about 8 percent in 1950 to 10 percent in 1968. Of course, a major factor contributing to this increase is that many federal grants are channeled through states and, consequently, appear as part of the SLG final demand for purposes of this study. Although the annual growth rate of SLG net purchases between 1970 and 1980 is projected to decrease slightly from that observed during the 1957–1968 period, a continuing upward trend is expected.

Unlike most of the other components of final demand, the state and local government component has a comprehensive data base as disaggregated time series data for each state are published in the *Census of Governments* [71–73] and *Governmental Finance Series* [92–100] of the Bureau of the Census. The greatest difficulty in estimating 1970 and 1980 purchases was in determining whether the rapid rate of increase in many states during recent years would continue. Because this has often been a catching-up process due to a previous lag, the trends for individual states usually differed considerably from the trend for the total. The historical growth rate for each state was therefore independently analyzed wherever data permitted. As with all components, the SLG projections have been adjusted so that the sum of the 51 regions (50 states plus the District of Columbia) equals the national control totals obtained from the Bureau of Labor Statistics (BLS). Adjustments to bring about this equality are discussed fully in a later section.

The major components and selected subcomponents of SLG net purchases are shown in Table 5-1. Although the BLS, in deriving their 1980 national projections, worked with eleven functional categories, the level of aggregation was reduced to seven functions for this study. The reason for this aggregation was that the state time-series data available from the Bureau of the Census (Census) would best conform to seven categories. The seven basic functional categories are: education; highways; hospitals, health, & sanitation; natural resources; local parks & recreation; public enterprises; and a residual category. The data for 1957 and 1967 shown in Table 5-1 are "direct general expenditures" for fiscal years, while the projections for 1970 and 1980 are "net

Table 5-1
Major Components of State and Local Government Expenditures and Net Purchases of Goods and Services
(millions of 1958 dollars)

| Component | Direct General Expenditures[a] (Fiscal Year) | | | | Projections of Net Purchases of Goods & Services (Calendar Year) | |
| | 1957 | | 1967 | | 1970 | 1980 |
	Total	Capital Outlay	Total	Capital Outlay		
Education	$14,525	$ 3,320	$28,447	$ 5,799	$30,828	$ 43,714
Elementary, secondary & other	12,513	2,826	21,746	3,657	21,950	32,956
Higher	2,012	494	6,701	2,142	8,878	10,758
Highways	7,087	4,468	11,349	8,098	11,439	15,386
Hospitals, health, & sanitation	3,758	356	5,647	600	6,079	10,374
Health & hospitals	3,206	356	4,981	538	5,404	9,482
Sanitation (excluding sewerage)[b]	552	n.a.	666	62	675	892
Natural resources	958	277	1,758	777	1,784	3,005
Local parks & recreation	625	159	968	368	1,093	3,457
Enterprises	3,442	3,442	4,119	4,119	5,190	12,095
Water-supply systems	–	764	–	928	1,147	2,250
Gas-supply systems	–	35	–	32	31	60
Electric-power systems	–	437	–	490	514	992
Transit systems	–	123	–	283	602	2,250
Sewerage	–	658	–	940	1,142	2,504
Housing & urban renewal	–	289	–	821	981	2,491
Water transport & terminals	–	109	–	162	202	387
Air transportation[c]	–	172	–	253	280	484
Highway toll facilities	–	855	–	209	291	677
Other	7,500	n.a.	13,942	n.a.	16,987	36,569
Police	1,509	n.a.	2,287	120	2,463	3,913
Fire	832	n.a.	1,125	91	1,172	1,792
Correction	477	74	825	130	917	1,463
Public welfare[d]	697	n.a.	2,679	n.a.	4,179	12,616
Libraries	205	n.a.	389	n.a.	493	1,061
General government[e]	2,013	n.a.	2,895	n.a.	3,058	4,717
Other & unallocable[f]	1,767	n.a.	3,742	n.a.	4,705	11,007
Total	$37,895	$12,888	$66,230	$20,102	$73,400[g]	$124,600

[a]The nonresidential construction deflator was used to deflate capital outlay expenditures, while the state and local government deflator was used for the total direct expenditures.

[b]Capital outlay for hospitals only; other data were not available.

[c]State government toll facilities expenditures only, since data were not available for local governments.

[d]Excludes cash assistance payments.

[e]Includes employment security administration, financial administration, and general contract.

[f]Includes general public buildings and all other expenditures not elsewhere classified.

[g]This total has not been reconciled with that given in the appendix, Table B-9 ($74,500 million).

n.a. = Not available.

Source: Expenditures [71–73], deflators [134; 136].

purchases of goods and services" for calendar years. Since data were not directly available for net purchases of goods and services on a calendar-year basis, projections were made in terms of fiscal-year expenditures and then converted to calendar-year purchases.

The next section of this chapter presents the general approach and basic sources of data that are common to the projections of each of the seven functions, while the third major section describes the detailed procedures used for each function.

General Methodology and Basic Data Sources

The general procedure used to make the 1970 and 1980 projections of this final demand component can be summarized as follows: (1) development of the national control totals for each of the two projection years for each input-output industry; (2) projection of the totals for the seven basic functional categories for each state; and (3) distribution of purchases from the functional categories to input-output industries. The 1970 and 1980 control totals are those published by the BLS [162; 158].

The state projections were generally calculated function by function from regressions with data for the period 1957-1968.[1] The historical fit of expenditures was examined closely in relation to time, population variables, and personal income before choosing a projection method. For example, after testing several alternative combinations of independent variables for the education function, it was found that the school-age population, that is, age class 5-17, and a time trend appeared to produce the best fit. Although the same independent variables were used for each state for this functional category, the time-series regression coefficients did change considerably from state to state. Since most of the available data are for direct general expenditures for fiscal years, these data were used in the equations. Each of the projections was then converted to a calendar-year basis by extrapolating the fiscal-year series to time period 1970.5 and 1980.5 for 1970 and 1980, respectively.

The adjustment from direct general expenditures to net purchases of goods and services was accomplished in the reconciliation with national projections. In the case of public welfare expenditures, sufficient data were available to enable assistance payments to be subtracted from the direct general expenditures; thus, it was possible to obtain a closer approximation to net purchases for this category. The conversion from direct general expenditures to purchases of goods and services is shown in Table 5-2.

The 1970 distribution of the state and local government net purchases of

---

1. For Alaska, projections were usually based on data from 1959-1968; for Hawaii, from 1960-1967.

Table 5–2

Conversion of State and Local Government Direct General
Expenditures to Purchases of Goods and Services (Office of Business
Economics Procedure Current in 1970)

	(1)	Total state and local government expenditures (direct general expenditures plus utilities, liquor stores, and insurance trusts)
minus:	(2)	Insurance benefits
	(3)	Interest on debt
	(4)	Assistance and subsidies plus payments for foster children in private homes and aid to higher education in schools run by local authorities
	(5)	Purchases of land and existing structures
	(6)	Current operations of government enterprises
	(7)	New construction
	(8)	Personal services to general government (wages plus salaries)
	(9)	Wage supplement (income other than wages and salaries) other than payments to self-administered retirement funds
plus:	(10)	General government force account compensation
equals:	(11)	Other gross purchases
minus:	(12)	Sales, other than structures
equals:	(13)	Other purchases
plus:	(14)	Compensation of general government (employees)
	(15)	Structures (including new construction less force account compensation)
	(16)	Purchases less sales of existing structures
equals:	(17)	Net purchases of goods and services
plus:	(18)	Sales of goods and services
equals:	(19)	Gross purchases of goods and services

Source: Karen R. Polenske and others. *State Estimates of the Gross National Product, 1947, 1958, 1963.* [58, p. 118]

goods and services to input-output industries was based on coefficients supplied by the BLS, which give for each function the percentage distribution of purchases among the input-output producing industries. Table 5–3 gives the coefficients that were used in distributing total state and local government net purchases to input-output industries. As shown in the table, for 1980 the BLS did not provide coefficients for distributing expenditures by function to input-output industries. Only a set of coefficients for the total is therefore listed for 1980.

Although the coefficients in Table 5–3 are for the nation, they were used for each state by assuming that the purchases of goods and services by function was uniform for all states. Even though this assumption introduces some error,

Table 5-3

Coefficients for the Distribution of 1970 and 1980 State and Local Government Net Purchases of Goods and Services to Input-Output Industries

Ind. No.	Industry Title	1970							1980
		Education	Highways	Hospitals, health, & sanitation	Natural resources	Local parks & recreation	Enterprises	Other	Total
1	Livestock & livestock products	.00004	a	.00134	.00016	.00009	—	.00097	.00051
2	Other agricultural products	-.00008	a	.00368	.00194	.00110	—	.00038	.00064
3	Forestry & fishery products	.00001	a	.00001	.00001	a	—	.00002	.00002
4	Agricultural, forestry, & fishery services	.00050	—	.00029	-.07188	-.04079	—	.00047	-.00372
5	Iron & ferroalloy ores mining	—	—	—	—	—	—	—	—
6	Nonferrous metal ores mining	—	—	—	—	—	—	—	—
7	Coal mining	.00095	a	.00320	.00068	.00039	—	.00380	.00226
8	Crude petroleum & natural gas	—	—	—	—	—	—	—	—
9	Stone & clay mining & quarrying	—	-.00139	—	—	—	—	—	-.00034
10	Chemical & fertilizer mineral mining	—	.00138	—	—	—	—	—	.00034
11	New construction	.16002	.66251	.08647	.30212	.30784	.86054	.10845	.28604
12	Maintenance & repair construction	.02555	.25643	.00672	.03921	.19767	—	.03366	.06124
13	Ordnance & accessories	—	—	—	—	—	—	.00073	.00023
14	Food & kindred products	.00515	.00002	.03472	.00445	.00252	—	.01060	.01100
15	Tobacco manufactures	—	—	.00007	—	—	—	.00001	.00002
16	Broad & narrow fabrics, yarn & thread mills	—	—	—	—	—	—	—	—
17	Miscellaneous textile goods & floor coverings	a	—	.00038	.00088	.00050	—	.00071	.00034
18	Apparel	.00004	.00011	.00027	.00006	.00004	—	—	.00005
19	Miscellaneous fabricated textile products	.00001	—	.01067	.00938	.00532	—	.00632	.00411
20	Lumber & wood products, except containers	—	a	.00003	.00002	.00001	—	.00003	.00002

(continued)

Table 5-3, continued

Ind. No.	Industry Title	1970							1980
		Education	Highways	Hospitals, health, & sanitation	Natural resources	Local parks & recreation	Enterprises	Other	Total
21	Wooden containers	a	–	.00001	.00027	.00015	–	.00001	.00002
22	Household furniture	.00051	.00148	.00087	.00006	.00004	.00019	.00702	.00317
23	Other furniture & fixtures	.00316	.00137	.00436	.00370	.00210	.01106	.00742	.00649
24	Paper & allied products, except containers & boxes	.00036	–	–	.00002	.00001	–	–	.00019
25	Paperboard containers & boxes	–	–	–	–	–	–	.00001	–
26	Printing & publishing	.00716	.00020	.00032	.01741	.00988	–	.01243	.00903
27	Chemicals & selected chemical products	.00168	.00397	.00922	.09594	.05444	–	.00863	.01152
28	Plastics & synthetic materials	–	–	–	.00206	.00117	–	–	–
29	Drugs, cleaning, & toilet preparations	.00116	.00032	.03831	.00002	.00001	–	.00159	.00621
30	Paints & allied products	–	–	a	.06950	.03944	–	a	–
31	Petroleum refining & related industries	.00201	.00691	.00525	.00244	.00138	–	.03739	.02014
32	Rubber & miscellaneous plastics products	.00031	.00021	.00107	–	–	–	.01206	.00461
33	Leather tanning & industrial leather products	–	–	–	–	–	–	–	–
34	Footwear & other leather products	–	–	.00006	–	–	–	.00015	.00005
35	Glass & glass products	–	–	–	–	–	–	–	–
36	Stone & clay products	.00003	.00002	.00008	.00031	.00018	–	.00049	.00021
37	Primary iron & steel manufacturing	.00001	.00004	.00001	.00033	.00019	–	.00005	.00005
38	Primary nonferrous metal manufacturing	–	–	–	–	–	–	–	–
39	Metal containers	–	–	–	–	–	–	–	–
40	Heating, plumbing, & fabricated structural metal products	–	–	–	–	–	–	–	–

41	Screw machine products, bolts, nuts, etc., & metal stampings	a	.00047	.00001	a	—	—	.00016	.00019
42	Other fabricated metal products	.00133	.00074	.00254	.00102	.00058	.00304	.00121	.00202
43	Engines & turbines	—	—	.00001	.00051	.00029	.00153	—	.00021
44	Farm machinery & equipment	.00053	.00024	.00069	.00582	.00330	—	.00017	.00081
45	Construction, mining, oil field machinery & equipment	—	.00197	—	.00040	.00023	.00120	.00034	.00076
46	Materials handling machinery & equipment	.00220	—	.00330	.00579	.00329	—	.00035	.00204
47	Metalworking machinery & equipment	a	—	.00002	.00086	.00049	.00258	.00004	.00036
48	Special industry machinery & equipment	.00061	—	.00119	.00080	.00045	.00239	.00281	.00175
49	General industrial machinery & equipment	.00012	.00001	.00006	.00023	.00013	.00069	.00028	.00026
50	Machine shop products	.00226	.00018	.00001	.00004	.00002	.00011	.00056	.00144
51	Office, computing, & accounting machines	.00650	.00027	.00094	.00010	.00006	.00031	.00271	.00456
52	Service industry machines	.00031	—	.00086	.00081	.00046	.00243	.00184	.00120
53	Electric transmission & distribution equipment, & electrical industrial apparatus	a	—	.00002	.00077	.00044	.00231	.00009	.00034
54	Household appliances	—	—	.00001	.00008	.00004	.00023	.00001	.00005
55	Electric lighting & wiring equipment	.00055	a	.00001	—	—	—	.00015	.00034
56	Radio, TV, & communication equipment	.00003	.00497	.00004	.00025	.00014	.00074	.00334	.00246
57	Electronic components & accessories	—	—	—	.00011	.00006	—	—	—
58	Miscellaneous electrical machinery, equipment & supplies	.00232	.00004	.00001	.00011	.00006	.00026	.00017	.00131
59	Motor vehicles & equipment	.00959	.00974	.00915	.00725	.00411	.02168	.02782	.02087
60	Aircraft & parts	—	—	—	.00007	.00004	—	a	—

(continued)

Table 5-3, continued

Ind. No.	Industry Title	1970							1980
		Education	Highways	Hospitals, health, & sanitation	Natural resources	Local parks & recreation	Enterprises	Other	Total
61	Other transportation equipment	—	.00001	a	.00645	.00366	.01930	.00012	.00256
62	Professional, scientific, & controlling instruments & supplies	.00127	.00192	.00649	.00399	.00226	.01192	.00094	.00385
63	Optical, ophthalmic, & photographic equipment & supplies	.00056	.00042	.00032	.00006	.00003	.00016	.00078	.00073
64	Miscellaneous manufacturing	.00678	.00044	.00181	.00159	.00090	.00475	.01258	.00880
65	Transportation & warehousing	.01499	.00095	.00815	.02498	.01418	—	.01503	.01568
66	Communications, except radio & TV broadcasting	.00439	a	.00317	.01384	.00786	—	.01722	.00937
67	Radio & TV broadcasting	—	—	—	—	—	—	—	—
68	Electric, gas, water, & sanitary services	.02834	.00004	−.00252	−.03822	−.02169	—	.01660	.01795
69	Wholesale & retail trade	−.00402	.00511	.01290	.04414	.02505	—	.02384	.01145
70	Finance & insurance	.00671	.00015	.00028	.01900	.01078	—	.01119	.00848
71	Real estate & rental	.00165	a	.00340	.00564	.00320	—	.03668	.01411
72	Hotels & lodging places; personal & repair services, except automobile repair	−.00430	.00014	.01131	.00894	.00507	—	.00797	.00242
73	Business services	.00643	−.00141	.03691	.07789	.04420	—	.03890	.02544
74	Research & development	—	—	—	—	—	—	—	—
75	Automobile repair & services	.00014	.00003	.00217	.01654	.00939	—	.01035	.00485
76	Amusements	.00328	a	.00001	.00222	.00126	—	.00028	−.00149
77	Medical, educational services, & nonprofit organizations	.00041	a	.06290	.00242	.00137	—	.00058	.00815
78	Federal government enterprises	.00055	.00004	.00162	.00102	.00058	—	.00860	.00351

79	State & local government enterprises	—	—	—	—	—	—	.00120	.00039
80	Directly allocated imports	—	—	—	.00257	.00146	—	—	.00016
81	Business travel, entertainment, & gifts	—	—	—	—	—	—	—	—
82	Office supplies	.00152	.00017	.00214	.00566	.00322	—	.01705	.00725
83	Scrap, used & secondhand goods	.00046	.02622	.00265	.01758	.00998	.05258	.00012	.01192
84	Government industry	.70328	.01356	.61992	.27952	.27933	—	.48444	.37900
85	Rest of the world industry	—	—	—	—	—	—	—	—
86	Household industry	—	—	—	—	—	—	—	—
87	Inventory valuation adjustment	—	—	—	—	—	—	—	—

NOTE: — coefficient is zero
a coefficient is less than .00001

Source: Unpublished data from the United States Department of Labor, Bureau of Labor Statistics [159].

data limitations precluded any other approach since there are many factors that produce substantial interregional differences in the types of goods and services purchased by state and local governments for a given function. A second source of error was undoubtedly introduced by the fact that only a single industrial distribution for SLG purchases was available for 1980. For this case, the assumption had to be made that either the relative magnitude of purchases by function is the same or the percentage distribution among input-output industries is the same for all functions. Examination of the projections presented in a later section, however, readily reveals that states vary considerably in the input-output industry distribution of purchases among functions.

In Table 5-4, the five largest industries supplying goods and services are shown for each of the seven functions. This table indicates that a few industries supply most of the goods and services for a specific function, but that the major supplying industries are not the same for all functions. The top five suppliers for government enterprises, for example, provide 96.7 percent of the total goods for this function. This high percentage can be explained by the fact that only capital outlay purchases are represented in this total. On the other extreme, purchases from the top five industries in the "other" function comprise only 70.5 percent of the total purchases.

The historical data used in making projections are from *Governmental Finances* [92-100], *State Government Finances* [112-114], and *Census of Governments* [71-73]. The third source presents greater detail but provides data on a state-by-state basis for only 1957, 1962, and 1967. In the *Census of Governments, 1967* [73], a convenient compilation of relevant statistics from 1957-1967 is given; but for the years before 1957, state-by-state data are available only for 1942. *State Government Finances* [112-114] also contains statistics for some components. A few additional data are available in special reports concerning the subject areas for each functional category. In some cases, national projections for 1975 and 1980 are available from sources other than the BLS; an example is the set of education projections from the Office of Education, Department of Health, Education, and Welfare [147]. These projections were evaluated in developing methodology, but they were not substituted for BLS projections for use as control figures. The reports by the Council of State Governments [39-43] on 1970 projections of state and local finances provided some assistance in obtaining and understanding trends for various other components. Council data, however, were also not directly used in this project.

Detailed Projection Methodologies for Specific Functions

The primary purpose of this section of the chapter is to present a detailed description of the methodologies used to make state projections of each of the

Table 5-4
The Five Input-Output Industries with the Greatest Percentage of the State and Local Government Net Purchases by Function, 1970

Ind. No.	Industry Title	Education	Highways	Hospitals, Health, & sanitation	Natural resources	Local parks & recreation	Enterprises	Other
		(Percent)						
11	New construction	16.0	66.3	8.6	30.2	30.8	86.1	10.8
12	Maintenance & repair construction	2.6	25.6			19.8		
27	Chemicals & selected chemical products			3.8	9.6	5.4		
29	Drugs, cleaning, & toilet preparations							
30	Paints & allied products				7.0			
31	Petroleum refining & related industries							3.7
59	Motor vehicles & equipment		1.0				2.2	
61	Other transportation equipment						1.9	
62	Professional, scientific, & controlling instruments & supplies						1.2	
65	Transportation & warehousing	1.5						
68	Electric, gas, water, & sanitary services	2.8						
71	Real estate & rental					4.4		
73	Business services			3.7	7.8			3.7
77	Medical, educational services, & nonprofit organizations			6.3				3.9
83	Scrap, used & secondhand goods		2.6			27.9		48.4
84	Government industry	70.3	1.4	62.0	28.0		5.3	
	Total for 5 industries	93.2	96.9	84.4	82.6	88.3	96.7	70.5

Source: Unpublished data from the U.S. Department of Labor, Bureau of Labor Statistics [159].

major functions and subfunctions within the state and local government component. For each function, specific definitions, coverage, and some general
description of the historical growth rate are included, together with the major
data sources and comments on their limitations.

Education

State and local government purchases for education include all state-
operated schools regardless of whether funds come from the state treasury,
federal grants, or student tuition. Private schools and federally operated institutions within the state are not included. Also excluded are some small amounts
spent for manpower training programs and certain antipoverty programs funded
by the Office of Economic Opportunity. Although these programs are sometimes
operated from public school buildings, they are included under federal purchases
of goods and services, since their funds do not go directly to the state. On the
other hand, most adult education is included under SLG final demand because the
federal funds are channeled through the state governments.

In 1967, public education expenditures comprised 78 percent of the total
of both public and private institutions. Of the total public portion, approximately 94 percent is considered to be purchases by state and local governments.
The national control total for these education purchases for 1980, as projected
by the BLS, indicates an expected 3.7 percent annual growth rate, which is
substantially lower than the 7.0 percent growth witnessed during the 1957–
1967 period. Undoubtedly, the expected slowing in the growth of the school-age
population (age class 5–17) is the primary reason for this change.

In turning to the data base, more information is available for education than
for most of the other functions within this component. The most complete
historical data are from the Bureau of the Census, which provides state-by-state
education data for 1942 and annually from 1957 to the present [73]. For 1957,
1962, and 1967, more detailed data are available than for the other years. In
addition, some independent projections of education purchases for the nation
and some selected states are available from publications of the Office of
Education, Department of Health, Education, and Welfare [147].

Two factors, which contribute to substantial differences in per capita
education expenditures among states, severely complicated the individual state
projections for this function. The first factor was the recent high annual rate of
increase in states that historically have had low per capita expenditures but are
catching up as a result of federal grants and increased public pressure for better
schools. The second was a substantial decrease in the growth of capital outlay
because the postwar boom in school-age population is subsiding in most states.
For projection purposes, education was divided into three subfunctions—elementary and secondary, higher, and other. Although each subfunction possessed

a unique trend, the "other" category was so small in value terms that it was projected using the same methodology as that of the elementary and secondary portion.

The following method of projecting the two basic subfunctions was chosen:

Step 1. Projection of 1970 and 1980 purchases of goods and services for higher education, equation (5.1), and for elementary, secondary, and other education, equation (5.2):

$$\text{log of } E_t^i = a_0 + a_1 t \tag{5.1}$$

$$E_t^i = b_0 + b_1 \, (P \, 5\text{-}17)_{t-1}^i \tag{5.2}$$

where

E^i = the expenditures in state i

t = the year

$(P \, 5\text{-}17)^i$ = the population in age-class 5–17 for state i.

$a_0, a_1,$

b_0, b_1 = least squares estimates using data from 1957 through 1968.

The population in age class 5–17 was lagged one year because education expenditures for any fiscal year are more closely correlated with population at the beginning than at the end of the year. An exception to the methodology expressed in the higher-education equation was made in the case of the District of Columbia. Unlike the states, it supported no higher education in 1957 and 1958. Expenditures were $1.3 million in 1959 and increased gradually to $1.8 million in 1967; however, they jumped to $4.1 million in 1968. In view of this pattern, the coefficients for equation (5.1) were determined using data for the period 1959–1968.

Step 2. Total education expenditures for each state was determined by summing the expenditures for higher education, elementary and secondary, and the "other" category.

Step 3. For each state, the share of the national total from Step 2 was then applied to the BLS national projection to make the final 1970 and 1980 state projections of education purchases. The conversion from expenditures to purchases was accomplished in this reconciliation.

Step 4. For 1970, the total purchases for education were converted to input-output industries by use of the coefficients in Table 5–3. For 1980, the total was added to the projections of the other six major functions before allocating them to industries.

Highways

State and local government net purchases for highways consist of the provision and maintenance of highway facilities, bridges, tunnels, and barriers, as well as regular roads, city streets, street-lighting, and snow and ice removal. Although the Census definition includes provision and maintenance of toll roads and other toll facilities, for the purpose of this study they have been excluded. Separate projections were made for the two subcomponents, namely, current operation and capital outlay. Capital outlay, which constitutes about 75 percent of the total, is composed of construction expenses and purchases of equipment and land; current operation is primarily compensation of employees, although it also includes purchases of other small items not classified under capital outlay.

Between 1957 and 1968, the growth rate for highways was about 4.2 percent per year. The capital outlay portion grew fastest, with a 5.1 percent growth rate, while current operation purchases lagged, with only a 1.2 percent annual growth. Purchases of goods and services for highways have declined as a share of total state and local government purchases, and this trend is expected to continue through the 1970s. In dollar terms, however, purchases will continue to rise considerably as state and local governments are confronted with the need for an expanded system of highways and streets.

As with the education component, considerable variations occur among states with respect to the absolute amount and annual rate of increase in expenditures for highways. There is a noticeable difference, therefore, in the degree to which expenditures can be explained by regression equations using time, population, and income as explanatory variables. An additional consideration that complicated the projection of this component is the fact that a large portion of the state highway funds comes from the federal government. In 1967, $4.1 billion of the total $11.2 billion state and local government highway expenditures was financed by federal grants [73]. In the federal-aid program, costs are generally shared on a 90 percent federal and a 10 percent state basis for interstate projects and on an equal basis for other federal-aid projects [166]. Consequently, expenditures by a state fluctuate from year to year, in part, according to how the federal government administers its funds.

Separate projections were made for capital outlay and for current operations because each component appeared to reflect a different trend. In addition, the mix between capital outlay and daily operating expenditures differed considerably among states. A certain degree of accuracy would therefore have been sacrificed if the two components had been combined and a single projection made. Also, by separating the two components, different deflators could be used for each. To produce a constant dollar historical series, the nonresidential construction deflator was applied to the current dollar capital outlay data, and the SLG deflator was used for the current operation data.

After testing several independent variables, the equation that was finally chosen for both capital outlays and current operations was:

$$E_t^i = a_0 + a_1 t \tag{5.3}$$

where

E^i = expenditures in state i

t = the year

a_0, a_1 = least squares estimates using data from 1957 through 1968

In the case of a few states where there was no significant trend, the least squares fit of the equations was very poor, and the 1968 purchases were therefore used as estimates for 1970 and 1980. This procedure was used for Idaho, Kansas, and Vermont for the projection of current operations and for Massachusetts for the projection of capital outlay.

The values obtained from equation (5.3) were used to estimate each state's share of the national total. These shares were then applied to the national BLS projection of total highway purchases in estimating the final projections for this function before allocating the 1970 total to input-output industries. The 1980 total was aggregated with projections of the other major components before distributing it to industries.

Hospitals, Health, and Sanitation

State and local government net purchases for hospitals comprise the establishment and operation of hospital facilities, provision of hospital care, and support of private hospitals. The health component encompasses research, clinics, immunization, and other general public-health activities. Sanitation (other than sewerage) includes street-cleaning and collection and disposal of garbage and other waste. Whereas the BLS lists expenditures to reduce water and air pollution under the sanitation category, the Census lists these under health. For the purpose of making the projections, this function was divided into two subcomponents: (1) health and hospitals, and (2) sanitation. This division was based upon the availability of Census data. Separate figures for hospitals and for health are available on a state-by-state basis for 1957, 1962, and 1967. Data on the two categories combined and on sanitation other than sewerage are available annually from 1957 through 1968, however.

Historically, the annual growth rate of this component has been about 3.9 percent. Within this total, the health and hospitals subcomponent has grown 4.2 percent per year, while sanitation has lagged considerably, with only a 1.9 percent annual growth. The BLS national projection indicates that the total component is expected to increase about 5.6 percent a year during the coming decade. Because of the recent concern over environmental control, an unprecedented increase in the percent of SLG purchases allocated to this component will undoubtedly occur. The problem of solid-waste accumulation has also begun to plague our nation's cities, requiring new and expanded methods of disposal. Added to these complications is the undefinable impact of federal programs, such as Medicare and Medicaid, and an increasing concern with the plight of the poverty-stricken, whose health needs are a major problem. The large federal-grants program adds another complicating factor to the development of reliable projections. As with highways, federal grants for such purposes as hospital construction and development of solid-waste management programs are a significant percentage of state expenditures. Since the federal grants have little correlation with historical trends in state expenditures, there is great difficulty in making reliable projections for the component.

Actual data from the calendar year 1970 are too recent to show the effect of the above-mentioned issues on SLG purchases, and the economic situation of 1970 and 1971 will act as a restraint to their expansion. But by 1980, as is evident in the national projection for this component, purchases are expected to increase considerably. Because of the many special problems, the projections for individual states were especially difficult to make. The degree to which any state is responsive to the increasing needs of health, hospitals, and sanitation is largely undeterminable. In spite of its limitations, the best procedure was to rely on relationships observed in the past. As with the other functions, data on expenditures in past years show a wide variation from state to state, and therefore projection equations had to be developed using historical data on expenditures in each state.

A change in the Census data classification occurred in 1960. Before that year, vendor payments for health and hospital services provided as part of public assistance programs were classified under "health" or "hospitals" as applicable. As of 1960, these payments are classified under "public welfare". In the *Census of Governments, 1967* [73] , revised state-by-state figures for 1957 are included insofar as state government vendor payments are concerned. Exact data on vendor payments by local governments in 1957 are not available, but indications are that the amount is relatively small. Consequently, the revised figures for 1957 may be considered comparable to Census figures for 1960–1968.

After a thorough examination of historical data on the relationship between expenditures and time, population, and income for the nation, as well as for a number of states, the following equations were selected for hospitals and sanitation, respectively:

Log of $E_t^i = a_0 + a_1 t$ $\qquad\qquad\qquad\qquad\qquad\qquad\qquad\qquad$ (5.4)

$E_t^i = b_0 + b_1 t$ $\qquad\qquad\qquad\qquad\qquad\qquad\qquad\qquad\qquad$ (5.5)

where

E^i $\quad$ = expenditures for state i

t $\qquad$ = time

a_0, a_1 = least squares estimates using data for 1957[2] and for 1960 through 1968

b_0, b_1 = least squares estimates using data from 1957 through 1968.

Regression equations for a few states (Indiana, Michigan, Minnesota, Missouri, and Pennsylvania) indicated a poor fit. For these states, the expenditures for 1968 were used as projections for 1970 and 1980.

Natural Resources

The natural-resources function includes purchases for conservation and the development of agriculture, fish and game, forestry, soil resources (irrigation, drainage, and flood control), state parks, agricultural experiment stations, and extension services. Parks and recreational facilities, water supply, and electric utilities of local governments and state hydroelectric power activities are excluded from state and local government net purchases of goods and services.

Although population growth will necessitate additional parks and recreational facilities, the expenditures by a state for natural resources cannot be related to changes in its population, since much of the demand for its facilities comes from out-of-state visitors. The amount of money committed to the development of natural resources depends largely on the physical characteristics of the state, its forests, lakes, and rivers, for example. Because of the vastly different opportunities for resource development, large variations among states can be expected. A comparison between Michigan and New Jersey, two states fairly similar in population and personal income, illustrates this point. In 1967, New Jersey spent $37,734,000 on natural resources, whereas Michigan, a state much more bountiful in lakes and forests, spent $68,273,000. As shown in Table 5-5, the extremes for 1967 were Delaware, where state and local govern-

---

2. Revised in conjunction with a change in data classification made in 1960.

Table 5-5
Variation Among States in State and Local Government Expenditures and Net Purchases for Natural Resources (1958 dollars)

	Smallest[a]			Largest			U.S. Mean	
	State		Amount	State		Amount		Amount
Actual expenditures (in millions of dollars)								
1957	Delaware	=	$1.8	California	=	$217.9		$21.6
1967	Delaware	=	3.2	California	=	582.2		34.5
Projected net purchases (in millions of dollars)								
1970	Delaware	=	3.2	California	=	590.3		35.0
1980	Delaware	=	5.4	California	=	995.4		58.9
Per capita expenditures (in dollars)								
1957	Massachusetts	=	1.96	Nevada	=	30.44		6.22
1967	Massachusetts	=	2.29	California	=	30.40		8.88
Annual growth rate[b] 1957–1967	New York	=	-0.4%	California	=	13.9%		8.6%

[a] District of Columbia had no expenditures.
[b] Based on current dollars.

ments spent $3.2 million on natural resources, and California, where $582.2 million was spent.

As with the data for health and hospitals, a change in classification was made in 1960 for this function. Revised figures by the Census for 1957 through 1959 do, however, incorporate this change [73]. While national data are available on an annual basis, state-by-state expenditures data are available for only 1957, 1962, and 1967. Because of the lack of more state data for this component, it appeared that the best method would be to distribute the national projection to states based on the 1967 actual distribution. This would allow the national total to change between the base and projection years, but not the relative share of each state. The procedure can be summarized in the following three steps:

Step 1. Determine for each state the share of the national total of expenditures for natural resources for the base period 1967.

Step 2. Apply the percentage shares derived in Step 1 to the BLS national projection of purchases for natural resources in both 1970 and 1980. It is assumed, of course, that the share of expenditures and purchases for a state are similar.

Step 3. Distribute the 1970 total purchases for natural resources of each state to input-output industries based on the coefficients obtained from the BLS and given in Table 5-3. For 1980, the estimates for this function were aggregated with those of the other components before distributing them to industries.

Local Parks and Recreation

This category includes net purchases for local government parks, playgrounds and playing fields, swimming pools and bathing beaches, and special facilities for recreation and cultural-scientific activities, such as auditoriums, museums, stadiums, zoos, auto camps, and local boat harbors. Purchases for this category are restricted to local governments.

For the period 1957–1967, the annual growth rate in expenditures for local parks and recreation was about 4.5 percent, which is just slightly above that of the total economy. The BLS projection for this category does indicate that this growth rate should accelerate substantially during the 1970s. Among states, however, a great variation occurs in both the historical and projected growth rates for this component. In deriving reliable projections for local parks and recreation, the lack of annual state-by-state data on metropolitan population was a severe handicap. Most of the outlays are for parks and recreation in metropolitan areas that have had significant changes in population. Because data on state population obscure internal movement within a state to the cities, the reliability of the projections was reduced by the necessity of basing projections on changes in the total state population rather than on changes in urban population.

The specific methodology used to make the 1970 and 1980 projections for this component are summarized in the following four steps.

Step 1. Projection of per capita state and local government expenditures for local parks and recreation for the nation:

$$\text{Log of } PCN_t = a_0 + a_1 t \tag{5.6}$$

where

PCN = per capita expenditures for the nation

t = the year

a_0, a_1 = least squares estimates using data from 1957 through 1968.

Step 2. Projection of expenditures for each state:

$$E_t^i = \left[E_{1968}^i\right] \left[\frac{PCN_t}{PCN_{1968}}\right] \left[\frac{P_t^i}{P_{1968}^i}\right] \tag{5.7}$$

where

E^i = the expenditures for state i

PCN = per capita expenditures for the nation

P^i = the population of state i

t = the year.

Step 3. For each state, the share of the national total was then calculated from the estimates obtained in Step 2 and applied to the BLS national projection of purchases for local parks and recreation to calculate state-by-state purchases for both 1970 and 1980.

Step 4. The 1970 input-output distribution was determined for this category by applying the coefficients from Table 5–3 to the state-by-state purchases as estimated in Step 3. The 1980 total for each state was added to the estimates of the other six functions before allocating to industries, since coefficients are not available for each function.

Enterprises

This component comprises the activities of the state and local government agencies that cover over half of their current operating costs by the sale of goods and services to the general public. This includes water-supply systems, gas-supply systems, electric-power systems, transit systems, sewerage, housing and urban renewal, water transportation, air transportation, and highway toll facilities. In addition to the above, there is some SLG outlay for parking facilities and miscellaneous other commercial activities, but the amounts were so small that they have been ignored in this study. The percentage distribution of the major subfunctions in 1967 is shown in Table 5-6.

While the historical growth in enterprises has been only about 1.6 percent per year, the national projection indicates that this growth rate is expected to accelerate to 8.0 percent per year during the decade 1970-1980. This increase in the growth rate can largely be explained by the greatly increasing needs in urban renewal and new transit facilities. In addition, the number of transit facilities that have been changing from private to public ownership has also increased substantially in recent years, and the trend is expected to continue.

State and local government capital outlays for enterprises varies considerably among states. For example, per capita expenditures for water-supply systems in Kansas were nearly 10 times those of West Virginia. In 1967 California spent 250 times as much as Vermont for water-supply systems. Many states have no discernible time trend, and in a few regions, such as the District of Columbia, the trend has been negative. Because the historical expenditures patterns for other enterprises are as erratic as those for water-supply systems, it was difficult to make reliable projections. Each of the components identified in Table 5-6, nevertheless, was analyzed individually, and separate projections were made for each subfunction.

An additional factor that complicated the projections was the scarcity of data available on the state-to-state distribution of expenditures or purchases. Although complete data are available for sewerage, water-supply systems, and highway toll facilities, information for the other subfunctions is limited to 1957, 1962, and 1967.

The following section presents the detailed equations for each of the nine subfunctions of state and local government enterprises.

Water-Supply Systems. Projections of capital outlay for each state for 1970 and 1980

$$CO_t^i = a_0 + a_1 P_t^i \tag{5.8}$$

where

Table 5-6
Percentage Distribution of Subfunctions Within State and Local Government Enterprises, 1967

Subfunctions	Percentage
Water-supply systems	23.1
Gas-supply systems	0.8
Electricity	11.9
Transit facilities	6.9
Sewerage	22.0
Housing & urban renewal	20.0
Water transportation & terminals[a]	4.1
Air transportation[b]	6.1
Highway toll facilities	5.1
Total	100.0

[a]Water transportation and terminals involves the provision, operation, and support of canals and other waterways, harbors, docks, wharves, and related terminal facilities.

[b]Air transportation includes provision of airports and related activities.

Source: Census of Governments, 1967 [73].

CO^i = capital outlay of state i

t = the year

P^i = the civilian population of state i as of July 1st of each year

a_0, a_1 = least squares estimates using data from 1961–1968

For a few states where there was no trend, the least squares fit of the equation was not acceptable, and the state-by-state expenditures for 1968 were therefore used to represent the projections for both 1970 and 1980.

Gas-Supply Systems. The 1970 and 1980 projections of capital outlay for this component were made by first projecting the national total and then relating the individual state changes to the national change as shown by the following equations:

$$CON_t = a_0 + a_1 t \tag{5.9}$$

where

CON = the national capital outlay

t = the year

a_0, a_1 = least squares estimates using data from 1957 through 1968;

$$CO_t = \left[CO^i_{1967} \right] \left[\frac{CON_t}{CON_{1967}} \right] \tag{5.10}$$

where

CO^i = capital outlay of state i.

Electricity. As with gas-supply systems, the projections of the capital outlay for this subfunction were made by relating the state projections to independent national projections as follows:

$$CON_t = a_0 + a_1 P_t \tag{5.11}$$

where

CON = the national capital outlay total

t = time

P = population

a_0, a_1 = least squares estimates using data from 1957 to 1968;

$$CO^i_t = CO^i_{1967} + a_1 \left[P_t - P_{1967} \right]^i \tag{5.12}$$

where

CO^i = capital outlay in state i

P^i = population in state i

t = the year

a_1 = the least squares estimates from equation (5.11).

Transit Facilities. Given the fact that there are a very limited number of transit systems and their capital outlays are normally planned many years in advance, the projections for this component are based on information obtained from the various transit authorities. Specifically, the various authorities in Boston, Chicago, Cleveland, New Jersey, New York, Philadelphia, San Francisco, Washington, and Atlanta were contacted for their own projections of capital outlays for both 1970 and 1980.

Sewerage. The 1970 and 1980 projections were derived in the following manner:

Step 1. Projection of per capita expenditures for each state for 1970 and 1980

$$PE_t^i = a_0 + a_1 t \qquad\qquad (5.13)$$

where

PE^i = per capita expenditures for state i

t = the year

a_0, a_1 = least squares estimates using data from 1957 and 1968.

In the case of a few states where there was no significant trend, the least squares fit of the equation was not acceptable, and the observed outlays in the state for 1967 were therefore used as projections for 1970 and 1980.

Step 2. Calculation of the 1970 and 1980 capital outlay for each state

$$CO_t^i = \left[PE_t^i \right] \left[P_t^i \right] \qquad\qquad (5.14)$$

where

CO^i = the capital outlay for state i

PE_t^i = estimate from equation (5.13)

P^i = population for state i

t = the year.

Housing and Urban Renewal. The same procedure used to project capital outlay of electricity was followed for this subfunction.

Water Transportation and Terminals. The projection of this subcomponent was made in the following three steps:

Step 1. Projections of 1970 and 1980 capital outlay for the nation

$$CON_t = a_0 + a_1 t \qquad\qquad (5.15)$$

where

CON = capital outlay for the nation

t = the year

a_0, a_1 = least squares estimates using data from 1957 through 1968.

Step 2. Estimates of 1967 capital outlay for each state[3]

$$CO_t^i = 0.60\,E_t \qquad (5.16)$$

where

CO^i =   capital outlay for state i

E_t =   direct general expenditures in year t.

Step 3. State capital outlay projections for 1970 and 1980

$$CO_t^i = \left[CO_{1967}^i\right]\left[\frac{CON_t}{CON_{1967}}\right] \qquad (5.17)$$

where CO^i is capital outlay for state i, and the second term on the right is the ratio of capital outlay computed from Step 1 and the observed capital outlay for 1967.

Air Transportation. The procedure followed for projecting water transportation and terminals was used, except that in Step 2, direct general expenditures were multiplied by a factor of 0.67 to estimate capital outlay.

Highway Toll Facilities. Capital outlay 1970 and 1980 projections for each state were calculated as follows:

$$CO_t^i = a_0 + a_1 t \qquad (5.18)$$

where

CO^i =   capital outlay for state i

t =   the year

a_0, a_1 =   least squares estimates using data for the time period 1960 through 1968.

In the case of a few states where there was no significant time trend, the least squares estimate was unacceptable, and the 1968 capital outlays for that state were used as projections for 1970 and 1980. The estimates obtained for each of the nine subfunctions of state and local enterprises were then aggregated for each state for both 1970 and 1980. The state-by-state percentage share of expenditures was then multiplied by the national projection of total enterprises

---

3. Capital outlay in 1967 amounted to 60 percent of the direct general expenditures for water transport and terminals for the nation.

Table 5-7
Percentage Distribution of Subfunctions Within
the All Other Category (fiscal year 1967)

Subfunction	Percentage
1. Police	16.4
2. Fire	8.1
3. Correction	5.9
4. Public welfare[a]	19.2
5. Libraries	2.8
6. General government	20.8
General control	
Financial administration	
Social security administration	
7. Other	26.8
Total	100.0

[a]Excludes assistance payments.
Source: Census of Governments, 1967 [73].

purchases to determine a final estimate for each state. The 1970 estimates were distributed to input-output industries in accordance with the vector given in column 6 of Table 5-3. For 1980, the enterprises total was added to the estimates for all the other six functions before distributing to input-output industries.

The All Other Category

This component consists of all items not elsewhere classified. The percentage distribution among the subfunctions is given in Table 5-7. Expenditures for police protection include highway police patrols, crime-prevention activities, detention and custody of persons awaiting trial, traffic safety, vehicle inspection, and the like. Fire protection is limited to activities of local government; however, the state expenditures for forest-fire fighting are classified under natural resources. Expenditures on correction include confinement and correction of adults and minors convicted of offenses against the law, as well as pardon, probation, and parole activities. "Other public welfare" spending consists of vendor payments[4] under welfare programs, institutional care of the needy, and administration of welfare activities. The category "libraries" encompasses public libraries operated by the government (except school libraries primarily for students and teachers) as well as support of other publicly and privately operated libraries. The "general control" function is comprised of activities of govern-

---

4. Vendor payments are payments made directly to private vendors for medical care and other goods and services provided under welfare programs for the needy.

mental chief executives and their staffs, legislative bodies, administration of justice, and agencies concerned with personnel administration, law, records, planning, and zoning.

As a percentage of total SLG purchases, the all other category is expected to increase throughout the 1970s. Because of the increasing concern for helping the disadvantaged in our country and improving public safety, public welfare and police will probably be among the most rapidly growing subfunctions. Moreover, as state and local governments become larger and more complex, administrative costs will increase.

The specific methodology used to project each of the subfunctions is detailed in the remaining part of this section.

Police.   The projection of this subfunction was completed in the following three steps:

Step 1.   Projection of national per capita expenditures for 1970 and 1980

$$PEN_t = a_0 + a_1 t \qquad\qquad\qquad\qquad (5.19)$$

where

PEN = per capita expenditures for the nation

t = the year

a_0, a_1 = least squares estimates from data for 1957 through 1968.

Step 2.   Projection of 1970 and 1980 per capita expenditures for each state

$$PE_t^i = \left[PE_{1967}^i\right] \left[\frac{PEN_t}{PEN_{1967}}\right] \qquad\qquad (5.20)$$

Step 3.   Calculation of 1970 and 1980 total expenditures for each state

$$E_t^i = \left[PE_t^i\right]\left[P_t^i\right] \qquad\qquad\qquad (5.21)$$

where

E^i = total expenditures for state i

PE_t^i = per capita expenditures for state i in year t

P_t^i = population of state i in year t,

Fire.

$$E_t^i = a_0 + a_1 Y_t^i \tag{5.22}$$

where

E^i $\quad$ = expenditures for state i

Y^i $\quad$ = personal income of state i

t $\quad$ = the year

a_0, a_1 = least squares estimates using data from 1957 through 1968.

Correction.

$$E_t^i = \begin{bmatrix} \text{Ratio of correction} \\ \text{expenditures to} \\ \text{police expenditures} \end{bmatrix}_{1967}^{i} \begin{bmatrix} \text{Police} \\ \text{expenditures} \end{bmatrix}_{t}^{i} \tag{5.23}$$

Public Welfare.

$$\log \text{ of } E_t^i = a_0 + a_1 t \tag{5.24}$$

where

E^i $\quad$ = expenditures for state i

t $\quad$ = the year

a_0, a_1 = least squares estimates using data from 1957, 1962, and 1967.

General Government and Other Categories. The state expenditures for these items were projected using the same equation as that of public welfare above.

Libraries. The state expenditures for libraries were projected to be 0.03 percent of the sum of the previous six categories, that is, police, fire, correction, public welfare, general government, and other expenditures.

The estimates for the nine subfunctions were then aggregated for each state. This represented the 1970 total for the all other category which was distributed to input-output industries using the coefficients given in Table 5-3. For 1980, this total was aggregated with the totals from the other six major functions prior to allocating the industries.

Conclusions

In this chapter, the methodology used in making 1970 and 1980 projections of state and local government net purchases of goods and services for each state was described. The general procedure consisted of subdividing the total purchases into functional categories and using the individual historical patterns within each state to project purchases in each of the functional categories, usually by means of regression analysis. For each function, the historical trend of expenditures was examined closely in relation to time, population, and personal income before the most appropriate method of projection was chosen. State projections were reconciled so that the sum equalled the national control totals. Finally, the state-by-state projections were allocated to input-output industries according to conversion vectors provided by the BLS.

Although the annual growth rate between 1970 and 1980 is projected to decrease slightly from that observed during the 1957-1968 period, a continuing upward trend is expected. For each of the seven functions, the SLG purchases are expected to increase, but at different rates. The rate of growth of the enterprise function, for example, is projected to be 8.8 percent per year for the period 1970-1980, while for highways, it is expected to be only 3.0 percent per year. This in turn will, of course, affect the percentage distribution of SLG purchases among functions. From 1967 to 1980, purchases for parks and recreation, enterprises, and the "other" category will show relative increases at the expense of education and highways. These shifts can be explained in terms of a decreasing rate of growth of the school-age population, a slowing of various highway expenditures, and an increasing demand for additional recreational activity. The proportion of purchases allocated to hospitals, health, sanitation, and natural resources is projected to change only slightly between 1967 and 1980.

Before more reliable projections could be obtained for this SLG component, certain improvements would be necessary in the data. Components having serious data limitations are welfare, hospitals, and natural resources. The lack of regional variation in the conversion coefficients from function to input-output industries is also a limitation. In addition, a separate set of coefficients for the distribution of purchases of input-output industries for each of the functional categories in 1980 would be beneficial. If it is not feasible to develop a distribution pattern for each function for 1980, the existing distribution pattern of the BLS should at least be reviewed. A greater proportion of total purchases seems, for example, to have been allocated to local parks and recreation than appears justified based on analysis in this study.

The final 1970 and 1980 projections for each state for each of the seven functions are shown in Tables 5-8 and 5-9. As has been emphasized throughout this chapter, there are large variations among states in the relative size of functional categories and in their historical growth rates.

Table 5-8

Functional Distribution by State for 1970 State and Local Government Net Purchases of Goods and Services (millions of 1958 dollars)

State	Education	Highways	Hospitals, health, & sanitation	Natural resources	Local parks & recreation	Enterprises	Other	Total
Alabama	441	209	83	18	7	59	186	1,004
Arizona	341	133	38	20	11	53	143	740
Arkansas	224	114	42	16	2	35	104	538
California	374	1,154	687	590	208	781	3,184	6,978
Colorado	437	120	65	19	15	33	177	865
Connecticut	395	186	72	11	18	87	266	1,035
Delaware	104	59	14	3	1	13	66	261
District of Columbia	94	54	66	0	12	183	121	530
Florida	847	293	237	70	49	172	432	2,101
Georgia	583	223	178	34	14	104	221	1,357
Idaho	100	58	17	18	2	6	57	258
Illinois	1,560	477	331	43	76	214	810	3,512
Indiana	844	267	129	25	16	65	219	1,565
Iowa	491	225	72	21	11	31	191	1,041
Kansas	353	147	56	21	9	37	127	750
Kentucky	436	202	73	24	6	92	233	1,066
Louisiana	483	257	89	45	13	90	237	1,214
Maine	129	68	15	11	2	11	64	300
Maryland	605	171	137	20	33	189	296	1,449
Massachusetts	659	209	190	13	21	158	594	1,843
Michigan	1,535	390	295	52	45	195	735	3,247
Minnesota	649	279	127	30	18	82	297	1,483
Mississippi	268	150	65	18	4	31	135	670
Missouri	614	257	120	23	19	87	246	1,366
Montana	118	89	12	12	2	13	46	292
Nebraska	212	115	34	19	5	63	94	541
Nevada	103	65	25	7	3	20	75	298
New Hampshire	90	51	14	4	2	13	42	217

New Jersey	897	275	182	29	39	177	565	2,164
New Mexico	231	84	26	15	4	19	77	455
New York	3,508	849	1,060	85	144	508	2,559	8,713
North Carolina	639	217	112	28	10	84	233	1,323
North Dakota	122	62	10	10	6	9	81	300
Ohio	1,317	570	214	39	37	186	552	2,916
Oklahoma	360	141	61	19	7	39	270	896
Oregon	418	158	44	33	10	63	164	891
Pennsylvania	1,492	587	233	55	47	212	729	3,355
Rhode Island	123	55	24	7	3	19	102	334
South Carolina	282	103	65	12	5	40	133	640
South Dakota	118	81	8	9	2	7	41	266
Tennessee	459	254	121	22	12	140	224	1,232
Texas	1,478	620	224	75	51	267	500	3,214
Utah	243	88	20	11	6	12	79	459
Vermont	73	56	7	6	0	7	34	183
Virginia	618	338	101	27	16	118	260	1,477
Washington	597	230	67	40	14	222	273	1,443
West Virginia	224	150	34	13	3	11	104	540
Wisconsin	863	288	121	34	35	77	379	1,796
Wyoming	80	67	13	9	1	2	23	195
Alaska	74	101	8	7	2	19	82	293
Hawaii	153	41	28	13	13	34	122	404

0 = smaller than 0.500

NOTE: The numbers in this table have not been completely reconciled with those given in the appendix, Table B–9.

Table 5-9

Functional Distribution by State for 1980 State and Local Government Net Purchases of Goods and Services (millions of 1958 dollars)

State	Education	Highways	Hospitals, health, & sanitation	Natural resources	Local Parks & recreation	Enterprises	Other	Total
Alabama	663	288	167	30	22	111	471	1,752
Arizona	593	209	78	35	41	119	338	1,413
Arkansas	290	162	81	28	7	80	390	1,038
California	4,561	1,688	1,221	995	726	1,921	7,608	18,720
Colorado	660	153	128	33	48	69	476	1,567
Connecticut	409	260	105	19	59	185	545	1,582
Delaware	147	96	25	5	4	27	230	534
District of Columbia	127	79	116	0	39	573	251	1,185
Florida	1,399	401	468	118	178	405	987	3,956
Georgia	855	309	379	57	42	241	529	2,412
Idaho	128	75	30	31	7	16	160	447
Illinois	2,127	545	603	72	232	603	1,611	5,793
Indiana	1,021	379	219	43	48	138	306	2,154
Iowa	606	265	117	35	30	116	381	1,550
Kansas	407	166	83	35	26	75	204	996
Kentucky	769	284	152	40	16	197	718	2,176
Louisiana	561	351	172	76	41	237	450	1,888
Maine	168	84	19	19	5	19	105	419
Maryland	864	223	260	33	107	556	788	2,831
Massachusetts	891	226	251	21	63	330	1,182	2,964
Michigan	1,790	432	444	88	135	426	2,031	5,346
Minnesota	745	373	132	50	55	168	780	2,303
Mississippi	390	204	134	31	11	90	365	1,225
Missouri	950	350	214	39	57	196	468	2,274
Montana	128	127	15	20	6	47	76	419
Nebraska	255	147	54	32	16	99	215	818
Nevada	142	106	70	11	10	49	192	580
New Hampshire	118	63	20	8	8	33	65	315

New Jersey	1,039	400	275	48	126	448	891	3,227
New Mexico	354	113	45	25	14	51	184	786
New York	4,500	1,318	2,361	182	548	1,478	5,456	15,843
North Carolina	922	302	194	46	31	179	455	2,129
North Dakota	167	72	14	16	17	13	201	500
Ohio	1,800	701	304	65	115	393	673	4,051
Oklahoma	460	175	115	32	21	80	773	1,656
Oregon	612	215	74	56	32	144	317	1,450
Pennsylvania	1,691	817	307	93	135	415	1,272	4,730
Rhode Island	159	78	39	12	8	42	256	594
South Carolina	341	134	118	21	14	82	345	1,055
South Dakota	137	105	12	15	5	14	61	349
Tennessee	703	360	256	36	37	327	544	2,263
Texas	1,913	795	389	127	158	523	1,084	4,989
Utah	382	133	37	19	18	30	232	851
Vermont	120	81	10	9	2	20	79	321
Virginia	779	530	170	45	50	330	565	2,469
Washington	864	335	91	67	43	423	732	2,555
West Virginia	261	237	59	22	8	19	274	880
Wisconsin	1,759	357	181	57	105	165	911	3,535
Wyoming	122	96	20	15	3	5	36	297
Alaska	135	199	13	11	6	32	187	583
Hawaii	407	60	42	21	39	.67	269	905

0 = smaller than 0.500

NOTE: The numbers in this table have not been completely reconciled with those given in the appendix, Table B-10.

6 Federal Government Purchases of Goods and Services

Federal government purchases have generally been one of the smaller final demand components, comprising about 10 percent of GNP. By 1980, the federal government's share is expected to decline to approximately 7.5 percent of the total, which implies an annual growth rate of less than 1 percent per year. Federal expenditures, in the national income accounts, are divided into two components: defense and nondefense. Since trust fund expenditures are not included in final demand, the defense portion is the dominant category, representing about 70 percent of all federal purchases.

Although the same basic methodology was employed to obtain 1970 and 1980 projections of the other final demand components, this could not be done for the federal government component. Instead, most of the resources were committed to determining a relatively good 1970 projection, since the limited historical data provided little basis for projecting the state distribution of federal government purchases for a year as distant as 1980. The 1980 projection was then obtained by adjusting each state's 1970 industrial distribution according to the expected change in its share of output by industry between 1970 and 1980.

The remaining sections of this chapter summarize the methodologies used to project the following categories: (1) Department of Defense (DOD) purchases for 1970; (2) nondefense purchases for 1970; and (3) total federal government purchases for 1980.

Department of Defense Purchases for 1970

Department of Defense purchases is one of the more difficult final demand components to project, since it depends heavily on world conditions which can change rapidly. As a percentage of GNP, it has fluctuated from a high of 42 percent toward the end of World War II to a low of about 4 percent in 1947. It represented about 8.5 percent of GNP in 1970. The BLS national projection was made under the assumption that there will be no major future conflicts; consequently, defense purchases are expected to decline to 4 percent of GNP by 1980.

No other component of final demand is as concentrated as defense expenditures, both in terms of input-output producing industries and geographic regions. For example, over 60 percent of these expenditures is concentrated in five input-output industries.[1] Approximately 33 percent is concentrated in eight states: California, Connecticut, Illinois, New York, Ohio, Pennsylvania, Texas, and Virginia.

Methodology

The choice of projection methodology was severely limited by the general lack of any reliable historical data on the regional distribution of defense purchases. The estimates by HERP for 1947, 1958, and 1963 represent the only comprehensive historical data available [58]. The reliance of those estimates on measures of output, however, limits their usefulness for developing estimating relationships.

Given the data limitations, and the fact that the BLS national projections would represent the control totals for each input-output industry, the decision was made to accept the most recently observed state-by-state distribution for calculating 1970 state shares. In general, the most recently observed data were for 1967 and 1968. A major factor in the decision to use the distribution patterns for a recent year was that most DOD production contracts run for several years; therefore, patterns change slowly, and the 1967 regional distribution of purchases was probably quite similar to that of 1970. This is particularly true for major weapons systems, such as aircraft, ships, and missiles, which represent a significant portion of purchases.

Although a state distribution was often determined from actual expenditures data, many proxy variables had to be used when these were not available. The overall procedure employed was as follows:

1. Determine the most recent expenditures or proxy series that most closely represents each input-output industry.
2. Derive state-by-state percentage shares of the national purchase or proxy total.
3. Apply the state percentages from (2) to the BLS 1970 national projection by input-output industry to determine the value for each state for each industry.

General Data Sources

The five basic data sources used to develop the state-by-state distribution of DOD expenditures are as follows:

---

1. The input-output industries represented in the 60 percent for 1970 are IO-13, Ordnance & accessories; IO-56, Radio, television & communication equipment; IO-60, Aircraft & parts; IO-61, Other transportation equipment; and IO-84, Government industry.

1. *Military Prime Contract Awards by Region and State, 1968* [145]. This publication, hereafter referred to as *Prime Contracts,* yields data recording the dollar value of contracts signed by various agencies of the United States government for some 25 categories of military procurement by state. While constituting the best available data on defense purchases, there are some limitations in the use of these data for this study. The primary limitation is that often the contract is coded to the location of corporate headquarters and not necessarily to the actual production facility. Another is that the categories described in the publication are in terms of DOD programs which are not easily related to input-output industries.

2. "Construction Appropriation Data by State for Fiscal Year 1970" from the Department of Defense [141]. In this unpublished source, the planned construction purchases by military installation are listed. The data have two limitations: they are based on appropriations which are not necessarily equal to expenditures; and they are reported on a fiscal-year instead of a calendar-year basis.

3. "Data on Civilian and Military Employment by State" from the Department of Defense [142]. These unpublished data specify total Department of Defense employment as of June 30, 1969.

4. *County Business Patterns, 1967* [84]. This publication gives the number of employees by SIC industry by state. However, the lack of detailed data on SIC categories presented difficulties in converting the numbers from the SIC to the input-output classification.

5. *Shipments of Defense-Oriented Industries MA-175, 1967* [111]. This source, hereafter referred to as *Shipments,* specifies the value of shipments purchased by the Department of Defense. Not only is information on prime contracts presented for sixteen types of expenditures for nine Census regions, but some limited information is available on subcontracts. A disadvantage is that the tiers of subcontracts are mixed, and the classification system is not easily converted to input-output industries.

Specific Data Sources and Procedures

This section specifies which expenditures or proxy series was employed to determine the state-by-state distribution of defense purchases for each input-output industry.

County Business Patterns, 1967. For many industries, no defense purchases data were available to determine the state distribution; consequently, purchases were assumed to take place where production and, therefore, employment occurred. Regression analysis of cross-section data on states for some selected industries indicated that production, employment, and defense purchases in a

Table 6-1
Defense Purchases Allocated According to Employment Data from
County Business Patterns, 1967

Industry Number	Industry Title
6	Nonferrous metal ores mining
7	Coal mining
10	Chemical & fertilizer mineral mining
14	Food & kindred products
15	Tobacco manufactures
16	Broad & narrow fabrics, yarn & thread mills
17	Miscellaneous textile goods & floor coverings
18	Apparel
19	Miscellaneous fabricated textile products
20	Lumber & wood products, except containers
21	Wooden containers
22	Household furniture
23	Other furniture & fixtures
24	Paper & allied products, except containers & boxes
25	Paperboard containers & boxes
26	Printing & publishing
28	Plastics & synthetic materials
29	Drugs, cleaning, & toilet preparations
30	Paints & allied products
33	Leather tanning & industrial leather products
34	Footwear & other leather products
35	Glass & glass products
36	Stone & clay products
39	Metal containers
40	Heating, plumbing, & fabricated structural metal products
43	Engines & turbines
44	Farm machinery & equipment
51	Office, computing, & accounting machines
52	Service industry machines
54	Household appliances
65	Transportation & warehousing
69	Wholesale & retail trade
70	Finance & insurance
71	Real estate & rental
72	Hotels & lodging places; personal & repair services, except automobile repair
75	Automobile repair & services
76	Amusements
77	Medical, educational services, & nonprofit organizations

state have a high positive correlation.[2] The industries allocated according to the above data are specified in Table 6-1.

---

2. Regressions were done on input-output industries IO-13, Ordnance & accessories, and IO-60, Aircraft & parts.

Prime Contracts and *County Business Patterns, 1967 (CBP).*   Industries that were allocated based on *Prime Contracts* as the main data source and *CBP* as a secondary source are presented in Table 6-2. Because the *Prime Contracts* distribution does not take account of the significant amount of subcontracting, an adjustment had to be made to this distribution. Previous studies indicated that, in general, 50 percent of the value of prime contracts is subcontracted to other establishments, and, of that total, 30 percent is subcontracted to firms in the state where the prime contract was awarded. Consequently, 65 percent of the total value of each prime contract was coded to the state of origin. On the assumption that subcontracts and employment by industry are highly correlated, the remaining 35 percent was distributed to the other states based on the employment data from *CBP.*[3]

Shipments and *County Business Patterns, 1967.*   The industries allocated according to these two sources are presented in Table 6-3. The DOD shipments data by category are given for only nine census regions of the United States. The state-by-state distribution within each of the census regions, therefore, was determined by use of *CBP* employment data. Here again the assumption was made that the state-by-state distribution of production and DOD expenditures is similar.

Defense Employment.   IO-84, Government industry, as well as an additional eight industries, was distributed to states on the basis of DOD employment. Table 6-4 specifies these industries. Here the defense purchases were assumed to be local purchases—purchases that are made in the area around military posts and other installations primarily to support the day-to-day operations of the establishment. Consequently, the state where the military installation is located and the state where the purchase takes place are identical. With the exeption of IO-84, Government industry, which is really purchases of labor services, the dollar value in each of these industries is quite small.

Nondefense Purchases for 1970

Although the federal budget for nondefense purchases is specified in terms of functions, that is, space research, education, welfare, and others, this category of direct federal purchases is so small that the BLS projections do not include detail by function. Instead, the BLS projection for total nondefense purchases

---

3. Unfortunately, after making this adjustment to account for subcontracts, it was found that the adjustment caused some minor distortion, since the shipments of components made under subcontract are actually in the interregional flow estimates and therefore should not be part of final demand. This part of the 1970 and 1980 methodology also differed from that used for the 1947, 1958, and 1963 state estimates.

Table 6-2

Defense Purchases Allocated According to *Prime Contracts* and Employment from *County Business Patterns*, 1967

Input-Output Industry		Prime Contracts Industry	
Number	Title	Number[a]	Title
13	Ordnance & accessories	6, 8 and 9	Combat vehicles, weapons & ammunition
31	Petroleum refining & related industries	11 and 12	Petroleum & other fuels & lubricants
45	Construction, mining, oil field machinery & equipment	20	Construction equipment
46	Materials handling machinery & equipment	23	Materials handling equipment
47	Metalworking machinery & equipment	18	Production equipment
48	Special industry machinery & equipment	18	Production equipment
50	Machine shop products	18	Production equipment
59	Motor vehicles & equipment	7	Noncombat vehicles
60	Aircraft & parts	1, 2 and 3	Airframes & related assemblies & spares
			Aircraft engines & related spares
			Other aircraft equipment & supplies
61	Other transportation equipment	5 and 17	Ships & transportation equipment
63	Optical, ophthalmic, & photographic equipment & supplies	22	Photographic equipment & supplies
64	Miscellaneous manufacturing	24	All other supplies & equipment

[a]The industry breakdown published in *Prime Contracts* is numbered sequentially starting with Industry 1, Airframes & related assemblies & spares, through Industry 25, Services, for purposes of this project [145].

Table 6-3
Defense Purchases Allocated According to *Shipments* and Employment from *County Business Patterns*, 1967

Input-Output Industry		Shipments Industry	
Number	Title	Number[a]	Title
27	Chemicals & selected chemical products	12	Selected chemicals & allied products
32	Rubber & miscellaneous plastics products	14	Fabricated rubber products, n.e.c.
37	Primary iron & steel manufacturing	15	Selected primary metal industries
38	Primary nonferrous metals manufacturing	15	Selected primary metal industries
41	Screw machine products, bolts, nuts, etc., & metal stampings	10	Selected fabricated metal products
42	Other fabricated metal products	10	Selected fabricated metal products
49	General industrial machinery & equipment	8	Other machinery
53	Electric transmission & distribution equipment & electrical industrial apparatus	9	Electric transmission & industrial apparatus; wiring devices, & miscellaneous electrical equipment
55	Electric lighting & wiring equipment	9	Electric transmission & industrial apparatus; wiring devices, & miscellaneous electrical equipment
58	Miscellaneous electrical machinery, equipment, & supplies	9	Electric transmission & industrial apparatus; wiring devices, & miscellaneous electrical equipment
62	Professional, scientific, & controlling instruments & supplies	6 and 7	Scientific instruments, mechanical measuring devices, optical instruments, & surgical & dental equipment, etc.

[a]The industrial breakdown published in *Shipments* is numbered sequentially starting with Industry 1, Turbines, construction machinery, machine tools, & computers, & related products, through Industry 16, Miscellaneous industries, for purposes of this project [111].

Table 6-4

Industries Allocated According to Defense Employment by State

Industry Number	Industry Title
4	Agricultural, forestry, & fisheries services
12	Maintenance & repair construction
66	Communications, except radio & TV broadcasting
68	Electric, gas, water, & sanitary services
73	Business services
78	Federal government enterprises
79	State & local government enterprises
82	Office supplies
84	Government industry

Table 6-5

Projected Percentage Distribution of Selected Industries for 1970 Nondefense Purchases

Industry Number	Industry Title	Percentage
11	New construction	23.0
13	Ordnance & accessories	5.5
56	Radio, TV, & communication equipment	3.5
60	Aircraft & parts	4.4
77	Medical, educational services, & nonprofit organizations	6.0
84	Government industry	28.0
Total		70.4

was distributed directly to input-output industries on the basis of historical data. These nondefense purchases are mostly a housekeeping function of branch offices of the various government agencies throughout the nation. The purchases, therefore, are also concentrated in a very few industries, as Table 6-5 indicates.

Methodology

In general, the procedure previously described for the defense purchases component was used. More specifically, usually 1967 or 1968 data on purchases or proxy variables were employed to calculate the 1970 state distribution of the national input-output industry total as projected by the BLS.

From these data, state shares were computed which were then applied to the BLS 1970 national projection by input-output industry to determine the final state values for each industry. While the national total can change between the base year (1967 or 1968) and the projection year, the state distribution was assumed to remain constant. Given the rather small dollar value of total purchases for this category, as well as the unavailability of historical data, this approach appears realistic.

Numerous sources of data were utilized in deriving purchase or proxy variables. Each will be described in the following section. Some of the general limitations of the data are as follows: (1) for most of the input-output categories, purchases data are not on a state basis, and proxy variables had to be utilized; (2) where purchases data were available, they were not current due to the lags between compiling and publishing; and (3) because of restrictions on disclosure, only partial data were available.

Specific Data Sources and Procedures

This section presents the specific data sources and procedures that were used to derive the state-by-state distribution for each input-output industry. The first part presents those data sources and methods that were used to calculate distributions for a large number of industries, while the second part presents descriptions for individual input-output industries.

Nondefense Employment. The purchases of input-output industries presented in Table 6-6 required their being allocated according to federal non-military employment. In general, they are overhead purchases made in the daily operation of all federal government agencies. Although it would have been preferable to use a stock figure of the value of government buildings for IO-4,

Table 6-6
Nondefense Purchases Allocated According to Nondefense Employment

Industry Number	Industry Title
4	Agricultural, forestry, & fisheries services
12	Maintenance & repair construction
51	Office, computing, & accounting machines
64	Miscellaneous manufacturing
66	Communications, except radio & TV broadcasting
68	Electric, gas, water, & sanitary services
71	Real estate & rental
72	Hotels & lodging places; personal & repair services, except automobile repair
75	Automobile repair & services
79	State & local government enterprises
82	Office supplies
84	Government industry

Table 6-7
Nondefense Purchases Allocated According to *Shipments* and Employment from *County Business Patterns*, 1967

Input-Output Industry		Shipments Industry	
Number	Title	Number[a]	Title
27	Chemicals & selected chemical products	12	Selected chemicals and allied products
32	Rubber & miscellaneous plastics products	14	Fabricated rubber products, n.e.c.
37	Primary iron & steel manufacturing	15	Selected primary metal industries
38	Primary nonferrous metals manufacturing	15	Selected primary metal industries
41	Screw machine products, bolts, nuts, etc., & metal stampings	10	Selected fabricated metal products
42	Other fabricated metal products	10	Selected fabricated metal products
49	General industrial machinery & equipment	8	Other machinery
53	Electric transmission & distribution equipment & electrical industrial apparatus	9	Electric transmission & industrial apparatus; wiring devices, & miscellaneous electrical equipment
55	Electric lighting & wiring equipment	9	Electric transmission & industrial apparatus; wiring devices, & miscellaneous electrical equipment
56	Radio, TV, & communication equipment	2	Communication equipment
57	Electronic components & accessories	3	Electronic components & accessories
58	Miscellaneous electrical machinery, equipment, & supplies	9	Electric transmission & industrial apparatus; wiring devices, & miscellaneous electrical equipment
62	Professional, scientific, & controlling instruments & supplies	6 and 7	Scientific instruments, mechanical measuring devices, optical instruments, & surgical & dental equipment, etc.

[a]The industry breakdown published in *Shipments* is numbered sequentially, starting with Industry 1, Turbines, construction machinery, machine tools, & computers & related products, through Industry 16, Miscellaneous industries, for purposes of this project [111].

Agricultural, forestry, & fisheries services, IO-12, Maintenance & repair construction, and IO-68, Electric, gas, water, & sanitary services, this estimate was not available. State-by-state employment figures were taken from the *Statistical Abstract of the United States, 1969* [122]. The Department of Defense employment was subtracted from total government employment for each state to determine the nonmilitary employment allocation vector.

Shipments **and** *County Business Patterns, 1967.* For the industries designated in Table 6-7, the nondefense purchases were distributed among the states using the same general two-part methodology as that used for defense purchases. The data were first distributed by region according to the pattern developed from data in *Shipments* [111] and then distributed among the states within each region by means of employment figures from *County Business Patterns, 1967* [84].

The first step in allocating these data was to subtract DOD shipments from total government shipments for each industry group. In some cases where the basic data were given as a range of values instead of absolute figures, an initial estimate was made based on the midpoint of the given range. These estimates were then adjusted from the midpoint, as necessary, to make the regional totals consistent with the United States totals.

The next step was to allocate the data for each industry group among the states within each region. Employment figures were taken from *CBP* by SIC codes and summed for each appropriate input-output industry. Where no employment figures were published, because of disclosure problems, estimates were made based on the number of establishments in each employment range. The initial estimate of employment in each class was based on the midpoint of each size class and then adjusted to conform with results obtained for residual employment calculated by subtracting known three-digit or four-digit employment figures from the two-digit or three-digit total for a state. All figures were checked for consistency with the United States total employment figures for each SIC industry or SIC group.

County Business Patterns, 1967. The state allocation for each of the industries specified in Table 6-8 is based on employment data. Since neither direct expenditures nor output data were available on any comprehensive scale, employment was used as a proxy. The employment figures were taken from *CBP* by SIC code and summed, where necessary, into input-output industry totals.

Consumption and Production Data. The industries specified in Table 6-9 are designated as local industries, that is, industries in which a substantial portion of the demand is to support the day-to-day operations of federal government employees. Assuming that federal demand for the products of these industries would generally be supplied from nearby industries, the final allocation was

Table 6–8
Nondefense Purchases Allocated According to Employment Data from
County Business Patterns, 1967

Industry Number	Industry Title
14	Food & kindred products
16	Broad & narrow fabrics, yarn & thread mills
18	Apparel
19	Miscellaneous fabricated textile products
21	Wooden containers
28	Plastics & synthetic materials
29	Drugs, cleaning, & toilet preparations
31	Petroleum refining & related industries
34	Footwear & other leather products
40	Heating, plumbing, & fabricated structural metal products
45	Construction, mining, oil field machinery & equipment
47	Metalworking machinery & equipment
48	Special industry machinery & equipment
50	Machine shop products
52	Service industry machines
54	Household appliances
59	Motor vehicles & equipment
61	Other transportation equipment

Table 6-9
Nondefense Purchases Allocated According to a Combination of
Consumption and Production Data

Industry Number	Industry Title
23	Other furniture & fixtures
24	Paper & allied products, except containers & boxes
25	Paperboard containers & boxes
26	Printing & publishing
30	Paints & allied products
44	Farm machinery & equipment

made according to a combination of the distribution of production and the distribution of consumption. The distribution of production for each industry was based on industrial employment figures and the distribution of consumption on federal nonmilitary employment. Equal weights were attached to each distribution.

The input-output industries presented below were somewhat unique and, consequently, individual distributions frequently had to be calculated from several data sources.

IO-1, Livestock & livestock products. The state allocation for the projected nine million dollars of federal nonmilitary purchases was based on the state distribution of sales for various livestock groups. The cash values received from the sales of cattle, calves, beef, veal, hogs, pork, lard, sheep, lambs, mutton, wool, chickens, turkeys, and eggs were summed to obtain total sales in the state. The data for this distribution are from *Agricultural Statistics, 1969* [66, tt. 454, 479, 490, 501, 589, 605, and 614].

IO-2, Other agricultural products. Net Commodity Credit Corporation (CCC) loans on all crops (*Agricultural Statistics, 1969* [66, t. 743]) were used to distribute the purchases from this input-output industry since most of the purchases are those made largely by the CCC under price stabilization programs.

IO-3, Forestry & fishery products. The nonmilitary portion of federal purchases from this industry was projected to be negative since it is comprised of receipts from the sale of timber on federal land. The distribution was made using data on payments to states, where the payment to each state is made as a result of sales of timber on federal land in that state. These data were obtained from *Agricultural Statistics, 1969* [66, t. 749].

IO-6, Nonferrous metal ores mining. The development of this distribution of purchases involved two steps. First, data from the *Statistical Supplement Stockpile Report to the Congress* [26] were used to divide government purchases among the various minerals included in the industry. Second, the estimated purchases of each mineral were distributed among the states on the basis of production figures given in the *Minerals Yearbook, 1967* [153]. Exact figures were not given for some of the minerals, and the value of these was included with that of other minerals in a category entitled "value of items that cannot be disclosed." The exact state distribution was available only for antimony, bauxite, copper, lead, mercury, silver, and zinc. Since aluminum comes from bauxite ore, the aluminum component was distributed in the same manner as bauxite. The exact distributions came to 75.2 percent of the total, which left 24.8 percent undistributed for beryl, platinum group, rare earths, rutile, tin, vanadium, and zirconium. The value of the other minerals was distributed using the state data on "value of items that cannot be disclosed." Although the undisclosed total included minerals other than those in IO-6, Nonferrous metal ores mining, their values could not be removed from the total since the figures are not available for each mineral separately. Estimates for all the different categories of minerals in each state were summed to produce the final distribution for this industry.

IO-11, New construction. Federal nonmilitary purchases fall into three broad categories—nonresidential buildings, highways, and conservation development. To obtain a state-by-state distribution, data were assembled on the purchases of the several government agencies constituting the major portion of new construction purchases.

The nonresidential buildings category, comprising about 37 percent of the total nonmilitary federal construction, was distributed to states in accordance with unpublished construction figures from the General Services Administration [25] and the National Aeronautics and Space Administration (NASA) [47], as well as published figures from the Atomic Energy Commission [64] and the Veterans Administration [122, t. 394]. The development and conservation portion of construction is about 53 percent of the total and was distributed using unpublished construction data from the Bureau of Reclamation [154], Tennessee Valley Authority [62], Bonneville Power Administration [152], and published data from the Corps of Civil Engineers [68].

Federal expenditures for highways were available by agency and parts of these were available by state in *Highway Statistics, 1967* [166]. This series has limited value since the majority of total funds administered by the Federal Highway Administration are transfers of funds to states. However, most of the forest highway funds administered by the Federal Highway Administration are direct construction purchases. The same applies to funds transferred from the park service. A series for forest highway funds and other funds including park service [166] is available and was used to distribute this component of federal construction.

IO-13, Ordnance & accessories.   According to the BLS, the federal non-military purchases from this industry are primarily purchases by NASA. The state distributon of their prime contracts and subcontracts obtained from the *NASA Annual Procurement Report* [45] was used to distribute the data for this industry.

IO-20, Lumber & wood products, except containers.   The nonmilitary portion of federal purchases from this industry was projected to be negative and represents receipts for the sale of timber from federal land. It was distributed using data on payments to states obtained from *Agricultural Statistics, 1969* [66, t. 794], where the payment to each state is made as a result of sales of timber on federal land in that state.

IO-43, Engines & turbines, and IO-60, Aircraft & parts.   Federal non-military purchases from these industries appear to be mainly in the field of research and development (R&D). The 1963 input-output table eliminated the R&D category as a separate industry by allocating it back to the performing industries, requiring that the state allocation of federal funds for R&D be used to distribute the purchases from these two industries. Data on R&D by state were obtained from the National Science Foundation publication, *Federal Funds for Research, Development, and Other Scientific Activities, Fiscal Years, 1968, 1969, and 1970* [50, t. C-84, p. 229].

IO-69, Wholesale & retail trade, and IO-70, Finance & insurance. Purchases from IO-69 consist of trade margins on all purchases made by the federal government, while purchases from IO-70 are miscellaneous charges on federal government transactions. Therefore, purchases for both were allocated according to the geographic distribution of total federal nonmilitary purchases.

IO-73, Business services. SIC 7391, Commercial research & development laboratories, was put into IO-73 from IO-74 when the latter was eliminated as a separate industry in the 1963 input-output table. Half of this industry was, therefore, allocated using the state distribution for R&D [50]. The remaining half of IO-73 was allocated on the basis of federal civilian employment on the assumption that these business services were used in conjunction with the normal government operations.

IO-76, Amusements. Federal nonmilitary purchases from IO-76 consist of training and educational films purchases from the movie industry. These purchases were allocated according to the state distribution of movie production and distribution. These figures are available from the *Census of Business: Selected Services* [70].

IO-77, Medical, educational services, & nonprofit organizations. Federal nonmilitary purchases from this industry are 50 percent medical expenditures and 50 percent veterans' educational assistance. The state-by-state distribution of veterans' education and training benefits was calculated from data in the *Statistical Abstract of the United States, 1969* [122, t. 394, p. 266]. For medical expenditures, the data were distributed by the federal employment vector, the assumption being that federal workers receive medical care in the states where they work.

IO-78, Federal government enterprises. Most of the purchases were made by the Post Office. State-by-state figures for Post Office employees, available on a state-by-state basis from the *Statistical Abstract of the United States, 1969* [122], were used to allocate the national total to states.

Total Federal Government Purchases for 1980

Most of the traditional long-run projection procedures could not be used because of the extremely limited data base on the state distribution of both defense and nondefense purchases. Because this limitation would obviously restrict the reliability of any long-term projection, the 1980 projection for both categories of federal purchases was calculated in a simple but systematic way. This allowed the resources for this study to be used in other areas where more reliable estimates could be obtained.

Since the 1970 projections of both the military and nonmilitary categories were considered fairly reliable, they were used as the initial estimates of the distribution among states for the 1980 projections. The initial estimates were obtained by applying the state-by-state distributions of the 1970 BLS projected national totals to the 1980 BLS projected total by input-output industry. This dollar value was then adjusted by the change in each state's share of projected output between 1970 and 1980. Estimates were then reconciled with the BLS national projection. The procedure is formularized as follows:

$$EXP_{ij}^{80} = \left[SS_{ij}^{70} \right] \left[T_j^{80} \right] \left[\frac{X_{ij}^{80}}{X_{ij}^{70}} \right] \tag{6.1}$$

where

X_{ij}^{70} = projected output in 1970 for state i and input-output industry j

X_{ij}^{80} = projected output in 1980 for state i and input-output industry j

T_j^{80} = total 1980 purchases as projected by BLS for input-output industry j

SS_{ij}^{70} = projected state share of purchases in 1970 for state i and input-output industry j

EXP_{ij}^{80} = 1980 federal government purchases for state i and input-output industry j

i = 1, . . . , 51

j = 1, . . . , 87

The estimates from equation (6.1) were then reconciled with the national total.

Conclusions and Recommendations

Since large gaps often occurred in the purchase data, and proxy variables were therefore frequently used, even the 1970 projection is open to substantial error. Obviously, the 1980 projection, due to the very nature of long-range projections, is open to greater error. Given the data limitations, however, this had to be accepted.

It is extremely unfortunate that there is such a scarcity of published data on the state distribution of federal government purchases. Relevant information is undoubtedly available in many government agencies and needs only to be systematically tabulated. The assembly of such data would require no new survey, which indicates that it might well be one of the least expensive data series to develop. A good data base would be extremely beneficial to policy-makers, as federal purchases can be used to promote differential state economic effects. Additional federal government purchases data will become available when the Regional Economics Division of the Office of Business Economics, U.S. Department of Commerce, develops its long-awaited gross state product estimates.

**Appendix A:
Input-Output Industry Numbers, Titles,
and Related SIC Codes**

Table A-1
Input-Output Industry Numbers, Titles, and Related SIC Codes

Industry Number	Industry Title	Related SIC Codes (1957 edition)[a]
1	Livestock & livestock products	013, pt. 014, 0193, pt. 02, pt. 0729
2	Other agricultural products	011, 012, pt. 014, 0192, 0199, pt. 02
3	Forestry & fishery products	074, 081, 082, 084, 086, 091
4	Agricultural, forestry, & fishery services	071, 0723, pt. 0729, 085, 098
5	Iron & ferroalloy ores mining	1011, 106
6	Nonferrous metal ores mining	102, 103, 104, 105, 108, 109
7	Coal mining	11, 12
8	Crude petroleum & natural gas	1311, 1321
9	Stone & clay mining & quarrying	141, 142, 144, 145, 148, 149
10	Chemical & fertilizer mineral mining	147
11	New construction	138, pt. 15, 16, pt. 17, pt. 6561
12	Maintenance & repair construction	pt. 15, pt. 16, pt. 17
13	Ordnance & accessories	19
14	Food & kindred products	20
15	Tobacco manufactures	21
16	Broad & narrow fabrics, yarn & thread mills	221, 222, 223, 224, 226, 228
17	Miscellaneous textile goods & floor coverings	227, 229
18	Apparel	225, 23 (excluding 239), 3992
19	Miscellaneous fabricated textile products	239
20	Lumber & wood products, except containers	24 (excluding 244)
21	Wooden containers	244
22	Household furniture	251
23	Other furniture & fixtures	25 (excluding 251)
24	Paper & allied products, except containers & boxes	26 (excluding 265)
25	Paperboard containers & boxes	265

Industry no.	Title	SIC codes
26	Printing & publishing	27
27	Chemicals & selected chemical products	281 (excluding alumina pt. of 2819), 286, 287, 289
28	Plastics & synthetic materials	282
29	Drugs, cleaning, & toilet preparations	283, 284
30	Paints & allied products	285
31	Petroleum refining & related industries	29
32	Rubber & miscellaneous plastics products	30
33	Leather tanning & industrial leather products	311, 312
34	Footwear & other leather products	31 (excluding 311, 312)
35	Glass & glass products	321, 322, 323
36	Stone & clay products	324, 325, 326, 327, 328, 329
37	Primary iron & steel manufacturing	331, 332, 3391, 3399
38	Primary nonferrous metals manufacturing	2819 (alumina only), 333, 334, 335, 336, 3392
39	Metal containers	3411, 3491
40	Heating, plumbing, & fabricated structural metal products	343, 344
41	Screw machine products, bolts, nuts, etc., & metal stampings	345, 346
42	Other fabricated metal products	342, 347, 348, 349 (excluding 3491)
43	Engines & turbines	351
44	Farm machinery & equipment	352
45	Construction, mining, oil field machinery & equipment	3531, 3532, 3533
46	Materials handling machinery & equipment	3534, 3535, 3536, 3537
47	Metalworking machinery & equipment	354
48	Special industry machinery & equipment	355
49	General industrial machinery & equipment	356
50	Machine shop products	359
51	Office, computing, & accounting machines	357
52	Service industry machines	358
53	Electric transmission & distribution equipment, & electrical industrial apparatus	361, 362
54	Household appliances	363
55	Electric lighting & wiring equipment	364
56	Radio, TV, & communication equipment	365, 366

Table A–1, cont.

Industry Number	Industry Title	Related SIC Codes (1957 edition)[a]
57	Electronic components & accessories	367
58	Miscellaneous electrical machinery, equipment, & supplies	369
59	Motor vehicles & equipment	371
60	Aircraft & parts	372
61	Other transportation equipment	373, 374, 375, 379
62	Professional, scientific, & controlling instruments & supplies	381, 382, 384, 387
63	Optical, ophthalmic, & photographic equipment & supplies	383, 385, 386
64	Miscellaneous manufacturing	39 (excluding 3992)
65	Transportation & warehousing	40, 41, 42, 44, 45, 46, 47
66	Communications, except radio & TV broadcasting	481, 482, 489
67	Radio & TV broadcasting	483
68	Electric, gas, water, & sanitary services	49
69	Wholesale & retail trade	50 (excluding manufacturers sales offices), 52, 53, 54, 55, 56, 57, 58, 59, pt. 7399
70	Finance & insurance	60, 61, 62, 63, 64, 66, 67
71	Real estate & rental	65 (excluding 6541 and pt. 6561)
72	Hotels & lodging places; personal & repair services, except automobile repair	70, 72, 76 (excluding 7694 and 7699)
73	Business services	6541, 73 (excluding 7361, 7391, and pt. 7399), 7694, 7699, 81, 89 (excluding 8921)
74	Research & development	(eliminated in 1963 study)
75	Automobile repair & services	75
76	Amusements	78, 79
77	Medical, educational services, & nonprofit organizations	0722, 7361, 80, 82, 84, 86, 8921

78	Federal government enterprises ....
79	State & local government enterprises ....
80a	Directly allocated imports of goods & services
80b	Transferred imports of goods & services ....
81	Business travel, entertainment, & gifts ....
82	Office supplies ....
83	Scrap, used, & secondhand goods ....
84	Government industry ....
85	Rest of the world industry ....
86	Household industry ....
87	Inventory valuation adjustment ....
88	Personal consumption expenditures ....
89	Gross private fixed capital formation
90	Net inventory change
91	Net exports
92	Federal government purchases
93	State & local government net purchases

[a]These are the SIC codes assigned to industries in the 1958 input-output study. They differ slightly from those assigned in the 1963 study.

Appendix B:
1970 and 1980 State Projections
of Final Demands
(MRIO Data Set 3)

This data set provides state projections of final demands for 1970 and 1980. The data for each year are separated into the six major components of the gross national product:

PCE   Personal Consumption Expenditures
GPCF Gross Private Capital Formation
NINV Net Inventory Change
NEXP Net Foreign Exports
SLG   State and Local Government Net Purchases of Goods and Services
FG   Federal Government Purchases

A detailed description of these components as they are defined for the national input-output tables prepared by the Office of Business Economics (OBE) is provided in *State Estimates of the Gross National Product, 1947, 1958, 1963,* by Karen R. Polenske and others [58]. The methodology used to project the final demands to 1970 and 1980 is described in Chapters 2 through 6 of this volume.

The national projected final demands for the six components are given in two publications of the Bureau of Labor Statistics (BLS):

1.   1970: *Projections of the Post-Vietnam Economy, 1975,* BLS Bulletin No. 1733, Appendix A (GPO: 1972).
2.   1980: *Patterns of U.S. Economic Growth,* BLS Bulletin No. 1672, Appendix D (GPO: 1970).

If the final demands are to be used for the implementation of the multi-regional input-output model, they must be adjusted. A summary of the required adjustments is given in Display B-1.

Notes About the State Projections of Final Demands

1.   The row sums of the state final demand matrices are identical to the national final demand figures listed in the two respective BLS tables. Throughout the estimation process, an attempt was made to project the

Display B-1
Adjustments Necessary for Comparison of Final Demands for Five Years, 1947, 1958, 1963, 1970, and 1980

Adjustments	1947	1958	1963	1970	1980	Comments
1. Alaska and Hawaii (see note 1.b)			X	X	X	No regional data were assembled for Alaska and Hawaii for 1947 and 1958.
2. Deflation (see note 2.a)	X	X		X	X	All data at present can only be converted to 1963 dollars. The national deflators are given in Display B-2.
3. IO-74, Research & development (see note 4)	X	X		X	X	Research and development was eliminated as a separate industry in the 1963 national table. The 1970 and 1980 projections, however, still contain data for the industry.
4. IO-82, Business travel, entertainment, & gifts (see note 7)	X	X	X	X	X	This industry was created by the Office of Business Economics, and no regional data were assembled for it in any of the five years.
5. Personal consumption expenditures of foreigners visiting the United States (see note 14.a)	X	X	X			Total final demand is not affected by this adjustment. It only shifts the expenditures from the PCE column to the net export column. (This adjustment was therefore not made for the multiregional calculations, but it should be made if PCE is separated from the other final demand components for analysis.)
6. Commodity Credit Corporation (see note 14.b)			X			Information was only available to make the adjustment for 1963. For 1970 and 1980, no adjustment is required. For 1947, CCC is already included as part of federal government final demand. For 1958, information was not available to make the adjustment.
7. Inventory depletion (see note 14.c)			X			Inventory depletions must be removed from the final demands for the balancing of the 1963 regional input-output tables with the trade flows, but they must be included in final demand to obtain the direct coefficients. Whether they are included or excluded from the final demands for the actual implementation of the multiregional model will depend upon whether the output figures are to reflect the total output produced that year or the total output supplied that year, respectively. The latter includes output produced in a previous year.

state figures on a basis comparable with the national input-output projections. Whenever an irreconcilable discrepancy occurred between the sum of the state figures and the national controls, the discrepancy was allocated to the states in proportion to the original entries in the state tables.

    a.   The rows are the 87 industries listed in the BLS tables plus row 88 of state totals.

    b.   The columns are the 51 regions (50 states and the District of Columbia), arranged in alphabetical order, plus a column 52 of residuals and a column 53 of industry totals. Alaska and Hawaii, however, are listed as states 50 and 51 because they did not become states until 1958, and some of the other sets of multiregional data assembled for 1947 and 1958 did not contain values for these two states.

    c.   Column 52 contains values for data that were not allocated to the states. These represent either figures for which state estimates seemed very arbitrary and were therefore not made (such as the inventory valuation adjustment component of 1970 net inventory change) or for purchases or payments made outside the 51 regions (such as purchases for the Panama Canal, wage payments to overseas military employees, etc.).

2.   The data for the three years are given in thousands of current dollars and are in producer prices.

    a.   Deflators. For comparisons of the sets of final demands for the two years, the figures must be deflated to constant dollars. The national final demand deflators were used for deflation of the projections in the multiregional input-output calculations. For those calculations, the national final demand deflators for 1958 ($63) were applied to the state final demand projections, which had been estimated in constant 1958 dollars. The 1958 deflators, which were obtained from Jack Faucett Associates, were separated by component. These deflators are given in Display B-2.[1]

    b.   Significant digits. The final adjustments to the two sets of data were made using double precision on the Harvard IBM 360/65.

    c.   Producer prices. It is customary for the input-output data to be given in producer prices. The margins on the goods (the differences between the producer prices and the purchaser prices) are then recorded as parts of IO-65, Transportation & warehousing; IO-69, Wholesale & retail trade; and IO-70, Finance & insurance. Some of the final demand projections were made in purchaser prices and were then converted to producer

---

    1. The deflators that are listed as being 1.0000 mean either that there were no price changes for those items between 1958 and 1963 or that the entries were zero. The 1's were inserted throughout to replace any zeros to assure that no actual entries were made zero in the deflation process.

Display B-2
1947 ($58) and 1958 ($63) Final Demand Deflators

	1947 ($58)			1958 ($63)			
	1 Total	2 PCE	3 GPCF	4 NINV	5 NEXP	6 SLG	7 FG
1 Livestock, prdts.	.6605	.8613	1.0000	.9938	.8230	.8569	.8532
2 Other agricultural prdts.	1.1186	.9099	1.0000	1.0963	1.0515	.9634	1.5848
3 Forestry, fisheries	2.1598	1.1261	1.0000	.9560	1.1261	1.1261	1.1261
4 Agri., fores., fish. serv.	1.5175	1.1050	1.0000	1.1270	1.1050	1.1050	1.1050
5 Iron, ferro. ores mining	1.6420	1.0000	1.0000	.9264	.9259	1.0000	.9259
6 Nonferrous ores mining	1.2531	1.0000	1.0000	.9886	1.0753	1.0000	1.0753
7 Coal mining	1.4085	1.0515	1.0000	.9104	1.0515	1.0515	1.0515
8 Crude petro., natural gas	1.6077	1.0000	1.0000	.9860	.9606	1.0000	1.0000
9 Stone, clay mining	1.6502	.8913	1.0000	1.0275	.8913	.8913	.8913
10 Chem., fert. min. mining	1.4859	1.0152	1.0893	.9838	.9009	.9009	1.0000
11 New construction	1.4556	1.0000	1.0000	1.1021	1.0893	.9294	.8953
12 Maint., repair constr.	1.6313	1.0000	1.0000	1.0859	1.0000	1.1587	1.1587
13 Ordnance, accessories	1.6750	1.0288	1.0000	.7184	1.0331	1.0288	1.0449
14 Food, kindred prdts.	1.1223	1.0132	1.0000	.9670	.9833	.9833	.9833
15 Tobacco manufactures	1.3316	1.0627	1.0000	1.1305	1.0299	1.0299	1.0000
16 Fabrics	.8811	1.0288	1.0000	1.0387	.9980	.9980	1.0101
17 Textile prdts.	1.1919	1.0121	1.0121	.9954	.9653	1.0000	1.0121
18 Apparel	.9208	1.0604	1.0000	1.0149	1.0225	1.0277	1.0395
19 Misc. textile prdts.	.9001	1.0718	1.0000	.9970	1.0395	1.0395	1.0515
20 Lumber, wood prdts.	1.2626	1.0449	1.0132	.9601	1.0132	1.0132	1.0246
21 Wooden containers	1.2121	1.0000	1.0000	.9989	.9930	1.0000	1.0050
22 Household furniture	1.2626	1.0858	1.0526	1.0336	1.0526	1.0526	1.0650
23 Other furniture	1.6234	1.0638	1.0288	1.0732	1.0288	1.0288	1.0406
24 Paper, allied prdts.	1.4451	1.0101	1.0000	.9776	.9794	.9794	.9901
25 Paperboard containers	1.2870	1.0142	1.0000	.9684	.9921	.9921	1.0040
26 Printing, publishing	1.5723	1.1429	1.0000	1.1369	1.1429	1.1429	1.1429
27 Chemicals, select. prdts.	1.1834	1.0040	1.0000	.9281	.9728	.9728	.9843
28 Plastics, synthetics	1.2888	.9390	1.0000	.8626	.9009	1.0000	.9107

29 Drugs, cosmetics	.9452	.9950	1.0000	.9418	.9643	.9643	.9747
30 Paint, allied prdts.	1.2346	1.0638	1.0000	.9985	1.0215	1.0215	1.0331
31 Petroleum, related inds.	1.3158	1.0050	1.0000	.9718	.9737	.9737	.9852
32 Rubber, misc. plastics	1.4706	.9551	.9259	.8863	.9259	.9259	.9372
33 Leather tanning, prdts.	.9671	1.0000	1.0000	1.0997	1.0799	1.0000	1.0929
34 Footwear, leather prdts.	1.2151	1.1148	1.0000	1.0493	1.1143	1.1148	1.1148
35 Glass, glass prdts.	1.7301	1.0215	1.0000	.9881	.9891	.9891	1.0000
36 Stone, clay prdts.	1.4903	1.0504	1.0000	1.0280	1.0173	1.0173	1.0288
37 Primary iron, steel mfr.	1.9920	1.0482	1.0000	.9563	1.0060	1.0060	1.0183
38 Primary nonferrous mfr.	1.9763	1.1050	1.0604	1.0210	1.0604	1.0000	1.0604
39 Metal containers	1.7483	1.0000	1.0331	1.0401	1.0331	1.0000	1.0449
40 Fabricated metal prdts.	1.3643	1.0000	.9718	.9522	.9718	1.0000	.9833
41 Screw mach. prdts., etc.	1.6584	1.1351	1.0001	1.0110	1.1001	1.1001	1.1136
42 Other fab. metal prdts.	1.6750	1.0661	1.0331	.9631	1.0331	1.0331	1.0449
43 Engines, turbines	1.7483	1.0091	.9785	.8740	.9785	1.0000	.9891
44 Farm mach., equip.	1.5823	1.1416	1.0953	1.0203	1.0953	1.0953	1.1074
45 Construc. mach., equip.	1.7730	1.0000	1.0695	1.0036	1.0695	1.0695	1.0695
46 Material handling mach.	1.7825	1.0000	1.0537	1.0239	1.0537	1.0537	1.0661
47 Metalworking machinery	1.8904	1.1494	1.1136	1.1507	1.1111	1.1136	1.1274
48 Special mach., equip.	1.6393	1.1211	1.0858	1.0793	1.0858	1.0858	1.0989
49 General mach., equip.	1.7212	1.0000	1.0309	1.0276	1.0309	1.0309	1.0428
50 Machine shop prdts.	1.6420	1.0604	1.0173	.9815	1.0000	1.0173	1.0288
51 Office, comput. machines	1.3333	1.0661	1.0225	1.0615	1.0225	1.0225	1.0352
52 Service ind. machines	1.3106	.9320	.9033	.8690	.9033	.9033	.9132
53 Elect. transmiss. equip.	1.6051	.9950	.9551	.9417	.9551	.9551	.9662
54 Household appliances	1.1601	.9268	.8977	.9229	.8977	.8977	.9083
55 Electric lighting equip.	1.6260	1.0858	1.0471	1.0121	1.0471	1.0471	1.0593
56 Radio, TV, etc., equip.	1.1050	.9615	.9320	.9179	.9320	.9320	.9434
57 Electronic components	1.2484	1.0142	.9833	.9434	.9833	.9833	.9940
58 Misc. electrical mach.	1.5528	1.0571	1.0235	.9778	1.0235	1.0235	1.0363
59 Motor vehicles, equip.	1.5361	1.0341	1.0020	.9683	1.0020	1.0020	1.0142
60 Aircraft, parts	1.6750	1.0661	1.0331	1.0897	1.0331	1.0000	1.0449
61 Other transport. equip.	1.6129	1.0438	1.0121	.9710	1.0121	1.0121	1.0235
62 Profess., scien. instru.	1.4903	1.0881	1.0537	1.4717	1.0537	1.0537	1.0661
63 Medical, photo. equip.	1.3298	1.0929	1.0593	1.0053	1.0593	1.0593	1.0707
64 Misc. manufacturing	1.1834	1.0526	1.0204	1.0051	1.0204	1.0204	1.0320

Display B-2 (continued)

	1947 ($58)	1958 ($63)					
	1 *Total*	*2* *PCE*	*3* *GPCF*	*4* *NINV*	*5* *NEXP*	*6* *SLG*	*7* *FG*
65 Transport., warehousing	1.6181	1.0493	.9814	1.0153	1.0834	1.1001	1.0341
66 Communica., exc. brdcast.	1.2821	1.0428	1.0428	1.0433	1.0267	1.0267	1.0267
67 Radio, TV broadcasting	1.3228	1.0000	1.0000	1.2253	1.2255	1.2255	1.0000
68 Elec., gas, water, san. ser.	1.2673	1.0753	1.0000	1.0331	1.0707	1.0320	1.0604
69 Wholesale, retail trade	1.1786	1.0482	1.0256	1.0441	.9891	.8091	.9881
70 Finance, insurance	1.7301	1.1792	1.1521	1.1324	1.1521	1.1494	1.2330
71 Real estate, rental	1.4164	1.0695	1.0893	1.1138	1.0672	1.0672	1.0672
72 Hotels, personal serv.	1.4451	1.1111	1.0000	1.1322	1.1038	1.1161	1.1211
73 Business services	1.8657	1.2453	1.0000	1.1724	1.2788	1.1561	1.1494
74 Research, development	1.6694	1.0000	1.0000	1.2598	1.0000	1.0000	1.0000
75 Auto repair, services	1.4859	1.0718	1.0000	1.0650	1.0000	1.0718	1.0718
76 Amusements	1.3928	1.1710	1.0000	1.1963	1.2516	1.1249	1.2019
77 Med., educ. services	1.5083	1.1834	1.0000	1.1838	1.2937	1.1765	1.2136
78 Federal govt. enterprise	1.4368	1.3245	1.0000	1.3245	1.3245	1.3245	1.3245
79 State, local govt. ent.	1.0000	1.0000	1.0000	1.0877	1.0000	1.0000	1.0000
80 Imports	1.0000	1.0000	1.0000	1.0000	1.0000	1.0000	1.0000
81 Bus. travel, ent., gifts.	1.0000	1.0000	1.0000	1.0000	1.0000	1.0000	1.0000
82 Office supplies	1.0000	1.0000	1.0000	1.0000	1.0000	1.0000	1.0000
83 Scrap, used goods	1.0000	1.0000	1.0000	1.0000	1.0000	1.0000	1.0000
84 Government industry	.5763	1.0000	1.0000	1.0000	1.0000	.8224	.8224
85 Rest of world industry	1.0000	1.0000	1.0000	1.0000	1.0000	1.0000	1.0000
86 Household industry	.7442	.8570	1.0000	1.0000	1.0000	1.0000	1.0000
87 Inventory valuation adj.	1.0000	1.0000	1.0000	1.0000	1.0000	1.0000	1.0000
88 Total	1.1816	1.0560	1.0608	.9786	1.0195	.9294	.9233

prices using the transportation, trade, and insurance margins from the national input-output projections.

3.   IO-11, New construction. All purchases of new construction are recorded in the final demand sector of the input-output table, that is, no purchases from this industry are considered to be intermediate purchases. Because the output of new construction is assumed to be used in the region in which it is produced, the total output must equal the total consumption in each state. The total output of the industry, therefore, can be obtained state by state by adding the respective state elements that appear in row 11 of the state final demand tables for gross private capital formation, net foreign exports, state and local government net purchases of goods and services, and federal government purchases.

4.   IO-74, Research & development. For 1947 and 1958, values appear in the state final demand matrices for IO-74 because the industry was given in the national input-output table. For 1963, this industry was eliminated in the national input-output table, and the values were included as part of the industry where the research and development was actually performed. For 1970 and 1980, only the SIC 7391, Commercial research & development laboratories, portion was given for this industry. To use the 1970 and 1980 state final demand projections for the multiregional input-output calculations, entries in row 74 must be added to those in row 73, Business services.

5.   IO-78, Federal government enterprises. For this industry, a value, representing Panama Canal tolls, appears in the residual column 52 in the 1958 and 1963 net export tables. Because these data were not available for 1970 and 1980, a value was estimated by multiplying the 1970 and 1980 total net export figure for the industry by the 1963 ratio of Panama Canal tolls to total net exports of IO-78.

6.   IO-80, Imports. No state estimates were made for imports in the gross private capital formation, net foreign exports, and federal government tables. The total value for transferred (competitive) plus directly allocated (noncompetitive) imports is given in the column 52 of residuals and in the column 53 of totals.

7.   IO-81, Business travel, entertainment, & gifts, and IO-82, Office supplies. These two industries are especially constructed for the input-output accounts. For the multiregional input-output calculations, the national input-output final demand projections were adjusted first to provide accurate control totals for the sum of the state final demands. (In the final demands, values appear only for IO-82.) The adjustment was made by taking column 82 in the national input-output table and calculating a co-

efficient vector from it. The values in row 82 of the national projections were then distributed to the other elements in the respective columns in proportion to the coefficients formed from column 82.

For the multiregional input-output calculations, the state values for IO-82 were redistributed to the appropriate industries using a procedure similar to the one used for the national controls, that is, the elements in row 82 of each matrix of state final demands were distributed to the other elements in each respective column according to the coefficients formed from the national column 82. For each table of state final demands, the column sums remain unchanged through this redistribution, but the row sums naturally change.

8. IO-83, Scrap, used & secondhand goods. If the output of scrap is not to be generated during the input-output calculations, special adjustments must be made to the column of scrap in the input-output tables. These adjustments, however, do not affect the final demand estimates.

9. Value added in final demand: IO-84, Government industry, IO-85, Rest of the world industry, and IO-86, Household industry. For these industries, figures appear only in the value added portion of the final demand sector of an input-output table and represent payments to government employees; purchases by foreigners and foreign interest payments and receipts; and payments to household employees, respectively. The following balances should therefore exist between the final demand values given in the accompanying set of statistical tables and any projections that would be made for payrolls and outputs of these three industries:

$$\text{IO-84 PAYROLLS} = \text{IO-84 OUTPUT} = \text{IO-84 SLG} + \text{IO-84 FG}$$
$$\text{IO-85 OUTPUT} = \text{IO-85 PCE} + \text{IO-85 NEXP}$$
$$+ \text{IO-85 FG}$$
$$\text{IO-86 PAYROLLS} = \text{IO-86 OUTPUT} = \text{IO-86 PCE}$$

Part of the value of IO-84 represents wages paid to government employees overseas; this value appears in column 52 of the federal government final demand tables. It was calculated by multiplying the total 1970 and 1980 value for the industry by the 1963 ratio of column 52 to column 53 for the industry.

10. IO-87, Inventory valuation adjustment. No state estimates were made for this; the total value appears in columns 52 and 53, and the item appears only in the net inventory change final demand table for 1970.

11. Row 88 is the state total for the particular final demand component, obtained by summing all elements in each column.

12. Column 52 contains values for data that were not allocated to the states (explained above under 1).

13. Column 53 is the industry total for the particular final demand component. As explained under 1 above, this total was forced to equal the respective national final demand projections for the industry.

14. For certain regional analyses, one additional adjustment would have to be made to the state final demand projections:

    The personal consumption expenditures column published by the OBE varies conceptually from that of the BLS. Each element in the OBE column is the same as or larger than the corresponding element in the BLS column because in the BLS data the purchases by foreign visitors are entirely excluded from the personal consumption expenditures column and are included in the net export column. For comparisons with the 1947, 1958, and 1963 state estimates of personal consumption expenditures and net exports which are described in MRIO DATA SET 1, the state data should therefore be adjusted to account for the difference between the OBE and the BLS handling of these purchases because the projected final demands were constructed using the BLS concepts.[2] (This does not, of course, affect total final demand since the purchases are merely shifted from the personal consumption expenditures column to the net foreign exports column.) It should be noted that if the BLS conventions are used, the IO-85 entry for personal consumption expenditures becomes zero, and the IO-85 entry in the net foreign exports column is altered by the amount of the original entry for IO-85 in the personal consumption expenditures column.

    The 12 tables of state final demand projections follow.

---

2. For a detailed description of MRIO DATA SET 1, refer to the first volume of this series, *State Estimates of the Gross National Product, 1947, 1958, 1963* [58].

MRIO Data Set 3
State Projections of Final Demands

TABLE 8-1

STATE ESTIMATES OF 1970
PERSONAL CONSUMPTION EXPENDITURES
(THOUSANDS OF 1958 DOLLARS)

INDUSTRY TITLE	1 ALABAMA	2 ARIZONA	3 ARKANSAS	4 CALIFORNIA	5 COLORADO	6 CONNECTICUT	7 DELAWARE	8 DISTRICT OF COLUMBIA	9 FLORIDA
1 LIVESTOCK, PRDTS.	30793	15121	17067	191037	20526	28871	5443	7169	59960
2 OTHER AGRICULTURE PRDTS.	41154	21468	23193	303720	30519	45208	8280	11724	84095
3 FORESTRY, FISHERIES	5096	2939	2965	44506	4273	6770	1110	1762	11427
4 AGRI.,FORES.,FISH. SERV.	0	0	0	0	0	0	0	0	0
5 IRON, FERRO. ORES MINING	0	0	0	0	0	0	0	0	0
6 NONFERROUS ORES MINING	0	0	0	0	0	0	0	0	0
7 COAL MINING	2094	766	1232	7578	850	2805	291	497	4285
8 CRUDE PETRO.,NATURAL GAS	0	0	0	0	0	0	0	0	0
9 STONE, CLAY MINING	393	207	227	3387	312	435	95	130	785
10 CHEM.,FERT. MIN. MINING	0	0	0	0	0	0	0	0	0
11 NEW CONSTRUCTION	0	0	0	0	0	0	0	0	0
12 MAINT., REPAIR CONSTR.	0	0	0	0	0	0	0	0	0
13 ORDNANCE, ACCESSORIES	4031	2475	2254	42790	3966	5545	1141	1466	9225
14 FOOD, KINDRED PRDTS.	792436	459025	459025	6803881	658621	1029120	168363	273775	1777845
15 TOBACCO MANUFACTURES	79043	35518	45698	522378	50376	92455	16018	22742	159725
16 FABRICS	20758	10583	11580	160559	15856	19011	4813	6693	43023
17 TEXTILE PRDTS.	20415	10440	12025	176564	16274	36054	6197	7841	37678
18 APPAREL	237148	109772	134790	1828438	167966	324249	59674	81813	486779
19 MISC. TEXTILE PRDTS.	31261	15054	17919	241769	22804	39210	7792	10355	66161
20 LUMBER, WOOD PRDTS.	6087	1862	3861	15434	2618	1991	543	506	5671
21 WOODEN CONTAINERS	0	0	0	0	0	0	0	0	0
22 HOUSEHOLD FURNITURE	53399	22893	31052	379489	35706	60240	12848	17491	112306
23 OTHER FURNITURE	3097	1537	1753	23301	2276	3438	754	911	6159
24 PAPER, ALLIED PRDTS.	22022	10549	12707	158423	15227	24302	4917	6921	45597
25 PAPERBOARD CONTAINERS	939	420	526	6727	647	1202	235	277	1828
26 PRINTING, PUBLISHING	52220	28809	29731	472764	43510	72602	13236	20408	112280
27 CHEMICALS,SELECT. PRDTS.	5537	2718	3152	40075	3907	5587	1180	1556	11159
28 PLASTICS, SYNTHETICS	327	161	184	2369	232	395	73	96	656
29 DRUGS, COSMETICS	124237	60383	71097	885034	86007	119219	26169	37001	253403
30 PAINT, ALLIED PRDTS.	397	160	226	2437	233	664	95	130	851
31 PETROLEUM, RELATED INDS.	143715	91532	90810	1125090	132965	235704	53312	32453	336534
32 RUBBER, MISC. PLASTICS	43150	22002	24286	349022	32986	44624	10306	13747	87810
33 LEATHER TANNING, PRDTS.	0	0	0	0	0	0	0	0	0
34 FOOTWEAR, LEATHER PRDTS.	41457	20920	23601	331092	31652	50023	9700	12895	84163
35 GLASS, GLASS PRDTS.	2860	1558	1621	26228	2416	3610	728	927	5788
36 STONE, CLAY PRDTS.	4508	2270	2547	35255	3384	5868	1056	1325	9057
37 PRIMARY IRON, STEEL MFR.	387	162	224	2059	211	510	70	109	803
38 PRIMARY NONFERROUS MFR.	311	138	177	2172	209	376	76	93	628

#	Industry	C1	C2	C3	C4	C5	C6	C7	C8	C9
39	METAL CONTAINERS	1475	637	904	8761	924	1536	264	383	3716
40	FABRICATED METAL PRDTS.	5273	2783	3006	47547	4328	6423	1289	1725	10840
41	SCREW MACH. PRDTS., ETC.	10037	5018	5701	77374	7451	10931	2376	3070	20174
42	OTHER FAB. METAL PRDTS.	4960	2465	2098	54778	4577	2606	1050	1492	15657
43	ENGINES, TURBINES	243	126	137	1822	180	258	56	69	479
44	FARM MACH., EQUIP.	0	0	0	0	0	0	0	0	0
45	CONSTRUC. HANDLING MACH.	0	0	0	0	0	0	0	0	0
46	MATERIAL HANDLING MACH.	0	0	0	0	0	0	0	0	0
47	METALWORKING MACHINERY	785	399	441	6094	598	903	198	228	1524
48	SPECIAL MACH., EQUIP.	525	265	293	4062	399	603	133	153	1011
49	GENERAL MACH., EQUIP.	0	0	0	0	0	0	0	0	0
50	MACHINE SHOP PRDTS.	0	0	0	0	0	0	0	0	0
51	OFFICE, COMPUT. MACHINES	1652	799	928	12645	1223	1895	434	493	3302
52	SERVICE IND. MACHINES	18264	2230	10315	36345	3557	6853	4688	9005	38365
53	ELECT. TRANSMISS. EQUIP.	396	200	224	3034	297	448	99	116	783
54	HOUSEHOLD APPLIANCES	74534	39620	42374	556664	54958	73052	15046	19940	154115
55	ELECTRIC LIGHTING EQUIP.	9369	4809	5282	74524	7200	10646	2372	2828	18898
56	RADIO, TV, ETC., EQUIP.	60117	32721	34414	542137	49650	71758	14034	21825	127706
57	ELECTRONIC COMPONENTS	6314	3448	3620	56958	5221	7536	1466	2278	13418
58	MISC. ELECTRICAL MACH.	9050	4623	5081	73453	6914	9244	2195	2910	18187
59	MOTOR VEHICLES, EQUIP.	276976	154800	176817	2524333	222663	398166	92290	98633	713974
60	AIRCRAFT, PARTS	904	549	467	13084	1019	581	234	332	3485
61	OTHER TRANSPORT. EQUIP.	0	0	0	0	0	0	0	0	0
62	PROFESS., SCIEN. INSTRU.	44225	26835	22851	639180	49797	28456	11439	16242	170252
63	MEDICAL, PHOTO. EQUIP.	10865	5096	6464	85216	8001	11670	2538	3893	21131
64	MISC. MANUFACTURING	18639	11726	10363	185818	17663	23079	4638	6287	40863
65	TRANSPORT., WAREHOUSING	72397	40709	41006	682789	63091	91043	18784	24921	155557
66	COMMUNICA.-EXC. BRDCAST.	173752	108416	102151	1655946	152045	265141	42458	67450	387496
67	RADIO, TV BROADCASTING	127205	65498	73369	1053138	96963	166222	28865	46775	264937
68	ELEC.,GAS,WATER,SAN.SER.	232027	107664	133642	1580651	153239	216248	48740	71935	479749
69	WHOLESALE, RETAIL TRADE	1412148	757046	819532	1392827	1105999	1814985	337973	458807	3082941
70	FINANCE, INSURANCE	265930	130522	150636	2237992	200463	1150396	69951	95554	563727
71	REAL ESTATE, RENTAL	873765	520841	508035	8406616	781759	1321075	202356	340372	1889468
72	HOTELS, PERSONAL SERV.	123114	135886	87816	1424700	153464	134154	37583	255435	99548
73	BUSINESS SERVICES	21959	13223	7170	459119	20842	17192	7472	45364	98077
74	RESEARCH, DEVELOPMENT	0	0	0	0	0	0	0	0	0
75	AUTO. REPAIR, SERVICES	95239	48319	53236	754062	71608	93320	22919	30044	191372
76	AMUSEMENTS	23279	18107	21035	548375	30718	25207	20837	63803	253526
77	MED.,EDUC. SERVICES	516737	234810	299524	3984552	361172	645352	132927	176111	1083544
78	FEDERAL GOVT. ENTERPRISE	13168	8031	7559	127697	11858	18067	3170	5187	28722
79	STATE, LOCAL GOVT. ENT.	10226	5347	5807	83446	7906	9201	2409	3280	20880
80	IMPORTS	119460	65172	68980	1005382	96228	155377	26836	40622	262607
81	BUS.TRAVEL, ENT., GIFTS.	0	0	0	0	0	0	0	0	0
82	OFFICE SUPPLIES	0	0	0	0	0	0	0	0	0
83	SCRAP, USED GOODS	-1667	-798	-952	-13033	-1218	-1762	-408	-520	-3358
84	GOVERNMENT INDUSTRY	0	0	0	0	0	0	0	0	0
85	REST OF WORLD INDUSTRY	0	0	0	0	0	0	0	0	0
86	HOUSEHOLD INDUSTRY	0	0	0	0	0	0	0	0	0
87	INVENTORY VALUATION ADJ.	51239	13691	29194	342380	23838	49852	19528	20520	114981
88	STATE TOTAL	6464366	3523619	3756048	54922748	5163023	9097801	1593754	2510371	15062064

TABLE 8-1

STATE ESTIMATES OF 1970
PERSONAL CONSUMPTION EXPENDITURES
(THOUSANDS OF 1958 DOLLARS)

INDUSTRY TITLE	10 GEORGIA	11 IDAHO	12 ILLINOIS	13 INDIANA	14 IOWA	15 KANSAS	16 KENTUCKY	17 LOUISIANA	18 MAINE
1 LIVESTOCK, PRODTS.	41528	8630	101799	44618	30595	23359	32374	29478	9040
2 OTHER AGRICULTURE PRODTS.	55748	10401	156177	67191	40332	31294	40518	40808	12921
3 FORESTRY, FISHERIES	6924	1145	21863	9474	4990	4002	4646	5317	1856
4 AGRI.+FORES.,FISH. SERV.	0	0	0	0	0	0	0	0	0
5 IRON, FERRO. ORES MINING	0	0	0	0	0	0	0	0	0
6 NONFERROUS ORES MINING	0	0	0	0	0	0	0	0	0
7 COAL MINING	2754	478	9761	4381	2964	2426	2004	2127	1223
8 CRUDE PETRO.,NATURAL GAS	0	0	0	0	0	0	0	0	0
9 STONE, CLAY MINING	525	80	1715	721	360	282	346	403	104
10 CHEM.+FERT. MIN. MINING	0	0	0	0	0	0	0	0	0
11 NEW CONSTRUCTION	0	0	0	0	0	0	0	0	0
12 MAINT.+REPAIR CONSTR.	0	0	0	0	0	0	0	0	0
13 ORDNANCE, ACCESSORIES	5606	1113	19634	8359	4146	3150	3610	4669	1337
14 FOOD, KINDRED PRODTS.	1079581	186444	3312286	1437559	778453	622495	736740	824531	291633
15 TOBACCO MANUFACTURES	103318	13949	285179	130442	66672	54690	72976	80950	27226
16 FABRICS	29149	4693	69905	29884	16132	13172	20190	21494	5250
17 TEXTILE PRODTS.	27228	3829	104608	45783	24230	18649	17413	19951	7768
18 APPAREL	325636	47507	1091818	444753	230699	176605	218807	246093	77173
19 MISC. TEXTILE PRODTS.	42539	6688	129350	54409	27860	21607	28531	33371	9567
20 LUMBER, WOOD PRODTS.	6571	1617	9295	5818	6647	3514	7880	4445	1186
21 WOODEN CONTAINERS	0	0	0	0	0	0	0	0	0
22 HOUSEHOLD FURNITURE	73931	9463	223845	97749	47829	37096	49102	56169	14574
23 OTHER FURNITURE	4288	710	12945	5538	2952	2257	2930	3157	885
24 PAPER, ALLIED PRODTS.	29948	4492	76530	34072	17818	14291	20209	22838	6659
25 PAPERBOARD CONTAINERS	1313	194	3347	1507	754	600	880	952	307
26 PRINTING, PUBLISHING	72728	12490	252332	106035	55234	43009	47562	55968	18420
27 CHEMICALS,SELECT. PRDTS.	7453	1202	19850	8984	4797	3870	5152	5630	1607
28 PLASTICS. SYNTHETICS	447	73	1198	551	287	232	304	334	109
29 DRUGS, COSMETICS	166537	26824	413104	185531	98140	79161	115065	127249	33481
30 PAINT, ALLIED PRDTS.	552	68	1870	766	414	333	356	421	160
31 PETROLEUM, RELATED INDS.	240700	32146	609223	333175	189616	126688	133988	141187	83372
32 RUBBER, MISC. PLASTICS	59265	10381	160085	69468	37077	28805	40026	44521	11831
33 LEATHER TANNING, PRDTS.	0	0	0	0	0	0	0	0	0
34 FOOTWEAR, LEATHER PRDTS.	56510	9311	181002	77279	40753	31690	38675	42788	12546
35 GLASS, GLASS PRDTS.	3998	609	12133	5203	2802	2113	2691	2935	884
36 STONE, CLAY PRDTS.	6226	1034	19021	8361	4511	3515	4277	4635	1516
37 PRIMARY IRON, STEEL MFR.	519	92	1783	779	492	395	369	400	191
38 PRIMARY NONFERROUS MFR.	433	61	1057	469	239	191	288	319	98

	col1	col2	col3	col4	col5	col6	col7	col8	col9
39 METAL CONTAINERS	0	0	0	0	0	0	0	0	0
40 FABRICATED METAL PRDTS.	2023	394	5168	2430	1308	970	1474	1700	443
41 SCREW MACH. PRDTS., ETC.	7323	1041	20997	9059	4913	3753	4963	5435	1589
42 OTHER FAB. METAL PRDTS.	13753	2242	39203	17668	9039	7029	9356	10285	2834
43 ENGINES, TURBINES	6173	682	12968	5443	2821	2102	3593	7253	823
44 FARM MACH., EQUIP.	334	58	969	417	229	176	232	246	70
45 CONSTRUC. MACH., EQUIP.	0	0	0	0	0	0	0	0	0
46 MATERIAL HANDLING MACH.	0	0	0	0	0	0	0	0	0
47 METALWORKING MACHINERY	1096	192	3408	1455	779	591	753	798	228
48 SPECIAL MACH., EQUIP.	729	128	2279	971	519	394	500	530	152
49 GENERAL MACH., EQUIP.	0	0	0	0	0	0	0	0	0
50 MACHINE SHOP PRDTS.	0	0	0	0	0	0	0	0	0
51 OFFICE, COMPUT. MACHINES	2322	380	7276	3009	1605	1203	1557	1695	472
52 SERVICE IND. MACHINES	23457	1281	40572	16798	8205	6026	14950	19792	1343
53 ELECT. TRANSMISS. EQUIP.	552	94	1709	717	388	293	376	403	114
54 HOUSEHOLD APPLIANCES	101787	18301	259771	117708	64630	50953	71390	76512	21493
55 ELECTRIC LIGHTING EQUIP.	-2995	2230	40233	16865	9026	6831	8788	9665	2703
56 RADIO, TV, ETC., EQUIP.	8094	13415	280383	120429	62431	47769	52940	63448	18031
57 ELECTRONIC COMPONENTS	8483	1399	29404	12693	6574	5032	5539	6667	1891
58 MISC. ELECTRICAL MACH.	12419	2167	33755	14537	7675	5971	8344	9231	2425
59 MOTOR VEHICLES, EQUIP.	429565	76725	1432043	696001	294927	242245	247502	282551	95178
60 AIRCRAFT, PARTS	1374	152	2887	1211	628	468	800	1615	183
61 OTHER TRANSPORT. EQUIP.	67213	7437	141392	59349	30764	22924	39149	78885	8977
62 PROFESS., SCIEN. INSTRU.	14375	2332	44427	17985	9706	6929	9272	11005	2894
63 MEDICAL, PHOTO. EQUIP.	25485	5260	93457	39450	20513	15738	17687	20329	6078
64 MISC. MANUFACTURING	59577	17492	334572	138210	70881	54282	66349	78698	21925
65 TRANSPORT., WAREHOUSING	240473	38238	801298	346152	178784	135875	156005	182652	69869
66 COMMUNICA., EXC. BRDCAST.	173077	24650	543144	234979	120010	95581	112952	131749	44750
67 RADIO, TV BROADCASTING									
68 ELEC.,GAS,WATER,SAN.SER.	311551	47220	912149	406591	218668	176622	211480	239871	62691
69 WHOLESALE, RETAIL TRADE	1968563	316994	5890825	2606612	1392833	1082113	1310815	1466785	500969
70 FINANCE, INSURANCE	376151	54673	1240062	518838	266413	207808	244415	287730	85321
71 REAL ESTATE, RENTAL	119717	175126	4120147	1796489	914670	741619	764890	938999	350138
72 HOTELS, PERSONAL SERV.	23434	33435	929840	267944	138886	100668	136212	171971	57435
73 BUSINESS SERVICES	4876	6503	358160	30164	17366	9223	17621	36460	1510
74 RESEARCH, DEVELOPMENT	0	0	0	0	0	0	0	0	0
75 AUTO. REPAIR, SERVICES	131265	23648	335940	146053	78189	61250	88951	97098	25222
76 AMUSEMENTS	5400	4810	285042	67142	37496	27316	40994	52894	6298
77 MED.,EDUC. SERVICES	720136	94473	2200652	902499	478179	364907	483106	544998	150958
78 FEDERAL GOVT. ENTERPRISE	17921	3265	59573	25291	13464	10441	12043	14210	4761
79 STATE, LOCAL GOVT. ENT.	13936	2434	35677	15619	8154	6442	9287	10538	2479
80 IMPORTS	163118	26376	510689	219759	115690	91882	109634	124882	41438
81 BUS.TRAVEL, ENT., GIFTS.	0	0	0	0	0	0	0	0	0
82 OFFICE SUPPLIES	0	0	0	0	0	0	0	0	0
83 SCRAP, USED GOODS	-2287	-387	-7842	-3118	-1627	-1244	-1537	-1679	-456
84 GOVERMENT INDUSTRY	0	0	0	0	0	0	0	0	0
85 REST OF WORLD INDUSTRY	0	0	0	0	0	0	0	0	0
86 HOUSEHOLD INDUSTRY	94449	4633	189972	54943	27174	20459	44680	57485	7818
87 INVENTORY VALUATION ADJ.									
88 STATE TOTAL	9105667	1465213	28534916	12146633	6349707	4962130	5954974	6866527	2233971

TABLE B-1

STATE ESTIMATES OF 1970
PERSONAL CONSUMPTION EXPENDITURES
(THOUSANDS OF 1958 DOLLARS)

INDUSTRY TITLE	19 MARYLAND	20 MASSA-CHUSETTS	21 MICHIGAN	22 MINNESOTA	23 MISSISSIPPI	24 MISSOURI	25 MONTANA	26 NEBRASKA	27 NEVADA
1 LIVESTOCK, PRDTS.	34350	49211	79277	37829	20486	44797	7947	18053	5969
2 OTHER AGRICULTURE PRDTS.	50134	77206	115150	50899	25350	61624	10482	21681	8578
3 FORESTRY, FISHERIES	6536	11755	15477	6432	2911	8028	1311	2375	1243
4 AGRI.,FORES.,FISH. SERV.	0	0	0	0	0	0	0	0	0
5 IRON, FERRO. ORES MINING	0	0	0	0	0	0	0	0	0
6 NONFERROUS ORES MINING	0	0	0	0	0	0	0	0	0
7 COAL MINING	1949	4884	7780	3626	1463	4707	381	1836	224
8 CRUDE PETRO.,NATURAL GAS	0	0	0	0	0	0	0	0	0
9 STONE, CLAY MINING	541	719	1189	463	213	597	94	161	70
10 CHEM.,FERT. MIN. MINING	0	0	0	0	0	0	0	0	0
11 NEW CONSTRUCTION	0	0	0	0	0	0	0	0	0
12 MAINT.,REPAIR CONSTR.	0	0	0	0	0	0	0	0	0
13 ORDNANCE, ACCESSORIES	6212	8962	13402	5388	2012	6264	1223	1783	926
14 FOOD, KINDRED PRDTS.	1001745	1797944	2361901	1000550	462187	1244662	206796	379584	194649
15 TOBACCO MANUFACTURES	96037	161568	207201	85117	45666	107830	16070	31271	11759
16 FABRICS	28948	32896	50034	20849	11859	25485	4960	8202	3835
17 TEXTILE PRDTS.	31133	59323	75618	31045	10316	35020	4652	11842	3725
18 APPAREL	338269	543880	758694	297377	128284	362771	51529	107171	39674
19 MISC. TEXTILE PRDTS.	43824	65361	90058	35939	17037	43853	7211	12919	5281
20 LUMBER, WOOD PRDTS.	3250	3065	7579	7249	5320	7684	1668	3112	506
21 WOODEN CONTAINERS	0	0	0	0	0	0	0	0	0
22 HOUSEHOLD FURNITURE	73018	101705	153105	62234	30090	73275	10950	20739	8029
23 OTHER FURNITURE	4299	5689	9138	3782	1746	4400	748	1425	533
24 PAPER, ALLIED PRDTS.	28712	41216	55082	22678	12538	28345	4948	8409	3536
25 PAPERBOARD CONTAINERS	1352	1958	2404	967	502	1136	209	338	154
26 PRINTING, PUBLISHING	75004	124685	176079	70931	28342	87784	13606	25443	10202
27 CHEMICALS,SELECT. PRDTS.	7020	9418	14693	6063	3183	7561	1282	2356	903
28 PLASTICS, SYNTHETICS	438	671	885	363	181	449	77	136	55
29 DRUGS, COSMETICS	157562	203907	301996	124140	71344	157170	28434	47019	20026
30 PAINT, ALLIED PRDTS.	543	1101	1352	529	220	690	74	213	50
31 PETROLEUM, RELATED INDS.	213467	407881	476314	227932	93144	245021	60011	104705	47155
32 RUBBER, MISC. PLASTICS	59720	74069	114791	47332	23758	56239	10566	17877	7757
33 LEATHER TANNING, PRDTS.									
34 FOOTWEAR, LEATHER PRDTS.	56269	84135	128354	52225	23202	62409	10007	19470	7300
35 GLASS, GLASS PRDTS.	4104	5996	8648	3569	1580	4091	715	1327	531
36 STONE, CLAY PRDTS.	6162	9668	13919	5703	2553	6799	1084	2198	773
37 PRIMARY IRON, STEEL MFR.	433	870	1352	611	251	775	80	287	51
38 PRIMARY NONFERROUS MFR.	434	620	755	307	171	371	68	110	49

120

#	Commodity	1	2	3	4	5	6	7	8	9
39	METAL CONTAINERS	1613	0	0	0	0	0	0	0	0
40	FABRICATED METAL PRDTS.	7339	2616	3814	1651	974	1893	353	599	227
41	SCREW MACH. PRDTS., ETC.	13701	10752	15168	6238	2968	7302	1261	2352	937
42	OTHER FAB. METAL PRDTS.	6405	18240	28044	11537	5607	13714	2403	4307	1728
43	ENGINES, TURBINES	327	4019	9031	3633	1927	4080	1022	1276	930
44	FARM MACH. EQUIP.	0	428	694	292	140	343	60	115	42
45	CONSTRUC. MACH., EQUIP.	0	0	0	0	0	0	0	0	0
46	MATERIAL HANDLING MACH.	1130	0	0	0	0	0	0	0	0
47	METALWORKING MACHINERY	756	1480	2419	996	437	1140	198	374	142
48	SPECIAL MACH., EQUIP.	0	988	1616	664	289	759	132	248	95
49	GENERAL MACH., EQUIP.	0	0	0	0	0	0	0	0	0
50	MACHINE SHOP PRDTS.	2414	0	0	0	0	0	0	0	0
51	OFFICE, COMPUT. MACHINES	26392	3086	5050	2063	902	2371	397	773	286
52	SERVICE IND. MACHINES	561	11606	27157	10387	8778	12575	1231	3095	866
53	ELECT. TRANSMISS. EQUIP.	93885	735	1202	496	222	572	98	189	69
54	HOUSEHOLD APPLIANCES	13295	123796	193609	82182	43825	96457	18324	32445	12776
55	ELECTRIC LIGHTING EQUIP.	81325	17441	28159	11582	5184	13471	2346	4365	1687
56	RADIO, TV, ETC., EQUIP.	8497	121029	197011	79695	32352	95386	15193	27792	11513
57	ELECTRONIC COMPONENTS	12678	12716	20698	8386	3395	10017	1598	2919	1209
58	MISC. ELECTRICAL MACH.	0	15261	24023	9835	4915	11762	2208	3667	1636
59	MOTOR VEHICLES, EQUIP.	467439	591341	1214894	347145	138934	449628	75680	147246	61856
60	AIRCRAFT, PARTS	1426	895	2010	809	428	908	228	284	207
61	OTHER TRANSPORT. EQUIP.	63736	43899	98468	39623	20995	44496	11128	13925	10122
62	PROFESS., SCIEN. INSTRU.	14035	19669	30651	12100	6218	14562	2505	4276	1806
63	MEDICAL, PHOTO. EQUIP.	27321	38745	64379	26563	9910	31639	5536	9476	4304
64	MISC. MANUFACTURING	105182	149640	230672	91415	38537	110366	19406	32236	14572
65	TRANSPORT., WAREHOUSING	234646	463600	556102	230477	99586	279913	47070	80299	40548
66	COMMUNICA.,EXC. BRDCAST.	170454	287422	378926	153447	70955	195853	29165	53150	22193
67	RADIO, TV BROADCASTING	292756	375154	665965	276554	134106	349251	50510	106996	35705
68	ELEC.,GAS,WATER,SAN.SER.	1891869	3094901	4265981	1766946	810851	2149198	364440	683846	300836
69	WHOLESALE, RETAIL TRADE	403540	588875	869227	344950	142232	412740	60019	124684	48115
70	FINANCE, INSURANCE	1180242	2339403	2906475	1167255	479390	1523886	224020	402336	177133
71	REAL ESTATE, RENTAL	219047	345997	494554	223423	78014	281079	37906	76982	455952
72	HOTELS, PERSONAL SERV.	32427	34190	157064	55493	7616	60739	2235	11242	5752
73	BUSINESS SERVICES	133123	153957	241817	100015	52129	119201	23308	38299	17127
74	RESEARCH, DEVELOPMENT	0	0	0	0	0	0	0	0	0
75	AUTO. REPAIR, SERVICES	104958	62589	149180	59524	13062	72428	4791	23938	25164
76	AMUSEMENTS	0	0	0	0	0	0	0	0	0
77	MED.,EDUC. SERVICES	755466	1086228	1528187	611520	278330	742238	109842	223384	88080
78	FEDERAL GOVT. ENTERPRISE	18260	31091	41286	17279	7425	21388	3621	6288	2687
79	STATE, LOCAL GOVT. ENT.	14022	15264	25528	10439	5571	12684	2519	3855	1849
80	IMPORTS	156977	267364	360933	148898	67535	183945	29660	54998	26551
81	BUS.TRAVEL, ENT., GIFTS.	0	0	0	0	0	0	0	0	0
82	OFFICE SUPPLIES	0	0	0	0	0	0	0	0	0
83	SCRAP, USED GOODS	-2330	-2876	-5441	-2090	-914	-2584	-382	-767	-297
84	GOVERNMENT INDUSTRY	0	0	0	0	0	0	0	0	0
85	REST OF WORLD INDUSTRY	0	0	0	0	0	0	0	0	0
86	HOUSEHOLD INDUSTRY	86728	73654	121364	36113	24695	58271	10663	12640	9211
87	INVENTORY VALUATION ADJ.	0	0	0	0	0	0	0	0	0
88	STATE TOTAL	9029111	14295560	20198171	8160436	3623427	10073506	1617876	3046169	1767170

TABLE 8-1

STATE ESTIMATES OF 1970
PERSONAL CONSUMPTION EXPENDITURES
(THOUSANDS OF 1958 DOLLARS)

INDUSTRY TITLE	28 NEW HAMPSHIRE	29 NEW JERSEY	30 NEW MEXICO	31 NEW YORK	32 NORTH CAROLINA	33 NORTH DAKOTA	34 OHIO	35 OKLAHOMA	36 OREGON
1 LIVESTOCK, PRDTS.	6853	66425	8942	175252	48310	8159	91786	24231	19044
2 OTHER AGRICULTURE PRDTS.	10110	104506	12376	272852	62916	9479	137786	33297	27562
3 FORESTRY, FISHERIES	1479	15904	1641	41554	7591	1008	19253	4252	3779
4 AGRI.,FORES.,FISH. SERV.	0	0	0	0	0	0	0	0	0
5 IRON, FERRO. ORES MINING	0	0	0	0	0	0	0	0	0
6 NONFERROUS ORES MINING	0	0	0	0	0	0	0	0	0
7 COAL MINING	846	6598	433	18002	3103	763	9159	1597	809
8 CRUDE PETRO.,NATURAL GAS	0	0	0	0	0	0	0	0	0
9 STONE, CLAY MINING	87	981	119	2463	576	67	1479	323	279
10 CHEM.,FERT. MIN. MINING	0	0	0	0	0	0	0	0	0
11 NEW CONSTRUCTION	0	0	0	0	0	0	0	0	0
12 MAINT., REPAIR CONSTR.	0	0	0	0	0	0	0	0	0
13 ORDNANCE, ACCESSORIES	1135	12491	1441	31781	5999	741	16630	3425	3536
14 FOOD, KINDRED PRDTS.	229956	2416952	257110	6360744	1192971	163627	2923630	659563	583325
15 TOBACCO MANUFACTURES	20565	215026	20423	555783	117080	13071	264526	64319	47826
16 FABRICS	4218	43161	6169	110519	32121	3507	61262	17238	13909
17 TEXTILE PRDTS.	6766	79809	6044	198794	29960	4927	90597	17760	14206
18 APPAREL	64718	736604	62976	1870487	357861	44556	921176	200499	151605
19 MISC. TEXTILE PRDTS.	7941	89002	8652	222900	46648	5357	111169	26218	20592
20 LUMBER, WOOD PRDTS.	710	4134	1255	12661	11806	2402	8880	4139	2864
21 WOODEN CONTAINERS	0	0	0	0	0	0	0	0	0
22 HOUSEHOLD FURNITURE	12103	136035	13263	341580	80686	8608	192049	45132	32847
23 OTHER FURNITURE	721	7559	907	19038	4670	593	11075	2589	2118
24 PAPER, ALLIED PRDTS.	5312	55190	6132	141572	33016	3519	69328	18206	14109
25 PAPERBOARD CONTAINERS	258	2626	246	6466	1428	142	3027	788	610
26 PRINTING, PUBLISHING	15098	165599	16631	431815	78624	10573	217797	44025	39143
27 CHEMICALS,SELECT. PRDTS.	1261	12882	1573	33055	8279	984	18289	4514	3602
28 PLASTICS, SYNTHETICS	88	918	93	2354	493	57	1118	268	219
29 DRUGS, COSMETICS	26405	274976	34904	706988	185449	19658	378630	101737	79336
30 PAINT, ALLIED PRDTS.	131	1455	90	3676	599	88	1630	335	209
31 PETROLEUM, RELATED INDS.	63651	895788	72966	1003956	264052	58289	492386	156530	145040
32 RUBBER, MISC. PLASTICS	9569	99266	12411	253038	65335	7441	140452	35940	29652
33 LEATHER TANNING, PRDTS.	0	0	0	0	0	0	0	0	0
34 FOOTWEAR, LEATHER PRDTS.	10299	112971	12156	285116	62438	8122	156808	34459	28757
35 GLASS, GLASS PRDTS.	736	8157	878	20571	4347	553	10411	2408	2108
36 STONE, CLAY PRDTS.	1244	13167	1311	33079	6819	919	16892	3743	3058
37 PRIMARY IRON, STEEL MFR.	138	1174	92	3137	576	119	1611	306	190
38 PRIMARY NONFERROUS MFR.	80	837	81	2091	471	46	948	260	193

Industry	1	2	3	4	5	6	7	8	9
39 METAL CONTAINERS	0	0	0	0	0	0	0	0	0
40 FABRICATED METAL PRDTS.	352	3184	386	8005	2246	250	4678	1243	909
41 SCREW MACH. PRDTS., ETC.	2318	14736	1549	37317	8020	982	18348	4418	3726
42 OTHER FAB. METAL PRDTS.	2309	24471	2911	61963	15103	1798	34429	8353	6846
43 ENGINES. TURBINES	635	5559	1182	14132	6163	530	10841	3348	3113
44 FARM MACH., EQUIP.	56	568	74	1442	364	48	837	201	168
45 CONSTRUC. MACH., EQUIP.	0	0	0	0	0	0	0	0	0
46 MATERIAL HANDLING MACH.	0	0	0	0	0	0	0	0	0
47 METALWORKING MACHINERY	188	1962	235	4899	1193	155	2916	661	561
48 SPECIAL MACH., EQUIP.	125	1309	155	3264	794	104	1948	440	373
49 GENERAL MACH., EQUIP.	0	0	0	0	0	0	0	0	0
50 MACHINE SHOP PRDTS.	0	0	0	0	0	0	0	0	0
51 OFFICE. COMPUT. MACHINES	389	4075	472	10184	2499	320	6036	1395	1111
52 SERVICE IND. MACHINES	1189	15615	1321	38676	25850	1306	33193	15339	3349
53 ELECT. TRANSMISS. EQUIP.	94	978	119	2460	598	79	1439	333	274
54 HOUSEHOLD APPLIANCES	16756	163511	22814	417199	113395	13609	235774	61209	51201
55 ELECTRIC LIGHTING EQUIP.	2213	23370	2837	59010	14070	1810	33836	7851	6572
56 RADIO, TV, ETC., EQUIP.	14649	157621	18670	397286	89851	11598	242696	49941	44598
57 ELECTRONIC COMPONENTS	1535	16506	1969	41479	9423	1218	25519	5233	4695
58 MISC. ELECTRICAL MACH.	1566	20427	2599	51928	13671	1525	29480	7546	6205
59 MOTOR VEHICLES, EQUIP.	84363	869003	90112	1610046	461464	68015	1229349	265661	213677
60 AIRCRAFT, PARTS	142	1238	263	3146	1371	118	2413	745	693
61 OTHER TRANSPORT. EQUIP.	6927	60702	12875	154298	67123	5787	118204	36468	33893
62 PROFESS., SCIEN. INSTRU.	2364	25969	2960	66274	16221	1757	36565	8979	7570
63 MEDICAL, PHOTO. EQUIP.	4561	51811	6678	132426	28163	3956	79290	15727	15967
64 MISC. MANUFACTURING	18353	205942	23502	519886	108320	13381	283372	61110	56938
65 TRANSPORT., WAREHOUSING	56698	649620	62696	1619233	264654	35395	679582	147968	138794
66 COMMUNICA.,EXC. BRDCAST.	36101	395488	36660	1060796	190806	22217	479029	106027	87132
67 RADIO, TV BROADCASTING	0	0	0	0	0	0	0	0	0
68 ELEC.,GAS,WATER,SAN.SER.	43671	499348	61682	1303983	345211	44650	827714	189555	142171
69 WHOLESALE, RETAIL TRADE	400170	4437333	446274	10348383	2172843	302851	5128305	1209172	1014281
70 FINANCE, INSURANCE	70903	806064	72825	2045160	401960	50396	1050123	225069	178953
71 REAL ESTATE, RENTAL	280235	3082748	290852	8237587	1320720	170178	3701965	733153	697022
72 HOTELS, PERSONAL SERV.	55510	455140	56518	1616676	244288	30952	576731	143308	100795
73 BUSINESS SERVICES	1692	49140	6487	425932	28307	2068	132973	23871	15478
74 RESEARCH, DEVELOPMENT	0	0	0	0	0	0	0	0	0
75 AUTO. REPAIR, SERVICES	20304	206091	27080	526637	144569	15936	296317	79508	64433
76 AMUSEMENTS	10251	87323	8510	766660	50410	6834	195507	33750	16314
77 MED.,EDUC. SERVICES	128008	1451545	135154	3725226	775762	93058	1836700	437969	322720
78 FEDERAL GOVT. ENTERPRISE	3837	41689	4530	111098	19683	2617	51525	11026	10555
79 STATE, LOCAL GOVT. ENT.	1989	20431	2999	52022	15374	1606	31642	8513	7153
80 IMPORTS	33366	361963	36720	938685	178999	23233	446772	99829	85407
81 BUS.,TRAVEL, ENT., GIFTS.	0	0	0	0	0	0	0	0	0
82 OFFICE SUPPLIES	0	0	0	0	0	0	0	0	0
83 SCRAP, USED GOODS	-373	-3916	-454	-10031	-2532	-316	-6578	-1408	-1088
84 GOVERNMENT INDUSTRY	0	0	0	0	0	0	0	0	0
85 REST OF WORLD INDUSTRY	0	0	0	0	0	0	0	0	0
86 HOUSEHOLD INDUSTRY	10951	105578	12089	271005	76631	5087	143012	45427	21647
87 INVENTORY VALUATION ADJ.	0	0	0	0	0	0	0	0	0
88 STATE TOTAL	1821728	19894335	2015624	49835694	9927809	1312479	24374261	5557041	4634731

TABLE B-1

STATE ESTIMATES OF 1970
PERSONAL CONSUMPTION EXPENDITURES
(THOUSANDS OF 1958 DOLLARS)

INDUSTRY TITLE	37 PENNSYL-VANIA	38 RHODE ISLAND	39 SOUTH CAROLINA	40 SOUTH DAKOTA	41 TENNESSEE	42 TEXAS	43 UTAH	44 VERMONT	45 VIRGINIA
1 LIVESTOCK, PRDTS.	108561	7856	22689	7983	38604	88017	8022	4015	46201
2 OTHER AGRICULTURE PRDTS.	165019	12139	29572	9490	49982	131201	12024	5473	61772
3 FORESTRY, FISHERIES	24488	1846	3546	1047	5960	18347	1710	750	7566
4 AGRI.,FORES.,FISH. SERV.	0	0	0	0	0	0	0	0	0
5 IRON, FERRO. ORES MINING	0	0	0	0	0	0	0	0	0
6 NONFERROUS ORES MINING	0	0	0	0	0	0	0	0	0
7 COAL MINING	11658	913	1600	833	2525	6249	335	535	2754
8 CRUDE PETRO.,NATURAL GAS	0	0	0	0	0	0	0	0	0
9 STONE, CLAY MINING	1501	109	266	70	453	1415	129	41	584
10 CHEM.,FERT. MIN. MINING	0	0	0	0	0	0	0	0	0
11 NEW CONSTRUCTION	0	0	0	0	0	0	0	0	0
12 MAINT., REPAIR CONSTR.	0	0	0	0	0	0	0	0	0
13 ORDNANCE, ACCESSORIES	19634	1332	2623	774	4780	16465	1530	556	6799
14 FOOD, KINDRED PRDTS.	3747613	282947	557161	168479	934136	2822141	261041	120227	1185711
15 TOBACCO MANUFACTURES	327920	26829	54907	13974	91946	273768	21948	10824	111780
16 FABRICS	66529	5128	15247	3490	24946	74219	6216	2173	32396
17 TEXTILE PRDTS.	122811	8575	12913	4727	23239	76242	6781	3144	30339
18 APPAREL	1112820	82390	163997	43996	280648	865145	66313	30995	369957
19 MISC. TEXTILE PRDTS.	136569	10006	21285	5469	36885	116243	9284	3762	48204
20 LUMBER, WOOD PRDTS.	10579	502	3410	2207	8379	11143	1159	879	7926
21 WOODEN CONTAINERS	0	0	0	0	0	0	0	0	0
22 HOUSEHOLD FURNITURE	215666	15273	37201	8921	64118	194433	15329	5898	78934
23 OTHER FURNITURE	12194	873	2185	599	3734	10783	945	362	4712
24 PAPER, ALLIED PRDTS.	87062	6593	15347	3697	25929	78091	6445	2666	32474
25 PAPERBOARD CONTAINERS	4172	301	641	145	1128	3384	282	131	1417
26 PRINTING, PUBLISHING	255684	19646	36245	10783	61606	195947	17089	7338	83122
27 CHEMICALS,SELECT. PRDTS.	20542	1516	3888	1018	6532	18882	1649	646	8113
28 PLASTICS, SYNTHETICS	1434	108	225	59	387	1149	102	44	488
29 DRUGS, COSMETICS	431582	33083	88304	20584	145548	428854	36272	13305	180698
30 PAINT, ALLIED PRDTS.	2278	166	271	81	467	1447	97	68	615
31 PETROLEUM, RELATED INDS.	635826	59894	121737	62598	167093	624241	53965	41873	253485
32 RUBBER, MISC. PLASTICS	159419	11436	29840	7546	51331	152993	13265	4928	66441
33 LEATHER TANNING, PRDTS.	0	0	0	0	0	0	0	0	0
34 FOOTWEAR, LEATHER PRDTS.	174269	13096	28917	8143	49283	146740	12888	5023	63111
35 GLASS, GLASS PRDTS.	12761	908	1989	551	3459	10186	979	358	4482
36 STONE, CLAY PRDTS.	20682	1499	3188	922	5438	15680	1386	623	6916
37 PRIMARY IRON, STEEL MFR.	2011	153	289	129	466	1247	82	83	550
38 PRIMARY NONFERROUS MFR.	1323	96	214	48	371	1113	89	40	469

124

#	Industry									
39	METAL CONTAINERS	0	0	0	0	0	0	0	0	5878
40	FABRICATED METAL PRDTS.	2198	197	379	5339	1844	290	1151	398	22858
41	SCREW MACH. PRDTS., ETC.	8190	639	1759	18717	6368	976	3675	1635	33623
42	OTHER FAB. METAL PRDTS.	15183	1149	3097	35380	11961	1834	6985	2839	9664
43	ENGINES, TURBINES	8888	355	1438	22739	5193	517	2637	626	921
44	FARM MACH., EQUIP.	366	28	75	825	292	49	173	67	0
45	CONSTRUC. MACH., EQUIP.	0	0	0	0	0	0	0	0	0
46	MATERIAL HANDLING MACH.	1214	95	249	2749	954	157	553	226	3151
47	METALWORKING MACHINERY	809	63	166	1831	635	104	368	151	2111
48	SPECIAL MACH., EQUIP.	0	0	0	0	0	0	0	0	0
49	GENERAL MACH., EQUIP.	0	0	0	0	0	0	0	0	0
50	MACHINE SHOP PRDTS.	0	0	0	0	0	0	0	0	0
51	OFFICE, COMPUT. MACHINES	2611	196	484	5821	2000	317	1159	461	6711
52	SERVICE IND. MACHINES	27963	488	1419	76521	19862	1337	10784	1762	20961
53	ELECT. TRANSMISS. EQUIP.	613	47	120	1378	478	78	280	112	1585
54	HOUSEHOLD APPLIANCES	109210	8926	23749	256065	90000	13705	53452	19323	272525
55	ELECTRIC LIGHTING EQUIP.	14605	1109	2870	33093	11248	1817	6553	2649	37758
56	RADIO, TV, ETC., EQUIP.	90222	7458	20327	224970	69586	11746	39897	18380	254628
57	ELECTRONIC COMPONENTS	9438	782	2147	23669	10719	1234	4170	1929	26741
58	MISC. ELECTRICAL MACH.	13913	1020	2790	32048		1550	6212	2332	32951
59	MOTOR VEHICLES, EQUIP.	486138	45282	97430	1268088	365921	55830	180723	87674	1244724
60	AIRCRAFT, PARTS	1978	79	320	5062	1156	115	587	140	2152
61	OTHER TRANSPORT. EQUIP.	96711	3874	15657	247356	56560	5643	28734	6835	105480
62	PROFESS., SCIEN. INSTRU.	14941	1118	3180	38144	12379	1612	7544	3053	40369
63	MEDICAL, PHOTO. EQUIP.	30186	2590	6902	70018	22083	4143	13403	5907	82066
64	MISC. MANUFACTURING	115273	8860	25149	274240	85980	13592	49206	22641	315875
65	TRANSPORT., WAREHOUSING	269647	28327	61288	636203	203252	36929	122065	71187	929121
66	COMMUNICA., EXC. BROCAST.	188668	18003	39830	460405	147494	23482	88429	45834	614773
67	RADIO, TV BROADCASTING	0	0	0	0	0	0	0	0	0
68	ELEC.,GAS,WATER,SAN.SER.	336586	25027	64140	810962	270586	46552	164173	61140	799120
69	WHOLESALE, RETAIL TRADE	2179239	212682	445999	5183985	1675881	307678	1000205	478785	6299339
70	FINANCE, INSURANCE	426074	35524	79610	1000050	314453	51250	182730	88378	1227945
71	REAL ESTATE, RENTAL	1322179	137591	319153	323822	1004675	178650	598286	373140	4808369
72	HOTELS, PERSONAL SERV.	282834	35019	42730	815143	197209	31103	100205	40515	598592
73	BUSINESS SERVICES	44243	634	8044	155178	49047	1625	11475	3898	67644
74	RESEARCH, DEVELOPMENT	0	0	0	0	0	0	0	0	0
75	AUTO. REPAIR, SERVICES	147303	10708	28835	334518	113524	16143	65880	23670	336033
76	AMUSEMENTS	59438	6204	10518	174264	42788	10590	19215	9467	90541
77	MED.,EDUC. SERVICES	818815	60597	143652	1892410	612521	92330	364308	165516	2236125
78	FEDERAL GOVT. ENTERPRISE	20638	1908	4778	48784	15501	2737	9316	4900	65597
79	STATE, LOCAL GOVT. ENT.	15456	1038	3251	36699	12006	1650	6983	2364	32994
80	IMPORTS	179825	16694	38489	430682	140534	23921	83145	41731	558134
81	BUS.TRAVEL, ENT., GIFTS.	0	0	0	0	0	0	0	0	0
82	OFFICE SUPPLIES	0	0	0	0	0	0	0	0	0
83	SCRAP, USED GOODS	-2482	-192	-492	-5921	-1983	-318	-1147	-442	-6208
84	GOVERNMENT INDUSTRY	0	0	0	0	0	0	0	0	0
85	REST OF WORLD INDUSTRY	0	0	0	0	0	0	0	0	0
86	HOUSEHOLD INDUSTRY	90598	2885	8904	222868	60565	4399	33372	10539	164140
87	INVENTORY VALUATION ADJ.	0	0	0	0	0	0	0	0	0
88	STATE TOTAL	10127726	943769	2065791	24549872	7729941	1333951	4526587	2264976	29243106

125

TABLE 8-1

STATE ESTIMATES OF 1970
PERSONAL CONSUMPTION EXPENDITURES
(THOUSANDS OF 1958 DOLLARS)

INDUSTRY TITLE	46 WASHINGTON	47 WEST VIRGINIA	48 WISCONSIN	49 WYOMING	50 ALASKA	51 HAWAII	52 NO STATE ALLOCATION	53 NATIONAL TOTAL
1 LIVESTOCK, PRDTS.	32202	17404	45387	3608	3876	6520	0	1885000
2 OTHER AGRICULTURE PRDTS.	48052	21348	64129	4790	5408	9963	0	2747000
3 FORESTRY, FISHERIES	6671	2375	8282	617	753	1445	0	379000
4 AGRI.,FORES.,FISH. SERV.	0	0	0	0	0	0	0	0
5 IRON, FERRO. ORES MINING	0	0	0	0	0	0	0	0
6 NONFERROUS ORES MINING	0	0	0	0	0	0	0	0
7 COAL MINING	1206	1075	3999	161	182	298	0	151000
8 CRUDE PETRO.,NATURAL GAS	0	0	0	0	0	0	0	0
9 STONE, CLAY MINING	505	169	645	41	42	101	0	27000
10 CHEM.,FERT. MIN. MINING	0	0	0	0	0	0	0	0
11 NEW CONSTRUCTION	0	0	0	0	0	0	0	0
12 MAINT., REPAIR CONSTR.	0	0	0	0	0	0	0	0
13 ORDNANCE, ACCESSORIES	6835	1777	7649	527	581	1272	0	321000
14 FOOD, KINDRED PRDTS.	1026382	377833	1270044	97390	118078	223563	0	58323000
15 TOBACCO MANUFACTURES	78886	37184	106886	7268	6420	15961	0	5127000
16 FABRICS	24932	10200	26848	2246	2380	5131	0	1284000
17 TEXTILE PRDTS.	27573	7217	41618	2079	2240	5021	0	1679000
18 APPAREL	274039	109528	417126	22701	24188	55306	0	17247000
19 MISC. TEXTILE PRDTS.	37456	13955	48984	3169	3207	7315	0	2168000
20 LUMBER, WOOD PRDTS.	4178	2689	8545	724	275	577	0	237000
21 WOODEN CONTAINERS	0	0	0	0	0	0	0	0
22 HOUSEHOLD FURNITURE	56502	24478	86425	4901	4279	11013	0	3554000
23 OTHER FURNITURE	3693	1485	5174	330	311	700	0	208000
24 PAPER, ALLIED PRDTS.	23967	10278	28910	2186	2084	4898	0	1410000
25 PAPERBOARD CONTAINERS	71004	461	1262	93	83	195	0	62000
26 PRINTING, PUBLISHING	6205	23316	94724	5856	6387	14533	0	4044000
27 CHEMICALS,SELECT. PRDTS.	364	2686	7636	570	539	1239	0	352000
28 PLASTICS, SYNTHETICS	134601	161	448	35	31	73	0	22000
29 DRUGS, COSMETICS	365	58965	156115	12595	12139	28033	0	7608000
30 PAINT, ALLIED PRDTS.	232367	182	707	33	34	74	0	30000
31 PETROLEUM, RELATED INDS.	53961	59931	281948	32414	22049	32081	0	11842000
32 RUBBER, MISC. PLASTICS	51442	20661	62522	4662	4702	10691	0	2809000
33 LEATHER TANNING, PRDTS.							0	
34 FOOTWEAR, LEATHER PRDTS.	3897	19745	70873	4422	4429	10062	0	2913000
35 GLASS, GLASS PRDTS.	5480	1357	4835	312	312	781	0	207000
36 STONE, CLAY PRDTS.	325	2231	7487	481	466	1062	0	321000
37 PRIMARY IRON, STEEL MFR.	337	190	720	35	39	71	0	28000
38 PRIMARY NONFERROUS MFR.		149	404	30	29	65	0	20000

39 METAL CONTAINERS	0	0	0	0	0	0	0
40 FABRICATED METAL PRDTS.	1524	755	1989	155	139	262	0	92000
41 SCREW MACH. PRDTS., ETC.	6914	2515	8210	552	550	1426	0	372000
42 OTHER FAB. METAL PRDTS.	12003	4772	15350	1061	1012	2348	0	664000
43 ENGINES, TURBINES	8429	2107	5182	396	683	1680	0	283000
44 FARM MACH., EQUIP.	289	118	390	26	25	55	0	16000
45 CONSTRUC. MACH., EQUIP.	0	0	0	0	0	0	0	0
46 MATERIAL HANDLING MACH.	0	0	0	0	0	0	0	0
47 METALWORKING MACHINERY	983	385	1363	87	82	181	0	54000
48 SPECIAL MACH., EQUIP.	656	256	911	58	55	120	0	36000
49 GENERAL MACH., EQUIP.	0	0	0	0	0	0	0	0
50 MACHINE SHOP PRDTS.	0	0	0	0	0	0	0	0
51 OFFICE, COMPUT. MACHINES	2051	788	2959	172	178	381	0	113000
52 SERVICE IND. MACHINES	6039	6758	15047	530	502	1056	0	691000
53 ELECT. TRANSMISS. EQUIP.	491	140	693	42	42	92	0	27000
54 HOUSEHOLD APPLIANCES	85057	38604	101573	3388	7308	17131	0	4711000
55 ELECTRIC LIGHTING EQUIP.	11964	4416	16232	1019	1039	2263	0	643000
56 RADIO, TV, ETC., EQUIP.	79548	26177	108609	6737	6822	16438	0	4364000
57 ELECTRONIC COMPONENTS	8348	2737	11410	709	711	1724	0	458000
58 MISC. ELECTRICAL MACH.	11312	4287	13133	977	990	2254	0	586000
59 MOTOR VEHICLES, EQUIP.	320737	122358	498836	34223	22895	66794	0	21739000
60 AIRCRAFT, PARTS	1876	469	1153	88	152	374	0	63000
61 OTHER TRANSPORT. EQUIP.	91678	22945	56494	4314	7425	18261	0	3082000
62 PROFESS., SCIEN. INSTRU.	12637	4321	16482	1092	1116	2530	0	709000
63 MEDICAL, PHOTO. EQUIP.	29960	8825	36361	2437	2499	5687	0	1447000
64 MISC. MANUFACTURING	104305	32894	127828	8487	9014	20541	0	5369000
65 TRANSPORT., WAREHOUSING	240576	75541	367809	21713	22162	52063	0	13869000
66 COMMUNICA.,EXC. BRDCAST.	152836	55774	200723	12862	13657	32536	0	9275000
67 RADIO, TV BROADCASTING	0	0	0	0	0	0	0	0
68 ELEC.,GAS,WATER,SAN.SER.	241281	107045	348154	22303	22290	49919	0	14730000
69 WHOLESALE, RETAIL TRADE	1762300	659910	2300267	169872	175123	355483	0	101714000
70 FINANCE, INSURANCE	335721	123881	466477	26573	29751	68159	0	20500000
71 REAL ESTATE, RENTAL	1215266	370152	1469219	101163	104389	263254	0	70353000
72 HOTELS, PERSONAL SERV.	158046	65882	264506	40474	55734	82702	0	13726000
73 BUSINESS SERVICES	25292	19137	41866	1039	2838	7151	0	2758000
74 RESEARCH, DEVELOPMENT	0	0	0	0	0	0	0	0
75 AUTO. REPAIR, SERVICES	117244	46223	131291	10324	10390	23326	0	6023000
76 AMUSEMENTS	32317	24301	63381	3992	3418	12485	0	3841000
77 MED.,EDUC. SERVICES	578110	238389	869861	47910	54677	120259	0	35993000
78 FEDERAL GOVT. ENTERPRISE	18894	5743	22558	1588	1706	3986	0	1019000
79 STATE, LOCAL GOVT. ENT.	12779	4750	13723	1122	1105	2553	0	635000
80 IMPORTS	151210	56084	194546	13736	16151	32154	0	8723000
81 BUS.,TRAVEL, ENT., GIFTS.	0	0	0	0	0	0	0	0
82 OFFICE SUPPLIES	0	0	0	0	0	0	0	0
83 SCRAP, USED GOODS	-2087	-772	-2952	-171	-171	-387	0	-114000
84 GOVERNMENT INDUSTRY	0	0	0	0	0	0	0	0
85 REST OF WORLD INDUSTRY	0	0	0	0	0	0	0	0
86 HOUSEHOLD INDUSTRY	40149	20321	64215	2823	4473	9147	0	3031000
87 INVENTORY VALUATION ADJ.	0	0	0	0	0	0	0	0
88 STATE TOTAL	8091304	2988071	10661184	763150	806477	1724435	0	478600000

TABLE B-2

STATE ESTIMATES OF 1980
PERSONAL CONSUMPTION EXPENDITURES
(THOUSANDS OF 1958 DOLLARS)

INDUSTRY TITLE	1 ALABAMA	2 ARIZONA	3 ARKANSAS	4 CALIFORNIA	5 COLORADO	6 CONNECTICUT	7 DELAWARE	8 DISTRICT OF COLUMBIA	9 FLORIDA
1 LIVESTOCK, PRDTS.	36188	18944	19295	264547	26009	36538	7426	10205	83691
2 OTHER AGRICULTURE PRDTS.	58384	31183	31984	481150	45118	65562	13086	19005	137572
3 FORESTRY, FISHERIES	7672	4469	4394	72008	6629	10004	1788	2870	19320
4 AGRI.,FORES.,FISH. SERV.	0	0	0	0	0	0	0	0	0
5 IRON, FERRO. ORES MINING	0	0	0	0	0	0	0	0	0
6 NONFERROUS ORES MINING	0	0	0	0	0	0	0	0	0
7 COAL MINING	1326	564	759	5791	551	2003	223	333	3238
8 CRUDE PETRO.,NATURAL GAS	0	0	0	0	0	0	0	0	0
9 STONE, CLAY MINING	750	360	415	6353	561	783	190	263	1593
10 CHEM.,FERT. MIN. MINING	0	0	0	0	0	0	0	0	0
11 NEW CONSTRUCTION	0	0	0	0	0	0	0	0	0
12 MAINT., REPAIR CONSTR.	0	0	0	0	0	0	0	0	0
13 ORDNANCE, ACCESSORIES	9173	4636	4816	87940	7917	10516	2475	4608	18016
14 FOOD, KINDRED PRDTS.	1149495	684089	656205	10789003	995082	1481614	263327	433461	2922443
15 TOBACCO MANUFACTURES	114337	51617	65552	787477	73464	130811	25451	36264	265074
16 FABRICS	28324	13739	15497	221964	20831	24311	6876	9777	65001
17 TEXTILE PRDTS.	36599	15764	20657	278182	25040	56725	10544	14629	69689
18 APPAREL	365811	165125	201819	2891456	250895	464433	94112	134233	794462
19 MISC. TEXTILE PRDTS.	42945	18554	23617	324525	29248	48599	10973	16692	90903
20 LUMBER, WOOD PRDTS.	7090	2448	4347	25452	3475	2972	846	912	7630
21 WOODEN CONTAINERS	0	0	0	0	0	0	0	0	0
22 HOUSEHOLD FURNITURE	110012	42496	61005	743493	67811	115911	27324	47978	238032
23 OTHER FURNITURE	5958	2658	3258	42930	4021	6119	1519	2146	12700
24 PAPER, ALLIED PRDTS.	42582	19367	23981	309330	28323	44841	10168	14680	96354
25 PAPERBOARD CONTAINERS	1812	750	1006	12356	1152	2044	460	616	4046
26 PRINTING, PUBLISHING	87111	43797	48335	773902	67739	106848	22398	36503	192624
27 CHEMICALS,SELECT. PRDTS.	9788	4640	5441	74279	6827	9606	2280	3071	21937
28 PLASTICS, SYNTHETICS	419	198	235	2987	279	476	99	130	981
29 DRUGS, COSMETICS	233768	110805	131529	1733858	158476	218163	53946	75858	538498
30 PAINT, ALLIED PRDTS.	725	257	403	4456	400	1217	181	267	1598
31 PETROLEUM, RELATED INDS.	181282	117354	113210	1574537	174070	295941	72575	48091	483513
32 RUBBER, MISC. PLASTICS	69730	33081	38299	578961	51303	66909	17339	25040	152391
33 LEATHER TANNING, PRDTS.	0	0	0	0	0	0	0	0	0
34 FOOTWEAR, LEATHER PRDTS.	53065	25764	29340	438284	39710	59824	13099	17864	116275
35 GLASS, GLASS PRDTS.	4701	2233	2596	42257	3721	5375	1210	1596	10032
36 STONE, CLAY PRDTS.	7229	3399	3970	57967	5240	8790	1787	2320	15812
37 PRIMARY IRON, STEEL MFR.	589	259	328	3709	339	796	125	193	1354
38 PRIMARY NONFERROUS MFR.	562	228	311	3796	350	621	142	188	1227

	C1	C2	C3	C4	C5	C6	C7	C8	C9
39 METAL CONTAINERS	3023	1512	1640	21662	2158	3899	618	1425	0
40 FABRICATED METAL PRDTS.	8595	4053	4791	78817	6843	9732	2149	2831	6705
41 SCREW MACH. PRDTS., ETC.	17593	8080	9746	134353	12342	17848	4373	6102	18718
42 OTHER FAB. METAL PRDTS.	10785	5641	4471	154786	11902	4773	2535	12051	38490
43 ENGINES, TURBINES	401	190	220	2927	276	403	101	136	18626
44 FARM MACH., EQUIP.	0	0	0	0	0	0	0	0	864
45 CONSTRUC. MACH., EQUIP.	933	445	536	7174	678	1017	255	342	0
46 MATERIAL HANDLING MACH.	903	408	492	6594	623	936	235	315	2098
47 METALWORKING MACHINERY	0	0	0	0	0	0	0	0	1924
48 SPECIAL MACH., EQUIP.	0	0	0	0	0	0	0	0	0
49 GENERAL MACH., EQUIP.	0	0	0	0	0	0	0	0	0
50 MACHINE SHOP PRDTS.	0	0	0	0	0	0	0	0	0
51 OFFICE, COMPUT. MACHINES	2827	1180	1513	20492	1893	2884	754	1010	5727
52 SERVICE IND. MACHINES	18235	2107	10703	36216	3382	6403	4673	8650	44027
53 ELECT. TRANSMISS. EQUIP.	723	317	386	5219	488	740	186	248	1481
54 HOUSEHOLD APPLIANCES	132949	70297	73794	1073775	99563	139594	29237	42907	319206
55 ELECTRIC LIGHTING EQUIP.	13141	5932	7094	100569	9278	13677	3435	4798	27078
56 RADIO, TV, ETC., EQUIP.	131199	67053	74740	1194173	105667	146300	31545	54080	299655
57 ELECTRONIC COMPONENTS	14610	7470	8342	132609	11766	16309	3497	6005	33389
58 MISC. ELECTRICAL MACH.	15815	7391	8707	129495	11463	15031	3969	5563	34594
59 MOTOR VEHICLES, EQUIP.	414217	224964	256427	3952637	331362	555590	141605	176835	1153937
60 AIRCRAFT, PARTS	2570	1344	1065	36889	1837	604	604	2872	4439
61 OTHER TRANSPORT. EQUIP.	46744	24440	19391	670071	51537	20750	10989	52144	80775
62 PROFESS., SCIEN. INSTRU.	16189	8373	9280	137046	11917	17055	4093	6008	34032
63 MEDICAL, PHOTO. EQUIP.	27652	16133	14846	281925	25033	30787	7037	11669	61213
64 MISC. MANUFACTURING	138307	70581	74679	1266394	111875	155604	36059	58165	287503
65 TRANSPORT., WAREHOUSING	295723	175312	168842	2828931	249399	432062	75044	120256	690367
66 COMMUNICA., EXC. BRDCAST.	235333	120038	135246	2056146	179592	308075	56497	92543	556230
67 RADIO, TV BROADCASTING	0	0	0	0	0	0	0	0	0
68 ELEC., GAS, WATER, SAN. SER.	368965	170156	209256	2657176	241838	339979	85036	124571	857732
69 WHOLESALE, RETAIL TRADE	2205205	1161233	1248739	18915207	1737757	2750376	565067	824130	5235902
70 FINANCE, INSURANCE	473443	219794	261170	3969410	342683	582916	122435	182161	1007591
71 REAL ESTATE, RENTAL	1760469	996369	1006001	16846296	1494624	2540919	424512	721879	4047284
72 HOTELS, PERSONAL SERV.	226325	250365	150389	2657146	278098	226335	67783	488415	1922884
73 BUSINESS SERVICES	31800	19145	9971	707699	30023	24641	11623	73528	145312
74 RESEARCH, DEVELOPMENT	0	0	0	0	0	0	0	0	0
75 AUTO. REPAIR, SERVICES	162704	75716	89283	1310497	115168	148472	40643	56208	357532
76 AMUSEMENTS	44318	31323	37764	994907	54738	43723	39299	138580	474241
77 MED., EDUC. SERVICES	962818	418238	526242	7436452	641401	1121262	252683	347988	2106179
78 FEDERAL GOVT. ENTERPRISE	23913	13189	13324	229248	20179	30651	5993	10428	53616
79 STATE, LOCAL GOVT. ENT.	19693	9584	10976	163855	14588	16716	4854	6863	43886
80 IMPORTS	17781	96103	100585	1581890	144485	223541	42334	66363	429786
81 BUS. TRAVEL, ENT., GIFTS.	0	0	0	0	0	0	0	0	0
82 OFFICE SUPPLIES	0	0	0	0	0	0	0	0	0
83 SCRAP, USED GOODS	-455	-213	-254	-3746	-333	-454	-115	-173	-998
84 GOVERNMENT INDUSTRY	0	0	0	0	0	0	0	0	0
85 REST OF WORLD INDUSTRY	0	0	0	0	0	0	0	0	0
86 HOUSEHOLD INDUSTRY	73618	18053	38896	379015	29991	59861	23639	32653	130308
87 INVENTORY VALUATION ADJ.	0	0	0	0	0	0	0	0	0
88 STATE TOTAL	10747074	5721095	6101897	9406902	8482695	13287897	2767245	4700642	26898339

STATE ESTIMATES OF 1940
PERSONAL CONSUMPTION EXPENDITURES
(THOUSANDS OF 1958 DOLLARS)

INDUSTRY TITLE	10 GEORGIA	11 IDAHO	12 ILLINOIS	13 INDIANA	14 IOWA	15 KANSAS	16 KENTUCKY	17 LOUISIANA	18 MAINE
1 LIVESTOCK, PRDTS.	48966	8655	115996	51334	32516	24971	35625	34750	10425
2 OTHER AGRICULTURE PRDTS.	78921	13530	207000	92102	51376	40622	53854	57577	17378
3 FORESTRY, FISHERIES	10372	1809	29961	13588	6789	5599	6621	7894	2587
4 AGRI.,FORES.,FISH. SERV.	0	0	0	0	0	0	0	0	0
5 IRON,FERRO.ORES MINING	0	0	0	0	0	0	0	0	0
6 NONFERROUS ORES MINING	0	0	0	0	0	0	0	0	0
7 COAL MINING	1750	215	6651	2953	1927	1570	1218	1401	766
8 CRUDE PETRO.,NATURAL GAS	0	0	0	0	0	0	0	0	0
9 STONE, CLAY MINING	993	150	2822	1261	601	486	632	745	179
10 CHEM.,FERT.MIN. MINING	0	0	0	0	0	0	0	0	0
11 NEW CONSTRUCTION	0	0	0	0	0	0	0	0	0
12 MAINT.,REPAIR CONSTR.	0	0	0	0	0	0	0	0	0
13 ORDNANCE, ACCESSORIES	12354	2186	33862	15401	7350	5793	7629	9632	2489
14 FOOD, KINDRED PRDTS.	1561353	276443	4412903	1996158	1021306	839391	1007668	1179369	395077
15 TOBACCO MANUFACTURES	150493	20224	388964	184215	87891	74532	98208	118376	35867
16 FABRICS	38609	5789	82938	37472	19046	15899	25465	28727	6503
17 TEXTILE PRDTS.	47144	6426	134447	62054	31780	25165	29070	37000	12548
18 APPAREL	490829	67767	1445308	637688	317423	251558	314551	366776	109693
19 MISC. TEXTILE PRDTS.	57095	8217	148395	66751	32567	26359	36412	44320	11525
20 LUMBER, WOOD PRDTS.	7884	1792	12436	7371	7444	4078	8653	5423	1355
21 WOODEN CONTAINERS	0	0	0	0	0	0	0	0	0
22 HOUSEHOLD FURNITURE	147090	18817	408394	189879	89256	71443	92843	119635	27481
23 OTHER FURNITURE	7967	1172	22131	10023	5069	3967	5181	6065	1540
24 PAPER, ALLIED PRDTS.	57117	8037	130436	60403	29679	24648	36752	43823	11566
25 PAPERBOARD CONTAINERS	2448	331	5294	2510	1189	994	1574	1829	529
26 PRINTING, PUBLISHING	118192	18564	344757	152654	76012	61353	74160	88211	25878
27 CHEMICALS,SELECT. PRDTS.	13117	1973	31657	14705	7389	6135	8582	9891	2555
28 PLASTICS, SYNTHETICS	567	82	1304	620	302	258	369	423	128
29 DRUGS, COSMETICS	313998	45936	704248	326321	162076	135863	204329	239126	57437
30 PAINT, ALLIED PRDTS.	993	113	2936	1276	664	550	624	765	281
31 PETROLEUM, RELATED INDS.	301263	37546	693921	390394	209087	141383	157368	177906	97062
32 RUBBER, MISC. PLASTICS	93924	14719	223012	101155	51059	40721	60547	70673	16963
33 LEATHER TANNING, PRDTS.	0	0	0	0	0	0	0	0	0
34 FOOTWEAR, LEATHER PRDTS.	70914	11119	207940	93843	47132	37597	46167	53437	14817
35 GLASS, GLASS PRDTS.	6272	996	16828	7553	3879	2995	4065	4720	1282
36 STONE, CLAY PRDTS.	9700	1498	26547	12126	6211	4952	6371	7246	2213
37 PRIMARY IRON, STEEL MFR.	784	111	2593	1154	683	550	527	609	260
38 PRIMARY NONFERROUS MFR.	759	100	1597	745	360	297	488	567	156

	C1	C2	C3	C4	C5	C6	C7	C8	C9
39 METAL CONTAINERS PRDTS.	4032	0	11880	0	2829	2202	0	0	1096
40 FABRICATED METAL PRDTS.	11444	735	28986	5466	6704	5251	2713	3644	2312
41 SCREW MACH. PRDTS., ETC.	23534	1807	60431	12986	13267	11053	7443	8678	4477
42 OTHER FAB. METAL PRDTS.	15718	3518	22357	27571	5058	3892	15233	17869	1343
43 ENGINES, TURBINES	536	2999	1459	10000	341	267	8722	16097	105
44 FARM MACH., EQUIP.		82		659			352	405	
45 CONSTRUC. MACH., EQUIP.									
46 MATERIAL HANDLING MACH.									
47 METALWORKING MACHINERY	1317	199	3694	1671	849	663	860	985	258
48 SPECIAL MACH., EQUIP.	1211	183	3401	1538	780	609	790	905	236
49 GENERAL MACH., EQUIP.									
50 MACHINE SHOP PRDTS.	3796	545	10650	4740	2412	1842	2463	2811	709
51 OFFICE, COMPUT. MACHINES	24072	1064	34369	15726	7704	5985	14282	17038	1366
52 SERVICE IND. MACHINES	953	142	2707	1210	622	479	622	711	184
53 ELECT. TRANSMISS. EQUIP.	180357	29652	447937	204670	107803	87424	119352	137346	38915
54 HOUSEHOLD APPLIANCES	17586	2672	49099	21940	11181	8625	11387	13177	3369
55 ELECTRIC LIGHTING EQUIP.	17571	28486	555763	248665	123573	97723	108843	138775	36723
56 RADIO, TV, ETC., EQUIP.	19541	3167	52056	22848	13826	10930	12082	15496	4101
57 ELECTRONIC COMPONENTS	21296	3282	50636	22883	11450	9137	13698	15852	3768
58 MISC. ELECTRICAL MACH.									
59 MOTOR VEHICLES, EQUIP.	626487	102496	1893985	1000245	405873	350090	344497	439084	127374
60 AIRCRAFT, PARTS	3746	715	5328	2383	1205	927	2079	3836	320
61 OTHER TRANSPORT. EQUIP.	68111	12988	97072	43419	21962	16900	37811	69714	5838
62 PROFESS., SCIEN. INSTRU.	21296	3212	61147	26563	13318	10321	13325	16958	4009
63 MEDICAL, PHOTO. EQUIP.	37630	6998	117030	52819	25909	20528	24266	28434	7923
64 MISC. MANUFACTURING	185330	30450	521365	232061	113774	90153	117648	141241	36441
65 TRANSPORT., WAREHOUSING	402954	65604	1208786	549015	270004	212899	249089	303979	106669
66 COMMUNICA., EXC. BRDCAST.	319049	47253	898945	406474	198160	163011	198996	247947	76968
67 RADIO, TV BROADCASTING	495621	69283	1333101	610729	310521	258071	319490	381037	90468
68 ELEC., GAS, WATER, SAN. SER.	3043140	476472	8361929	3870426	1956245	1560618	1914123	2261913	718341
69 WHOLESALE, RETAIL TRADE	655985	91916	1817844	803405	392809	318924	409543	485053	131776
70 FINANCE, INSURANCE	2334828	374676	6997729	3146516	1523494	1299250	1464911	1858341	626813
71 REAL ESTATE, RENTAL	411408	60286	1490028	452290	225688	169661	229159	293923	96777
72 HOTELS, PERSONAL SERV.	59701	8419	465202	40574	22151	11972	23811	49455	2006
73 BUSINESS SERVICES	219700	33928	489960	222536	112608	9091	142191	162634	38066
74 RESEARCH, DEVELOPMENT	100543	8679	454441	113640	61018	46153	73643	93372	10825
75 AUTO. REPAIR, SERVICES	1306974	170979	3511897	1541278	788531	612905	840372	953809	260366
76 AMUSEMENTS	32093	5454	91204	40594	20239	16287	20368	24680	7563
77 MED., EDUC. SERVICES	26491	4167	59754	27302	13520	10975	16940	19977	4283
78 FEDERAL GOVT. ENTERPRISE	240222	39563	680951	308307	154134	125884	153629	182626	56743
79 STATE, LOCAL GOVT. ENT.									
80 IMPORTS									
81 BUS. TRAVEL, ENT., GIFTS.									
82 OFFICE SUPPLIES									
83 SCRAP, USED GOODS	-515	-95	-1914	-825	-412	-331	-394	-480	-113
84 GOVERNMENT INDUSTRY									
85 REST OF WORLD INDUSTRY									
86 HOUSEHOLD INDUSTRY	110243	9361	187661	68110	32990	27284	61246	72967	10172
87 INVENTORY VALUATION ADJ.									
88 STATE TOTAL	14913949	2275654	41954141	18699343	9280763	7508384	9301138	11197205	3385130

TABLE B-2

STATE ESTIMATES OF 1980
PERSONAL CONSUMPTION EXPENDITURES
(THOUSANDS OF 1958 DOLLARS)

INDUSTRY TITLE	19 MARYLAND	20 MASSA-CHUSETTS	21 MICHIGAN	22 MINNESOTA	23 MISSISSIPPI	24 MISSOURI	25 MONTANA	26 NEBRASKA	27 NEVADA
1 LIVESTOCK, PRDTS.	45185	58817	97865	43157	23230	49233	8891	17345	7270
2 OTHER AGRICULTURE PRDTS.	74801	106535	166651	69080	35081	81071	13790	26635	11840
3 FORESTRY, FISHERIES	9762	16464	22923	9266	4439	11214	1847	3443	1779
4 AGRI.,FORES.,FISH. SERV.	0	0	0	0	0	0	0	0	0
5 IRON, FERRO. ORES MINING	0	0	0	0	0	0	0	0	0
6 NONFERROUS ORES MINING	0	0	0	0	0	0	0	0	0
7 COAL MINING	1432	2976	5813	2499	909	3126	227	1045	158
8 CRUDE PETRO.,NATURAL GAS	0	0	0	0	0	0	0	0	0
9 STONE, CLAY MINING	995	1266	2179	811	405	1001	152	294	110
10 CHEM.,FERT. MIN. MINING	0	0	0	0	0	0	0	0	0
11 NEW CONSTRUCTION	0	0	0	0	0	0	0	0	0
12 MAINT., REPAIR CONSTR.	0	0	0	0	0	0	0	0	0
13 ORDNANCE, ACCESSORIES	12588	16760	26300	10002	4920	11496	2216	3510	1557
14 FOOD, KINDRED PRDTS.	1458883	2447461	3385919	1393096	676916	1678868	282443	521284	273956
15 TOBACCO MANUFACTURES	139542	210258	291674	119575	66330	148672	22036	44938	15724
16 FABRICS	37901	39983	65281	25992	15895	31523	6008	9994	4517
17 TEXTILE PRDTS.	47972	91639	111540	42689	17468	48240	6716	16037	4703
18 APPAREL	492009	757503	1168665	426914	199528	516386	68129	159577	53710
19 MISC. TEXTILE PRDTS.	56506	77889	116812	43956	23437	53965	8282	16536	5815
20 LUMBER, WOOD PRDTS.	4659	4384	10887	8343	5812	8881	1909	3391	678
21 WOODEN CONTAINERS	0	0	0	0	0	0	0	0	0
22 HOUSEHOLD FURNITURE	141940	184774	316225	120756	57483	141852	18853	43027	12968
23 OTHER FURNITURE	7954	9625	17742	6814	3239	7901	1226	2510	827
24 PAPER, ALLIED PRDTS.	54723	71158	99877	40162	24288	49382	8407	15143	5980
25 PAPERBOARD CONTAINERS	2442	3137	4027	1632	969	1940	346	613	242
26 PRINTING, PUBLISHING	117378	172509	268000	102730	47972	124507	18859	37977	14284
27 CHEMICALS,SELECT. PRDTS.	12631	15174	24695	9977	5632	12115	2046	3806	1424
28 PLASTICS, SYNTHETICS	555	750	990	411	240	510	86	160	59
29 DRUGS, COSMETICS	300295	347229	540246	218704	134188	271206	47682	83320	33869
30 PAINT, ALLIED PRDTS.	997	1945	2369	882	407	1101	116	345	80
31 PETROLEUM, RELATED INDS.	274740	479929	573478	267977	120856	282125	71004	112778	55655
32 RUBBER, MISC. PLASTICS	93433	105118	175923	69021	38455	81125	14501	25663	10417
33 LEATHER TANNING, PRDTS.	0	0	0	0	0	0	0	0	0
34 FOOTWEAR, LEATHER PRDTS.	70016	95462	165652	63585	29819	74610	11384	23527	8087
35 GLASS, GLASS PRDTS.	6295	8616	13511	5213	2491	5979	977	1917	689
36 STONE, CLAY PRDTS.	9660	13871	21243	8351	4042	9792	1520	3146	1047
37 PRIMARY IRON, STEEL MFR.	717	1211	2162	897	366	1108	111	360	77
38 PRIMARY NONFERROUS MFR.	751	975	1235	489	307	585	104	182	73

Industry	Col1	Col2	Col3	Col4	Col5	Col6	Col7	Col8	Col9
39 METAL CONTAINERS	3393	5749	9476	3791	2025	4590	760	1433	0
40 FABRICATED METAL PRDTS.	11296	15677	23172	9019	4621	10566	1738	3385	468
41 SCREW MACH. PRDTS.. ETC.	23250	28248	47596	18670	9709	21986	3637	6937	1242
42 OTHER FAB. METAL PRDTS.	14863	7181	18322	6823	6487	7567	2287	2430	2521
43 ENGINES. TURBINES	531	632	1175	457	224	533	87	171	1762
44 FARM MACH.. EQUIP.	0	0	0	0	0	0	0	0	58
45 CONSTRUC. MACH.. EQUIP.	0	0	0	0	0	0	0	0	0
46 MATERIAL HANDLING MACH.	0	0	0	0	0	0	0	0	0
47 METALWORKING MACHINERY	1335	1586	2962	1144	531	1318	210	424	141
48 SPECIAL MACH.. EQUIP.	1231	1459	2726	1052	487	1210	192	389	129
49 GENERAL MACH.. EQUIP.	0	0	0	0	0	0	0	0	0
50 MACHINE SHOP PRDTS.	0	0	0	0	0	0	0	0	0
51 OFFICE. COMPUT. MACHINES	3897	4533	8702	3225	1510	3691	562	1171	381
52 SERVICE IND. MACHINES	23375	10629	27544	10212	10233	11660	1017	3575	677
53 ELECT. TRANSMISS. EQUIP.	366	1165	2207	833	387	954	149	305	101
54 HOUSEHOLD APPLIANCES	171136	219003	354711	146424	78370	170060	30814	55804	21372
55 ELECTRIC LIGHTING EQUIP.	17303	21641	39856	14980	7139	17226	2770	5460	1894
56 RADIO. TV. ETC.. EQUIP.	168212	230595	433341	167321	70999	194004	28859	55903	21192
57 ELECTRONIC COMPONENTS	18534	25671	48373	18719	7907	21645	3218	6690	2353
58 MISC. ELECTRICAL MACH.	21333	23598	39832	15492	8613	18251	3230	5726	2329
59 MOTOR VEHICLES. EQUIP.	658205	797785	1868385	504234	199498	644093	100466	218877	76203
60 AIRCRAFT. PARTS	354	1712	4366	1626	1546	1803	545	579	420
61 OTHER TRANSPORT. EQUIP.	64501	31225	79543	29627	28111	32864	9912	10554	7634
62 PROFESS.. SCIEN. INSTRU.	20411	27562	49018	17816	8526	22464	3331	6778	2677
63 MEDICA_. PHOTO. EQUIP.	38142	49594	91628	35178	15316	41645	7039	12690	5294
64 MISC. MANUFACTURING	186615	249934	414897	153793	74989	183528	30774	56403	22653
65 TRANSPORT.. WAREHOUSING	384572	724312	934646	365932	165711	435112	69669	132574	61170
66 COMMUNICA..EXC. BROCAST.	308840	501478	674503	267813	130858	327615	48799	97393	37527
67 RADIO. TV BROADCASTING	0	0	0	0	0	0	0	0	0
68 ELEC.+GAS.WATER.SAN.SER.	471725	547114	1028136	417515	214681	510071	72713	157746	52517
69 WHOLESALE. RETAIL TRADE	2927025	4447136	6686222	2624528	1263695	3120944	513530	1000197	428023
70 FINANCE. INSURANCE	681024	916655	1409005	538464	258239	631257	90479	194806	72942
71 REAL ESTATE. RENTAL	2283425	4179037	5157143	2071887	982129	2641167	395498	778139	312192
72 HOTELS. PERSONAL SERV.	369173	570080	873308	380917	139940	466829	62479	133649	772962
73 BUSINESS SERVICES	119220	47864	222670	75069	11209	77951	2874	14551	7440
74 RESEARCH. DEVELOPMENT	22024	231582	386482	152351	89443	179000	33224	56841	0
75 AUTO. REPAIR. SERVICES	185656	106438	267135	102113	25764	121025	7763	41863	23861
76 AMUSEMENTS	1329499	1830299	2786977	1055138	526606	1218003	170563	377811	39989
77 MED.+EDUC. SERVICES	31587	49562	68249	2736	13390	33807	5499	10122	142408
78 FEDERAL GOVT. ENTERPRISE	26240	26163	46503	18309	10916	21781	4136	6774	4063
79 STATE. LOCAL GOVT. ENT.	229372	365608	528365	209558	101448	252263	40217	77976	2964
80 IMPORTS	0	0	0	0	0	0	0	0	36500
81 BUS.+TRAVEL. ENT.. GIFTS.	0	0	0	0	0	0	0	0	0
82 OFFICE SUPPLIES	-605	-715	-1542	-559	-242	-682	-93	-210	-67
83 SCRAP. USED GOODS	0	0	0	0	0	0	0	0	0
84 GOVERNMENT INDUSTRY	0	0	0	0	0	0	0	0	0
85 REST OF WORLD INDUSTRY	105111	95333	146372	44949	39740	64493	9410	17838	0
86 HOUSEHOLD INDUSTRY	0	0	0	0	0	0	0	0	9200
87 INVENTORY VALUATION ADJ.	0	0	0	0	0	0	0	0	0
88 STATE TOTAL	14601815	21731143	32481890	12624745	6055879	15221808	2378225	4736257	2702787

TABLE B-2

STATE ESTIMATES OF 1990
PERSONAL CONSUMPTION EXPENDITURES
(THOUSANDS OF 1958 DOLLARS)

INDUSTRY TITLE	28 NEW HAMPSHIRE	29 NEW JERSEY	30 NEW MEXICO	31 NEW YORK	32 NORTH CAROLINA	33 NORTH DAKOTA	34 OHIO	35 OKLAHOMA	36 OREGON
1 LIVESTOCK, PRDTS.	8569	84475	10103	202785	55033	8880	110435	26466	20098
2 OTHER AGRICULTURE PRDTS.	14717	152226	16441	362466	87263	12098	194065	44103	33494
3 FORESTRY, FISHERIES	2210	23488	2327	56334	11322	1373	27870	6027	4802
4 AGRI.,FORES.,FISH. SERV.	0	0	0	0	0	0	0	0	0
5 IRON, FERRO. ORES MINING	0	0	0	0	0	0	0	0	0
6 NONFERROUS ORES MINING	0	0	0	0	0	0	0	0	0
7 COAL MINING	570	4599	275	11322	1975	514	6653	952	477
8 CRUDE PETRO.,NATURAL GAS	0	0	0	0	0	0	0	0	0
9 STONE, CLAY MINING	163	1791	190	4127	1088	107	2603	572	398
10 CHEM.,FERT. MIN. MINING	0	0	0	0	0	0	0	0	0
11 NEW CONSTRUCTION	0	0	0	0	0	0	0	0	0
12 MAINT., REPAIR CONSTR.	0	0	0	0	0	0	0	0	0
13 ORDNANCE, ACCESSORIES	2195	24259	2535	53854	13386	1302	31058	6850	5604
14 FOOD, KINDRED PRDTS.	333225	346739	355324	8376236	1710649	215244	4102884	901191	724562
15 TOBACCO MANUFACTURES	29799	306295	27781	737648	168288	16775	372669	87771	57633
16 FABRICS	5589	55707	7410	132515	42476	4150	78382	21789	14929
17 TEXTILE PRDTS.	11599	127724	8210	287385	52930	6731	127834	29047	17815
18 APPAREL	97389	1074390	84761	2457397	540847	62184	1358120	282997	182544
19 MISC. TEXTILE PRDTS.	10368	111411	9924	257322	62802	6293	140204	32848	21060
20 LUMBER, WOOD PRDTS.	898	6306	1501	16424	13206	2569	12394	4722	3343
21 WOODEN CONTAINERS	0	0	0	0	0	0	0	0	0
22 HOUSEHOLD FURNITURE	25273	258745	22814	608652	163418	15651	379544	84195	48672
23 OTHER FURNITURE	1368	13651	1446	31554	8776	1010	20705	4554	3060
24 PAPER, ALLIED PRDTS.	9986	102265	10480	241285	62951	5824	124437	32780	21284
25 PAPERBOARD CONTAINERS	467	4554	413	10490	2704	233	5078	1406	864
26 PRINTING, PUBLISHING	22697	244438	23096	578561	129628	14621	320588	67611	48818
27 CHEMICALS,SELECT. PRDTS.	2161	22277	2505	51187	14417	1525	30415	7419	5121
28 PLASTICS, SYNTHETICS	107	1117	106	2573	624	63	1270	324	214
29 DRUGS, COSMETICS	48881	504770	59349	1190061	345044	32552	675888	178803	119100
30 PAINT, ALLIED PRDTS.	261	2671	139	6259	1070	142	2768	567	281
31 PETROLEUM, RELATED INDS.	80672	1138906	87031	1161254	326170	65434	594219	182153	152940
32 RUBBER, MISC. PLASTICS	14833	150541	17320	348608	103380	10301	209571	53410	36849
33 LEATHER TANNING, PRDTS.	0	0	0	0	0	0	0	0	0
34 FOOTWEAR, LEATHER PRDTS.	13026	137117	13705	316560	78312	9380	194858	40652	29277
35 GLASS, GLASS PRDTS.	1149	12285	1194	28008	6945	781	15753	3631	2560
36 STONE, CLAY PRDTS.	1935	20118	1809	46071	10683	1297	25195	5519	3826
37 PRIMARY IRON, STEEL MFR.	206	1797	133	4302	871	165	2519	437	252
38 PRIMARY NONFERROUS MFR.	138	1403	126	3229	831	70	1522	432	261

134

	Col1	Col2	Col3	Col4	Col5	Col6	Col7	Col8	Col9
39 METAL CONTAINERS	0	0	0	0	0	0	0	0	0
40 FABRICATED METAL PRDTS.	947	7992	824	13045	4390	587	11440	2148	1754
41 SCREW MACH. PRDTS., ETC.	2068	22418	2158	51472	12729	1383	27416	6646	4585
42 OTHER FAB. METAL PRDTS.	3936	40491	4366	94034	25979	2761	56956	13509	9178
43 ENGINES, TURBINES	1126	10607	2726	23351	15677	983	20641	6455	6601
44 FARM MACH., EQUIP.	91	901	103	2092	590	70	1371	306	215
45 CONSTRUC. MACH., EQUIP.	0	0	0	0	0	0	0	0	0
46 MATERIAL HANDLING MACH.	229	2260	244	5191	1452	172	3463	755	521
47 METALWORKING MACHINERY	210	2078	223	4768	1335	158	3187	694	477
48 SPECIAL MACH., EQUIP.	0	0	0	0	0	0	0	0	0
49 GENERAL MACH., EQUIP.	0	0	0	0	0	0	0	0	0
50 MACHINE SHOP PRDTS.	0	0	0	0	0	0	0	0	0
51 OFFICE, COMPUT. MACHINES	541	6354	645	14418	4137	472	9878	2144	1404
52 SERVICE IND. MACHINES	1256	15097	1149	34650	27279	1315	31861	14833	2512
53 ELECT. TRANSMISS. EQUIP.	164	1651	173	3765	1045	125	2522	543	371
54 HOUSEHOLD APPLIANCES	32853	309913	38266	711618	198633	23798	426607	100559	74869
55 ELECTRIC LIGHTING EQUIP.	2996	30700	3232	69746	19224	2204	45605	9979	6923
56 RADIO, TV, ETC., EQUIP.	32904	322305	35593	754598	195127	23120	511846	102247	73985
57 ELECTRONIC COMPONENTS	3683	35822	3974	83856	21711	2581	57190	11383	8245
58 MISC. ELECTRICAL MACH.	3321	33636	3869	77707	23417	2266	47379	12167	8175
59 MOTOR VEHICLES, EQUIP.	119722	1236243	121153	2085610	671213	95280	1806880	362359	252122
60 AIRCRAFT, PARTS	258	2528	650	5565	3736	234	4919	1538	1573
61 OTHER TRANSPORT. EQUIP.	4834	46108	11816	101534	67950	4270	89629	27997	28600
62 PROFESS., SCIEN. INSTRU.	3621	38479	4192	90567	24004	2622	57613	12543	9447
63 MEDICAL, PHOTO. EQUIP.	5825	70333	8458	160400	40707	4896	107927	21058	18284
64 MISC. MANUFACTURING	32508	356674	37209	812414	202946	21520	485525	105002	80843
65 TRANSPORT., WAREHOUSING	92017	1047499	93778	2349382	444792	52839	1104754	233480	187324
66 COMMUNICA.+EXC. BRDCAST.	65016	724428	62027	1695553	352586	35775	834727	185325	129758
67 RADIO, TV BROADCASTING	0	0	0	0	0	0	0	0	0
68 ELEC.+GAS+WATER+SAN.SER.	76625	778472	89886	1858371	545199	62888	1265772	283430	184652
69 WHOLESALE, RETAIL TRADE	620094	6756794	632588	14349178	3337432	425796	7792966	1752465	1288478
70 FINANCE, INSURANCE	119667	1303325	117464	3059129	695746	74338	1642432	364958	252102
71 REAL ESTATE, RENTAL	543897	5865897	514466	14172795	2635839	286419	6576093	1379606	1095796
72 HOTELS, PERSONAL SERV.	97856	768036	97098	2544426	428883	53822	978358	240773	158292
73 BUSINESS SERVICES	2497	71431	8332	564610	40441	2617	181148	31953	17807
74 RESEARCH, DEVELOPMENT	0	0	0	0	0	0	0	0	0
75 AUTO. REPAIR, SERVICES	33196	331608	39479	767412	241510	22924	461018	125116	83287
76 AMUSEMENTS	18114	153550	13990	1205737	94624	11590	333743	58760	24212
77 MED.,EDUC. SERVICES	231224	2598249	215696	5849551	1411540	150177	3206189	745411	457892
78 FEDERAL GOVT. ENTERPRISE	6555	69794	6929	165511	35463	3834	84794	18558	14310
79 STATE, LOCAL GOVT. ENT.	3735	37498	5011	86893	29136	2646	56192	15201	10548
80 IMPORTS	48953	521799	50149	1237597	262904	31068	635792	138644	104470
81 BUS.,TRAVEL, ENT., GIFTS.	0	0	0	0	0	0	0	0	0
82 OFFICE SUPPLIES	0	0	0	0	0	0	0	0	0
83 SCRAP, USED GOODS	-99	-1027	-112	-2399	-679	-82	-1782	-354	-235
84 GOVERNMENT INDUSTRY	0	0	0	0	0	0	0	0	0
85 REST OF WORLD INDUSTRY	0	0	0	0	0	0	0	0	0
86 HOUSEHOLD INDUSTRY	9807	139756	11450	288767	105833	5976	166841	55753	19610
87 INVENTORY VALUATION ADJ.	0	0	0	0	0	0	0	0	0
88 STATE TOTAL	2963873	31820764	3007702	72982983	16241619	1910713	38298393	8553202	6179125

STATE ESTIMATES OF 1940
PERSONAL CONSUMPTION EXPENDITURES
(THOUSANDS OF 1958 DOLLARS)

INDUSTRY TITLE	37 PENNSYL-VANIA	38 RHODE ISLAND	39 SOUTH CAROLINA	40 SOUTH DAKOTA	41 TENNESSEE	42 TEXAS	43 UTAH	44 VERMONT	45 VIRGINIA
1 LIVESTOCK, PRDTS.	120836	9489	27729	8463	44841	102114	9181	4401	56265
2 OTHER AGRICULTURE PRDTS.	211848	16880	43265	11928	69295	185036	15828	6933	88054
3 FORESTRY, FISHERIES	32247	2589	5509	1420	8786	27319	2329	984	11104
4 AGRI.,FORES.,FISH. SERV.	0	0	0	0	0	0	0	0	0
5 IRON, FERRO. ORES MINING	0	0	0	0	0	0	0	0	0
6 NONFERROUS ORES MINING	0	0	0	0	0	0	0	0	0
7 COAL MINING	7080	689	1042	535	1572	3987	214	355	1880
8 CRUDE PETRO.,NATURAL GAS									
9 STONE, CLAY MINING	2425	193	527	115	837	2641	200	66	1076
10 CHEM.,FERT. MIN. MINING	0	0	0	0	0	0	0	0	0
11 NEW CONSTRUCTION	0	0	0	0	0	0	0	0	0
12 MAINT., REPAIR CONSTR.	0	0	0	0	0	0	0	0	0
13 ORDNANCE, ACCESSORIES	31769	2545	6894	1380	10505	33828	2681	958	13992
14 FOOD, KINDRED PRDTS.	4789089	387240	836828	220067	1328876	4047614	347887	154060	1686771
15 TOBACCO MANUFACTURES	426036	37108	80480	18266	128904	401444	28443	13071	159390
16 FABRICS	77632	6286	21159	4100	32345	98679	7293	2553	42340
17 TEXTILE PRDTS.	169936	13624	22273	6364	37551	142282	8857	4740	49893
18 APPAREL	1427066	116026	259016	60953	413210	1294229	86745	40439	537118
19 MISC. TEXTILE PRDTS.	152564	12130	30953	6352	48853	155105	10360	4278	62475
20 LUMBER, WOOD PRDTS.	12528	723	4211	2369	9494	14597	1409	951	9506
21 WOODEN CONTAINERS	0	0	0	0	0	0	0	0	0
22 HOUSEHOLD FURNITURE	373561	28334	76392	16618	118013	410576	25244	10857	162093
23 OTHER FURNITURE	19619	1524	4245	1019	6723	20877	1491	607	8767
24 PAPER, ALLIED PRDTS.	144049	11640	30626	6123	48459	149384	10568	4417	61412
25 PAPERBOARD CONTAINERS	6577	502	1248	237	2057	6396	441	211	2626
26 PRINTING, PUBLISHING	334284	27922	63487	14890	98082	309540	23390	9639	130206
27 CHEMICALS,SELECT. PRDTS.	30869	2473	7066	1568	11302	33029	2526	988	14156
28 PLASTICS, SYNTHETICS	1535	123	303	64	487	1435	109	48	609
29 DRUGS, COSMETICS	707326	57523	171159	33985	267171	803969	59210	21744	337865
30 PAINT, ALLIED PRDTS.	3820	308	532	133	832	2605	145	114	1098
31 PETROLEUM, RELATED INDS.	702177	73639	161445	69660	207508	772681	62303	46952	315875
32 RUBBER, MISC. PLASTICS	210790	16749	49852	10464	79514	241169	18036	6742	103043
33 LEATHER TANNING, PRDTS.	189924	15101	38118	9415	60782	183556	14187	5520	77154
34 FOOTWEAR, LEATHER PRDTS.	16905	1320	3210	773	5206	16372	1293	486	6839
35 GLASS, GLASS PRDTS.	27839	2181	5204	1287	8316	24547	1877	847	10649
36 STONE, CLAY PRDTS.	2676	247	455	173	683	1913	121	117	862
37 PRIMARY IRON, STEEL MFR.	1973	155	394	72	642	1956	130	61	818
38 PRIMARY NONFERROUS MFR.									

39 METAL CONTAINERS	0	0	0	0	0	0	0	0	0
40 FABRICATED METAL PRDTS.	12275	945	2669	611	3665	11218	827	479	4660
41 SCREW MACH. PRDTS., ETC.	30652	2393	5840	1357	9491	29792	2356	868	12421
42 OTHER FAB. METAL PRDTS.	56866	4478	12482	2308	19935	61498	4523	1714	25598
43 ENGINES, TURBINES	14093	1395	11975	961	13740	46880	3266	593	21014
44 FARM MACH., EQUIP.	1297	102	290	71	458	1381	103	41	588
45 CONSTRUC. MACH., EQUIP.	0	0	0	0	0	0	0	0	0
46 MATERIAL HANDLING MACH.	0	0	0	0	0	0	0	0	0
47 METALWORKING MACHINERY	3255	251	700	172	1119	3420	253	102	1449
48 SPECIAL MACH., EQUIP.	2955	231	643	157	1028	3146	233	94	1334
49 GENERAL MACH., EQUIP.	0	0	0	0	0	0	0	0	0
50 MACHINE SHOP PRDTS.	0	0	0	0	0	0	0	0	0
51 OFFICE, COMPUT. MACHINES	9161	705	2015	471	3226	9739	665	286	4207
52 SERVICE IND. MACHINES	19610	1598	12678	1342	20350	68012	1218	387	25281
53 ELECT. TRANSMISS. EQUIP.	2348	183	509	124	812	2464	177	73	1051
54 HOUSEHOLD APPLIANCES	445835	35419	99809	23170	156382	449164	37743	16137	196682
55 ELECTRIC LIGHTING EQUIP.	43026	3385	9441	2216	14971	45645	3291	1327	19441
56 RADIO, TV, ETC., EQUIP.	474206	36479	90914	23807	143607	483429	37409	14663	188513
57 ELECTRONIC COMPONENTS	53061	4056	10082	2660	15971	53993	4184	1640	20884
58 MISC. ELECTRICAL MACH.	47143	3732	11157	2314	17943	54606	4035	1516	23288
59 MOTOR VEHICLES, EQUIP.	1533303	119103	271577	77276	507294	1935588	124432	56528	712264
60 AIRCRAFT, PARTS	3359	332	2854	229	3275	11173	778	141	5008
61 OTHER TRANSPORT. EQUIP.	61295	6060	51856	4173	59538	203088	14151	2575	91024
62 PROFESS., SCIEN. INSTRU.	53729	4270	10804	2674	17157	60170	4345	1455	22288
63 MEDICAL, PHOTO. EQUIP.	95556	7700	21659	5168	31923	98488	8565	3169	42452
64 MISC. MANUFACTURING	476365	38313	100980	21860	156847	493940	39028	13600	205892
65 TRANSPORT., WAREHOUSING	1311361	110045	209458	55192	326597	1095982	89688	40744	437705
66 COMMUNICA., EXC. BRDCAST.	957190	82649	169851	38543	260070	859920	64505	29189	344170
67 RADIO, TV BROADCASTING	0	0	0	0	0	0	0	0	0
68 ELEC.,GAS,WATER,SAN.SER.	1103944	90479	273540	65653	421467	1287982	90078	34852	530456
69 WHOLESALE, RETAIL TRADE	8473632	697993	1621348	428639	2529107	8003565	613001	288971	3317441
70 FINANCE, INSURANCE	1766254	140584	339307	75918	537157	1673962	122304	53632	713315
71 REAL ESTATE, RENTAL	8087009	672894	1256850	300951	1946398	6532944	539667	232671	2547422
72 HOTELS, PERSONAL SERV.	932628	66877	183103	51428	338709	1409375	68877	56631	477455
73 BUSINESS SERVICES	85956	5484	17697	2085	69736	214894	10139	804	61423
74 RESEARCH, DEVELOPMENT	0	0	0	0	0	0	0	0	0
75 AUTO. REPAIR, SERVICES	466177	37024	115587	23275	186119	555683	40917	15540	241185
76 AMUSEMENTS	121475	16085	39766	17454	79493	307601	16627	9861	104692
77 MED.,EDUC. SERVICES	3437325	283987	709767	152509	1105580	3349523	222099	96382	1433891
78 FEDERAL GOVT. ENTERPRISE	96165	8154	17925	4114	26584	85882	7092	2935	35771
79 STATE, LOCAL GOVT. ENT.	52742	4203	14028	2733	22429	69016	5243	1720	28654
80 IMPORTS	715533	57308	127586	31779	203296	630093	50668	21509	259005
81 BUS.TRAVEL, ENT., GIFTS.	0	0	0	0	0	0	0	0	0
82 OFFICE SUPPLIES	0	0	0	0	0	0	0	0	0
83 SCRAP, USED GOODS	-1414	-111	-318	-81	-507	-1663	-115	-45	-670
84 GOVERNMENT INDUSTRY	0	0	0	0	0	0	0	0	0
85 REST OF WORLD INDUSTRY	0	0	0	0	0	0	0	0	0
86 HOUSEHOLD INDUSTRY	155687	15265	52609	5531	90389	268810	9457	3193	111188
87 INVENTORY VALUATION ADJ.	0	0	0	0	0	0	0	0	0
88 STATE TOTAL	41437178	3405313	7832660	1938197	12391602	39959283	2984327	1349116	16222378

137

TABLE B-2

STATE ESTIMATES OF 1980
PERSONAL CONSUMPTION EXPENDITURES
(THOUSANDS OF 1958 DOLLARS)

INDUSTRY TITLE	46 WASHINGTON	47 WEST VIRGINIA	48 WISCONSIN	49 WYOMING	50 ALASKA	51 HAWAII	52 NO STATE ALLOCATION	53 NATIONAL TOTAL
1 LIVESTOCK, PRDTS.	38184	22921	50885	4040	3898	7837	0	2255002
2 OTHER AGRICULTURE PRDTS.	66471	32500	83986	6182	6233	13802	0	3856002
3 FORESTRY, FISHERIES	9649	3724	11312	840	846	2081	0	552003
4 AGRI.,FORES.,FISH. SERV.	0	0	0	0	0	0	0	0
5 IRON, FERRO. ORES MINING	0	0	0	0	0	0	0	0
6 NONFERROUS ORES MINING	0	0	0	0	0	0	0	0
7 COAL MINING	780	813	2868	101	136	189	0	101002
8 CRUDE PETRO.,NATURAL GAS	0	0	0	0	0	0	0	0
9 STONE, CLAY MINING	845	334	1055	62	70	165	0	48000
10 CHEM.,FERT. MIN. MINING	0	0	0	0	0	0	0	0
11 NEW CONSTRUCTION	0	0	0	0	0	0	0	0
12 MAINT., REPAIR CONSTR.	0	0	0	0	0	0	0	0
13 ORDNANCE, ACCESSORIES	12403	3916	12780	906	1015	2242	0	614999
14 FOOD, KINDRED PRDTS.	1445958	573129	1682080	129472	130337	315326	0	82447001
15 TOBACCO MANUFACTURES	107090	56370	143370	9381	9100	21322	0	7212000
16 FABRICS	30729	14409	32027	2591	2864	6184	0	1648000
17 TEXTILE PRDTS.	39008	11827	53988	2798	3112	7006	0	2543001
18 APPAREL	376752	168621	568245	28850	33025	76714	0	24833998
19 MISC. TEXTILE PRDTS.	44439	19053	56976	3442	3712	8480	0	2711999
20 LUMBER, WOOD PRDTS.	5291	3235	9825	817	375	754	0	298000
21 WOODEN CONTAINERS	0	0	0	0	0	0	0	0
22 HOUSEHOLD FURNITURE	100015	49122	153895	7723	7629	19188	0	6823002
23 OTHER FURNITURE	6061	2841	8667	513	533	1128	0	373001
24 PAPER, ALLIED PRDTS.	41532	20608	49082	3521	3675	8409	0	2566002
25 PAPERBOARD CONTAINERS	1707	896	1982	145	140	335	0	107997
26 PRINTING, PUBLISHING	102328	38419	130805	7798	9068	20832	0	6014002
27 CHEMICALS, SELECT. PRDTS.	10118	5048	12098	860	911	1988	0	594000
28 PLASTICS, SYNTHETICS	406	220	490	36	37	82	0	26000
29 DRUGS, COSMETICS	231639	117666	264901	20080	22399	47942	0	13740001
30 PAINT, ALLIED PRDTS.	591	344	1160	46	54	113	0	52001
31 PETROLEUM, RELATED INDS.	283486	80192	321567	36047	27793	38848	0	14493997
32 RUBBER, MISC. PLASTICS	77975	34116	86112	6062	6767	15310	0	4226996
33 LEATHER TANNING, PRDTS.	0	0	0	0	0	0	0	0
34 FOOTWEAR, LEATHER PRDTS.	59741	25894	80860	4772	5229	11528	0	3533001
35 GLASS, GLASS PRDTS.	5619	2202	6572	396	431	1071	0	309000
36 STONE, CLAY PRDTS.	7913	3672	10358	629	673	1503	0	479998
37 PRIMARY IRON, STEEL MFR.	506	314	1066	48	60	105	0	42000
38 PRIMARY NONFERROUS MFR.	522	276	605	43	44	102	0	33000

#	Industry	1	2	3	4	5	6	7
39	METAL CONTAINERS	3297	0	0	0	0	0	0
40	FABRICATED METAL PRDTS.	10267	1606	4489	324	316	567	204999
41	SCREW MACH. PRDTS., ETC.	18483	4088	11286	597	768	1999	557999
42	OTHER FAB. METAL PRDTS.	18483	8478	23293	1518	1591	3549	1086998
43	ENGINES, TURBINES	19562	5343	8833	803	1259	3620	621002
44	FARM MACH., EQUIP.	414	196	576	36	38	78	25000
45	CONSTRUC. MACH., EQUIP.	0	0	0	0	0	0	0
46	MATERIAL HANDLING MACH.	1028	476	1449	88	90	188	62004
47	METALWORKING MACHINERY	945	437	1334	81	82	173	57001
48	SPECIAL MACH., EQUIP.	0	0	0	0	0	0	0
49	GENERAL MACH., EQUIP.	0	0	0	0	0	0	0
50	MACHINE SHOP PRDTS.	2927	1336	4232	234	255	527	175999
51	OFFICE, COMPUT. MACHINES	5233	6531	13567	*33	446	937	662999
52	SERVICE IND. MACHINES	747	339	1075	62	67	136	45001
53	ELECT. TRANSMISS. EQUIP.	144875	74977	173113	13162	12528	28410	8407004
54	HOUSEHOLD APPLIANCES	14256	6155	19391	1153	1265	2619	830998
55	ELECTRIC LIGHTING EQUIP.	158291	57669	210613	11880	12996	31668	9020999
56	RADIO, TV, ETC. EQUIP.	17598	6404	23499	1323	1435	3512	1005001
57	ELECTRONIC COMPONENTS	17446	7660	19483	1350	1514	3439	950997
58	MISC. ELECTRICAL MACH.	432373	183512	690775	44038	31204	93697	3128997
59	MOTOR VEHICLES, EQUIP.	2662	1273	2105	191	300	863	147995
60	AIRCRAFT, PARTS	84658	23159	38349	3482	5454	15673	2692001
61	OTHER TRANSPORT. EQUIP.	17292	6393	23859	1436	1605	3705	1046995
62	PROFESS., SCIEN. INSTRU.	38625	13137	44673	2997	3189	7351	1957998
63	MEDICAL, PHOTO. EQUIP.	170304	62019	202194	12766	14417	32986	9220001
64	MISC. MANUFACTURING	367668	125750	455581	30918	30961	77251	22050001
65	TRANSPORT., WAREHOUSING	264742	105534	331358	20003	23708	55473	16383002
66	COMMUNICA., EXC. BRDCAST.	354376	180623	504282	30566	32819	72724	22608996
67	RADIO, TV BROADCASTING	2586764	1055713	3283845	229397	228522	516101	152669004
68	ELEC., GAS, WATER, SAN. SER.	530517	213098	679872	38005	44927	107257	31727000
69	WHOLESALE, RETAIL TRADE	2156127	760459	2526175	164892	186733	461466	129768998
70	FINANCE, INSURANCE	256634	115865	425993	69674	33744	149666	23481000
71	REAL ESTATE, RENTAL	33917	28274	52953	1247	3790	9688	3845004
72	HOTELS, PERSONAL SERV.	177000	80862	189480	13957	15667	35009	9541000
73	BUSINESS SERVICES	53651	45321	107251	6502	5589	21155	6585999
74	RESEARCH, DEVELOPMENT	953468	446554	1363552	71287	82913	201561	62013997
75	AUTO. REPAIR, SERVICES	30048	10269	33668	2285	2616	6090	1678004
76	AMUSEMENTS	21978	9480	22739	1731	1888	4344	1148003
77	MED., EDUC. SERVICES	211664	86130	259817	17943	18482	44748	12413000
78	FEDERAL GOVT. ENTERPRISE	0	0	0	0	0	0	0
79	STATE, LOCAL GOVT. ENT.	0	0	0	0	0	0	0
80	IMPORTS	-518	-213	-752	-40	-43	-100	-29998
81	BUS. TRAVEL, ENT., GIFTS.	0	0	0	0	0	0	0
82	OFFICE SUPPLIES	0	0	0	0	0	0	0
83	SCRAP, USED GOODS	45689	28554	73230	2587	4155	14352	3583003
84	GOVERNMENT INDUSTRY	0	0	0	0	0	0	0
85	REST OF WORLD INDUSTRY	0	0	0	0	0	0	0
86	HOUSEHOLD INDUSTRY	0	0	0	0	0	0	0
87	INVENTORY VALUATION ADJ.	0	0	0	0	0	0	0
88	STATE TOTAL	12334806	5057143	15666849	1077209	1087456	2643068	751909006

139

TABLE 8-3

STATE ESTIMATES OF 1970
GROSS PRIVATE CAPITAL FORMATION
(THOUSANDS OF 1958 DOLLARS)

INDUSTRY TITLE	1 ALABAMA	2 ARIZONA	3 ARKANSAS	4 CALIFORNIA	5 COLORADO	6 CONNECTICUT	7 DELAWARE	8 DISTRICT OF COLUMBIA	9 FLORIDA
1 LIVESTOCK, PRDTS.	0	0	0	0	0	0	0	0	0
2 OTHER AGRICULTURE PRDTS.	0	0	0	0	0	0	0	0	0
3 FORESTRY, FISHERIES	0	0	0	0	0	0	0	0	0
4 AGRI.,FORES.,FISH. SERV.	0	0	0	0	0	0	0	0	0
5 IRON, FERRO. ORES MINING	0	0	0	0	0	0	0	0	0
6 NONFERROUS ORES MINING	0	0	0	0	0	0	0	0	0
7 COAL MINING	0	0	0	0	0	0	0	0	0
8 CRUDE PETRO.,NATURAL GAS	0	0	0	0	0	0	0	0	0
9 STONE, CLAY MINING	0	0	0	0	0	0	0	0	0
10 CHEM.,FERT. MIN. MINING	0	0	0	0	0	0	0	0	0
11 NEW CONSTRUCTION	602859	457835	314260	5267269	583419	624900	144390	187627	1579482
12 MAINT., REPAIR CONSTR.	0	0	0	0	0	0	0	0	0
13 ORDNANCE, ACCESSORIES	0	0	0	0	0	0	0	0	0
14 FOOD, KINDRED PRDTS.	0	0	0	0	0	0	0	0	0
15 TOBACCO MANUFACTURES	0	0	0	0	0	0	0	0	0
16 FABRICS	0	0	0	0	0	0	0	0	0
17 TEXTILE PRDTS.	1078	809	465	11883	1058	1410	294	648	3164
18 APPAREL	0	0	0	0	0	0	0	0	0
19 MISC. TEXTILE PRDTS.	0	0	0	0	0	0	0	0	0
20 LUMBER, WOOD PRDTS.	85	33	84	790	105	54	15	12	217
21 WOODEN CONTAINERS	0	0	0	0	0	0	0	0	0
22 HOUSEHOLD FURNITURE	2003	1986	1003	24024	2333	2747	552	1433	8690
23 OTHER FURNITURE	22503	17056	9439	222400	21271	28439	6491	10872	64340
24 PAPER, ALLIED PRDTS.	0	0	0	0	0	0	0	0	0
25 PAPERBOARD CONTAINERS	0	0	0	0	0	0	0	0	0
26 PRINTING, PUBLISHING	0	0	0	0	0	0	0	0	0
27 CHEMICALS,SELECT. PRDTS.	0	0	0	0	0	0	0	0	0
28 PLASTICS, SYNTHETICS	0	0	0	0	0	0	0	0	0
29 DRUGS, COSMETICS	0	0	0	0	0	0	0	0	0
30 PAINT, ALLIED PRDTS.	0	0	0	0	0	0	0	0	0
31 PETROLEUM, RELATED INDS.	0	0	0	0	0	0	0	0	0
32 RUBBER, MISC. PLASTICS	974	613	446	4249	910	353	149	77	1335
33 LEATHER TANNING, PRDTS.	0	0	0	0	0	0	0	0	0
34 FOOTWEAR, LEATHER PRDTS.	0	0	0	0	0	0	0	0	0
35 GLASS, GLASS PRDTS.	0	0	0	0	0	0	0	0	0
36 STONE, CLAY PRDTS.	0	0	0	0	0	0	0	0	0
37 PRIMARY IRON, STEEL MFR.	0	0	0	0	0	0	0	0	0
38 PRIMARY NONFERROUS MFR.	0	0	0	0	0	0	0	0	0

39	METAL CONTAINERS	205	94	178	1961	243	153	42	39	549
40	FABRICATED METAL PRDTS.	20134	10147	7892	107046	14988	11363	4960	3307	34290
41	SCREW MACH. PRDTS., ETC.	0	0	1606	3491	3435	4189	1077	1651	0
42	OTHER FAB. METAL PRDTS.	4209	2975	10057	96915	19747	8398	3541	1708	9189
43	ENGINES, TURBINES	21589	14890	39794	215099	39474	11106	7373	2190	30391
44	FARM MACH., EQUIP.	35941	33899	10617	228582	34445	18656	4649	8962	73218
45	CONSTRUC. MACH., EQUIP.	20794	23856	7557	113360	11695	15475	4170	3227	56054
46	MATERIAL HANDLING MACH.	16155	9823	11530	234843	16761	45008	8586	3618	26878
47	METALWORKING MACHINERY	35485	18493	24678	200524	18820	25248	9901	5741	37142
48	SPECIAL MACH., EQUIP.	50464	12723	10566	157672	16616	22161	7966	4304	60967
49	GENERAL MACH., EQUIP.	31413	14020	0	0	0	0	0	0	43744
50	MACHINE SHOP PRDTS.	0	0	0	0	0	0	0	0	0
51	OFFICE, COMPUT. MACHINES	58183	41675	26951	524286	56489	78781	19555	30763	157235
52	SERVICE IND. MACHINES	29725	20593	13828	296276	26505	33548	8307	12209	87324
53	ELECT. TRANSMISS. EQUIP.	41400	24970	17526	208726	31343	18983	5875	4825	63374
54	HOUSEHOLD APPLIANCES	1995	1429	972	18553	1780	2258	518	842	6058
55	ELECTRIC LIGHTING EQUIP.	2130	1320	1144	11890	1780	1122	452	388	3459
56	RADIO, TV, ETC., EQUIP.	36136	17935	15370	238039	26891	17340	6450	8107	77949
57	ELECTRONIC COMPONENTS	1356	895	665	17396	1120	1557	1011	534	3061
58	MISC. ELECTRICAL MACH.	5225	2545	2142	32760	3493	4033	1507	1112	7454
59	MOTOR VEHICLES, EQUIP.	119247	99730	83288	1165939	133862	118024	30719	57105	359613
60	AIRCRAFT, PARTS	18915	14717	15487	251919	29767	30061	3687	15593	76695
61	OTHER TRANSPORT. EQUIP.	21825	14362	16109	230424	27034	21290	4386	12805	73890
62	PROFESS., SCIEN. INSTRU.	24917	13402	9956	144098	17824	21897	7058	4631	40323
63	MEDICAL, PHOTO. EQUIP.	14495	10786	6214	153737	14465	19703	4510	9956	44879
64	MISC. MANUFACTURING	7231	5429	3409	79541	7692	8672	2396	4423	24793
65	TRANSPORT., WAREHOUSING	17425	12002	9362	130172	15378	14880	4094	4839	36651
66	COMMUNICA.+EXC. BRDCAST.	14988	7723	6495	101224	11303	6249	2298	3340	36086
67	RADIO, TV BROADCASTING	0	0	0	0	0	0	0	0	0
68	ELEC.+GAS,WATER,SAN.SER.	0	0	0	0	0	0	0	0	0
69	WHOLESALE, RETAIL TRADE	114399	79466	63314	900658	101534	102281	28410	36022	257940
70	FINANCE, INSURANCE	0	0	0	0	0	0	0	0	0
71	REAL ESTATE, RENTAL	12956	14549	8644	188143	21349	9531	679	6176	54607
72	HOTELS, PERSONAL SERV.	0	0	0	0	0	0	0	0	0
73	BUSINESS SERVICES	0	0	0	0	0	0	0	0	0
74	RESEARCH, DEVELOPMENT	0	0	0	0	0	0	0	0	0
75	AUTO. REPAIR, SERVICES	0	0	0	0	0	0	0	0	0
76	AMUSEMENTS	0	0	0	0	0	0	0	0	0
77	MED.+EDUC. SERVICES	0	0	0	0	0	0	0	0	0
78	FEDERAL GOVT. ENTERPRISE	0	0	0	0	0	0	0	0	0
79	STATE, LOCAL GOVT. ENT.	0	0	0	0	0	0	0	0	0
80	IMPORTS	0	0	0	0	0	0	0	0	0
81	BUS.TRAVEL, ENT., GIFTS.	0	0	0	0	0	0	0	0	0
82	OFFICE SUPPLIES	0	0	0	0	0	0	0	0	0
83	SCRAP, USED GOODS	-7088	-5095	-3585	-51291	-8034	-5095	-1671	-1651	-15889
84	GOVERNMENT INDUSTRY	0	0	0	0	0	0	0	0	0
85	REST OF WORLD INDUSTRY	0	0	0	0	0	0	0	0	0
86	HOUSEHOLD INDUSTRY	0	0	0	0	0	0	0	0	0
87	INVENTORY VALUATION ADJ.	0	0	0	0	0	0	0	0	0
88	STATE TOTAL	1401256	997142	747664	11661594	1306872	1324778	334397	447436	3425151

141

TABLE 8-3

STATE ESTIMATES OF 1970
GROSS PRIVATE CAPITAL FORMATION
(THOUSANDS OF 1958 DOLLARS)

INDUSTRY TITLE	10 GEORGIA	11 IDAHO	12 ILLINOIS	13 INDIANA	14 IOWA	15 KANSAS	16 KENTUCKY	17 LOUISIANA	18 MAINE
1 LIVESTOCK, PRDTS.	0	0	0	0	0	0	0	0	0
2 OTHER AGRICULTURE PRDTS.	0	0	0	0	0	0	0	0	0
3 FORESTRY, FISHERIES	0	0	0	0	0	0	0	0	0
4 AGRI.,FORES.,FISH. SERV.	0	0	0	0	0	0	0	0	0
5 IRON, FERRO. ORES MINING	0	0	0	0	0	0	0	0	0
6 NONFERROUS ORES MINING	0	0	0	0	0	0	0	0	0
7 COAL MINING	0	0	0	0	0	0	0	0	0
8 CRUDE PETRO.,NATURAL GAS	0	0	0	0	0	0	0	0	0
9 STONE, CLAY MINING	0	0	0	0	0	0	0	0	0
10 CHEM.,FERT. MIN. MINING	0	0	0	0	0	0	0	0	0
11 NEW CONSTRUCTION	858646	132550	2553746	1085661	455107	454958	517299	1617767	117291
12 MAINT., REPAIR CONSTR.	0	0	0	0	0	0	0	0	0
13 ORDNANCE, ACCESSORIES	0	0	0	0	0	0	0	0	0
14 FOOD, KINDRED PRDTS.	0	0	0	0	0	0	0	0	0
15 TOBACCO MANUFACTURES	0	0	0	0	0	0	0	0	0
16 FABRICS	0	0	0	0	0	0	0	0	0
17 TEXTILE PRDTS.	1831	227	6926	1957	934	762	1038	1758	271
18 APPAREL	0	0	0	0	0	0	0	0	0
19 MISC. TEXTILE PRDTS.	175	38	322	168	264	52	76	54	38
20 LUMBER, WOOD PRDTS.	0	0	0	0	0	0	0	0	0
21 WOODEN CONTAINERS	0	0	0	0	0	0	0	0	0
22 HOUSEHOLD FURNITURE	3601	524	12281	3852	2206	1614	2127	2963	715
23 OTHER FURNITURE	38033	4890	128865	44227	19932	15374	22462	29497	5445
24 PAPER, ALLIED PRDTS.	0	0	0	0	0	0	0	0	0
25 PAPERBOARD CONTAINERS	0	0	0	0	0	0	0	0	0
26 PRINTING, PUBLISHING	0	0	0	0	0	0	0	0	0
27 CHEMICALS,SELECT. PRDTS.	0	0	0	0	0	0	0	0	0
28 PLASTICS, SYNTHETICS	0	0	0	0	0	0	0	0	0
29 DRUGS, COSMETICS	0	0	0	0	0	0	0	0	0
30 PAINT, ALLIED PRDTS.	0	0	0	0	0	0	0	0	0
31 PETROLEUM, RELATED INDS.	0	0	0	0	0	0	0	0	0
32 RUBBER, MISC. PLASTICS	991	218	3198	1613	575	553	750	1777	109
33 LEATHER TANNING, PRDTS.	0	0	0	0	0	0	0	0	0
34 FOOTWEAR, LEATHER PRDTS.	0	0	0	0	0	0	0	0	0
35 GLASS, GLASS PRDTS.	0	0	0	0	0	0	0	0	0
36 STONE, CLAY PRDTS.	0	0	0	0	0	0	0	0	0
37 PRIMARY IRON, STEEL MFR.	0	0	0	0	0	0	0	0	0
38 PRIMARY NONFERROUS MFR.	0	0	0	0	0	0	0	0	0

39 METAL CONTAINERS	424	83	858	393	545	124	181	154	84
40 FABRICATED METAL PRDTS.	18973	4667	6243	31937	12327	13312	21161	69790	2774
41 SCREW MACH. PRDTS., ETC.	4931	842	0	0	0	0	0	0	0
42 OTHER FAB. METAL PRDTS.	22267	5029	21220	8046	2925	2319	4086	5587	761
43 ENGINES, TURBINES	54614	23039	71668	36342	13629	12478	17035	38481	2481
44 FARM MACH., EQUIP.	22893	5108	105472	61307	121926	59265	36098	30378	12112
45 CONSTRUC. MACH., EQUIP.	24238	3537	103777	26208	12947	26860	31275	213803	2875
46 MATERIAL HANDLING MACH.	38867	4238	68062	33792	12714	9963	16603	26749	3709
47 METALWORKING MACHINERY	99317	9501	191021	117174	31466	16110	37476	17806	5080
48 SPECIAL MACH., EQUIP.	32183	6177	117094	57439	29636	15911	34819	32217	15987
49 GENERAL MACH., EQUIP.			103111	59890	19403	14746	30298	46403	4623
50 MACHINE SHOP PRDTS.	0	0	0	0	0	0	0	0	0
51 OFFICE, COMPUT. MACHINES	96755	12631	373087	126895	52472	45743	66389	86357	12985
52 SERVICE IND. MACHINES	58203	6916	161108	52439	27311	18024	27082	34764	8771
53 ELECT. TRANSMISS. EQUIP.	45515	7551	122177	68947	24871	20754	30011	42017	4943
54 HOUSEHOLD APPLIANCES	3710	440	9600	3125	2099	1700	1801	2805	567
55 ELECTRIC LIGHTING EQUIP.	2810	555	7537	3847	2117	1548	1681	3277	397
56 RADIO, TV, ETC., EQUIP.	50668	5324	73519	39992	22038	22292	28855	45402	4437
57 ELECTRONIC COMPONENTS	3663	245	7053	3725	1124	1609	2204	1488	260
58 MISC. ELECTRICAL MACH.	7593	936	19222	11567	3525	2991	4289	4093	978
59 MOTOR VEHICLES, EQUIP.	223372	43137	664940	214046	165282	106601	130963	222466	37621
60 AIRCRAFT, PARTS	49255	6714	199773	49452	22140	16748	27922	46130	7944
61 OTHER TRANSPORT. EQUIP.	48573	8668	145397	38965	19563	19931	22072	81046	10275
62 PROFESS., SCIEN. INSTRU.	27713	5789	100559	45691	17791	16601	29735	45852	3481
63 MEDICAL, PHOTO. EQUIP.	20536	3804	94013	26675	12311	11056	18534	34678	3375
64 MISC. MANUFACTURING	12147	1805	43137	14570	6441	4666	8238	31789	2138
65 TRANSPORT., WAREHOUSING	26093	4596	77696	32351	18540	12876	17490	21354	3967
66 COMMUNICA..EXC. BRDCAST.	21313	2173	22153	11613	8694	9388	12733		1451
67 RADIO, TV BROADCASTING	0	0	0	0	0	0	0	0	0
68 ELEC.,GAS,WATER,SAN.SER.	175953	3224	533852	212498	130227	87767	116120	196902	28075
69 WHOLESALE, RETAIL TRADE	0	0	0	0	0	0	0	0	0
70 FINANCE, INSURANCE	2343	3651	57531	27903	10699	11721	8985	16588	2885
71 REAL ESTATE, RENTAL	0	0	0	0	0	0	0	0	0
72 HOTELS, PERSONAL SERV.	0	0	0	0	0	0	0	0	0
73 BUSINESS SERVICES	0	0	0	0	0	0	0	0	0
74 RESEARCH, DEVELOPMENT	0	0	0	0	0	0	0	0	0
75 AUTO. REPAIR, SERVICES	0	0	0	0	0	0	0	0	0
76 AMUSEMENTS	0	0	0	0	0	0	0	0	0
77 MED.,EDUC. SERVICES	0	0	0	0	0	0	0	0	0
78 FEDERAL GOVT. ENTERPRISE	0	0	0	0	0	0	0	0	0
79 STATE, LOCAL GOVT. ENT.	0	0	0	0	0	0	0	0	0
80 IMPORTS	0	0	0	0	0	0	0	0	0
81 BUS.TRAVEL, ENT., GIFTS.	0	0	0	0	0	0	0	0	0
82 OFFICE SUPPLIES	0	0	0	0	0	0	0	0	0
83 SCRAP, USED GOODS	-9585	-1631	-29965	-13170	-5337	-5920	-6544	-30062	-1248
84 GOVERNMENT INDUSTRY	0	0	0	0	0	0	0	0	0
85 REST OF WORLD INDUSTRY	0	0	0	0	0	0	0	0	0
86 HOUSEHOLD INDUSTRY	0	0	0	0	0	0	0	0	0
87 INVENTORY VALUATION ADJ.	0	0	0	0	0	0	0	0	0
88 STATE TOTAL	2100213	346195	6232252	2541137	1278447	1050493	1321341	3031133	307654

TABLE 8-3

STATE ESTIMATES OF 1970
GROSS PRIVATE CAPITAL FORMATION
(THOUSANDS OF 1958 DOLLARS)

INDUSTRY TITLE	19 MARYLAND	20 MASSA-CHUSETTS	21 MICHIGAN	22 MINNESOTA	23 MISSISSIPPI	24 MISSOURI	25 MONTANA	26 NEBRASKA	27 NEVADA
1 LIVESTOCK, PRDTS.	0	0	0	0	0	0	0	0	0
2 OTHER AGRICULTURE PRDTS.	0	0	0	0	0	0	0	0	0
3 FORESTRY, FISHERIES	0	0	0	0	0	0	0	0	0
4 AGRI.,FORES.,FISH. SERV.	0	0	0	0	0	0	0	0	0
5 IRON, FERRO. ORES MINING	0	0	0	0	0	0	0	0	0
6 NONFERROUS ORES MINING	0	0	0	0	0	0	0	0	0
7 COAL MINING	0	0	0	0	0	0	0	0	0
8 CRUDE PETRO.,NATURAL GAS	0	0	0	0	0	0	0	0	0
9 STONE, CLAY MINING	0	0	0	0	0	0	0	0	0
10 CHEM.,FERT. MIN. MINING	0	0	0	0	0	0	0	0	0
11 NEW CONSTRUCTION	847604	987014	1791051	738431	390708	875758	163538	251584	158770
12 MAINT., REPAIR CONSTR.	0	0	0	0	0	0	0	0	0
13 ORDNANCE, ACCESSORIES	0	0	0	0	0	0	0	0	0
14 FOOD, KINDRED PRDTS.	0	0	0	0	0	0	0	0	0
15 TOBACCO MANUFACTURES	0	0	0	0	0	0	0	0	0
16 FABRICS	0	0	0	0	0	0	0	0	0
17 TEXTILE PRDTS.	1562	2790	4362	1748	495	2307	215	548	358
18 APPAREL	0	0	0	0	0	0	0	0	0
19 MISC. TEXTILE PRDTS.	0	0	0	0	0	0	0	0	0
20 LUMBER, WOOD PRDTS.	105	112	193	146	63	160	10	116	3
21 WOODEN CONTAINERS	0	0	0	0	0	0	0	0	0
22 HOUSEHOLD FURNITURE	3232	5377	7508	3312	1096	4333	488	1246	2109
23 OTHER FURNITURE	32780	53630	84730	33921	9685	44846	5169	12064	7600
24 PAPER, ALLIED PRDTS.	0	0	0	0	0	0	0	0	0
25 PAPERBOARD CONTAINERS	0	0	0	0	0	0	0	0	0
26 PRINTING, PUBLISHING	0	0	0	0	0	0	0	0	0
27 CHEMICALS,SELECT. PRDTS.	0	0	0	0	0	0	0	0	0
28 PLASTICS, SYNTHETICS	0	0	0	0	0	0	0	0	0
29 DRUGS, COSMETICS	0	0	0	0	0	0	0	0	0
30 PAINT, ALLIED PRDTS.	0	0	0	0	0	0	0	0	0
31 PETROLEUM, RELATED INDS.	0	0	0	0	0	0	0	0	0
32 RUBBER, MISC. PLASTICS	839	745	2267	1237	592	1030	250	282	190
33 LEATHER TANNING, PRDTS.	0	0	0	0	0	0	0	0	0
34 FOOTWEAR, LEATHER PRDTS.	0	0	0	0	0	0	0	0	0
35 GLASS, GLASS PRDTS.	0	0	0	0	0	0	0	0	0
36 STONE, CLAY PRDTS.	0	0	0	0	0	0	0	0	0
37 PRIMARY IRON, STEEL MFR.	0	0	0	0	0	0	0	0	0
38 PRIMARY NONFERROUS MFR.	0	0	0	0	0	0	0	0	0

39 METAL CONTAINERS	262	310	516	341	140	396	28	247	16
40 FABRICATED METAL PRDTS.	18835	19556	48163	18528	10744	20612	5098	6584	3844
41 SCREW MACH. PRDTS., ETC.	0	0	0	0	0	0	0	0	0
42 OTHER FAB. METAL PRDTS.	5212	7427	14023	6071	1597	6379	1015	1580	1268
43 ENGINES, TURBINES	19015	16918	50491	25054	13051	23320	5974	6593	4332
44 FARM MACH., EQUIP.	21626	12867	46496	76592	40342	63946	21324	64690	5995
45 CONSTRUC. MACH., EQUIP.	24543	30237	58769	38192	18080	29749	12428	13546	10312
46 MATERIAL HANDLING MACH.	13755	27277	59939	19749	7931	24301	4233	5973	3375
47 METALWORKING MACHINERY	45144	66169	198470	46578	11510	53312	6993	10815	4273
48 SPECIAL MACH., EQUIP.	34039	57390	87410	36495	19081	44353	5727	11576	4109
49 GENERAL MACH., EQUIP.	30426	36821	89959	26572	11197	34442	6345	8449	5132
50 MACHINE SHOP PRDTS.	0	0	0	0	0	0	0	0	0
51 OFFICE, COMPUT. MACHINES	80536	150232	256742	97272	27079	131536	11356	30607	14275
52 SERVICE IND. MACHINES	40470	63759	105519	42114	13240	58299	5878	15755	8158
53 ELECT. TRANSMISS. EQUIP.	39030	38849	103302	37895	21630	44383	9169	10993	6106
54 HOUSEHOLD APPLIANCES	2869	4191	6515	2905	1194	3592	466	1340	610
55 ELECTRIC LIGHTING EQUIP.	2183	2240	5978	2391	1275	2963	615	1118	435
56 RADIO, TV, ETC., EQUIP.	35381	36549	103079	31932	18465	46514	7115	10105	2435
57 ELECTRONIC COMPONENTS	2349	3024	11703	1938	805	4489	311	560	214
58 MISC. ELECTRICAL MACH.	6484	7941	19840	4974	2077	7947	1197	1692	574
59 MOTOR VEHICLES, EQUIP.	153584	235904	355251	209162	81339	248002	40666	98754	42641
60 AIRCRAFT, PARTS	40678	61860	96430	44947	12267	69675	5125	16680	6129
61 OTHER TRANSPORT. EQUIP.	35285	48146	68862	38035	17927	52380	7651	17184	5816
62 PROFESS., SCIEN. INSTRU	24879	39647	75075	28221	12013	35899	4659	7279	3848
63 MEDICAL, PHOTO. EQUIP.	21124	39751	54996	24200	6977	29139	3208	7112	8190
64 MISC. MANUFACTURING	11543	17703	27805	10523	3047	14167	1511	3814	10143
65 TRANSPORT., WAREHOUSING	19815	27522	52506	23847	9944	27815	4988	9863	4361
66 COMMUNICA., EXC. BROCAST.	13964	13568	42181	13370	8328	19225	2954	3876	573
67 RADIO, TV BROADCASTING	0	0	0	0	0	0	0	0	0
68 ELEC.,GAS,WATER,SAN.SER.	0	0	0	0	0	0	0	0	0
69 WHOLESALE, RETAIL TRADE	133344	188651	354828	165641	65615	192393	32809	71176	28875
70 FINANCE, INSURANCE	0	0	0	0	0	0	0	0	0
71 REAL ESTATE, RENTAL	12279	34488	39489	24646	7680	27851	3289	10877	5458
72 HOTELS, PERSONAL SERV.	0	0	0	0	0	0	0	0	0
73 BUSINESS SERVICES	0	0	0	0	0	0	0	0	0
74 RESEARCH, DEVELOPMENT	0	0	0	0	0	0	0	0	0
75 AUTO. REPAIR, SERVICES	0	0	0	0	0	0	0	0	0
76 AMUSEMENTS	0	0	0	0	0	0	0	0	0
77 MED.,EDUC. SERVICES	0	0	0	0	0	0	0	0	0
78 FEDERAL GOVT. ENTERPRISE	0	0	0	0	0	0	0	0	0
79 STATE, LOCAL GOVT. ENT.	0	0	0	0	0	0	0	0	0
80 IMPORTS	0	0	0	0	0	0	0	0	0
81 BUS.TRAVEL, ENT., GIFTS.	0	0	0	0	0	0	0	0	0
82 OFFICE SUPPLIES	0	0	0	0	0	0	0	0	0
83 SCRAP, USED GOODS	-9237	-9585	-20218	-8700	-5015	-10532	-2376	-3705	-2034
84 GOVERNMENT INDUSTRY	0	0	0	0	0	0	0	0	0
85 REST OF WORLD INDUSTRY	0	0	0	0	0	0	0	0	0
86 HOUSEHOLD INDUSTRY	0	0	0	0	0	0	0	0	0
87 INVENTORY VALUATION ADJ.	0	0	0	0	0	0	0	0	0
88 STATE TOTAL	1782515	2329081	4303830	1868281	842196	2234982	379428	710973	358493

TABLE 8-3

STATE ESTIMATES OF 1970
GROSS PRIVATE CAPITAL FORMATION
(THOUSANDS OF 1958 DOLLARS)

INDUSTRY TITLE	28 NEW HAMPSHIRE	29 NEW JERSEY	30 NEW MEXICO	31 NEW YORK	32 NORTH CAROLINA	33 NORTH DAKOTA	34 OHIO	35 OKLAHOMA	36 OREGON
1 LIVESTOCK, PRDTS.	0	0	0	0	0	0	0	0	0
2 OTHER AGRICULTURE PRDTS.	0	0	0	0	0	0	0	0	0
3 FORESTRY, FISHERIES	0	0	0	0	0	0	0	0	0
4 AGRI.,FORES.,FISH. SERV.	0	0	0	0	0	0	0	0	0
5 IRON, FERRO. ORES MINING	0	0	0	0	0	0	0	0	0
6 NONFERROUS ORES MINING	0	0	0	0	0	0	0	0	0
7 COAL MINING	0	0	0	0	0	0	0	0	0
8 CRUDE PETRO.,NATURAL GAS	0	0	0	0	0	0	0	0	0
9 STONE, CLAY MINING	0	0	0	0	0	0	0	0	0
10 CHEM.,FERT. MIN. MINING	0	0	0	0	0	0	0	0	0
11 NEW CONSTRUCTION	131982	1589275	410538	3594365	873746	119632	2240175	558650	390605
12 MAINT., REPAIR CONSTR.	0	0	0	0	0	0	0	0	0
13 ORDNANCE, ACCESSORIES	0	0	0	0	0	0	0	0	0
14 FOOD, KINDRED PRDTS.	0	0	0	0	0	0	0	0	0
15 TOBACCO MANUFACTURES	0	0	0	0	0	0	0	0	0
16 FABRICS	0	0	0	0	0	0	0	0	0
17 TEXTILE PRDTS.	256	3654	446	14141	1793	171	5012	827	861
18 APPAREL	0	0	0	0	0	0	0	0	0
19 MISC. TEXTILE PRDTS.	0	0	0	0	0	0	0	0	0
20 LUMBER, WOOD PRDTS.	10	297	15	317	135	6	278	21	65
21 WOODEN CONTAINERS	0	0	0	0	0	0	0	0	0
22 HOUSEHOLD FURNITURE	583	6734	970	25590	3837	404	9117	1712	1616
23 OTHER FURNITURE	5138	72749	8744	241847	38165	3761	101285	15818	16280
24 PAPER, ALLIED PRDTS.	0	0	0	0	0	0	0	0	0
25 PAPERBOARD CONTAINERS	0	0	0	0	0	0	0	0	0
26 PRINTING, PUBLISHING	0	0	0	0	0	0	0	0	0
27 CHEMICALS,SELECT. PRDTS.	0	0	0	0	0	0	0	0	0
28 PLASTICS, SYNTHETICS	0	0	0	0	0	0	0	0	0
29 DRUGS, COSMETICS	0	0	0	0	0	0	0	0	0
30 PAINT, ALLIED PRDTS.	0	0	0	0	0	0	0	0	0
31 PETROLEUM, RELATED INDS.	0	0	0	0	0	0	0	0	0
32 RUBBER, MISC. PLASTICS	141	1341	463	2260	897	102	3033	654	297
33 LEATHER TANNING, PRDTS.	0	0	0	0	0	0	0	0	0
34 FOOTWEAR, LEATHER PRDTS.	0	0	0	0	0	0	0	0	0
35 GLASS, GLASS PRDTS.	0	0	0	0	0	0	0	0	0
36 STONE, CLAY PRDTS.	0	0	0	0	0	0	0	0	0
37 PRIMARY IRON, STEEL MFR.	0	0	0	0	0	0	0	0	0
38 PRIMARY NONFERROUS MFR.	0	0	0	0	0	0	0	0	0

Sector	1	2	3	4	5	6	7	8	9
39 METAL CONTAINERS	28	726	43	1073	338	21	693	71	162
40 FABRICATED METAL PRDTS.	2656	39060	15039	68969	20586	3022	64848	18292	6914
41 SCREW MACH. PRDTS., ETC.	752	11518	1444	35069	0	388	17451	2350	2047
42 OTHER FAB. METAL PRDTS.	3155	31159	11266	51528	5262	2280	68058	14195	7403
43 ENGINES, TURBINES	3005	22822	17422	82454	20932	21520	61405	30870	20999
44 FARM MACH., EQUIP.	2891	47588	57557	192567	68013	10467	72112	51607	12835
45 CONSTRUC. MACH., EQUIP.	3547	39204	6922	93393	20493	1589	72133	9602	12380
46 MATERIAL HANDLING MACH.	7981	85841	4776	190063	24172	1339	223195	13483	16250
47 METALWORKING MACHINERY	10296	95128	4709	152468	31399	1744	132644	11340	31946
48 SPECIAL MACH., EQUIP.	4460	64250	9302	126774	122812	2229	11418	13699	12622
49 GENERAL MACH., EQUIP.					35116				
50 MACHINE SHOP PRDTS.									
51 OFFICE, COMPUT. MACHINES	13830	195655	19508	730014	92153	7697	299177	44144	39018
52 SERVICE IND. MACHINES	6551	110521	9670	294774	53109	4829	120337	19203	23298
53 ELECT. TRANSMISS. EQUIP.	6042	60773	12376	133214	42165	3970	132813	21765	14188
54 HOUSEHOLD APPLIANCES	451	6135	825	18249	4384	419	7262	1634	1378
55 ELECTRIC LIGHTING EQUIP.	320	3646	883	8468	2603	362	7649	1382	983
56 RADIO, TV, ETC., EQUIP.	3372	62773	10766	176516	44380	6400	105470	24416	18655
57 ELECTRONIC COMPONENTS	325	4109	374	16941	1928	176	10833	905	829
58 MISC. ELECTRICAL MACH.	953	11487	963	25208	6424	425	25253	2189	3583
59 MOTOR VEHICLES, EQUIP.	22451	375403	69036	1011755	226051	33747	456531	97675	127743
60 AIRCRAFT, PARTS	4257	128353	9634	215452	52444	4941	122315	16079	31275
61 OTHER TRANSPORT. EQUIP.	3418	93299	16773	177780	47966	6111	89649	22533	79441
62 PROFESS., SCIEN. INSTRU.	4512	59714	8928	121936	29280	2085	101282	14603	9962
63 MEDICAL, PHOTO. EQUIP.	3422	50655	7640	197895	23324	2333	67837	12417	10304
64 MISC. MANUFACTURING	1929	24751	2236	110900	12920	938	35183	4294	5992
65 TRANSPORT., WAREHOUSING	3175	42062	8985	110767	26943	3340	67049	12481	11716
66 COMMUNICA.*EXC. BRDCAST.	1024	24587	5003	69707	19519	3098	35823	11371	8074
67 RADIO, TV BROADCASTING	0	0	0	0	0	0	0	0	0
68 ELEC.*GAS*WATER*SAN.SER.									
69 WHOLESALE, RETAIL TRADE	20964	292603	54584	796369	184450	23444	440251	81198	82736
70 FINANCE, INSURANCE									
71 REAL ESTATE, RENTAL	3123	17811	7192	197748	21703	2869	43465	17616	10969
72 HOTELS, PERSONAL SERV.	0	0	0	0	0	0	0	0	0
73 BUSINESS SERVICES	0	0	0	0	0	0	0	0	0
74 RESEARCH, DEVELOPMENT	0	0	0	0	0	0	0	0	0
75 AUTO. REPAIR, SERVICES	0	0	0	0	0	0	0	0	0
76 AMUSEMENTS	0	0	0	0	0	0	0	0	0
77 MED.*EDUC. SERVICES	0	0	0	0	0	0	0	0	0
78 FEDERAL GOVT. ENTERPRISE	0	0	0	0	0	0	0	0	0
79 STATE, LOCAL GOVT. ENT.	0	0	0	0	0	0	0	0	0
80 IMPORTS	0	0	0	0	0	0	0	0	0
81 BUS.*TRAVEL, ENT., GIFTS.	0	0	0	0	0	0	0	0	0
82 OFFICE SUPPLIES	0	0	0	0	0	0	0	0	0
83 SCRAP, USED GOODS	-1168	-15405	-6988	-34053	-10048	-1732	-26001	-8438	-4189
84 GOVERNMENT INDUSTRY	0	0	0	0	0	0	0	0	0
85 REST OF WORLD INDUSTRY	0	0	0	0	0	0	0	0	0
86 HOUSEHOLD INDUSTRY	0	0	0	0	0	0	0	0	0
87 INVENTORY VALUATION ADJ.	0	0	0	0	0	0	0	0	0
88 STATE TOTAL	275911	3650280	788045	9252717	2149394	274128	5332037	1140637	1009238

TABLE B-3

STATE ESTIMATES OF 1970
GROSS PRIVATE CAPITAL FORMATION
(THOUSANDS OF 1958 DOLLARS)

INDUSTRY TITLE	37 PENNSYL-VANIA	38 RHODE ISLAND	39 SOUTH CAROLINA	40 SOUTH DAKOTA	41 TENNESSEE	42 TEXAS	43 UTAH	44 VERMONT	45 VIRGINIA
1 LIVESTOCK, PRDTS.	0	0	0	0	0	0	0	0	0
2 OTHER AGRICULTURE PRDTS.	0	0	0	0	0	0	0	0	0
3 FORESTRY, FISHERIES	0	0	0	0	0	0	0	0	0
4 AGRI.,FORES.,FISH. SERV.	0	0	0	0	0	0	0	0	0
5 IRON, FERRO. ORES MINING	0	0	0	0	0	0	0	0	0
6 NONFERROUS ORES MINING	0	0	0	0	0	0	0	0	0
7 COAL MINING	0	0	0	0	0	0	0	0	0
8 CRUDE PETRO.,NATURAL GAS	0	0	0	0	0	0	0	0	0
9 STONE, CLAY MINING	0	0	0	0	0	0	0	0	0
10 CHEM.,FERT. MIN. MINING	0	0	0	0	0	0	0	0	0
11 NEW CONSTRUCTION	1931453	140437	401274	92263	637849	3082386	307336	63948	865360
12 MAINT., REPAIR CONSTR.	0	0	0	0	0	0	0	0	0
13 ORDNANCE, ACCESSORIES	0	0	0	0	0	0	0	0	0
14 FOOD, KINDRED PRDTS.	0	0	0	0	0	0	0	0	0
15 TOBACCO MANUFACTURES	0	0	0	0	0	0	0	0	0
16 FABRICS	0	0	0	0	0	0	0	0	0
17 TEXTILE PRDTS.	4610	311	797	152	1522	4986	507	139	1544
18 APPAREL	0	0	0	0	0	0	0	0	0
19 MISC. TEXTILE PRDTS.	0	0	0	0	0	0	0	0	0
20 LUMBER, WOOD PRDTS.	324	15	33	34	132	274	30	14	117
21 WOODEN CONTAINERS	0	0	0	0	0	0	0	0	0
22 HOUSEHOLD FURNITURE	8946	621	1494	430	2874	9896	894	363	3343
23 OTHER FURNITURE	94635	6744	15523	3646	29849	99687	10282	2738	31122
24 PAPER, ALLIED PRDTS.	0	0	0	0	0	0	0	0	0
25 PAPERBOARD CONTAINERS	0	0	0	0	0	0	0	0	0
26 PRINTING, PUBLISHING	0	0	0	0	0	0	0	0	0
27 CHEMICALS,SELECT. PRDTS.	0	0	0	0	0	0	0	0	0
28 PLASTICS, SYNTHETICS	0	0	0	0	0	0	0	0	0
29 DRUGS, COSMETICS	0	0	0	0	0	0	0	0	0
30 PAINT, ALLIED PRDTS.	0	0	0	0	0	0	0	0	0
31 PETROLEUM, RELATED INDS.	0	0	0	0	0	0	0	0	0
32 RUBBER, MISC. PLASTICS	2437	107	455	83	613	3679	438	45	1023
33 LEATHER TANNING, PRDTS.	0	0	0	0	0	0	0	0	0
34 FOOTWEAR, LEATHER PRDTS.	0	0	0	0	0	0	0	0	0
35 GLASS, GLASS PRDTS.	0	0	0	0	0	0	0	0	0
36 STONE, CLAY PRDTS.	0	0	0	0	0	0	0	0	0
37 PRIMARY IRON, STEEL MFR.	0	0	0	0	0	0	0	0	0
38 PRIMARY NONFERROUS MFR.	0	0	0	0	0	0	0	0	0

	1	2	3	4	5	6	7	8	9
39 METAL CONTAINERS	787	40	83	73	303	712	75	31	285
40 FABRICATED METAL PRDTS.	57572	3266	14374	1432	26938	133878	9048	1064	22130
41 SCREW MACH. PRDTS., ETC.	0	0	0	0	0	0	0	0	0
42 OTHER FAB. METAL PRDTS.	16216	1360	3012	372	5460	17449	1929	370	5326
43 ENGINES, TURBINES	54528	2563	10846	2036	14701	81293	10224	1063	23137
44 FARM MACH., EQUIP.	53597	1972	16794	35912	29501	136347	9688	6980	27302
45 CONSTRUC. MACH., EQUIP.	67279	3440	11057	3499	26552	265632	25380	1463	32717
46 MATERIAL HANDLING MACH.	57314	4053	12595	1403	19505	63228	7010	1570	19864
47 METALWORKING MACHINERY	181337	9837	15097	1579	32117	89680	14858	3783	29470
48 SPECIAL MACH., EQUIP.	114733	11019	88367	3055	63597	123133	7844	3336	59062
49 GENERAL MACH., EQUIP.	101368	6899	24305	1746	41161	131305	11461	1943	32219
50 MACHINE SHOP PRDTS.	0	0	0	0	0	0	0	0	0
51 OFFICE, COMPUT. MACHINES	253969	18638	46328	7244	89493	303165	26643	6796	84975
52 SERVICE IND. MACHINES	117047	7764	22020	4615	38555	126405	11571	3210	41777
53 ELECT. TRANSMISS. EQUIP.	108757	6526	20673	3888	31449	114879	16637	2051	41341
54 HOUSEHOLD APPLIANCES	7846	536	1573	467	2773	8430	742	216	2829
55 ELECTRIC LIGHTING EQUIP.	5813	376	1206	446	1801	7593	848	175	2215
56 RADIC, TV, ETC., EQUIP.	80355	7310	21387	4974	42558	119961	14332	1657	38948
57 ELECTRONIC COMPONENTS	6170	498	952	158	1917	5600	534	135	2236
58 MISC. ELECTRICAL MACH.	17618	1486	3319	433	5384	13570	1956	425	5601
59 MOTOR VEHICLES, EQUIP.	*33954	29811	81291	40066	166577	568568	60657	17455	188510
60 AIRCRAFT, PARTS	-14809	8775	15922	2636	37843	86950	14111	3543	51781
61 OTHER TRANSPORT. EQUIP.	86507	6750	19977	4289	30435	133919	13576	2698	44981
62 PROFESS., SCIEN. INSTRU.	79357	5203	19767	1700	36473	128726	10032	2173	29868
63 MEDICAL, PHOTO. EQUIP.	63732	4500	12720	2005	26167	92133	6857	2188	21708
64 MISC. MANUFACTURING	31452	2420	6271	1178	11314	31503	3149	1186	10821
65 TRANSPORT., WAREHOUSING	58791	3938	13055	3582	21068	76567	8089	1811	21812
66 COMMUNICA.-EXC. BRDCAST.	28431	2571	9253	2250	18918	54449	6287	534	16820
67 RADIO, TV BROADCASTING	0	0	0	0	0	0	0	0	0
68 ELEC.,GAS,WATER,SAN.SER.	0	0	0	0	0	0	0	0	0
69 WHOLESALE, RETAIL TRADE	392259	26294	84520	27407	142675	506769	50419	12837	146617
70 FINANCE, INSURANCE	0	0	0	0	0	0	0	0	0
71 REAL ESTATE, RENTAL	33885	4202	8591	2925	17146	92565	5496	1121	17289
72 HOTELS, PERSONAL SERV.	0	0	0	0	0	0	0	0	0
73 BUSINESS SERVICES	0	0	0	0	0	0	0	0	0
74 RESEARCH, DEVELOPMENT	0	0	0	0	0	0	0	0	0
75 AUTO. REPAIR, SERVICES	0	0	0	0	0	0	0	0	0
76 AMUSEMENTS	0	0	0	0	0	0	0	0	0
77 MED.,EDUC. SERVICES	0	0	0	0	0	0	0	0	0
78 FEDERAL GOVT. ENTERPRISE	0	0	0	0	0	0	0	0	0
79 STATE, LOCAL GOVT. ENT.	0	0	0	0	0	0	0	0	0
80 IMPORTS	0	0	0	0	0	0	0	0	0
81 BUS.,TRAVEL, ENT., GIFTS.	0	0	0	0	0	0	0	0	0
82 OFFICE SUPPLIES	0	0	0	0	0	0	0	0	0
83 SCRAP, USED GOODS	-21688	-1309	-4350	-1027	-6986	-46478	-4491	-604	-8781
84 GOVERNMENT INDUSTRY	0	0	0	0	0	0	0	0	0
85 REST OF WORLD INDUSTRY	0	0	0	0	0	0	0	0	0
86 HOUSEHOLD INDUSTRY	0	0	0	0	0	0	0	0	0
87 INVENTORY VALUATION ADJ.	0	0	0	0	0	0	0	0	0
88 STATE TOTAL	4646520	328674	1000607	258050	1648233	6668842	664449	148458	1915871

149

TABLE B-3

STATE ESTIMATES OF 1970
GROSS PRIVATE CAPITAL FORMATION
(THOUSANDS OF 1958 DOLLARS)

INDUSTRY TITLE	46 WASHINGTON	47 WEST VIRGINIA	48 WISCONSIN	49 WYOMING	50 ALASKA	51 HAWAII	52 NO STATE ALLOCATION	53 NATIONAL TOTAL
1 LIVESTOCK, PRDTS.	0	0	0	0	0	0	0	0
2 OTHER AGRICULTURE PRDTS.	0	0	0	0	0	0	0	0
3 FORESTRY, FISHERIES	0	0	0	0	0	0	0	0
4 AGRI.,FORES.,FISH. SERV.	0	0	0	0	0	0	0	0
5 IRON, FERRO. ORES MINING	0	0	0	0	0	0	0	0
6 NONFERROUS ORES MINING	0	0	0	0	0	0	0	0
7 COAL MINING	0	0	0	0	0	0	0	0
8 CRUDE PETRO.,NATURAL GAS	0	0	0	0	0	0	0	0
9 STONE, CLAY MINING	0	0	0	0	0	0	0	0
10 CHEM.,FERT. MIN. MINING	0	0	0	0	0	0	0	0
11 NEW CONSTRUCTION	581356	276233	788425	227066	73075	163047	0	43300000
12 MAINT., REPAIR CONSTR.	0	0	0	0	0	0	0	0
13 ORDNANCE, ACCESSORIES	0	0	0	0	0	0	0	0
14 FOOD, KINDRED PRDTS.	0	0	0	0	0	0	0	0
15 TOBACCO MANUFACTURES	0	0	0	0	0	0	0	0
16 FABRICS	0	0	0	0	0	0	0	0
17 TEXTILE PRDTS.	1348	612	1738	172	128	376	0	97000
18 APPAREL	0	0	0	0	0	0	0	0
19 MISC. TEXTILE PRDTS.	0	0	0	0	0	0	0	0
20 LUMBER, WOOD PRDTS.	98	17	200	3	12	57	0	6000
21 WOODEN CONTAINERS	0	0	0	0	0	0	0	0
22 HOUSEHOLD FURNITURE	2503	929	3219	389	257	926	0	191000
23 OTHER FURNITURE	26253	12599	33441	2924	2303	7508	0	1879000
24 PAPER, ALLIED PRDTS.	0	0	0	0	0	0	0	0
25 PAPERBOARD CONTAINERS	0	0	0	0	0	0	0	0
26 PRINTING, PUBLISHING	0	0	0	0	0	0	0	0
27 CHEMICALS,SELECT. PRDTS.	0	0	0	0	0	0	0	0
28 PLASTICS, SYNTHETICS	0	0	0	0	0	0	0	0
29 DRUGS, COSMETICS	0	0	0	0	0	0	0	0
30 PAINT, ALLIED PRDTS.	0	0	0	0	0	0	0	0
31 PETROLEUM, RELATED INDS.	0	0	0	0	0	0	0	0
32 RUBBER, MISC. PLASTICS	346	763	938	367	55	143	0	47000
33 LEATHER TANNING, PRDTS.	0	0	0	0	0	0	0	0
34 FOOTWEAR, LEATHER PRDTS.	0	0	0	0	0	0	0	0
35 GLASS, GLASS PRDTS.	0	0	0	0	0	0	0	0
36 STONE, CLAY PRDTS.	0	0	0	0	0	0	0	0
37 PRIMARY IRON, STEEL MFR.	0	0	0	0	0	0	0	0
38 PRIMARY NONFERROUS MFR.	0	0	0	0	0	0	0	0

#	Industry								
39	METAL CONTAINERS	237	44	441	9	28	126	0	15000
40	FABRICATED METAL PRDTS.	14639	21725	17932	10017	1244	3083	0	1181000
41	SCREW MACH. PRDTS.+ETC.	0	0	0	0	0	0	0	0
42	OTHER FAB. METAL PRDTS.	4207	3828	5349	708	345	974	0	299000
43	ENGINES, TURBINES	8471	16956	21032	8173	1215	3236	0	1061000
44	FARM MACH.+ EQUIP.	29285	6457	63789	9772	1464	16550	0	2091000
45	CONSTRUC. MACH.+ EQUIP.	19219	35291	21147	36994	3942	6711	0	2117000
46	MATERIAL HANDLING MACH.	16095	11848	26856	3912	1228	2835	0	1092000
47	METALWORKING MACHINERY	27734	25390	81346	1970	1105	2652	0	2407000
48	SPECIAL MACH.+ EQUIP.	4141	24334	65200	2170	3536	6721	0	2302000
49	GENERAL MACH.+ EQUIP.	26136	31573	34044	5262	1591	3872	0	1716000
50	MACHINE SHOP PRDTS.	0	0	0	0	0	0	0	0
51	OFFICE, COMPUT. MACHINES	42968		104218	7430	6052	19199	0	5299000
52	SERVICE IND. MACHINES	35895	12304	46468	2516	3513	9924	0	2392000
53	ELECT. TRANSMISS. EQUIP.	20399	25076	38423	7422	1861	6859	0	1969000
54	HOUSEHOLD APPLIANCES	2188	639	2881	331	158	707	0	157000
55	ELECTRIC LIGHTING EQUIP.	1326	1271	2800	563	138	480	0	120000
56	RADIO, TV, ETC.+ EQUIP.	27594	14666	23790	3525	1589	9190	0	1893000
57	ELECTRONIC COMPONENTS	1243	791	4342	144	115	377	0	136000
58	MISC. ELECTRICAL MACH.	4158	2909	7783	398	348	935	0	311000
59	MOTOR VEHICLES, EQUIP.	145056		184136	31401	21662	54841	0	9962000
60	AIRCRAFT, PARTS	32885	16247	47860	3864	7361	13463	0	2279000
61	OTHER TRANSPORT. EQUIP.	52702	14935	34295	9632	22148	11289	0	2133000
62	PROFESS.+ SCIEN. INSTRU.	22721	27542	31027	5870	1662	3676	0	1567000
63	MEDICAL, PHOTO. EQUIP.	17804	14467	20907	3888	1580	5030	0	1370000
64	MISC. MANUFACTURING	9056	5576	11521	686	946	2792	0	675000
65	TRANSPORT.+ WAREHOUSING	16619	12598	25079	4836	1930	4746	0	1212000
66	COMMUNICA.+EXC. BRDCAST.	11790	5813	6313	1568	497	4182	0	767000
67	RADIO+ TV BROADCASTING	0	0	0	0	0	0	0	0
68	ELEC.+GAS+WATER+SAN.SER.	0	0	0	0	0	0	0	0
69	WHOLESALE+ RETAIL TRADE	115990	77553	169181	28048	12931	34000	0	8235000
70	FINANCE, INSURANCE	0	0	0	0	0	0	0	0
71	REAL ESTATE, RENTAL	13558	2919	19186	1782	1680	9183	0	1200000
72	HOTELS, PERSONAL SERV.	0	0	0	0	0	0	0	0
73	BUSINESS SERVICES	0	0	0	0	0	0	0	0
74	RESEARCH, DEVELOPMENT	0	0	0	0	0	0	0	0
75	AUTO. REPAIR, SERVICES	0	0	0	0	0	0	0	0
76	AMUSEMENTS	0	0	0	0	0	0	0	0
77	MED.,EDUC. SERVICES	0	0	0	0	0	0	0	0
78	FEDERAL GOVT. ENTERPRISE	0	0	0	0	0	0	0	0
79	STATE, LOCAL GOVT. ENT.	0	0	0	0	0	0	0	0
80	IMPORTS	0	0	0	0	0	0	25000	25000
81	BUS.TRAVEL, ENT.+ GIFTS.	0	0	0	0	0	0	0	0
82	OFFICE SUPPLIES	0	0	0	0	0	0	0	0
83	SCRAP, USED GOODS	-5639	-4491	-8237	-4713	-886	-2034	0	-503000
84	GOVERNMENT INDUSTRY	0	0	0	0	0	0	0	0
85	REST OF WORLD INDUSTRY	0	0	0	0	0	0	0	0
86	HOUSEHOLD INDUSTRY	0	0	0	0	0	0	0	0
87	INVENTORY VALUATION ADJ.	0	0	0	0	0	0	0	0
88	STATE TOTAL	1398370	818730	1937071	419199	176854	407657	25000	101000000

151

TABLE B-4

STATE ESTIMATES OF 1940
GROSS PRIVATE CAPITAL FORMATION
(THOUSANDS OF 1958 DOLLARS)

INDUSTRY TITLE	1 ALABAMA	2 ARIZONA	3 ARKANSAS	4 CALIFORNIA	5 COLORADO	6 CONNECTICUT	7 DELAWARE	8 DISTRICT OF COLUMBIA	9 FLORIDA
1 LIVESTOCK, PRDTS.	0	0	0	0	0	0	0	0	0
2 OTHER AGRICULTURE PRDTS.	0	0	0	0	0	0	0	0	0
3 FORESTRY, FISHERIES	0	0	0	0	0	0	0	0	0
4 AGRI.,FORES.,FISH. SERV.	0	0	0	0	0	0	0	0	0
5 IRON, FERRO. ORES MINING	0	0	0	0	0	0	0	0	0
6 NONFERROUS ORES MINING	0	0	0	0	0	0	0	0	0
7 COAL MINING	0	0	0	0	0	0	0	0	0
8 CRUDE PETRO.,NATURAL GAS	0	0	0	0	0	0	0	0	0
9 STONE, CLAY MINING	0	0	0	0	0	0	0	0	0
10 CHEM.,FERT. MIN. MINING	0	0	0	0	0	0	0	0	0
11 NEW CONSTRUCTION	1041135	904513	560575	9726956	1099385	1076638	251507	329700	3128581
12 MAINT., REPAIR CONSTR.	0	0	0	0	0	0	0	0	0
13 ORDNANCE, ACCESSORIES	0	0	0	0	0	0	0	0	0
14 FOOD, KINDRED PRDTS.	0	0	0	0	0	0	0	0	0
15 TOBACCO MANUFACTURES	0	0	0	0	0	0	0	0	0
16 FABRICS	0	0	0	0	0	0	0	0	0
17 TEXTILE PRDTS.	1849	1710	749	21833	2094	2351	518	1023	6585
18 APPAREL	0	0	0	0	0	0	0	0	0
19 MISC. TEXTILE PRDTS.	0	0	0	0	0	0	0	0	0
20 LUMBER, WOOD PRDTS.	81	32	80	729	98	53	12	10	223
21 WOODEN CONTAINERS	0	0	0	0	0	0	0	0	0
22 HOUSEHOLD FURNITURE	2764	3454	1333	37579	3774	4024	857	1954	14614
23 OTHER FURNITURE	29168	26808	11774	325723	31886	37630	9167	13774	104652
24 PAPER, ALLIED PRDTS.	0	0	0	0	0	0	0	0	0
25 PAPERBOARD CONTAINERS	0	0	0	0	0	0	0	0	0
26 PRINTING, PUBLISHING	0	0	0	0	0	0	0	0	0
27 CHEMICALS,SELECT. PRDTS.	0	0	0	0	0	0	0	0	0
28 PLASTICS, SYNTHETICS	0	0	0	0	0	0	0	0	0
29 DRUGS, COSMETICS	0	0	0	0	0	0	0	0	0
30 PAINT, ALLIED PRDTS.	0	0	0	0	0	0	0	0	0
31 PETROLEUM, RELATED INDS.	0	0	0	0	0	0	0	0	0
32 RUBBER, MISC. PLASTICS	770	587	368	3404	842	144	115	31	1215
33 LEATHER TANNING, PRDTS.	0	0	0	0	0	0	0	0	0
34 FOOTWEAR, LEATHER PRDTS.	0	0	0	0	0	0	0	0	0
35 GLASS, GLASS PRDTS.	0	0	0	0	0	0	0	0	0
36 STONE, CLAY PRDTS.	0	0	0	0	0	0	0	0	0
37 PRIMARY IRON, STEEL MFR.	0	0	0	0	0	0	0	0	0
38 PRIMARY NONFERROUS MFR.	0	0	0	0	0	0	0	0	0

39 METAL CONTAINERS	870	436	739	8375	1018	674	164	146	2588
40 FABRICATED METAL PRDTS.	21157	13182	8022	117974	18680	9974	4196	3294	43611
41 SCREW MACH. PRDTS., ETC.	5201	0	0	0	0	0	0	0	0
42 OTHER FAB. METAL PRDTS.	18055	4538	2070	45430	5134	4912	1239	2074	14573
43 ENGINES, TURBINES	55727	14223	8718	81962	19449	3846	2816	773	29096
44 FARM MACH., EQUIP.	33457	63828	65530	377818	61471	17738	12422	3840	143423
45 CONSTRUC. MACH., EQUIP.	16548	38198	13601	379723	59508	33470	7422	13275	105361
46 MATERIAL HANDLING MACH.	39557	12628	7873	132038	14796	13242	4404	3478	35247
47 METALWORKING MACHINERY	78775	32832	16875	371705	23575	43384	12709	5318	64537
48 SPECIAL MACH., EQUIP.	45652	26048	38998	364759	39943	34487	14880	9688	117617
49 GENERAL MACH., EQUIP.		26292	16072	262630	30734	28128	10648	6929	83601
50 MACHINE SHOP PRDTS.	0	0	0	0	0	0	0	0	0
51 OFFICE, COMPUT. MACHINES	127113	113811	59477	1510602	146874	152501	40297	64311	424763
52 SERVICE IND. MACHINES	35048	32586	16546	436794	39000	43650	11949	14617	139483
53 ELECT. TRANSMISS. EQUIP.	92372	65208	41931	487595	84065	21436	13503	5581	168794
54 HOUSEHOLD APPLIANCES	3547	3126	1715	36886	3549	4075	1022	1440	13099
55 ELECTRIC LIGHTING EQUIP.	3771	2893	2111	23031	3878	1526	823	660	7603
56 RADIO, TV, ETC., EQUIP.	155189	83807	67685	984624	122598	32891	26029	15873	371925
57 ELECTRONIC COMPONENTS	4821	3275	2422	52586	4257	3325	3229	1096	11411
58 MISC. ELECTRICAL MACH.	5222	3202	2396	36651	4496	3186	1624	1104	9460
59 MOTOR VEHICLES, EQUIP.	151805	156345	103019	1703872	197328	171754	42215	77646	576716
60 AIRCRAFT, PARTS	19362	21905	18992	367038	44773	40324	3688	23655	124641
61 OTHER TRANSPORT. EQUIP.	33071	32179	27606	469891	61814	47070	8213	28029	170082
62 PROFESS., SCIEN. INSTRU.	32155	21415	12777	195076	28117	23618	7426	6102	61793
63 MEDICAL, PHOTO. EQUIP.	36100	34028	14310	416992	44373	53492	10471	25873	140281
64 MISC. MANUFACTURING	6060	6542	2936	80528	9193	7965	2344	4565	29935
65 TRANSPORT., WAREHOUSING	31541	26442	17298	265043	32977	25216	7694	8834	83927
66 COMMUNICA.,EXC. BRDCAST.	32521	17655	14118	207624	25020	5039	4717	2694	82871
67 RADIO, TV BROADCASTING	0	0	0	0	0	0	0	0	0
68 ELEC.,GAS,WATER,SAN.SER.	0	0	0	0	0	0	0	0	0
69 WHOLESALE, RETAIL TRADE	172726	148158	96409	1544018	179674	150016	44328	55232	493558
70 FINANCE, INSURANCE	0	0	0	0	0	0	0	0	0
71 REAL ESTATE, RENTAL	42702	57065	31714	702128	82266	12850	0	17645	211896
72 HOTELS, PERSONAL SERV.	0	0	0	0	0	0	0	0	0
73 BUSINESS SERVICES	0	0	0	0	0	0	0	0	0
74 RESEARCH, DEVELOPMENT									
75 AUTO. REPAIR, SERVICES									
76 AMUSEMENTS									
77 MED.,EDUC. SERVICES									
78 FEDERAL GOVT. ENTERPRISE									
79 STATE, LOCAL GOVT. ENT.									
80 IMPORTS									
81 BUS.TRAVEL, ENT., GIFTS.									
82 OFFICE SUPPLIES									
83 SCRAP, USED GOODS	11161	8022	5644	80761	12651	8022	2632	2600	25018
84 GOVERNMENT INDUSTRY									
85 REST OF WORLD INDUSTRY									
86 HOUSEHOLD INDUSTRY									
87 INVENTORY VALUATION ADJ.									
88 STATE TOTAL	2391255	2006973	1292483	21859178	2537840	2118651	565280	752865	7043180

TABLE B-4

STATE ESTIMATES OF 1940
GROSS PRIVATE CAPITAL FORMATION
(THOUSANDS OF 1958 DOLLARS)

INDUSTRY TITLE	10 GEORGIA	11 IDAHO	12 ILLINOIS	13 INDIANA	14 IOWA	15 KANSAS	16 KENTUCKY	17 LOUISIANA	18 MAINE
1 LIVESTOCK, PRDTS.	0	0	0	0	0	0	0	0	0
2 OTHER AGRICULTURE PRDTS.	0	0	0	0	0	0	0	0	0
3 FORESTRY, FISHERIES	0	0	0	0	0	0	0	0	0
4 AGRI.,FORES.,FISH. SERV.	0	0	0	0	0	0	0	0	0
5 IRON, FERRO. ORES MINING	0	0	0	0	0	0	0	0	0
6 NONFERROUS ORES MINING	0	0	0	0	0	0	0	0	0
7 COAL MINING	0	0	0	0	0	0	0	0	0
8 CRUDE PETRO.,NATURAL GAS	0	0	0	0	0	0	0	0	0
9 STONE, CLAY MINING	0	0	0	0	0	0	0	0	0
10 CHEM.,FERT. MIN. MINING	0	0	0	0	0	0	0	0	0
11 NEW CONSTRUCTION	1562886	229765	4303505	1769849	747969	725278	899674	2630038	186329
12 MAINT., REPAIR CONSTR.	0	0	0	0	0	0	0	0	0
13 ORDNANCE, ACCESSORIES	0	0	0	0	0	0	0	0	0
14 FOOD, KINDRED PRDTS.	0	0	0	0	0	0	0	0	0
15 TOBACCO MANUFACTURES	0	0	0	0	0	0	0	0	0
16 FABRICS	0	0	0	0	0	0	0	0	0
17 TEXTILE PRDTS.	3428	374	11577	2994	1401	1185	1872	3016	396
18 APPAREL	0	0	0	0	0	0	0	0	0
19 MISC. TEXTILE PRDTS.	0	0	0	0	0	0	0	0	0
20 LUMBER, WOOD PRDTS.	166	34	173	137	210	28	54	30	37
21 WOODEN CONTAINERS	0	0	0	0	0	0	0	0	0
22 HOUSEHOLD FURNITURE	5507	719	16968	5109	2913	2210	3070	4257	967
23 OTHER FURNITURE	56163	6327	169983	52028	24336	19480	30933	39907	6466
24 PAPER, ALLIED PRDTS.	0	0	0	0	0	0	0	0	0
25 PAPERBOARD CONTAINERS	0	0	0	0	0	0	0	0	0
26 PRINTING, PUBLISHING	0	0	0	0	0	0	0	0	0
27 CHEMICALS,SELECT. PRDTS.	0	0	0	0	0	0	0	0	0
28 PLASTICS, SYNTHETICS	0	0	0	0	0	0	0	0	0
29 DRUGS, COSMETICS	0	0	0	0	0	0	0	0	0
30 PAINT, ALLIED PRDTS.	0	0	0	0	0	0	0	0	0
31 PETROLEUM, RELATED INDS.	0	0	0	0	0	0	0	0	0
32 RUBBER, MISC. PLASTICS	823	188	2485	1256	393	356	569	1365	40
33 LEATHER TANNING, PRDTS.	0	0	0	0	0	0	0	0	0
34 FOOTWEAR, LEATHER PRDTS.	0	0	0	0	0	0	0	0	0
35 GLASS, GLASS PRDTS.	0	0	0	0	0	0	0	0	0
36 STONE, CLAY PRDTS.	0	0	0	0	0	0	0	0	0
37 PRIMARY IRON, STEEL MFR.	0	0	0	0	0	0	0	0	0
38 PRIMARY NONFERROUS MFR.	0	0	0	0	0	0	0	0	0

#	Sector	(1)	(2)	(3)	(4)	(5)	(6)	(7)	(8)	(9)
39	METAL CONTAINERS	1353	330	2534	1458	1913	329	611	482	358
40	FABRICATED METAL PRDTS.	2066	5496	60548	30435	12676	11302	24049	75246	2124
41	SCREW MACH. PRDTS., ETC.	0	1128	26765	9135	3622	2800	5664	7145	763
42	OTHER FAB. METAL PRDTS.	6715	4480	58404	29559	9916	8587	13737	31244	1066
43	ENGINES, TURBINES	19465	37226	132270	91955	161991	89193	55260	51374	18448
44	FARM MACH., EQUIP.	5126	7339	153748	37951	17657	9895	45974	356244	4423
45	CONSTRUC. MACH., EQUIP.	39405	3914	65354	30151	12891	18653	18653	29208	3019
46	MATERIAL HANDLING MACHINERY	27081	6326	204708	120650	43588	25585	58767	25651	5727
47	METALWORKING MACHINERY	60069	17198	179550	90730	49723	25817	62169	45764	16657
48	SPECIAL MACH., EQUIP.	15723	10739	143878	30688	30688	21617	52024	27871	5349
49	GENERA MACH., EQUIP.	5178	17508	110739	76636	76636	52024	52024	52024	7853
50	MACHINE SHOP PRDTS.	0	0	0	0	0	0	0	0	0
51	OFFICE, COMPUT. MACHINES	226755	30579	780578	248155	107824	93983	159081	189181	24296
52	SERVICE IND. MACHINES	85185	9273	206027	62991	31679	20489	35979	46087	9771
53	ELECT. TRANSMISS. EQUIP.	110342	17508	230758	128269	49453	44367	67905	101912	5389
54	HOUSEHOLD APPLIANCES	681	837	16565	5480	3770	3377	3418	5305	811
55	ELECTRIC LIGHTING EQUIP.	5313	1105	12712	6277	3328	2534	3017	6007	514
56	RADIO, TV, ETC., EQUIP.	223741	19776	173704	100481	82239	93691	125299	207212	9013
57	ELECTRONIC COMPONENTS	12836	1007	15186	7819	3506	4874	7567	5557	546
58	MISC. ELECTRICAL MACH.	8472	1019	17586	9547	3590	3219	4670	4796	790
59	MOTOR VEHICLES, EQUIP.	299932	56044	872365	264524	187075	123149	173601	296167	46130
60	AIRCRAFT, PARTS	69235	8531	271214	58200	22929	15454	38154	62408	10396
61	OTHER TRANSPORT. EQUIP.	91806	15905	298603	75472	36587	36404	43253	162884	12920
62	PROFESS., SCIEN. INSTRU.	36564	8302	124773	52417	22030	19826	42030	56371	3054
63	MEDICAL, PHOTO. EQUIP.	55245	10081	241926	61926	28748	24799	51671	86140	7853
64	MISC. MANUFACTURING	12177	1616	41307	11561	5336	4118	8377	8488	1808
65	TRANSPORT., WAREHOUSING	51828	8888	135203	52870	31321	22075	33753	60605	6058
66	COMMUNICA., EXC. BRDCAST.	47341	3843	21202	12667	16072	19685	27397	46984	1172
67	RADIO, TV BROADCASTING	0	0	0	0	0	0	0	0	0
68	ELEC., GAS, WATER, SAN. SER.	0	0	0	0	0	0	0	0	0
69	WHOLESALE, RETAIL TRADE	292173	51827	784938	292353	182405	125611	187557	311316	36739
70	FINANCE, INSURANCE	0	0	0	0	0	0	0	0	0
71	REAL ESTATE, RENTAL	80284	13658	167664	98163	32943	41469	28321	57746	8816
72	HOTELS, PERSONAL SERV.	0	0	0	0	0	0	0	0	0
73	BUSINESS SERVICES	0	0	0	0	0	0	0	0	0
74	RESEARCH, DEVELOPMENT	0	0	0	0	0	0	0	0	0
75	AUTO. REPAIR, SERVICES	0	0	0	0	0	0	0	0	0
76	AMUSEMENTS	0	0	0	0	0	0	0	0	0
77	MED., EDUC. SERVICES	0	0	0	0	0	0	0	0	0
78	FEDERAL GOVT. ENTERPRISE	0	0	0	0	0	0	0	0	0
79	STATE, LOCAL GOVT. ENT.	0	0	0	0	0	0	0	0	0
80	IMPORTS	0	0	0	0	0	0	0	0	0
81	BUS. TRAVEL, ENT., GIFTS.	0	0	0	0	0	0	0	0	0
82	OFFICE SUPPLIES	0	0	0	0	0	0	0	0	0
83	SCRAP, USED GOODS	15092	2568	47181	20737	8403	9322	10305	47340	1966
84	GOVERNMENT INDUSTRY	0	0	0	0	0	0	0	0	0
85	REST OF WORLD INDUSTRY	0	0	0	0	0	0	0	0	0
86	HOUSEHOLD INDUSTRY	0	0	0	0	0	0	0	0	0
87	INVENTORY VALUATION ADJ.	0	0	0	0	0	0	0	0	0
88	STATE TOTAL	383134	593950	9991942	3919996	1981126	1683192	2324435	5136348	440211

155

STATE ESTIMATES OF 1980
GROSS PRIVATE CAPITAL FORMATION
(THOUSANDS OF 1958 DOLLARS)

INDUSTRY TITLE	19 MARYLAND	20 MASSA-CHUSETTS	21 MICHIGAN	22 MINNESOTA	23 MISSISSIPPI	24 MISSOURI	25 MONTANA	26 NEBRASKA	27 NEVADA
1 LIVESTOCK, PRDTS.	0	0	0	0	0	0	0	0	0
2 OTHER AGRICULTURE PRDTS.	0	0	0	0	0	0	0	0	0
3 FORESTRY, FISHERIES	0	0	0	0	0	0	0	0	0
4 AGRI.,FORES.,FISH. SERV.	0	0	0	0	0	0	0	0	0
5 IRON, FERRO. ORES MINING	0	0	0	0	0	0	0	0	0
6 NONFERROUS ORES MINING	0	0	0	0	0	0	0	0	0
7 COAL MINING	0	0	0	0	0	0	0	0	0
8 CRUDE PETRO.,NATURAL GAS	0	0	0	0	0	0	0	0	0
9 STONE, CLAY MINING	0	0	0	0	0	0	0	0	0
10 CHEM.,FERT. MIN. MINING	0	0	0	0	0	0	0	0	0
11 NEW CONSTRUCTION	1559384	1627337	2991786	1296484	673537	1531052	263184	487886	319372
12 MAINT., REPAIR CONSTR.	0	0	0	0	0	0	0	0	0
13 ORDNANCE, ACCESSORIES	0	0	0	0	0	0	0	0	0
14 FOOD, KINDRED PRDTS.	0	0	0	0	0	0	0	0	0
15 TOBACCO MANUFACTURES	0	0	0	0	0	0	0	0	0
16 FABRICS	0	0	0	0	0	0	0	0	0
17 TEXTILE PRDTS.	2898	4601	7098	3209	791	3906	347	909	807
18 APPAREL	0	0	0	0	0	0	0	0	0
19 MISC. TEXTILE PRDTS.	0	0	0	0	0	0	0	0	0
20 LUMBER, WOOD PRDTS.	88	89	172	82	60	114	6	87	3
21 WOODEN CONTAINERS	0	0	0	0	0	0	0	0	0
22 HOUSEHOLD FURNITURE	5070	7492	10443	4891	1427	5935	676	1838	3898
23 OTHER FURNITURE	47386	70167	105340	45681	12121	58939	6497	16358	13050
24 PAPER, ALLIED PRDTS.	0	0	0	0	0	0	0	0	0
25 PAPERBOARD CONTAINERS	0	0	0	0	0	0	0	0	0
26 PRINTING, PUBLISHING	0	0	0	0	0	0	0	0	0
27 CHEMICALS,SELECT. PRDTS.	0	0	0	0	0	0	0	0	0
28 PLASTICS, SYNTHETICS	0	0	0	0	0	0	0	0	0
29 DRUGS, COSMETICS	0	0	0	0	0	0	0	0	0
30 PAINT, ALLIED PRDTS.	0	0	0	0	0	0	0	0	0
31 PETROLEUM, RELATED INDS.	0	0	0	0	0	0	0	0	0
32 RUBBER, MISC. PLASTICS	627	265	1651	815	515	810	179	232	180
33 LEATHER TANNING, PRDTS.	0	0	0	0	0	0	0	0	0
34 FOOTWEAR, LEATHER PRDTS.	0	0	0	0	0	0	0	0	0
35 GLASS, GLASS PRDTS.	0	0	0	0	0	0	0	0	0
36 STONE, CLAY PRDTS.	0	0	0	0	0	0	0	0	0
37 PRIMARY IRON, STEEL MFR.	0	0	0	0	0	0	0	0	0
38 PRIMARY NONFERROUS MFR.	0	0	0	0	0	0	0	0	0

#	Sector	C1	C2	C3	C4	C5	C6	C7	C8	C9
39	METAL CONTAINERS	1031	1146	2115	934	587	1336	89	831	75
40	FABRICATED METAL PRDTS., ETC.	19848	15614	43190	19028	11626	21045	5316	7278	5209
41	SCREW MACH. PRDTS., ETC.	0	0	0	0	0	0	0	0	0
42	OTHER FAB. METAL PRDTS.	7049	8724	16592	7905	2145	8278	1250	2142	2196
43	ENGINES, TURBINES	15136	6688	38813	18695	11995	19269	4401	5679	4257
44	FARM MACH., EQUIP.	35767	17244	72148	110625	66073	99195	33001	94165	12233
45	CONSTRUC. MACH., EQUIP.	44795	44589	85603	51322	25476	25150	18487	22908	20607
46	MATERIAL HANDLING MACH.	20826	25509	49492	23037	8561	68697	4356	6561	4855
47	METALWORKING MACHINERY	61244	86115	189919	87498	16595	70115	10236	16822	7787
48	SPECIAL MACH., EQUIP.	56731	69015	114686	57805	29446	52293	9490	19347	9171
49	GENERAL MACH., EQUIP.	45937	50318	108371	45841	18016		9985	14196	10777
50	MACHINE SHOP PRDTS.	0	0	0	0	0	0	0	0	0
51	OFFICE, COMPUT. MACHINES	183141	310529	503840	236109	59843	287767	24784	69663	40275
52	SERVICE IND. MACHINES	57752	78449	132794	53036	16417	74015	7250	19503	13272
53	ELECT. TRANSMISS. EQUIP.	82417	48115	216101	85097	54116	99193	19450	22122	15486
54	HOUSEHOLD APPLIANCES	5729	6440	11186	5309	2007	6290	879	2794	1367
55	ELECTRIC LIGHTING EQUIP.	4029	3149	9085	4352	2456	5202	1059	1926	1031
56	RADIO, TV, ETC., EQUIP.	139252	84930	406493	126525	81366	185923	30974	25070	7894
57	ELECTRONIC COMPONENTS	8010	7960	23901	6197	2910	13132	1063	1501	575
58	MISC. ELECTRICAL MACH.	6924	7419	15402	5579	2387	8054	1240	1665	670
59	MOTOR VEHICLES, EQUIP.	239385	323430	475291	272830	101309	326683	49503	122562	71237
60	AIRCRAFT, PARTS	58257	84681	129272	69304	13890	94844	4867	20452	9146
61	OTHER TRANSPORT. EQUIP.	75159	82867	141500	74878	28500	108786	13492	38029	14049
62	PROFESS., SCIEN. INSTRU.	32768	47075	80546	40234	16192	46291	5777	9954	6150
63	MEDICAL, PHOTO. EQUIP.	51586	110113	134260	66359	15763	74156	7762	18598	29512
64	MISC. MANUFACTURING	12369	16335	24426	10736	2542	13029	1275	3782	15046
65	TRANSPORT., WAREHOUSING	39211	46915	87169	44264	18803	51781	8945	18142	10555
66	COMMUNICA., EXC. BRDCAST.	27327	14002	87668	26089	17856	38417	6514	4044	704
67	RADIO, TV BROADCASTING	0	0	0	0	0	0	0	0	0
68	ELEC., GAS, WATER, SAN. SER.	221386	272820	499595	262107	101560	297552	49194	108806	58126
69	WHOLESALE, RETAIL TRADE									
70	FINANCE, INSURANCE	37355	101262	137358	84426	27879	91575	11771	37558	21645
71	REAL ESTATE, RENTAL	0	0	0	0	0	0	0	0	0
72	HOTELS, PERSONAL SERV.	0	0	0	0	0	0	0	0	0
73	BUSINESS SERVICES	0	0	0	0	0	0	0	0	0
74	RESEARCH, DEVELOPMENT	0	0	0	0	0	0	0	0	0
75	AUTO. REPAIR, SERVICES	0	0	0	0	0	0	0	0	0
76	AMUSEMENTS	0	0	0	0	0	0	0	0	0
77	MED., EDUC. SERVICES	0	0	0	0	0	0	0	0	0
78	FEDERAL GOVT. ENTERPRISE	0	0	0	0	0	0	0	0	0
79	STATE, LOCAL GOVT. ENT.	0	0	0	0	0	0	0	0	0
80	IMPORTS	0	0	0	0	0	0	0	0	0
81	BUS. TRAVEL, ENT., GIFTS.	0	0	0	0	0	0	0	0	0
82	OFFICE SUPPLIES	0	0	0	0	0	0	0	0	0
83	SCRAP, USED GOODS	12963	15093	31835	13638	7895	16583	3742	5834	3202
84	GOVERNMENT INDUSTRY	0	0	0	0	0	0	0	0	0
85	REST OF WORLD INDUSTRY	0	0	0	0	0	0	0	0	0
86	HOUSEHOLD INDUSTRY	0	0	0	0	0	0	0	0	0
87	INVENTORY VALUATION ADJ.	0	0	0	0	0	0	0	0	0
88	STATE TOTAL	3233724*	3696497	6985141	3261580	1452662	3853376	617040	1229244	734419

TABLE 8-4

STATE ESTIMATES OF 1960
GROSS PRIVATE CAPITAL FORMATION
(THOUSANDS OF 1958 DOLLARS)

INDUSTRY TITLE	28 NEW HAMPSHIRE	29 NEW JERSEY	30 NEW MEXICO	31 NEW YORK	32 NORTH CAROLINA	33 NORTH DAKOTA	34 OHIO	35 OKLAHOMA	36 OREGON
1 LIVESTOCK, PRDTS.	0	0	0	0	0	0	0	0	0
2 OTHER AGRICULTURE PRDTS.	0	0	0	0	0	0	0	0	0
3 FORESTRY, FISHERIES	0	0	0	0	0	0	0	0	0
4 AGRI.,FORES.,FISH. SERV.	0	0	0	0	0	0	0	0	0
5 IRON, FERRO. ORES MINING	0	0	0	0	0	0	0	0	0
6 NONFERROUS ORES MINING	0	0	0	0	0	0	0	0	0
7 COAL MINING	0	0	0	0	0	0	0	0	0
8 CRUDE PETRO.,NATURAL GAS	0	0	0	0	0	0	0	0	0
9 STONE, CLAY MINING	0	0	0	0	0	0	0	0	0
10 CHEM.,FERT. MIN. MINING	0	0	0	0	0	0	0	0	0
11 NEW CONSTRUCTION	233091	2699761	713727	6023141	1591459	202062	3674654	870544	643002
12 MAINT., REPAIR CONSTR.	0	0	0	0	0	0	0	0	0
13 ORDNANCE, ACCESSORIES	0	0	0	0	0	0	0	0	0
14 FOOD, KINDRED PRDTS.	0	0	0	0	0	0	0	0	0
15 TOBACCO MANUFACTURES	0	0	0	0	0	0	0	0	0
16 FABRICS	455	6217	862	23670	3383	288	7999	1300	1415
17 TEXTILE PRDTS.	0	0	0	0	0	0	0	0	0
18 APPAREL	0	0	0	0	0	0	0	0	0
19 MISC. TEXTILE PRDTS.	0	0	0	0	0	0	0	0	0
20 LUMBER, WOOD PRDTS.	9	274	14	210	135	3	236	12	57
21 WOODEN CONTAINERS	0	0	0	0	0	0	0	0	0
22 HOUSEHOLD FURNITURE	907	9580	1529	36744	5899	586	12411	2295	2257
23 OTHER FURNITURE	7140	98269	12694	320917	56278	4893	124543	20599	21574
24 PAPER, ALLIED PRDTS.	0	0	0	0	0	0	0	0	0
25 PAPERBOARD CONTAINERS	0	0	0	0	0	0	0	0	0
26 PRINTING, PUBLISHING	0	0	0	0	0	0	0	0	0
27 CHEMICALS,SELECT. PRDTS.	0	0	0	0	0	0	0	0	0
28 PLASTICS, SYNTHETICS	0	0	0	0	0	0	0	0	0
29 DRUGS, COSMETICS	0	0	0	0	0	0	0	0	0
30 PAINT, ALLIED PRDTS.	0	0	0	0	0	0	0	0	0
31 PETROLEUM, RELATED INDS.	0	0	0	0	0	0	0	0	0
32 RUBBER, MISC. PLASTICS	105	782	380	780	782	68	2191	444	180
33 LEATHER TANNING, PRDTS.	0	0	0	0	0	0	0	0	0
34 FOOTWEAR, LEATHER PRDTS.	0	0	0	0	0	0	0	0	0
35 GLASS, GLASS PRDTS.	0	0	0	0	0	0	0	0	0
36 STONE, CLAY PRDTS.	0	0	0	0	0	0	0	0	0
37 PRIMARY IRON, STEEL MFR.	0	0	0	0	0	0	0	0	0
38 PRIMARY NONFERROUS MFR.	0	0	0	0	0	0	0	0	0

#	Industry									
39	METAL CONTAINERS	114	3074	197	3796	1530	64	2681	223	641
40	FABRICATED METAL PRDTS.	2338	31729	17248	60652	23863	3280	59662	16669	6522
41	SCREW MACH. PRDTS., ETC.	0	0	0	0	0	0	0	0	0
42	OTHER FAB. METAL PRDTS.	1023	13495	2031	44142	7554	484	20282	2793	2522
43	ENGINES, TURBINES	2464	19419	9431	20027	19112	1605	51557	10235	4812
44	FARM MACH., EQUIP.	3911	36502	29590	133441	121011	22926	95015	44322	28431
45	CONSTRUC. MACH., EQUIP.	5155	72712	95029	309480	33745	18766	113194	66907	18719
46	MATERIAL HANDLING MACH.	3784	36261	8008	94192	26086	1727	65315	9470	12242
47	METALWORKING MACHINERY	11920	103016	6933	264931	46870	2006	217070	18788	22408
48	SPECIAL MACH., EQUIP.	14395	135711	9511	202468	180322	2714	193602	18389	49276
49	GENERAL MACH., EQUIP.	7016	80375	15988	188880	57630	3646	150749	20205	19040
50	MACHINE SHOP PRDTS.	31587	391157	49825	1566272	220269	17248	600027	95332	84537
51	OFFICE, COMPUT. MACHINES	8533	140190	14445	379886	75537	5831	146401	23472	29914
52	SERVICE IND. MACHINES	11534	107203	30838	190588	103975	8805	250297	48359	28400
53	ELECT. TRANSMISS. EQUIP.	823	10935	1629	27016	7916	780	12545	3004	2448
54	HOUSEHOLD APPLIANCES	551	5792	1733	12883	5121	533	12251	2247	1590
55	ELECTRIC LIGHTING EQUIP.	7935	224460	51377	537546	199502	27757	348957	104017	73467
56	RADIO, TV, ETC., EQUIP.	1008	11120	1407	35072	7110	650	30004	3077	2661
57	ELECTRONIC COMPONENTS	979	10746	1231	22562	7352	490	21900	2449	3588
58	MISC. ELECTRICAL MACH.	31261	519868	96655	1351209	329353	38299	590357	114876	156213
59	MOTOR VEHICLES, EQUIP.	5451	201494	13048	253908	82098	6081	147041	15409	45391
60	AIRCRAFT, PARTS	6052	209909	36826	294090	101164	12940	176977	39382	115981
61	OTHER TRANSPORT. EQUIP.	6225	56560	12429	143941	41875	2615	115346	17825	11360
62	PROFESS., SCIEN. INSTRU.	10071	120423	21359	534483	67117	6062	166926	28986	25800
63	MEDICAL, PHOTO. EQUIP.	1942	23076	2502	131164	13101	816	31371	3746	5414
64	MISC. MANUFACTURING	5920	74082	17872	198890	53799	5682	111796	21471	20089
65	TRANSPORT., WAREHOUSING	823	43429	11528	107929	42792	6458	62193	23519	15571
66	COMMUNICA.,EXC. BRDCAST.	0	0	0	0	0	0	0	0	0
67	RADIO, TV BROADCASTING	0	0	0	0	0	0	0	0	0
68	ELEC.,GAS,WATER,SAN.SER.	32555	440104	91754	1206016	309018	32390	617695	116018	119232
69	WHOLESALE, RETAIL TRADE	10530	35628	28460	635325	77036	10143	138428	65929	38468
70	FINANCE, INSURANCE	0	0	0	0	0	0	0	0	0
71	REAL ESTATE, RENTAL	0	0	0	0	0	0	0	0	0
72	HOTELS, PERSONAL SERV.	0	0	0	0	0	0	0	0	0
73	BUSINESS SERVICES	0	0	0	0	0	0	0	0	0
74	RESEARCH, DEVELOPMENT	0	0	0	0	0	0	0	0	0
75	AUTO. REPAIR, SERVICES	0	0	0	0	0	0	0	0	0
76	AMUSEMENTS	0	0	0	0	0	0	0	0	0
77	MED.,EDUC. SERVICES	0	0	0	0	0	0	0	0	0
78	FEDERAL GOVT. ENTERPRISE	0	0	0	0	0	0	0	0	0
79	STATE, LOCAL GOVT. ENT.	0	0	0	0	0	0	0	0	0
80	IMPORTS	0	0	0	0	0	0	0	0	0
81	BUS.TRAVEL, ENT., GIFTS.	1839	0	0	0	0	0	0	0	0
82	OFFICE SUPPLIES	0	0	0	0	0	0	0	0	0
83	SCRAP, USED GOODS	24257	24257	11003	53618	15822	2727	40935	13286	6595
84	GOVERNMENT INDUSTRY	0	0	0	0	0	0	0	0	0
85	REST OF WORLD INDUSTRY	0	0	0	0	0	0	0	0	0
86	HOUSEHOLD INDUSTRY	0	0	0	0	0	0	0	0	0
87	INVENTORY VALUATION ADJ.	0	0	0	0	0	0	0	0	0
88	STATE TOTAL	470016	5997609	1419093	15409869	3935616	451425	8412608	1845599	1619817

159

STATE ESTIMATES OF 1980
GROSS PRIVATE CAPITAL FORMATION
(THOUSANDS OF 1958 DOLLARS)

INDUSTRY TITLE	37 PENNSYL-VANIA	38 RHODE ISLAND	39 SOUTH CAROLINA	40 SOUTH DAKOTA	41 TENNESSEE	42 TEXAS	43 UTAH	44 VERMONT	45 VIRGINIA
1 LIVESTOCK, PRDTS.	0	0	0	0	0	0	0	0	0
2 OTHER AGRICULTURE PRDTS.	0	0	0	0	0	0	0	0	0
3 FORESTRY, FISHERIES	0	0	0	0	0	0	0	0	0
4 AGRI.,FORES.,FISH. SERV.	0	0	0	0	0	0	0	0	0
5 IRON, FERRO. ORES MINING	0	0	0	0	0	0	0	0	0
6 NONFERROUS ORES MINING	0	0	0	0	0	0	0	0	0
7 COAL MINING	0	0	0	0	0	0	0	0	0
8 CRUDE PETRO.,NATURAL GAS	0	0	0	0	0	0	0	0	0
9 STONE, CLAY MINING	0	0	0	0	0	0	0	0	0
10 CHEM.,FERT. MIN. MINING	0	0	0	0	0	0	0	0	0
11 NEW CONSTRUCTION	2929613	224901	711309	158909	1126469	4793335	552843	110934	1536240
12 MAINT., REPAIR CONSTR.	0	0	0	0	0	0	0	0	0
13 ORDNANCE, ACCESSORIES	0	0	0	0	0	0	0	0	0
14 FOOD, KINDRED PRDTS.	0	0	0	0	0	0	0	0	0
15 TOBACCO MANUFACTURES	0	0	0	0	0	0	0	0	0
16 FABRICS	0	0	0	0	0	0	0	0	0
17 TEXTILE PRDTS.	6710	458	1372	250	2597	8460	981	239	2679
18 APPAREL	0	0	0	0	0	0	0	0	0
19 MISC. TEXTILE PRDTS.	0	0	0	0	0	0	0	0	0
20 LUMBER, WOOD PRDTS.	272	13	30	26	116	230	26	11	112
21 WOODEN CONTAINERS	0	0	0	0	0	0	0	0	0
22 HOUSEHOLD FURNITURE	11332	758	2142	635	4018	14531	1394	580	4850
23 OTHER FURNITURE	107053	7924	20796	4753	38609	139240	14482	3688	41830
24 PAPER, ALLIED PRDTS	0	0	0	0	0	0	0	0	0
25 PAPERBOARD CONTAINERS	0	0	0	0	0	0	0	0	0
26 PRINTING, PUBLISHING	0	0	0	0	0	0	0	0	0
27 CHEMICALS,SELECT. PRDTS.	0	0	0	0	0	0	0	0	0
28 PLASTICS, SYNTHETICS	0	0	0	0	0	0	0	0	0
29 DRUGS, COSMETICS	0	0	0	0	0	0	0	0	0
30 PAINT, ALLIED PRDTS.	0	0	0	0	0	0	0	0	0
31 PETROLEUM, RELATED INDS.	0	0	0	0	0	0	0	0	0
32 RUBBER, MISC. PLASTICS	1301	44	378	57	526	2676	381	16	831
33 LEATHER TANNING, PRDTS.	0	0	0	0	0	0	0	0	0
34 FOOTWEAR, LEATHER PRDTS.	0	0	0	0	0	0	0	0	0
35 GLASS, GLASS PRDTS.	0	0	0	0	0	0	0	0	0
36 STONE, CLAY PRDTS.	0	0	0	0	0	0	0	0	0
37 PRIMARY IRON, STEEL MFR.	0	0	0	0	0	0	0	0	0
38 PRIMARY NONFERROUS MFR.	0	0	0	0	0	0	0	0	0

Industry									
39 METAL CONTAINERS	2971	154	368	245	1176	2819	295	111	1226
40 FABRICATED METAL PRDTS.	44031	2823	17020	1337	28351	133121	10418	857	20205
41 SCREW MACH. PRDTS., ETC.	0	1172	0	0	0	0	0	0	0
42 OTHER FAB. METAL PRDTS.	16539	1179	4219	473	7237	22884	2595	476	6520
43 ENGINES, TURBINES	30970	2733	9431	1448	12931	62830	9000	418	19569
44 FARM MACH., EQUIP.	77769	4434	25326	50218	44209	226996	13833	10130	40366
45 CONSTRUC. MACH., EQUIP.	77042	13323	19218	5079	40753	324593	40522	2218	50817
46 MATERIAL HANDLING MACH.	46085	3594	13323	1413	20866	66379	8065	1486	20462
47 METALWORKING MACHINERY	168073	11432	22604	2116	46001	132432	19424	4793	44566
48 SPECIAL MACH., EQUIP.	144333	14447	132413	4827	103810	220396	15179	4028	83256
49 GENERAL MACH., EQUIP.	107329	9557	40849	2710	64628	212332	18425	2732	43419
50 MACHINE SHOP PRDTS.	0	0	0	0	0	0	0	0	0
51 OFFICE, COMPUT. MACHINES	460418	35794	106820	16248	202754	692332	65652	14716	183565
52 SERVICE IND. MACHINES	136541	8692	28264	5171	48527	174581	16160	3714	56504
53 ELECT. TRANSMISS. EQUIP.	155449	9055	48882	8552	77114	269400	40839	2359	98070
54 HOUSEHOLD APPLIANCES	12738	822	2741	925	4678	16233	1466	343	5187
55 ELECTRIC LIGHTING EQUIP.	7659	530	2200	716	3411	13406	1699	251	4093
56 RADIO, TV, ETC., EQUIP.	213309	21781	95503	20935	178284	525196	64688	3297	162316
57 ELECTRONIC COMPONENTS	12741	1254	3359	541	6916	19840	2055	323	7233
58 MISC. ELECTRICAL MACH.	12198	1400	3520	488	5996	15860	2272	386	6132
59 MOTOR VEHICLES, EQUIP.	497685	37634	108562	47160	218255	721917	86283	23089	250619
60 AIRCRAFT, PARTS	129008	12699	22401	2436	53639	88011	21014	4187	76988
61 OTHER TRANSPORT. EQUIP.	143938	13287	35611	8922	64112	228008	30516	4406	89938
62 PROFESS., SCIEN. INSTRU.	78139	5670	27378	2228	47184	165373	14648	2720	33134
63 MEDICAL, PHOTO. EQUIP.	142141	10520	34428	5427	67418	232513	19910	6610	50018
64 MISC. MANUFACTURING	23784	1976	5918	1221	10475	31059	3327	1308	9261
65 TRANSPORT., WAREHOUSING	84792	6260	24357	6342	39648	140130	15976	3119	40205
66 COMMUNICA.,EXC. BRDCAST.	39957	3583	20469	4631	38520	115300	13891	431	34262
67 RADIO, TV BROADCASTING	0	0	0	0	0	0	0	0	0
68 ELEC.,GAS,WATER,SAN.SER.	0	0	0	0	0	0	0	0	0
69 WHOLESALE, RETAIL TRADE	490717	35501	132127	39160	222102	779344	83315	18731	224556
70 FINANCE, INSURANCE	0	0	0	0	0	0	0	0	0
71 REAL ESTATE, RENTAL	77433	12367	28574	10251	57923	352872	19798	3082	58876
72 HOTELS, PERSONAL SERV.	0	0	0	0	0	0	0	0	0
73 BUSINESS SERVICES	0	0	0	0	0	0	0	0	0
74 RESEARCH, DEVELOPMENT	0	0	0	0	0	0	0	0	0
75 AUTO. REPAIR, SERVICES	0	0	0	0	0	0	0	0	0
76 AMUSEMENTS	0	0	0	0	0	0	0	0	0
77 MED.,EDUC. SERVICES	0	0	0	0	0	0	0	0	0
78 FEDERAL GOVT. ENTERPRISE	0	0	0	0	0	0	0	0	0
79 STATE, LOCAL GOVT. ENT.	0	0	0	0	0	0	0	0	0
80 IMPORTS	0	0	0	0	0	0	0	0	0
81 BUS.,TRAVEL, ENT., GIFTS.	0	0	0	0	0	0	0	0	0
82 OFFICE SUPPLIES	0	0	0	0	0	0	0	0	0
83 SCRAP, USED GOODS	34149	2061	6849	1617	11001	73182	7071	951	13825
84 GOVERNMENT INDUSTRY	0	0	0	0	0	0	0	0	0
85 REST OF WORLD INDUSTRY	0	0	0	0	0	0	0	0	0
86 HOUSEHOLD INDUSTRY	0	0	0	0	0	0	0	0	0
87 INVENTORY VALUATION ADJ.	0	0	0	0	0	0	0	0	0
88 STATE TOTAL	6524119	506509	1758761	417467	2900254	1101811	1218443	236739	3321131

TABLE B-4

STATE ESTIMATES OF 1980
GROSS PRIVATE CAPITAL FORMATION
(THOUSANDS OF 1958 DOLLARS)

INDUSTRY TITLE	46 WASHINGTON	47 WEST VIRGINIA	48 WISCONSIN	49 WYOMING	50 ALASKA	51 HAWAII	52 NO STATE ALLOCATION	53 NATIONAL TOTAL
1 LIVESTOCK, PRDTS.	0	0	0	0	0	0	0	0
2 OTHER AGRICULTURE PRDTS.	0	0	0	0	0	0	0	0
3 FORESTRY, FISHERIES	0	0	0	0	0	0	0	0
4 AGRI.,FORES.,FISH. SERV.	0	0	0	0	0	0	0	0
5 IRON, FERRO. ORES MINING	0	0	0	0	0	0	0	0
6 NONFERROUS ORES MINING	0	0	0	0	0	0	0	0
7 COAL MINING	0	0	0	0	0	0	0	0
8 CRUDE PETRO.,NATURAL GAS	0	0	0	0	0	0	0	0
9 STONE, CLAY MINING	0	0	0	0	0	0	0	0
10 CHEM.,FERT. MIN. MINING	0	0	0	0	0	0	0	0
11 NEW CONSTRUCTION	964008	408701	1319497	362626	128983	341883	0	74246000
12 MAINT., REPAIR CONSTR.	0	0	0	0	0	0	0	0
13 ORDNANCE, ACCESSORIES	0	0	0	0	0	0	0	0
14 FOOD, KINDRED PRDTS.	0	0	0	0	0	0	0	0
15 TOBACCO MANUFACTURES	0	0	0	0	0	0	0	0
16 FABRICS	0	0	0	0	0	0	0	0
17 TEXTILE PRDTS.	2205	792	2728	281	275	857	0	165994
18 APPAREL	0	0	0	0	0	0	0	0
19 MISC. TEXTILE PRDTS.	83	15	152	2	12	58	0	4996
20 LUMBER, WOOD PRDTS.	0	0	0	0	0	0	0	0
21 WOODEN CONTAINERS	0	0	0	0	0	0	0	0
22 HOUSEHOLD FURNITURE	3384	963	4338	557	542	2025	0	278000
23 OTHER FURNITURE	34019	12148	40668	3468	3991	13682	0	2525002
24 PAPER, ALLIED PRDTS.	0	0	0	0	0	0	0	0
25 PAPERBOARD CONTAINERS	0	0	0	0	0	0	0	0
26 PRINTING, PUBLISHING	0	0	0	0	0	0	0	0
27 CHEMICALS,SELECT. PRDTS.	0	0	0	0	0	0	0	0
28 PLASTICS, SYNTHETICS	0	0	0	0	0	0	0	0
29 DRUGS, COSMETICS	0	0	0	0	0	0	0	0
30 PAINT, ALLIED PRDTS.	0	0	0	0	0	0	0	0
31 PETROLEUM, RELATED INDS.	0	0	0	0	0	0	0	0
32 RUBBER, MISC. PLASTICS	168	509	684	308	47	134	0	33997
33 LEATHER TANNING, PRDTS.	0	0	0	0	0	0	0	0
34 FOOTWEAR, LEATHER PRDTS.	0	0	0	0	0	0	0	0
35 GLASS, GLASS PRDTS.	0	0	0	0	0	0	0	0
36 STONE, CLAY PRDTS.	0	0	0	0	0	0	0	0
37 PRIMARY IRON, STEEL MFR.	0	0	0	0	0	0	0	0
38 PRIMARY NONFERROUS MFR.	0	0	0	0	0	0	0	0

39 METAL CONTAINERS		153	1508	28	130	569	0	57996
40 FABRICATED METAL PRDTS.		19110	17484	11205	1570	4275	0	1179992
41 SCREW MACH. PRDTS., ETC.	901	0	0	0	0	0	0	0
42 OTHER FAB. METAL PRDTS.	1.951	4199	6579	928	566	1757	0	381000
43 ENGINES, TURBINES	527C	11972	16194	7237	1114	3225	0	811001
44 FARM MACH., EQUIP.	.582	8345	92757	14278	2019	33043	0	3273004
45 CONSTRUC. MACH., EQUIP.	4.607	39000	34887	59795	7839	14954	0	3222012
46 MATERIAL HANDLING MACH.	29529	10579	25863	4430	1579	4064	0	1110000
47 METALWCRKING MACHINERY	15966	28907	98640	2864	2002	5405	0	3024998
48 SPECIAL MACH., EQUIP.	38325	34987	97855	4473	6642	13531	0	3550013
49 GENERAL MACH., EQUIP.	6041E	41191	47930	8916	3081	8285	0	2528001
50 MACHINE SHOP PRDTS.	4.110S	0	0	0	0	0	0	0
51 OFFICE, COMPUT. MACHINES	16324C	80121	217461	16273	16223	56053	0	11610057
52 SERVICE IND. MACHINES	44618	11211	54771	2693	5766	16935	0	317002
53 ELECT. TRANSMISS. EQUIP.	35944	48457	69685	19287	4597	18857	0	4065031
54 HOUSEHOLD APPLIANCES	3855	971	4732	588	398	1887	0	281997
55 ELECTRIC LIGHTING EQUIP.	.983	1989	4508	1098	289	1073	0	206998
56 RADIO, TV, ETC., EQUIP.	9925	55259	53673	16338	6698	43768	0	7119009
57 ELECTRONIC COMPONENTS	3704	2557	11638	496	325	1337	0	376997
58 MISC. ELECTRICAL MACH.	3907	2602	7007	489	408	1264	0	305996
59 MOTOR VEHICLES, EQUIP.	175044	73797	234137	38736	31409	92524	0	13347060
60 AIRCRAFT, PARTS	38844	17444	63522	4019	11991	21270	0	3043006
61 OTHER TRANSPORT. EQUIP.	77232	24250	70641	19547	30177	29035	0	4092002
62 PROFESS., SCIEN. INSTRU.	28368	29773	36597	8194	2231	6326	0	1935002
63 MEDICAL, PHOTO. EQUIP.	44993	29524	49624	9517	5357	18368	0	3569017
64 MISC. MANUFACTURING	8342	4128	10025	612	1206	3831	0	674001
65 TRANSPORT., WAREHOUSING	28966	18729	42725	9123	3870	11703	0	221304
66 COMMUNICA.,EXC. BRDCAST.	20839	11309	5092	3485	1139	9611	0	1448004
67 RADIO, TV BROADCASTING	0	0	0	0	0	0	0	0
68 ELEC.,GAS,WATER,SAN.SER.	169681	95571	242728	43343	22270	69956	0	12654068
69 WHOLESALE, RETAIL TRADE	0	0	0	0	0	0	0	0
70 FINANCE, INSURANCE	42981	7325	64243	6681	6660	36385	0	4063018
71 REAL ESTATE, RENTAL	0	0	0	0	0	0	0	0
72 HOTELS, PERSONAL SERV.	0	0	0	0	0	0	0	0
73 BUSINESS SERVICES	0	0	0	0	0	0	0	0
74 RESEARCH, DEVELOPMENT	0	0	0	0	0	0	0	0
75 AUTO. REPAIR, SERVICES	0	0	0	0	0	0	0	0
76 AMUSEMENTS	0	0	0	0	0	0	0	0
77 MED.,EDUC. SERVICES	0	0	0	0	0	0	0	0
78 FEDERAL GOVT. ENTERPRISE	0	0	0	0	0	0	0	0
79 STATE, LOCAL GOVT. ENT.	0	0	0	0	0	0	0	0
80 IMPORTS	0	0	0	0	0	0	50000	50000
81 BUS.TRAVEL, ENT., GIFTS.	0	0	0	0	0	0	0	0
82 OFFICE SUPPLIES	0	0	0	0	0	0	0	0
83 SCRAP, USED GOODS	8878	7071	12969	7420	1395	3203	0	792000
84 GOVERNMENT INDUSTRY	0	0	0	0	0	0	0	0
85 REST OF WORLD INDUSTRY	0	0	0	0	0	0	0	0
86 HOUSEHCLD INDUSTRY	0	0	0	0	0	0	0	0
87 INVENTCRY VALUATION ADJ.	0	0	0	0	0	0	0	0
88 STATE TOTAL	226019E	1143659	3063542	689336	312801	891133	50000	171410275

TABLE B-5

STATE ESTIMATES OF 1970
NET INVENTORY CHANGE
(THOUSANDS OF 1958 DOLLARS)

INDUSTRY TITLE	1 ALABAMA	2 ARIZONA	3 ARKANSAS	4 CALIFORNIA	5 COLORADO	6 CONNECTICUT	7 DELAWARE	8 DISTRICT OF COLUMBIA	9 FLORIDA
1 LIVESTOCK, PRDTS.	3501	1943	1900	12664	4109	372	459	0	2769
2 OTHER AGRICULTURE PRDTS.	0	21223	13540	68925	0	589	2520	0	50547
3 FORESTRY, FISHERIES	415	85	326	1712	11	28	23	0	630
4 AGRI.,FORES.,FISH. SERV.	2064	1176	3068	5251	119	113	153	0	1661
5 IRON, FERRO. ORES MINING	612	64	55	3471	6416	0		0	0
6 NONFERROUS ORES MINING	56	11317	642	124	4406	24		0	308
7 COAL MINING	440	0	0	0	95	0		0	0
8 CRUDE PETRO.,NATURAL GAS	494	8	233	3349	2723	0		0	31
9 STONE, CLAY MINING	863	590	2077	7202	940	736	16	0	2860
10 CHEM.,FERT. MIN. MINING	0	0	0	0	0	0	0	0	0
11 NEW CONSTRUCTION	0	0	0	0	0	0	0	0	0
12 MAINT., REPAIR CONSTR.	0	0	0	0	0	0	0	0	0
13 ORDNANCE, ACCESSORIES	2335	3154	4	59599	1296	350	0	0	7118
14 FOOD, KINDRED PRDTS.	5396	2207	5312	47804	6459	3587	681	616	15311
15 TOBACCO MANUFACTURES	37	0	0	0	0	48	0	0	188
16 FABRICS	1819	1	101	180	0	328	188	0	43
17 TEXTILE PRDTS.	1750	8	1384	9909	19	1471	367	2	83
18 APPAREL	9135	736	2064	16251	251	638	1310	14	2916
19 MISC. TEXTILE PRDTS.	787	68	4	4178	80	273	87	11	409
20 LUMBER, WOOD PRDTS.	218	334	521	6792	144	113	46		398
21 WOODEN CONTAINERS	496	254	759	5867	67	101	9		1361
22 HOUSEHOLD FURNITURE	2224	604	5169	21212	893	2251	9	97	5151
23 OTHER FURNITURE	275	179	922	6787	179	1308	55	28	771
24 PAPER, ALLIED PRDTS.	9222	111	6160	15482	92	1320	106	426	9883
25 PAPERBOARD CONTAINERS	865	181	2653	22592	216	937	96	20	3509
26 PRINTING, PUBLISHING	818	777	526	13123	1276	1911	282	2732	3348
27 CHEMICALS,SELECT. PRDTS.	4366	771	1864	9705	743	1118	1093	25	8653
28 PLASTICS, SYNTHETICS	9373	0	20	8955	33	3817	4680	33	12223
29 DRUGS, COSMETICS	182	38	6	25328	645	14142	1513	10	1348
30 PAINT, ALLIED PRDTS.	116	22	37	1838	88	8	9	18	464
31 PETROLEUM, RELATED INDS.	1514	16	2222	30989	2862	638	13057	18	971
32 RUBBER, MISC. PLASTICS	8110	278	1838	18613	6223	4770	2538	4	534
33 LEATHER TANNING, PRDTS.	0	0	0	166	2	0	178	0	381
34 FOOTWEAR, LEATHER PRDTS.	113	11	1590	715	803	706	162	0	457
35 GLASS, GLASS PRDTS.	175	24	77	3278	10	101	13	2	
36 STONE, CLAY PRDTS.	1491	3714	1484	33860	4397	2254	1003	1250	14360
37 PRIMARY IRON, STEEL MFR.	9243	85	16	13341	2413	1458	709	0	491
38 PRIMARY NONFERROUS MFR.	8658	11921	1558	15312	108	6317	167	0	1726

	A	B	C	D	E	F	G	H	I
39 METAL CONTAINERS	220	0	0	17763	1360	0	0	0	4203
40 FABRICATED METAL PRDTS.	2628	864	1198	18039	1052	501	733	93	7405
41 SCREW MACH. PRDTS., ETC.	1396	42	312	11685	1043	4234	82	0	680
42 OTHER FAB. METAL PRDTS.	1523	180	994	17724	114	3728	274	10	1375
43 ENGINES, TURBINES	0	0	0	423	420	1075	107	0	81
44 FARM MACH., EQUIP.	2302	572	183	4136	1532	420	15	0	1325
45 CONSTRUC. MACH., EQUIP.	141	7	7	3670	33	48	0	0	37
46 MATERIAL HANDLING MACH.	264	0	264	3634	22	15	15	0	231
47 METALWORKING MACHINERY	67	54	106	3120	152	33	215	0	229
48 SPECIAL MACH., EQUIP.	1143	9	67	7348	415	1848	5	13	1064
49 GENERAL MACH., EQUIP.	88	58	344	10155	508	2257	32	0	109
50 MACHINE SHOP PRDTS.	316	315	95	5674	14	5158	0	52	1178
51 OFFICE, COMPUT. MACHINES	1	980	166	6565	19	1111	16	13	807
52 SERVICE IND. MACHINES	83	360	1978	1278	1996	1130	1	1	63
53 ELECT. TRANSMISS. EQUIP.	597	58	275	16445	13	114	116	37	280
54 HOUSEHOLD APPLIANCES	2	1	1693	5000	37	3484	99	2	53
55 ELECTRIC LIGHTING EQUIP.	487	10		3404	19	1763	4	10	142
56 RADIO, TV, ETC., EQUIP.	56	2058		52426	45	773	20	28	5923
57 ELECTRONIC COMPONENTS	513	1970		20536	153	1064	119	11	843
58 MISC. ELECTRICAL MACH.	183	3		1165		3222	0	1	648
59 MOTOR VEHICLES, EQUIP.	7166	5930		0		404	0	0	0
60 AIRCRAFT, PARTS	1477	94	27	14640		0	207	0	5723
61 OTHER TRANSPORT. EQUIP.	60	1139	1399	13639	108	3978	29	2	4525
62 PROFESS., SCIEN. INSTRU.	0	0	1911	16388	540	3615	431	13	1014
63 MEDICAL, PHOTO. EQUIP.	0	23		2917		1159	3	7	548
64 MISC. MANUFACTURING	112	45	302	2776	93	717	3	13	270
65 TRANSPORT., WAREHOUSING	472	573	588	11579	1611	1242	38	912	4376
66 COMMUNICA.,EXC. BROCAST.	0	0	0	0	0	0	0	0	0
67 RADIO, TV BROADCASTING	0	0	0	0	0	0	0	0	0
68 ELEC.,GAS,WATER,SAN.SER.	0	0	0	0	0	0	0	0	0
69 WHOLESALE, RETAIL TRADE	2078	1963	644	26358	2206	2516	800	581	8759
70 FINANCE, INSURANCE	0	0	0	0	0	0	0	0	0
71 REAL ESTATE, RENTAL	0	0	0	0	0	0	0	0	0
72 HOTELS, PERSONAL SERV.	0	0	0	0	0	0	0	0	0
73 BUSINESS SERVICES	0	0	0	0	0	0	0	0	0
74 RESEARCH, DEVELOPMENT	0	0	0	0	0	0	0	0	0
75 AUTO. REPAIR, SERVICES	0	0	0	0	503	0	0	0	0
76 AMUSEMENTS	172	0	0	0	0	0	74	78	1068
77 MED.,EDUC. SERVICES	0	0	0	0	0	0	0	0	0
78 FEDERAL GOVT. ENTERPRISE	0	0	0	0	0	0	0	0	0
79 STATE, LOCAL GOVT. ENT.	0	0	0	0	0	0	0	0	0
80 IMPORTS	0	0	0	0	0	0	0	0	0
81 BUS.TRAVEL, ENT., GIFTS.	0	0	0	0	0	0	0	0	0
82 OFFICE SUPPLIES	0	0	0	0	0	0	0	0	0
83 SCRAP, USED GOODS	0	0	0	0	0	0	0	0	0
84 GOVERNMENT INDUSTRY	0	0	0	0	0	0	0	0	0
85 REST OF WORLD INDUSTRY	0	0	0	0	0	0	0	0	0
86 HOUSEHOLD INDUSTRY	0	0	0	0	0	0	0	0	0
87 INVENTORY VALUATION ADJ.	0	0	0	0	0	0	0	0	0
88 STATE TOTAL	110539	79388	72001	788434	76945	97013	34963	7133	203859

TABLE B-5

STATE ESTIMATES OF 1970
NET INVENTORY CHANGE
(THOUSANDS OF 1958 DOLLARS)

INDUSTRY TITLE	10 GEORGIA	11 IDAHO	12 ILLINOIS	13 INDIANA	14 IOWA	15 KANSAS	16 KENTUCKY	17 LOUISIANA	18 MAINE
1 LIVESTOCK, PRDTS.	5067	1371	4346	1195	6861	4065	987	1023	1231
2 OTHER AGRICULTURE PRDTS.	6122	4207		14644		1032	6881	8462	0
3 FORESTRY, FISHERIES	1115	195	42	27	11	287	60	646	370
4 AGRI., FORES., FISH. SERV.	3640	211	747	413	606	0	162	639	613
5 IRON, FERRO. ORES MINING	92	49	0	0	0	0	0	0	0
6 NONFERROUS ORES MINING	4	676	662	0	0	2	0	0	4
7 COAL MINING	2	4	999	164	12	17	1820	0	0
8 CRUDE PETRO., NATURAL GAS	0	0	728	346	0	2096	624	42016	0
9 STONE, CLAY MINING	3166	256	3050	922	1744	733	2103	1221	21
10 CHEM., FERT. MIN. MINING	0	0	0	0	0	0	0	0	0
11 NEW CONSTRUCTION	0	0	0	0	0	0	0	0	0
12 MAINT., REPAIR CONSTR.	0	0	0	0	0	0	0	0	0
13 ORDNANCE, ACCESSORIES	40	10	258	1233	2350	0	0		385
14 FOOD, KINDRED PRDTS.	11079	2225	7464	8431	12762	79	3026	2141	2485
15 TOBACCO MANUFACTURES	47	0	96	0	7	2	5917	84	0
16 FABRICS	5066	0	57	449	9	5	21	0	357
17 TEXTILE PRDTS.	47951	0	2768	379	73	27	27	53	240
18 APPAREL	13698	19	1209	466	171	655	3937	610	866
19 MISC. TEXTILE PRDTS.	2264	21	2965	1068	105	67	472	200	83
20 LUMBER, WOOD PRDTS.	229	1244	461	64	233	27	118	161	745
21 WOODEN CONTAINERS	2671	67	209		1192	14	1665	236	32
22 HOUSEHOLD FURNITURE	4143	51	5444	9443	592	616	1630	450	335
23 OTHER FURNITURE	303	14	2685	1859	1031	344	234	41	41
24 PAPER, ALLIED PRDTS.	17965	1179	6927	2942	2611	100	1113	4059	5247
25 PAPERBOARD CONTAINERS	8817	142	12527	1976	1041	2880	1836	1103	404
26 PRINTING, PUBLISHING	1957	177	10755	2724	1806	840	1073	743	129
27 CHEMICALS, SELECT. PRDTS.	2404	3299	9566	5668	6864	2306	9654	11986	136
28 PLASTICS, SYNTHETICS	1472	0	5172	1162	2191	1386	14666	5226	4
29 DRUGS, COSMETICS	5615	0	44617	11181	150	3890	309	541	2
30 PAINT, ALLIED PRDTS.	491	2	2072	97	145	46	439	73	101
31 PETROLEUM, RELATED INDS.	987	0	17307	2431	4400	5584	5160	36046	1291
32 RUBBER, MISC. PLASTICS	2442	10	19908	15632	0	3677	769	215	366
33 LEATHER TANNING, PRDTS.	47	0	61	0	1	0	25	3	
34 FOOTWEAR, LEATHER PRDTS.	816	15	0	519		7	76	0	3979
35 GLASS, GLASS PRDTS.	807	0	3880	904		28	523	382	6
36 STONE, CLAY PRDTS.	2735	570	11117	9417	3367	5586	2223	7180	587
37 PRIMARY IRON, STEEL MFR.	324	12	17050	29051	1070	244	3308	604	2
38 PRIMARY NONFERROUS MFR.	1440	2492	12225	18631	7495	323	976	5129	24

39	METAL CONTAINERS	2513	217	807	594	0	746	430	3549	705
40	FABRICATED METAL PRDTS.	4235	351	8346	6455	1841	1638	561	2390	142
41	SCREW MACH. PRDTS., ETC.	1702	34	20176	6888	893	168	1587	84	5
42	OTHER FAB. METAL PRDTS.	708	0	13300	7349	2040	750	3775	665	59
43	ENGINES, TURBINES	5	0	3611	1140	835	0	0	18	0
44	FARM MACH., EQUIP.	4953	801	17994	5876	84738	5815	12744	1580	86
45	CONSTRUC. MACH., EQUIP.	752	7	56743	2168	2575	274	15	858	340
46	MATERIAL HANDLING MACH.	495	33	2180	99	132	264	231	66	0
47	METALWORKING MACHINERY	120	3	4185	1261	180	105	106	0	31
48	SPECIAL MACH., EQUIP.	2510	43	10241	1127	843	836	1107	614	123
49	GENERAL MACH., EQUIP.	400	0	8136	7641	419	920	1597	25	55
50	MACHINE SHOP PRDTS.	284	47	2030	1628	88	716	1151	429	103
51	OFFICE, COMPUT. MACHINES	39	0	1250	26	0	3	1435	8	13
52	SERVICE IND. MACHINES	208	7	1626	496	432	315	861	64	63
53	ELECT. TRANSMISS. EQUIP.	3801	0	12545	4519	1230	69	2194	48	2
54	HOUSEHOLD APPLIANCES	44	0	9031	5570	3050	3	15084	9	131
55	ELECTRIC LIGHTING EQUIP.	559	0	2857	1264	8	7	1268	13	104
56	RADIO, TV, ETC., EQUIP.	15	0	15460	11931	6101	93	614	11	330
57	ELECTRONIC COMPONENTS	36	13	4397	2364	1271	446	403	9	52
58	MISC. ELECTRICAL MACH.	250	0	1400	6569	318	610	52	13	0
59	MOTOR VEHICLES, EQUIP.	0	0	0	0	0	0	0	0	0
60	AIRCRAFT, PARTS	13477	74	5439	0	0	22511	87	2494	724
61	OTHER TRANSPORT. EQUIP.	3069	697	5424	12366	582	1989	948	5175	3367
62	PROFESS., SCIEN. INSTRU.	1178	10	16478	2260	2037	46	401	220	9
63	MEDICAL, PHOTO. EQUIP.	24	24	2357	1658	14	24	33	58	1
64	MISC. MANUFACTURING	497	19	2453	621	285	50	163	96	23
65	TRANSPORT., WAREHOUSING	2324	276	9203	1820	484	216	974	1874	356
66	COMMUNICA.,EXC. BRDCAST.	0	0	0	0	0	0	0	0	0
67	RADIO, TV BROADCASTING	0	0	0	0	0	0	0	0	0
68	ELEC.,GAS,WATER,SAN.SER.	0	0	0	0	0	0	0	0	0
69	WHOLESALE, RETAIL TRADE	5364	423	11667	3191	1337	802	1694	2581	478
70	FINANCE, INSURANCE	0	0	0	0	0	0	0	0	0
71	REAL ESTATE, RENTAL	0	0	0	0	0	0	0	0	0
72	HOTELS, PERSONAL SERV.	0	0	0	0	0	0	0	0	0
73	BUSINESS SERVICES	0	0	0	0	0	0	0	0	0
74	RESEARCH, DEVELOPMENT	0	0	0	0	0	0	0	0	0
75	AUTO. REPAIR, SERVICES	0	0	0	0	0	0	0	0	0
76	AMUSEMENTS	134	170	170	0	0	0	57	134	0
77	MED.,EDUC. SERVICES	0	0	0	0	0	0	0	0	0
78	FEDERAL GOVT. ENTERPRISE	0	0	0	0	0	0	0	0	0
79	STATE, LOCAL GOVT. ENT.	0	0	0	0	0	0	0	0	0
80	IMPORTS	0	0	0	0	0	0	0	0	0
81	BUS.TRAVEL, ENT., GIFTS.	0	0	0	0	0	0	0	0	0
82	OFFICE SUPPLIES	0	0	0	0	0	0	0	0	0
83	SCRAP, USED GOODS	0	0	0	0	0	0	0	0	0
84	GOVERNMENT INDUSTRY	0	0	0	0	0	0	0	0	0
85	REST OF WORLD INDUSTRY	0	0	0	0	0	0	0	0	0
86	HOUSEHOLD INDUSTRY	0	0	0	0	0	0	0	0	0
87	INVENTORY VALUATION ADJ.	0	0	0	0	0	0	0	0	0
88	STATE TOTAL	204635	21571	456881	250316	170630	76358	121405	154365	27391

TABLE B-5

STATE ESTIMATES OF 1970
NET INVENTORY CHANGE
(THOUSANDS OF 1958 DOLLARS)

INDUSTRY TITLE	19 MARYLAND	20 MASSA-CHUSETTS	21 MICHIGAN	22 MINNESOTA	23 MISSISSIPPI	24 MISSOURI	25 MONTANA	26 NEBRASKA	27 NEVADA
1 LIVESTOCK, PRDTS.	1203	33	205	3953	2786	433	1356	4878	132
2 OTHER AGRICULTURE PRDTS.	812	49	15048	1961	7340	29958	1428	2	366
3 FORESTRY, FISHERIES	194	577	108	85	510	62	81	0	0
4 AGRI.,FORES.,FISH. SERV.	650	53	245	795	2358	606	104	261	19
5 IRON, FERRO. ORES MINING	70	0	6106	24677	0	373	190	0	241
6 NONFERROUS ORES MINING	0	0	1774	182	0	288	2212	0	1790
7 COAL MINING	9	0	0	0	0	59	0	0	0
8 CRUDE PETRO.,NATURAL GAS	8	0	199	0	2102	8	3	1436	3
9 STONE, CLAY MINING	1792	236	1952	1082	836	1792	1413	1126	556
10 CHEM.,FERT. MIN. MINING	0	0	0	0	0	0	210	0	0
11 NEW CONSTRUCTION	0	0	0	0	0	0	0	0	0
12 MAINT.,REPAIR CONSTR.	0	0	0	0	0	0	0	0	0
13 ORDNANCE, ACCESSORIES	556	241	3062	302		4608	0	34	0
14 FOOD, KINDRED PRDTS.	5516	5340	11064	3694	4036	6394	308	5099	187
15 TOBACCO MANUFACTURES	11			7	37	104	0	0	0
16 FABRICS	201	868	8	700	2377	1157	0	1	0
17 TEXTILE PRDTS.	22	5520	2026	277	543	478	0	0	0
18 APPAREL	2538	11872	202	222	6212	1768	0	308	7
19 MISC. TEXTILE PRDTS.	595	2325	11239	625	255	271	5	13	6
20 LUMBER, WOOD PRDTS.	363	261	344	154	2225	320	1095	136	33
21 WOODEN CONTAINERS	626	121	96				0	7	0
22 HOUSEHOLD FURNITURE	1675	4973	3003	607	6470	1642	21	281	63
23 OTHER FURNITURE	1680	468	7544	647	358	592	0	248	14
24 PAPER, ALLIED PRDTS.	1746	7419	6849	6922	1073	2800	184	246	2
25 PAPERBOARD CONTAINERS	5531	2068	8035	1780	758	3801	417	417	0
26 PRINTING, PUBLISHING	1732	4224	3619	1333	208	4845	214	636	199
27 CHEMICALS,SELECT. PRDTS.	2018	1447	6037	3457	2338	6059	268	1059	918
28 PLASTICS, SYNTHETICS	1217	7288	7809	876	478	213	0	0	0
29 DRUGS, COSMETICS	11040	3390	13298	6731	2660	13558	9	658	122
30 PAINT, ALLIED PRDTS.	386	276	892	227	9	326	0	15	2
31 PETROLEUM, RELATED INDS.	500	696	7844	1580	2742	6036	4185	48	46
32 RUBBER, MISC. PLASTICS	5792	10550	6138	818	1476	3002	8	760	0
33 LEATHER TANNING, PRDTS.	19	0	72	83	0	57	0	0	0
34 FOOTWEAR, LEATHER PRDTS.	57	1732	632	124	894	625	0	0	0
35 GLASS, GLASS PRDTS.	1165	28	3520	205	296	618	0	5	0
36 STONE, CLAY PRDTS.	5050	938	3755	12079	3765	2233	113	2034	2078
37 PRIMARY IRON, STEEL MFR.	9853	624	27851	620	127	1883	7	65	7
38 PRIMARY NONFERROUS MFR.	10246	4975	7333	235	317	1246	9773	5306	1826

168

	39–88								
39 METAL CONTAINERS	1708	0	630	4933	157	5391	0	1218	0
40 FABRICATED METAL PRDTS.	352	2235	2204	669	1950	3703	157	2453	145
41 SCREW MACH. PRDTS., ETC.	2104	3811	12746	1465	904	1677	4	139	11
42 OTHER FAB. METAL PRDTS.	0	5734	14526	2095	1009	2953	0	379	11
43 ENGINES, TURBINES	20	4131	8213	290	0	115	114	0	0
44 FARM MACH., EQUIP.	44	33	22453	12072	5850	9956	0	5215	15
45 CONSTRUC. MACH. EQUIP.	297	148	1850	1436	592	925	0	170	0
46 MATERIAL HANDLING MACH.	854	198	5814	529	694	529	0	33	7
47 METALWORKING MACHINERY	3478	1555	9593	397	6	530	0	0	3
48 SPECIAL MACH., EQUIP.	286	7711	8766	1062	704	1168	0	5	0
49 GENERAL MACH., EQUIP.	458	2358	5071	1586	20	727	0	61	20
50 MACHINE SHOP PRDTS.	62	1266	1997	1147	279	1690	30	1062	8
51 OFFICE, COMPUT. MACHINES	452	1274	2272	5665	0	223	0	156	17
52 SERVICE IND. MACHINES	989	453	1674	1058	123	1518	0	3	0
53 ELECT. TRANSMISS. EQUIP.	164	2435	1968	917	388	2783	0	10	6
54 HOUSEHOLD APPLIANCES	17	291	2354	2726	1420	434	0	6	10
55 ELECTRIC LIGHTING EQUIP.	17646	678	148	321	1029	938	0	2179	105
56 RADIO, TV, ETC., EQUIP.	236	26245	606	924	264	2885	0	588	4
57 ELECTRONIC COMPONENTS	748	8912	1112	1484	186	232	0	27	2
58 MISC. ELECTRICAL MACH.	0	662	4471	131	58	592	0	5	0
59 MOTOR VEHICLES, EQUIP.	0	0	0	0	0	0	0	0	5
60 AIRCRAFT, PARTS	11296	4461	4078	332	649	32572	61	2288	2
61 OTHER TRANSPORT. EQUIP.	1001	10223	9422	5954	4406	6110	68	1513	0
62 PROFESS., SCIEN. INSTRU.	189	6004	10980	1664	103	2379	0	0	17
63 MEDICAL, PHOTO. EQUIP.	158	1123	136	453	304	219	16	142	320
64 MISC. MANUFACTURING	2023	2764	1138	1749	365	267	112	691	0
65 TRANSPORT., WAREHOUSING	0	0	3801	0	0	3321	0	0	0
66 COMMUNICA.,EXC. BRDCAST.	0	0	0	0	0	0	0	0	0
67 RADIO, TV BROADCASTING	0	0	0	0	0	0	0	0	0
68 ELEC.,GAS,WATER,SAN.SER.	0	0	0	0	0	0	0	0	0
69 WHOLESALE, RETAIL TRADE	3279	4119	7387	2481	786	3940	367	966	608
70 FINANCE, INSURANCE	0	0	0	0	0	0	0	0	0
71 REAL ESTATE, RENTAL	0	0	0	0	0	0	0	0	0
72 HOTELS, PERSONAL SERV.	0	0	0	0	0	0	0	0	0
73 BUSINESS SERVICES	0	0	0	0	0	0	0	0	0
74 RESEARCH, DEVELOPMENT	0	0	0	0	0	0	0	0	0
75 AUTO. REPAIR, SERVICES	0	0	0	0	0	0	0	0	0
76 AMUSEMENTS	269	0	105	0	0	0	0	60	1882
77 MED.,EDUC. SERVICES	0	0	0	0	0	0	0	0	0
78 FEDERAL GOVT. ENTERPRISE	0	0	0	0	0	0	0	0	0
79 STATE, LOCAL GOVT. ENT.	0	0	0	0	0	0	0	0	0
80 IMPORTS	0	0	0	0	0	0	0	0	0
81 BUS.TRAVEL, ENT., GIFTS.	0	0	0	0	0	0	0	0	0
82 OFFICE SUPPLIES	0	0	0	0	0	0	0	0	0
83 SCRAP, USED GOODS	0	0	0	0	0	0	0	0	0
84 GOVERNMENT INDUSTRY	0	0	0	0	0	0	0	0	0
85 REST OF WORLD INDUSTRY	0	0	0	0	0	0	0	0	0
86 HOUSEHOLD INDUSTRY	0	0	0	0	0	0	0	0	0
87 INVENTORY VALUATION ADJ.	0	0	0	0	0	0	0	0	0
88 STATE TOTAL	123006	177415	313425	130579	77828	185989	24115	44461	11791

STATE ESTIMATES OF 1970
NET INVENTORY CHANGE
(THOUSANDS OF 1958 DOLLARS)

INDUSTRY TITLE	28 NEW HAMPSHIRE	29 NEW JERSEY	30 NEW MEXICO	31 NEW YORK	32 NORTH CAROLINA	33 NORTH DAKOTA	34 OHIO	35 OKLAHOMA	36 OREGON
1 LIVESTOCK, PRDTS.	90	481	1497	2043	3375	573	0	1397	729
2 OTHER AGRICULTURE PRDTS.	0	2909	3634	6143	30615	0	17132	83	0
3 FORESTRY, FISHERIES	34	167	34	236	924	1	58	17	4745
4 AGRI.,FORES.,FISH. SERV.	45	93	210	221	1850	136	370	355	310
5 IRON, FERRO. ORES MINING	0	0	246	2291	234	0	0	0	222
6 NONFERROUS ORES MINING	0	243	7639	578	4	60	14	34	20
7 COAL MINING	0	0	0	0	0	66	1152	8	0
8 CRUDE PETRO.,NATURAL GAS	0	96	33	28	0	1759	81	7271	0
9 STONE, CLAY MINING	193	0	8881	2883	1630	236	1171	644	364
10 CHEM.,FERT. MIN. MINING	0	1593	695	0	0	0	0	0	0
11 NEW CONSTRUCTION	0	0	0	0	0	0	0	0	0
12 MAINT., REPAIR CONSTR.	0	0	0	0	0	0	0	0	6
13 ORDNANCE, ACCESSORIES	0	5	2449	210	1209	0	4670	8	0
14 FOOD, KINDRED PRDTS.	576	17949	982	11171	9228	0	14856	33	3663
15 TOBACCO MANUFACTURES	0	0	0	0	4372	0	0	10	0
16 FABRICS	278	477	1	438	19162	0	46	4	241
17 TEXTILE PRDTS.	235	3252	4	4379	6398	0	7130	1196	477
18 APPAREL	1151	13502	78	46666	29536	11	3116	86	1365
19 MISC. TEXTILE PRDTS.	20	4306	106	9195	1138	6	413	26	675
20 LUMBER, WOOD PRDTS.	234	73	1	974	871	0	504	522	8803
21 WOODEN CONTAINERS	72	630	36	237	417	21	175	69	541
22 HOUSEHOLD FURNITURE	878	4647	69	6808	29399	0	4267	473	818
23 OTHER FURNITURE	413	1790	0	4103	2051	24	2574	319	69
24 PAPER, ALLIED PRDTS.	2765	9741	7	9441	5468	128	10815	590	4665
25 PAPERBOARD CONTAINERS	478	7492	291	4328	3592	51	5788	860	969
26 PRINTING, PUBLISHING	534	7153	49	24186	1593	0	5409	29	589
27 CHEMICALS,SELECT. PRDTS.	49	15857	5	5554	2183	0	14118	107	900
28 PLASTICS, SYNTHETICS	301	7033	2	8250	15276	0	10455	18	593
29 DRUGS, COSMETICS	21	62053	1614	52056	3417	0	13506	0	118
30 PAINT, ALLIED PRDTS.	0	1260	131	217	203	0	885	0	39
31 PETROLEUM, RELATED INDS.	79	7662	13	12602	854	2525	18463	11660	56
32 RUBBER, MISC. PLASTICS	1438	13164	8	1415	125	0	41673	2313	268
33 LEATHER TANNING, PRDTS.	333	375	0	29	2847	0	0	0	9
34 FOOTWEAR, LEATHER PRDTS.	982	1763	1828	2252	406	515	6816	88	22
35 GLASS, GLASS PRDTS.	20	3617	0	1697	1103	1	6077	627	180
36 STONE, CLAY PRDTS.	904	5565	264	4297	3164	0	6077	2786	2532
37 PRIMARY IRON, STEEL MFR.	277	942	0	10863	175	0	31143	82	177
38 PRIMARY NONFERROUS MFR.	544	9683	264	10863	2255	0	25485	625	2796

39 METAL CONTAINERS	2098	0	10983	0	67	3216	0	11785	0
40 FABRICATED METAL PRDTS.	1595	3980	9971	222	2769	8160	118	7340	235
41 SCREW MACH. PRDTS.,ETC.	166	153	19100	77	1402	5923	8	9210	57
42 OTHER FAB. METAL PRDTS.	770	871	580	26	1868	8312	0	36	270
43 ENGINES, TURBINES	16	1	5705	0	3	6567	23	112	1
44 FARM MACH.,EQUIP.	860	445	4447	1328	2605	1330	74	518	3
45 CONSTRUC. MACH., EQUIP.	104	4928	2081	7	15	377	0	5550	755
46 MATERIAL HANDLING MACH.	264	33	5632	0	0	391	15	451	0
47 METALWORKING MACHINERY	7	23	9118	23	113	2378	11	9291	43
48 SPECIAL MACH.,EQUIP.	2411	643	10266	18	8101	7727	4	4729	2073
49 GENERAL MACH.,EQUIP.	39	1452	6113	1	183	7470	146	950	914
50 MACHINE SHOP PRDTS.	332	439	2182	34	404	3296	10	1312	80
51 OFFICE,COMPUT. MACHINES	10	10	1262	0	117	9094	12	428	49
52 SERVICE IND. MACHINES	54	188	10491	0	261	3519	10	2240	41
53 ELECT. TRANSMISS. EQUIP.	2615	493	21149	0	4028	16285	0	12031	2092
54 HOUSEHOLD APPLIANCES	38	16	2716	0	1467	1301	121	4505	1
55 ELECTRIC LIGHTING EQUIP.	44	2	4097	0	494	1937	40	557	28
56 RADIO, TV, ETC., EQUIP.	35	5202	3335	0	8351	40315	7	0	2223
57 ELECTRONIC COMPONENTS	29	77	1465	0	956	8550	0	0	1498
58 MISC. ELECTRICAL MACH.	87	101	0	0	1686	925	2	0	4
59 MOTOR VEHICLES, EQUIP.	0	0	14843	0	0	0	0	0	0
60 AIRCRAFT, PARTS	560	4204	2335	0	664	15277	2	4242	82
61 OTHER TRANSPORT. EQUIP.	2245	896	4454	3	1081	3148	7	9246	48
62 PROFESS., SCIEN. INSTRU.	313	288	94	9	1638	7811	159	2032	142
63 MEDICAL, PHOTO. EQUIP.	312	1	0	0	432	21677	0	0	0
64 MISC. MANUFACTURING	93	106	802	17	249	5767	4	1085	67
65 TRANSPORT., WAREHOUSING	1631	190	4638	199	2870	7079	376	7465	129
66 COMMUNICA.,EXC. BRDCAST.	0	0	0	0	0	0	0	0	0
67 RADIO, TV BROADCASTING	0	0	0	0	0	0	0	0	0
68 ELEC.,GAS,WATER,SAN.SER.	1674	1253	7310	328	4529	21411	878	8976	422
69 WHOLESALE, RETAIL TRADE	0	0	0	0	0	0	0	0	0
70 FINANCE, INSURANCE	0	0	0	0	0	0	0	0	0
71 REAL ESTATE, RENTAL	0	0	0	0	0	0	0	0	0
72 HOTELS, PERSONAL SERV.	0	0	0	0	0	0	0	0	0
73 BUSINESS SERVICES	0	0	0	0	0	0	0	0	0
74 RESEARCH, DEVELOPMENT	0	0	0	0	0	0	0	0	0
75 AUTO. REPAIR, SERVICES	0	0	0	0	0	0	0	0	0
76 AMUSEMENTS	0	0	271	0	48	9564	56	35	0
77 MED.,EDUC. SERVICES	0	0	0	0	0	0	0	0	0
78 FEDERAL GOVT. ENTERPRISE	0	0	0	0	0	0	0	0	0
79 STATE, LOCAL GOVT. ENT.	0	0	0	0	0	0	0	0	0
80 IMPORTS	0	0	0	0	0	0	0	0	0
81 BUS.TRAVEL, ENT., GIFTS.	0	0	0	0	0	0	0	0	0
82 OFFICE SUPPLIES	0	0	0	0	0	0	0	0	0
83 SCRAP, USED GOODS	0	0	0	0	0	0	0	0	0
84 GOVERNMENT INDUSTRY	0	0	0	0	0	0	0	0	0
85 REST OF WORLD INDUSTRY	0	0	0	0	0	0	0	0	0
86 HOUSEHOLD INDUSTRY	0	0	0	0	0	0	0	0	0
87 INVENTORY VALUATION ADJ.	0	0	0	0	0	0	0	0	0
88 STATE TOTAL	55362	58334	413803	8415	230622	466153	32888	324035	24201

TABLE B-5

STATE ESTIMATES OF 1970
NET INVENTORY CHANGE
(THOUSANDS OF 1958 DOLLARS)

INDUSTRY TITLE	37 PENNSYL-VANIA	38 RHODE ISLAND	39 SOUTH CAROLINA	40 SOUTH DAKOTA	41 TENNESSEE	42 TEXAS	43 UTAH	44 VERMONT	45 VIRGINIA
1 LIVESTOCK, PRDTS.	2290	21	439	3279	1014	6138	642	535	962
2 OTHER AGRICULTURE PRDTS.	4399	209	373	13	2911	48247	0	118	2088
3 FORESTRY, FISHERIES	110	58	699	156	104	1220	11	32	528
4 AGRI.,FORES.,FISH. SERV.	481	92	304	3	345	6164	93	8	667
5 IRON, FERRO. ORES MINING	2766	0	0	0	12	664	1330	0	95
6 NONFERROUS ORES MINING	190	0	16	612	246	276	5380	0	98
7 COAL MINING	1615	0	0	2	140	14	273		1254
8 CRUDE PETRO.,NATURAL GAS	160	0	0	0	3	32263	2487		14
9 STONE, CLAY MINING	994	142	1312	105	1256	3111	548	115	1497
10 CHEM.,FERT. MIN. MINING									
11 NEW CONSTRUCTION									
12 MAINT., REPAIR CONSTR.									
13 ORDNANCE, ACCESSORIES	1318	3	0	0	2071	1397	3620	0	1
14 FOOD, KINDRED PRDTS.	17034	832	1982	1535	7378	14404	1635	697	7440
15 TOBACCO MANUFACTURES	0	0	41	0	222	0	0	0	987
16 FABRICS	980	574	16719	0	1431	447	16	12	3659
17 TEXTILE PRDTS.	6431	1094	9978	0	4868	327	134	25	5809
18 APPAREL	21320	1814	7656	0	18497	8886	29	41	4268
19 MISC. TEXTILE PRDTS.	1910	42	287	14	601	465	75	3	206
20 LUMBER, WOOD PRDTS.	688	21	162	42	636	225	1	38	780
21 WOODEN CONTAINERS	163	5	651	1	1268	546	0	25	1162
22 HOUSEHOLD FURNITURE	8513	39	1787	42	10366	6048	429	1249	13891
23 OTHER FURNITURE	7049	372	193	0	1308	2065	179	0	1996
24 PAPER, ALLIED PRDTS.	12955	160	5006	3	8432	7041	201	576	4718
25 PAPERBOARD CONTAINERS	5319	247	2839	4	2284	4000	127	221	1616
26 PRINTING, PUBLISHING	6025	420	436	155	1943	4612	388	371	1489
27 CHEMICALS,SELECT. PRDTS.	4965	748	5883	44	17321	58357	251	22	3865
28 PLASTICS, SYNTHETICS	14222	1564	13554	0	19792	21270	0	60	17747
29 DRUGS, COSMETICS	33670	165	3494	50	5427	4256	60	5	5152
30 PAINT, ALLIED PRDTS.	720	25	110	0	86	977	6	23	99
31 PETROLEUM, RELATED INDS.	7584	71	874	0	670	105825	4656	2	2589
32 RUBBER, MISC. PLASTICS	8893	3757	2211	102	5054	8455	678	323	2640
33 LEATHER TANNING, PRDTS.	0	0	18	0	356	454	5	52	2
34 FOOTWEAR, LEATHER PRDTS.	3565	587	0	0	2701	569	15	141	328
35 GLASS, GLASS PRDTS.	2537	718	1625	0	2661	21502	4	0	139
36 STONE, CLAY PRDTS.	1838	478	2106	423	2649	6664	2807	110	7321
37 PRIMARY IRON, STEEL MFR.	44828	187	192	0	374	18142	3462	8	725
38 PRIMARY NONFERROUS MFR.	10268	5406	159	0	9401		5084	469	3713

	C1	C2	C3	C4	C5	C6	C7	C8	C9
39 METAL CONTAINERS	4436	0	42	0	30	1662	0	0	143
40 FABRICATED METAL PRDTS.	12373	90	1829	245	2905	11349	2147	28	3435
41 SCREW MACH. PRDTS., ETC.	4265	374	423	32	1154	1172	42	11	124
42 OTHER FAB. METAL PRDTS.	7461	568	621	0	2554	6858	98	38	1763
43 ENGINES, TURBINES	8203	3	0	0	1	582	0	0	0
44 FARM MACH., EQUIP.	3129	3	181	333	10559	1758	249	74	1361
45 CONSTRUC. MACH., EQUIP.	1828	0	15	0	67	16391	1199	89	163
46 MATERIAL HANDLING MACH.	5021	208	99	165	529	991	0	0	132
47 METALWORKING MACHINERY	2503	791	279	49	149	390	17	611	34
48 SPECIAL MACH., EQUIP.	6396	562	4921	78	876	4273	244	63	406
49 GENERAL MACH., EQUIP.	7311	129	409	88	425	2620	453	25	464
50 MACHINE SHOP PRDTS.	1338	1	352	0	478	1810	181	17	255
51 OFFICE, COMPUT. MACHINES	2573	21	75	0	0	98	2	123	602
52 SERVICE IND. MACHINES	978	176	7	0	362	1738	130	46	159
53 ELECT. TRANSMISS. EQUIP.	3083	27	774	0	2529	1913	150	78	3412
54 HOUSEHOLD APPLIANCES	899	398	209	0	4595	288	0	0	5
55 ELECTRIC LIGHTING EQUIP.	4530	155	15	0	567	279	2	176	10
56 RADIO, TV, ETC., EQUIP.	2531	603	46	3	6683	10319	270	0	961
57 ELECTRONIC COMPONENTS	9829	63	1167	37	734	1602	308	440	2824
58 MISC. ELECTRICAL MACH.	1016	0	6	0	404	403	5	184	109
59 MOTOR VEHICLES, EQUIP.	11720	0	0	0	0	0	0	0	0
60 AIRCRAFT, PARTS	4994	206	0	191	2111	12750	10669	1725	886
61 OTHER TRANSPORT. EQUIP.	10860	225	319	2	3486	7801	470	13	5137
62 PROFESS., SCIEN. INSTRU.	677	1354	1109	0	1283	4155	54	395	601
63 MEDICAL, PHOTO. EQUIP.	1538	139	340	7	8	345	15	99	495
64 MISC. MANUFACTURING	3885	783	231	52	506	369	58	14	411
65 TRANSPORT., WAREHOUSING	0	459	628	0	1787	907	727	123	2801
66 COMMUNICA., EXC. BRDCAST.	0	0	0	0	0	0	0	0	0
67 RADIO, TV BROADCASTING	0	0	0	0	0	0	0	0	0
68 ELEC., GAS, WATER, SAN. SER.	0	0	0	0	0	0	0	0	0
69 WHOLESALE, RETAIL TRADE	6836	420	1226	212	2053	9913	858	137	3232
70 FINANCE, INSURANCE	0	0	0	0	0	0	0	0	0
71 REAL ESTATE, RENTAL	0	0	0	0	0	0	0	0	0
72 HOTELS, PERSONAL SERV.	0	0	0	0	0	0	0	0	0
73 BUSINESS SERVICES	0	0	0	0	0	0	0	0	0
74 RESEARCH, DEVELOPMENT	0	0	0	0	0	0	0	0	0
75 AUTO. REPAIR, SERVICES	0	0	4	28	0	37	44	30	0
76 AMUSEMENTS	0	0	0	0	0	0	0	0	0
77 MED., EDUC. SERVICES	0	0	0	0	0	0	0	0	0
78 FEDERAL GOVT. ENTERPRISE	0	0	0	0	0	0	0	0	0
79 STATE, LOCAL GOVT. ENT.	0	0	0	0	0	0	0	0	0
80 IMPORTS	0	0	0	0	0	0	0	0	0
81 BUS. TRAVEL, ENT., GIFTS.	0	0	0	0	0	0	0	0	0
82 OFFICE SUPPLIES	0	0	0	0	0	0	0	0	0
83 SCRAP, USED GOODS	0	0	0	0	0	0	0	0	0
84 GOVERNMENT INDUSTRY	0	0	0	0	0	0	0	0	0
85 REST OF WORLD INDUSTRY	0	0	0	0	0	0	0	0	0
86 HOUSEHOLD INDUSTRY	0	0	0	0	0	0	0	0	0
87 INVENTORY VALUATION ADJ.	0	0	0	0	0	0	0	0	0
88 STATE TOTAL	371435	27622	96433	8115	180659	497845	53017	9820	129469

TABLE 8-5

STATE ESTIMATES OF 1970
NET INVENTORY CHANGE
(THOUSANDS OF 1958 DOLLARS)

INDUSTRY TITLE	46 WASHINGTON	47 WEST VIRGINIA	48 WISCONSIN	49 WYOMING	50 ALASKA	51 HAWAII	52 NO STATE ALLOCATION	53 NATIONAL TOTAL
1 LIVESTOCK, PRDTS.	909	0	3483	791	41	426	0	100000
2 OTHER AGRICULTURE PRDTS.	3363	378	8462		12	13268	0	400000
3 FORESTRY, FISHERIES	2038	54	97	12		76	0	20000
4 AGRI.,FORES.,FISH. SERV.	313	246	240	25	1417	1259	0	40000
5 IRON, FERRO. ORES MINING	68		38	1340	1		0	52000
6 NONFERROUS ORES MINING	420	0	30	3534	33	0	0	44000
7 COAL MINING	8	3775	0	15	280	0	0	12000
8 CRUDE PETRO.,NATURAL GAS	143	242	0	6575	23	0	0	118000
9 STONE, CLAY MINING	211	222	547	1004	264	0	0	59000
10 CHEM.,FERT. MIN. MINING	0	0			73	374	0	0
11 NEW CONSTRUCTION	0	0	0	0	0	0	0	0
12 MAINT., REPAIR CONSTR.	0	0	0	0	0	0	0	0
13 ORDNANCE, ACCESSORIES	200	2436	322	0	0	0	0	109000
14 FOOD, KINDRED PRDTS.	5171	977	8913	120	827	3942	0	308000
15 TOBACCO MANUFACTURES	0	34	0	0	0	0	0	12000
16 FABRICS	56	11	21	0	0	1	0	54000
17 TEXTILE PRDTS.	152	8	2100	0	0	22	0	131000
18 APPAREL	926	339	1865	0	8	775	0	241000
19 MISC. TEXTILE PRDTS.	283	40	117	1	136	44	0	48000
20 LUMBER, WOOD PRDTS.	2468	81	857	29	13	47	0	34000
21 WOODEN CONTAINERS	1054	12	368	0			0	25000
22 HOUSEHOLD FURNITURE	697	190	1249	0	6	450	0	172000
23 OTHER FURNITURE	358	179	1831	0	0	165	0	55000
24 PAPER, ALLIED PRDTS.	12720	178	21185	0	1623	227	0	229000
25 PAPERBOARD CONTAINERS	1247	129	4057	0		162	0	131000
26 PRINTING, PUBLISHING	731	361	3030	62	48	217	0	122000
27 CHEMICALS,SELECT. PRDTS.	7442	14556	652	12	41	455	0	253000
28 PLASTICS, SYNTHETICS	923	13651	1346	0	0	0	0	239000
29 DRUGS, COSMETICS	93	390	7830	0	0	99	0	355000
30 PAINT, ALLIED PRDTS.	136	14	76	0	0	0	0	13000
31 PETROLEUM, RELATED INDS.	11775	129	186	2795	145	953	0	335000
32 RUBBER, MISC. PLASTICS	493	154	4968	4	4	34	0	232000
33 LEATHER TANNING, PRDTS.	9	0	733	0	0	0	0	3000
34 FOOTWEAR, LEATHER PRDTS.	18	42	476	0	0	28	0	27000
35 GLASS, GLASS PRDTS.	91	1490	28	0	0	12	0	41000
36 STONE, CLAY PRDTS.	3817	216	4112	467	271	1175	0	213000
37 PRIMARY IRON, STEEL MFR.	700	5332	3882	0	0	92	0	224000
38 PRIMARY NONFERROUS MFR.	15444	11191	1449	0	0	0	0	269000

39	METAL CONTAINERS	2744	0	9474	0	0	1868	0	83000
40	FABRICATED METAL PRDTS.	2180	372	1605	7	36	302	0	148000
41	SCREW MACH. PRDTS., ETC.	335	222	6716	26	0	0	0	113000
42	OTHER FAB. METAL PRDTS.	458	1805	2096	20	0	32	0	148000
43	ENGINES, TURBINES	1	0	6856	0	0	0	0	43000
44	FARM MACH., EQUIP.	588	1066	30814	15	0	71	0	262000
45	CONSTRUC. MACH., EQUIP.	289	274	5084	0	0	0	0	111000
46	MATERIAL HANDLING MACH.	727	132	231	0	0	0	0	33000
47	METALWORKING MACHINERY	43	271	956	0	0	2	0	39000
48	SPECIAL MACH., EQUIP.	1311	38	9419	2	0	199	0	121000
49	GENERAL MACH., EQUIP.	178	61	4712	21	0	3	0	89000
50	MACHINE SHOP PRDTS.	750	232	624	0	13	27	0	41000
51	OFFICE, COMPUT. MACHINES	62	49	87	4	0	0	0	38000
52	SERVICE IND. MACHINES	95	1250	1348	2	0	2	0	23000
53	ELECT. TRANSMISS. EQUIP.	516	20	11845	0	0	4	0	130000
54	HOUSEHOLD APPLIANCES	52	1841	3378	0	0	0	0	83000
55	ELECTRIC LIGHTING EQUIP.	145	7	84	3	0	4	0	30000
56	RADIO, TV, ETC., EQUIP.	137	114	5048	0	4	8	0	258000
57	ELECTRONIC COMPONENTS	51	0	1106	13	0	2	0	87000
58	MISC. ELECTRICAL MACH.	11	1170	2376	5	3	0	0	28000
59	MOTOR VEHICLES, EQUIP.	0	517	0	54	0	0	0	0
60	AIRCRAFT, PARTS	42542	61	2160	3	2	53	0	234000
61	OTHER TRANSPORT. EQUIP.	20706	21	1657	45	44	5	0	158000
62	PROFESS., SCIEN. INSTRU.	21	519	45	0	5	3	0	126000
63	MEDICAL, PHOTO. EQUIP.	10	0	539	0	3	14	0	44000
64	MISC. MANUFACTURING	153	0	1911	60	475	778	0	25000
65	TRANSPORT., WAREHOUSING	1260	0	0	0	0	0	0	95000
66	COMMUNICA.,EXC. BRDCAST.	0	65	0	0	0	0	0	0
67	RADIO, TV BROADCASTING	0	0	0	0	0	0	0	0
68	ELEC.,GAS,WATER,SAN.SER.	0	0	2328	0	351	1026	0	175000
69	WHOLESALE, RETAIL TRADE	2117	0	0	0	0	0	0	0
70	FINANCE, INSURANCE	0	0	0	0	0	0	0	0
71	REAL ESTATE, RENTAL	0	0	0	0	0	0	0	0
72	HOTELS, PERSONAL SERV.	0	0	0	0	0	0	0	0
73	BUSINESS SERVICES	0	0	0	0	0	0	0	0
74	RESEARCH, DEVELOPMENT	0	0	0	0	39	132	0	0
75	AUTO. REPAIR, SERVICES	0	0	0	0	0	0	0	15000
76	AMUSEMENTS	6	0	0	0	0	0	0	0
77	MED.,EDUC. SERVICES	0	0	0	0	0	0	0	0
78	FEDERAL GOVT. ENTERPRISE	0	0	0	0	0	0	0	0
79	STATE, LOCAL GOVT. ENT.	0	0	0	0	0	0	0	0
80	IMPORTS	0	0	0	0	0	0	0	0
81	BUS.,TRAVEL, ENT., GIFTS.	0	0	0	0	0	0	0	0
82	OFFICE SUPPLIES	0	0	0	0	0	0	0	0
83	SCRAP, USED GOODS	0	0	0	0	0	0	0	0
84	GOVERNMENT INDUSTRY	0	0	0	0	0	0	0	0
85	REST OF WORLD INDUSTRY	0	0	0	0	0	0	0	0
86	HOUSEHOLD INDUSTRY	0	0	0	0	0	0	0	0
87	INVENTORY VALUATION ADJ.	0	0	0	0	0	0	-5000000	-5000000
88	STATE TOTAL	151986	57166	198050	17055	6241	28834	-5000000	2500000

STATE ESTIMATES OF 1980
NET INVENTORY CHANGE
(THOUSANDS OF 1958 DOLLARS)

INDUSTRY TITLE	1 ALABAMA	2 ARIZONA	3 ARKANSAS	4 CALIFORNIA	5 COLORADO	6 CONNECTICUT	7 DELAWARE	8 DISTRICT OF COLUMBIA	9 FLORIDA
1 LIVESTOCK, PRDTS.	9032	5013	4902	32673	10601	959	1184	0	7145
2 OTHER AGRICULTURE PRDTS.	3811	26504	23061	104890	664	1781	3207	0	62963
3 FORESTRY, FISHERIES	79	544	597	0	0	0	0	0	829
4 AGRI.,FORES.,FISH. SERV.	1026	666	1515	1947	16646	0	0	0	239
5 IRON, FERRO. ORES MINING	0	174	149	9412	5647		0	0	0
6 NONFERROUS ORES MINING	71	5630	353	0	0	30	0	0	
7 COAL MINING	258	3	0	1	15		0	0	
8 CRUDE PETRO.,NATURAL GAS	312	5	0	0	1668		0	0	16
9 STONE, CLAY MINING	832	708	2685	7927	1170	896	3	0	3589
10 CHEM.,FERT. MIN. MINING	0	0	0	0	0	0	0	0	0
11 NEW CONSTRUCTION	0	0	0	0	0	0	0	0	0
12 MAINT., REPAIR CONSTR.	0	0	0	0	0	0	0	0	0
13 ORDNANCE, ACCESSORIES	3097	5100	0	35142	2096	0	0	0	9968
14 FOOD, KINDRED PRDTS.	3799	1600	3752	33020	4483	2578	391	393	11290
15 TOBACCO MANUFACTURES	41	0	0	0	0	56	0	0	182
16 FABRICS	2215	3	334	719	0	0	836	0	196
17 TEXTILE PRDTS.	0	13	2586	18570	881	0	615	0	164
18 APPAREL	37025	3108	8368	59883	0	0	5505	0	12051
19 MISC. TEXTILE PRDTS.	925	92	0	4955	588	0	118	38	578
20 LUMBER, WOOD PRDTS.	0	1482	226	31368	0	395	164	0	903
21 WOODEN CONTAINERS	0	0	0	4947	0	0	0	0	43
22 HOUSEHOLD FURNITURE	1650	276	3722	12424	764	1565	46	65	5298
23 OTHER FURNITURE	218	564	921	5842	152	1211	0	10	729
24 PAPER, ALLIED PRDTS.	10767	180	7031	19867	0	206	0	509	11123
25 PAPERBOARD CONTAINERS	721	0	2705	21688	0	49	0	0	3307
26 PRINTING, PUBLISHING	849	169	588	15536	1472	2361	327	3080	4365
27 CHEMICALS,SELECT. PRDTS.	5448	1055	1791	11658	839	225	735	0	14857
28 PLASTICS, SYNTHETICS	16043	1394	3	12939	51	5041	805	0	20921
29 DRUGS, COSMETICS	236	32	1	31921	913	19086	2285	2	1935
30 PAINT, ALLIED PRDTS.	181	39	67	2438	121	0	17	23	788
31 PETROLEUM, RELATED INDS.	1226	0	1339	15251	2422	540	10880	0	805
32 RUBBER, MISC. PLASTICS	9162	376	2422	19712	8390	2100	2824	3	476
33 LEATHER TANNING, PRDTS.	0	0	0	0	0	0	728	0	0
34 FOOTWEAR, LEATHER PRDTS.	683	68	9424	724	4576	4281	955	0	2236
35 GLASS, GLASS PRDTS.	460	55	0	6368	0	0	36	6	1199
36 STONE, CLAY PRDTS.	367	1470	550	12821	1715	739	398	0	5732
37 PRIMARY IRON, STEEL MFR.	23022	394	0	74802	12753	0	3946	502	2919
38 PRIMARY NONFERROUS MFR.	18697	26765	1394	30980	0	0	432	0	4464

#	Industry	1	2	3	4	5	6	7	8	9
39	METAL CONTAINERS	297	0	0	25270	1984	0	0	0	6063
40	FABRICATED METAL PRDTS.	4958	2197	3259	42884	2500	1755	1985	185	21201
41	SCREW MACH. PRDTS., ETC.	131	41	318	11169	150	0	780	0	684
42	OTHER FAB. METAL PRDTS.	2409	467	2899	46565	2849	0	0	0	4022
43	ENGINES, TURBINES	0	419	0	1288	415	3912	0	0	359
44	FARM MACH., EQUIP.	1282	0	0	499	1	0	87	0	933
45	CONSTRUC. MACH., EQUIP.	0	3	159	2210	1030	0	12	0	124
46	MATERIAL HANDLING MACH.	170	352	677	19604	0	4453	0	0	1489
47	METALWORKING MACHINERY	362	0	29	8189	126	1005	0	16	1271
48	SPECIAL MACH., EQUIP.	1528	215	1234	31677	1157	7785	0	0	41
49	GENERAL MACH., EQUIP.	0	1146	629	18039	1848	1610	0	189	3801
50	MACHINE SHOP PRDTS.	939	1366	1232	94189	78	6517	0	173	11678
51	OFFICE, COMPUT. MACHINES	4	0	0	9387	121	0	140	10	247
52	SERVICE IND. MACHINES	14402	3055	2473	35027	4302	5978	0	82	620
53	ELECT. TRANSMISS. EQUIP.	167	125	4085	9369	21	0	230	5	117
54	HOUSEHOLD APPLIANCES	1174	0	1123	13155	111	867	392	42	566
55	ELECTRIC LIGHTING EQUIP.	0	42	3123	113732	110	22	7	53	10758
56	RADIO, TV, ETC., EQUIP.	1945	3952	15	124937	241	14057	110	7	5316
57	ELECTRONIC COMPONENTS	1	11178	8	2366	407	679	312	0	1786
58	MISC. ELECTRICAL MACH.	3237	25	1765	251174	2172	15050	83920	43	0
59	MOTOR VEHICLES, EQUIP.	453	0	20	0	10357	0	142	0	4064
60	AIRCRAFT, PARTS	2634	4276	3837	24477	0	11267	0	5	9482
61	OTHER TRANSPORT. EQUIP.	5165	0	3680	30778	978	0	828	0	1799
62	PROFESS., SCIEN. INSTRU.	318	2148	7	6848	35	2709	0	13	1320
63	MEDICAL, PHOTO. EQUIP.	0	55	2801	24643	671	1181	2	90	2585
64	MISC. MANUFACTURING	51	449	4089	88215	12979	9800	0	0	37555
65	TRANSPORT., WAREHOUSING	0	4327	10	145	18	3	3	7459	59
66	COMMUNICA.,EXC. BRDCAST.	1001	12	0	0	0	0	0	1	0
67	RADIO, TV BROADCASTING	1441	0	0	0	0	0	0	0	0
68	ELEC.,GAS,WATER,SAN.SER.	23	0	0	0	0	0	0	0	80881
69	WHOLESALE, RETAIL TRADE	18705	18051	5539	240990	20029	22637	7343	4926	0
70	FINANCE, INSURANCE	0	0	0	0	0	0	0	0	0
71	REAL ESTATE, RENTAL	0	0	0	0	0	0	0	0	0
72	HOTELS, PERSONAL SERV.	0	0	0	0	0	0	0	0	0
73	BUSINESS SERVICES	0	0	0	0	0	0	0	0	0
74	RESEARCH, DEVELOPMENT	0	0	0	0	0	0	0	0	0
75	AUTO. REPAIR, SERVICES	0	0	0	0	0	0	0	0	0
76	AMUSEMENTS	765	0	103	6484	1883	0	362	581	4656
77	MED.,EDUC. SERVICES	0	0	0	0	0	0	0	0	0
78	FEDERAL GOVT. ENTERPRISE	0	0	0	0	0	0	0	0	0
79	STATE, LOCAL GOVT. ENT.	0	0	0	0	0	0	0	0	0
80	IMPORTS	0	0	0	0	0	0	0	0	0
81	BUS.TRAVEL, ENT., GIFTS.	0	0	0	0	0	0	0	0	0
82	OFFICE SUPPLIES	0	0	0	0	0	0	0	0	0
83	SCRAP, USED GOODS	-18780	-21910	-12519	-279196	-31299	-14607	-1043	-9390	-81379
84	GOVERNMENT INDUSTRY	0	0	0	0	0	0	0	0	0
85	REST OF WORLD INDUSTRY	0	0	0	0	0	0	0	0	0
86	HOUSEHOLD INDUSTRY	0	0	0	0	0	0	0	0	0
87	INVENTORY VALUATION ADJ.	0	0	0	0	0	0	0	0	0
88	STATE TOTAL	184069	129280	112453	1647987	113799	140779	132049	9121	323408

STATE ESTIMATES OF 1980
NET INVENTORY CHANGE
(THOUSANDS OF 1958 DOLLARS)

INDUSTRY TITLE	10 GEORGIA	11 IDAHO	12 ILLINOIS	13 INDIANA	14 IOWA	15 KANSAS	16 KENTUCKY	17 LOUISIANA	18 MAINE
1 LIVESTOCK, PRDTS.	13074	3537	11213	3082	17701	10487	2547	2639	3177
2 OTHER AGRICULTURE PRDTS.	14683	10049	0	29621	14155	11871	16302	15042	1288
3 FORESTRY, FISHERIES	7119	1241	0	0	0	0	0	0	0
4 AGRI.,FORES.,FISH. SERV.	2433	0	0	0	0	0	0	0	467
5 IRON, FERRO. ORES MINING	57	134	0	0	0	0	0	0	0
6 NONFERROUS ORES MINING	0	0	699	0	0	0	0	0	6
7 COAL MINING	1	0	675	0	0	0	1442	0	0
8 CRUDE PETRO., NATURAL GAS		0		146		0	169	24026	0
9 STONE, CLAY MINING	3009	272	3079	490	1989	714	2439	1576	0
10 CHEM.,FERT. MIN. MINING	0	0	0	0	0	0	0	0	0
11 NEW CONSTRUCTION	0	0	0	0	0	0	0	0	0
12 MAINT., REPAIR CONSTR.	0	0	0	0	0	0	0	0	0
13 ORDNANCE, ACCESSORIES	0	0	0	0	3748	0	0	0	0
14 FOOD, KINDRED PRDTS.	7810	1507	1195	5258	7763	0	1574	2725	621
15 TOBACCO MANUFACTURES	52	0	108	0	0	0	6696	0	1778
16 FABRICS	10707	0	0	0	0	8	0	0	0
17 TEXTILE PRDTS.	88034	0	0	0	6	0	0	0	0
18 APPAREL	52970	80	956	561	16	2540	14462	1601	3320
19 MISC. TEXTILE PRDTS.	2057	33	2922	304	192	0	544	0	0
20 LUMBER, WOOD PRDTS.	0	5701	853	4583	43	46	0	0	3230
21 WOODEN CONTAINERS	4709	5	0	0	320	0	1450	0	0
22 HOUSEHOLD FURNITURE	1308	12	0	0	147	182	0	0	252
23 OTHER FURNITURE	167	5	0	1325	422	311	137	13	0
24 PAPER, ALLIED PRDTS.	23101	1634	5170	2488	1251	2732	1325	460	876
25 PAPERBOARD CONTAINERS	8750	132	9065	300	2478	840	1604	671	381
26 PRINTING, PUBLISHING	2212	216	9313	3218	882	2997	1132	17710	108
27 CHEMICALS,SELECT. PRDTS.	253	6805	6800	9613	3190	2106	20132	2577	0
28 PLASTICS, SYNTHETICS		0	7331	1233	11725	2612	24924	688	0
29 DRUGS, COSMETICS	7566	0	53511	2936	2509		466	82	0
30 PAINT, ALLIED PRDTS.	814	4	2430	0	163	84	520	26052	0
31 PETROLEUM, RELATED INDS.	711	0	8838	6809	106	1467	3953	289	81
32 RUBBER, MISC. PLASTICS	2902	14	24354	18378	5057	4417	190	15	1719
33 LEATHER TANNING, PRDTS.	195	0	0	0	0	0	25	0	1872
34 FOOTWEAR, LEATHER PRDTS.	4496	84	0	2630	0	19	0	694	21275
35 GLASS, GLASS PRDTS.	2111	0	5522	0	0	72	1375	2847	0
36 STONE, CLAY PRDTS.	864	217	3754	3454	1161	2128	786	3933	220
37 PRIMARY IRON, STEEL MFR.	0	32	31185	104797	6057	821	15301	13260	0
38 PRIMARY NONFERROUS MFR.	2935	5471	5565	35866	19377	298	0		0

Industry	1	2	3	4	5	6	7	8	9
39 METAL CONTAINERS	3635	317	0	666	0	1108	640	5114	1023
40 FABRICATED METAL PRDTS.	11370	976	14615	13155	3714	3300	0	6140	144
41 SCREW MACH. PRDTS., ETC.	1616	0	13966	5391	903	148	1550	22	0
42 OTHER FAB. METAL PRDTS.	1740	104	11693	16414	5211	2262	9918	2007	0
43 ENGINES, TURBINES	20	0	8721	200	3986	4395	0	84	68
44 FARM MACH., EQUIP.	3559	564	49122	921	63981	96	8261	1145	306
45 CONSTRUC. MACH., EQUIP.	440	14	668	96	12	133	59	669	48
46 MATERIAL HANDLING MACH.	276	19	12153	5715	305	613	451	48	177
47 METALWORKING MACHINERY	781	58	8992	76	632	926	1308	736	49
48 SPECIAL MACH., EQUIP.	2949	0	18618	19780	407	3421	5278	0	187
49 GENERAL MACH., EQUIP.	1463	141	0	0	0	1785	3744	1454	375
50 MACHINE SHOP PRDTS.	1033	60	7210	150	0	52	22476	110	375
51 OFFICE, COMPUT. MACHINES	632	0	7888	2982	0	2677	7315	485	74
52 SERVICE IND. MACHINES	1757	60	22457	2118	0	4719	4719	102	127
53 ELECT. TRANSMISS. EQUIP.	8315	0	9055	4700	7677	4800	33345	7	533
54 HOUSEHOLD APPLIANCES	0	0	6921	7677	0	0	5169	52	200
55 ELECTRIC LIGHTING EQUIP.	2255	0	316	3315	11271	105	1180	22	1953
56 RADIO, TV, ETC., EQUIP.	1	0	2810	12365	6736	2774	257	60	137
57 ELECTRONIC COMPONENTS	23	0	1859	1510	393	1685	1772	13	111
58 MISC. ELECTRICAL MACH.	210	71	1685	14036	1377	65822	79447	1772	521
59 MOTOR VEHICLES, EQUIP.	213262	257	51916	1377	14036	65822	79447	1772	111
60 AIRCRAFT, PARTS	9717	53	3922	0	0	16229	63	1761	521
61 OTHER TRANSPORT. EQUIP.	5775	1655	20105	770	23073	3899	2290	9616	8666
62 PROFESS., SCIEN. INSTRU.	2312	21	3359	3840	2891	483	370	370	1953
63 MEDICAL, PHOTO. EQUIP.	61	0	3881	17	1693	60	79	145	1
64 MISC. MANUFACTURING	4830	187	17860	4358	1693	367	1369	917	2559
65 TRANSPORT., WAREHOUSING	17703	1786	68772	11382	1383	6034	13182	917	33
66 COMMUNICA.,EXC. BRDCAST.	33	3	12	8	11	14	19	33	1
67 RADIO, TV BROADCASTING	0	0	0	0	0	0	0	0	0
68 ELEC.,GAS,WATER,SAN.SER.	0	0	0	0	0	0	0	0	0
69 WHOLESALE, RETAIL TRADE	4916	3737	104345	28253	11418	6710	15102	23286	4181
70 FINANCE, INSURANCE	0	0	0	0	0	0	0	0	0
71 REAL ESTATE, RENTAL	0	0	0	0	0	0	0	0	0
72 HOTELS, PERSONAL SERV.	0	0	0	0	0	0	0	0	0
73 BUSINESS SERVICES	0	0	0	0	0	0	0	0	0
74 RESEARCH, DEVELOPMENT	0	0	0	0	0	0	0	0	0
75 AUTO. REPAIR, SERVICES	0	0	0	0	0	0	0	0	0
76 AMUSEMENTS	845	0	3220	228	26	208	598	855	86
77 MED.,EDUC. SERVICES	0	0	0	0	0	0	0	0	0
78 FEDERAL GOVT. ENTERPRISE	0	0	0	0	0	0	0	0	0
79 STATE, LOCAL GOVT. ENT.	0	0	0	0	0	0	0	0	0
80 IMPORTS	0	0	0	0	0	0	0	0	0
81 BUS.TRAVEL, ENT., GIFTS.	0	0	0	0	0	0	0	0	0
82 OFFICE SUPPLIES	0	0	0	0	0	0	0	0	0
83 SCRAP, USED GOODS	-34430	-5217	-85553	-41733	-15650	-16693	-13563	-25939	-4173
84 GOVERNMENT INDUSTRY	0	0	0	0	0	0	0	0	0
85 REST OF WORLD INDUSTRY	0	0	0	0	0	0	0	0	0
86 HOUSEHOLD INDUSTRY	0	0	0	0	0	0	0	0	0
87 INVENTORY VALUATION ADJ.	0	0	0	0	0	0	0	0	0
88 STATE TOTAL	577459	41991	579560	375504	212893	148774	317086	161217	57947

TABLE B-6

STATE ESTIMATES OF 1980
NET INVENTORY CHANGE
(THOUSANDS OF 1958 DOLLARS)

#	INDUSTRY TITLE	19 MARYLAND	20 MASSA-CHUSETTS	21 MICHIGAN	22 MINNESOTA	23 MISSISSIPPI	24 MISSOURI	25 MONTANA	26 NEBRASKA	27 NEVADA
1	LIVESTOCK, PRDTS.	3104	84	530	10199	7189	1118	3499	12586	341
2	OTHER AGRICULTURE PRDTS.	3116	1354	24433	17796	17205	41923	6524	8044	746
3	FORESTRY, FISHERIES	18	0	0	0	1678		179	0	0
4	AGRI.,FORES.,FISH. SERV.	177	0	0	7076	730		0	0	0
5	IRON, FERRO. ORES MINING		0	2042	230	0	943	513	0	121
6	NONFERROUS ORES MINING			2035			0	720	1	1332
7	COAL MINING	0		0	0	0	34	0	0	0
8	CRUDE PETRO., NATURAL GAS	6				883				612
9	STONE, CLAY MINING	2101	0	1676	1259	1132	6	821	907	
10	CHEM.,FERT. MIN. MINING	0		0	0	0	1748	222	1483	0
11	NEW CONSTRUCTION	0		0	0	0	0	0	0	0
12	MAINT., REPAIR CONSTR.	0		0	0	0	0	0	0	0
13	ORDNANCE, ACCESSORIES	899	0	4953	0	0	7453		55	123
14	FOOD, KINDRED PRDTS.	3524	3206	7426	862	2858	3325	115	2891	0
15	TOBACCO MANUFACTURES	12	0	0	0	0	0	0	0	0
16	FABRICS	767		0	0	4426	0			0
17	TEXTILE PRDTS.	0	0	601	877	0	433			0
18	APPAREL	3865	40280	16163	0	24503	1307	0	1256	31
19	MISC. TEXTILE PRDTS.	543	2181	0	0	828	0	7	0	6
20	LUMBER, WOOD PRDTS.	1660	762	0	2658	0	764	5192	693	99
21	WOODEN CONTAINERS	282	0	0	0	2818	0	0	0	0
22	HOUSEHOLD FURNITURE	632		6257	523	6516	44		154	65
23	OTHER FURNITURE	1663	3249	1197	7014	322	2927	0	279	15
24	PAPER, ALLIED PRDTS.	1340	0	6305	1124	731	2690	252	345	0
25	PAPERBOARD CONTAINERS	5170	4232	3449	998	203	5237	0	642	298
26	PRINTING, PUBLISHING	2146	0	1210	6827	3148	7376	145	2075	1722
27	CHEMICALS,SELECT. PRDTS.	0	5850	12025	1499	789	365	517	173	173
28	PLASTICS, SYNTHETICS	210	890	13805	8489	4016	15642		27	
29	DRUGS, COSMETICS	13224	284	844	404	17	279	11	173	38
30	PAINT, ALLIED PRDTS.	600	0	5662	502	279	4975		3	3
31	PETROLEUM, RELATED INDS.	0	6482	1520	203	2278	3155	3383	38	0
32	RUBBER, MISC. PLASTICS	6518	0	3154	398	1120	251	10	833	0
33	LEATHER TANNING, PRDTS.	49	0	0	440	0	762	0	0	0
34	FOOTWEAR, LEATHER PRDTS.		0	0	0	5409	520		0	0
35	GLASS, GLASS PRDTS.	2621		8114	0	778	6089		12	12
36	STONE, CLAY PRDTS.	1861		924	4792	1476	0	12	779	809
37	PRIMARY IRON, STEEL MFR.	47370		119041		678		0	127	45
38	PRIMARY NONFERROUS MFR.	21785	7731	4068	821	821		22269	13290	4164

#	Industry									
39	METAL CONTAINERS	0	1792	0	7755	214	7280	884	0	2870
40	FABRICATED METAL PRDTS.	360	6614	384	7399	5511	0	0	3686	0
41	SCREW MACH. PRDTS., ETC.	4	141	0	1263	839	941	4856	2302	5757
42	OTHER FAB. METAL PRDTS.	34	1055		4608	2763	5421	17173	4957	
43	ENGINES, TURBINES	0	0	93	0	4516	404	20408	17129	0
44	FARM MACH., EQUIP.	11	3839		7852	495	6137	12035	0	
45	CONSTRUC. MACH., EQUIP.	0	15		479	422	10	0	90	167
46	MATERIAL HANDLING MACH.	8	0		297	39	248	3063	4024	5183
47	METALWORKING MACHINERY	0	75		2513	841	1680	42907	2167	4184
48	SPECIAL MACH., EQUIP.	12	0		604	1016	808	9598	3926	600
49	GENERAL MACH., EQUIP.	6	3850		1197	829	5378	9967	673	
50	MACHINE SHOP PRDTS.		488	90	336	808	2751	0	16416	578
51	OFFICE, COMPUT. MACHINES	58	42		2722	3138	87895	22425	841	3843
52	SERVICE IND. MACHINES	35			11522	4159	6234	5340	0	1680
53	ELECT. TRANSMISS. EQUIP.	0			3110		0	0	0	280
54	HOUSEHOLD APPLIANCES	0			0		4825	0		
55	ELECTRIC LIGHTING EQUIP.				2676	500	1210	12		33879
56	RADIO, TV, ETC., EQUIP.	201	3438		4646	1171	18	3123	45347	150
57	ELECTRONIC COMPONENTS	23	3713		1294	153	9169	11948	44989	1977
58	MISC. ELECTRICAL MACH.	5	32		1465				1120	
59	MOTOR VEHICLES, EQUIP.	8	5077		207780	8530	44440		11791	64556
60	AIRCRAFT, PARTS	3	3	164	23459	468	0	2812	0	25242
61	OTHER TRANSPORT. EQUIP.	6	6424	103	10247	12478	11587	21245	10428	1697
62	PROFESS., SCIEN. INSTRU.	0	2508		3907	176	4141	18142	14511	456
63	MEDICAL, PHOTO. EQUIP.		7	139	357	0		161	13648	15590
64	MISC. MANUFACTURING	153	1242		1234	2756	3654	9722	4684	19
65	TRANSPORT., WAREHOUSING	2472	4226		24396	2169	-12251	29382	20637	
66	COMMUNICA..EXC. BRDCAST.	0	2	5	27	12	18	61	8	
67	RADIO, TV BROADCASTING									
68	ELEC.,GAS,WATER,SAN.SER.									
69	WHOLESALE, RETAIL TRADE	5595	8408	3191	34839	6884	21687	66423	36292	29751
70	FINANCE, INSURANCE									
71	REAL ESTATE, RENTAL									
72	HOTELS, PERSONAL SERV.									
73	BUSINESS SERVICES									
74	RESEARCH, DEVELOPMENT									
75	AUTO. REPAIR, SERVICES									
76	AMUSEMENTS	6946	437	7	543	46	439	1699		1578
77	MED.,EDUC. SERVICES									
78	FEDERAL GOVT. ENTERPRISE									
79	STATE, LOCAL GOVT. ENT.									
80	IMPORTS									
81	BUS.TRAVEL, ENT., GIFTS.									
82	OFFICE SUPPLIES									
83	SCRAP, USED GOODS	-8347	-15650	-5217	-41733	-11477	-36516	-58426	-51123	-17737
84	GOVERNMENT INDUSTRY									
85	REST OF WORLD INDUSTRY									
86	HOUSEHOLD INDUSTRY									
87	INVENTORY VALUATION ADJ.									
88	STATE TOTAL	18338	84504	43350	436160	142008	276380	501394	285118	309116

TABLE B-6

STATE ESTIMATES OF 1980
NET INVENTORY CHANGE
(THOUSANDS OF 1958 DOLLARS)

INDUSTRY TITLE	28 NEW HAMPSHIRE	29 NEW JERSEY	30 NEW MEXICO	31 NEW YORK	32 NORTH CAROLINA	33 NORTH DAKOTA	34 OHIO	35 OKLAHOMA	36 OREGON
1 LIVESTOCK, PRDTS.	232	1241	3862	5272	8708	1479	0	3604	1881
2 OTHER AGRICULTURE PRDTS.	11	5664	5657	13983	46572	0	29593	6329	3393
3 FORESTRY, FISHERIES	0	0	185	0	5106	0	0	0	30281
4 AGRI.,FORES.,FISH. SERV.	0	0	17	0	809	0	0	0	3
5 IRON, FERRO. ORES MINING	0	0	665	2907	498	0	0	0	601
6 NONFERROUS ORES MINING	0	0	8647	328	0	71	19	0	26
7 COAL MINING	0	0	5	0	0	81	1341	0	0
8 CRUDE PETRO.,NATURAL GAS	0	0	5262	0	0	1110	0	2676	0
9 STONE, CLAY MINING	250	1284	917	2748	1859	301	0	641	5
10 CHEM.,FERT. MIN. MINING	0	0	0	0	0	0	0	0	59
11 NEW CONSTRUCTION	0	0	0	0	0	0	0	0	0
12 MAINT., REPAIR CONSTR.	0	0	0	0	0	0	0	0	0
13 ORDNANCE, ACCESSORIES	0	0	3961	0	1955	0	5865	9	2
14 FOOD, KINDRED PRDTS.	387	12373	710	5073	6718	0	9614	0	2431
15 TOBACCO MANUFACTURES	0	0	0	0	3871	0	0	0	0
16 FABRICS	0	0	4	0	69238	0	11878	45	1093
17 TEXTILE PRDTS.	0	0	0	0	4173	0	4259	0	935
18 APPAREL	4387	44566	0	52452	115382	0	0	4798	5066
19 MISC. TEXTILE PRDTS.	0	4535	117	5114	0	12	0	88	933
20 LUMBER, WOOD PRDTS.	783	0	338	3529	2139	24	1396	0	37944
21 WOODEN CONTAINERS	0	0	0	0	0	0	0	0	822
22 HOUSEHOLD FURNITURE	186	794	0	0	15505	13	0	166	0
23 OTHER FURNITURE	416	1507	73	783	1862	0	0	0	0
24 PAPER, ALLIED PRDTS.	2182	8417	0	0	4703	0	7592	584	4616
25 PAPERBOARD CONTAINERS	425	4591	7	0	3214	24	2286	159	935
26 PRINTING, PUBLISHING	608	8537	318	22538	1885	123	4595	522	552
27 CHEMICALS,SELECT. PRDTS.	0	5868	0	0	2548	5	18794	1663	1345
28 PLASTICS, SYNTHETICS	270	1211	0	7646	23501	0	9974	46	936
29 DRUGS, COSMETICS	5	70473	7	58640	4519	0	9896	128	31
30 PAINT, ALLIED PRDTS.	0	1048	4	0	331	0	538	5	14
31 PETROLEUM, RELATED INDS.	69	12530	1311	12770	109	2184	12761	7022	308
32 RUBBER, MISC. PLASTICS	1683	1292	164	0	3517	0	33497	2257	47
33 LEATHER TANNING, PRDTS.	1635	9169	0	0	0	0	0	0	32
34 FOOTWEAR, LEATHER PRDTS.	1220	6075	62	1816	2385	0	0	512	460
35 GLASS, GLASS PRDTS.	48	1594	20	0	2575	0	11042	252	252
36 STONE, CLAY PRDTS.	335	0	724	0	1135	204	1176	1051	975
37 PRIMARY IRON, STEEL MFR.	1712	0	0	0	516	8	17793	0	0
38 PRIMARY NONFERROUS MFR.	1408	0	0	0	5002	0	53579	0	6349

39 METAL CONTAINERS	0	16661	0	4197	100	0	0	0	3117
40 FABRICATED METAL PRDTS.	527	17161	244	13749	7133	606	15626	10139	3580
41 SCREW MACH. PRDTS., ETC.	543	8663	25	2003	1427	68	537	124	147
42 OTHER FAB. METAL PRDTS.	0	12936	0	8749	4965	33	40160	2414	1965
43 ENGINES, TURBINES	552	0	7	26807	14	0	0	0	68
44 FARM MACH., EQUIP.	0	0	74	0	1788	1094	0	113	582
45 CONSTRUC. MACH., EQUIP.	2056	3093	0	46	0	0	405	3633	0
46 MATERIAL HANDLING MACH.	3396	0	79	7875	638	7	11787	13	0
47 METALWORKING MACHINERY	20	9406	17	3787	10934	8	4496	115	3109
48 SPECIAL MACH., EQUIP.	770	7421	532	13931	592	153	18144	901	0
49 GENERAL MACH., EQUIP.	311	0	151	2198	922	24	7577	4818	28
50 MACHINE SHOP PRDTS.	4345	10991	90	108406	1835	123	12583	1598	385
51 OFFICE, COMPUT. MACHINES	0	10291	22	25597	2164	0	0	99	5644
52 SERVICE IND. MACHINES	92	6988	0	27797	8931	0	5361	1447	0
53 ELECT. TRANSMISS. EQUIP.	4270	0	230	2745	3245	0	35807	979	174
54 HOUSEHOLD APPLIANCES	9452	5797	256	61747	2012	0	6640	0	36
55 ELECTRIC LIGHTING EQUIP.	2	2367	20	14686	16036	0	1863	9484	184
56 RADIO, TV, ETC., EQUIP.	0	2878	1	220	4543	0	14827	486	129
57 ELECTRONIC COMPONENTS	233	71278	18	48427	4831	0	251	251	6769
58 MISC. ELECTRICAL MACH.	0	0	312	9620	2957	0	454092	3030	403
59 MOTOR VEHICLES, EQUIP.	327	2185	0	41898	471	0	9498	2539	5107
60 AIRCRAFT, PARTS	352	13819	3	38513	2677	0	0	359	511
61 OTHER TRANSPORT. EQUIP.	790	3893	2539	33989	3214	17	5095	2	759
62 PROFESS., SCIEN. INSTRU.	0	3247	8	72	1017	167	110	864	690
63 MEDICAL, PHOTO. EQUIP.	0	63974	0	0	2289	1223	2663	0	12963
64 MISC. MANUFACTURING	0	30	0	0	24478	4	31019	0	11
65 TRANSPORT., WAREHOUSING	3776	0	8022	0	30	0	42	16	0
66 COMMUNICA.,EXC. BRDCAST.	0	0	0	0	0	0	0	0	0
67 RADIO, TV BROADCASTING	0	81892	0	190010	41290	2816	64847	10956	14855
68 ELEC.,GAS,WATER,SAN.SER.	0	0	0	0	0	0	0	0	0
69 WHOLESALE, RETAIL TRADE	0	0	0	0	0	0	0	0	0
70 FINANCE, INSURANCE	0	0	0	0	0	0	0	0	0
71 REAL ESTATE, RENTAL	0	0	0	0	0	0	0	0	0
72 HOTELS, PERSONAL SERV.	0	0	0	0	0	0	0	0	0
73 BUSINESS SERVICES	0	0	0	0	0	0	0	0	0
74 RESEARCH, DEVELOPMENT	146	1637	305	40233	599	0	2650	123	149
75 AUTO. REPAIR, SERVICES	0	0	0	0	0	0	0	0	0
76 AMUSEMENTS	0	0	0	0	0	0	0	0	0
77 MED.,EDUC. SERVICES	0	0	0	0	0	0	0	0	0
78 FEDERAL GOVT. ENTERPRISE	0	0	0	0	0	0	0	0	0
79 STATE, LOCAL GOVT. ENT.	0	0	0	0	0	0	0	0	0
80 IMPORTS	0	0	0	0	0	0	0	0	0
81 BUS.,TRAVEL, ENT., GIFTS.	0	0	0	0	0	0	0	0	0
82 OFFICE SUPPLIES	0	0	0	0	0	0	0	0	0
83 SCRAP, USED GOODS	-4173	-26083	-10433	-294174	-32343	-4173	-64686	-26083	-16693
84 GOVERNMENT INDUSTRY	0	0	0	0	0	0	0	0	0
85 REST OF WORLD INDUSTRY	0	0	0	0	0	0	0	0	0
86 HOUSEHOLD INDUSTRY	0	0	0	0	0	0	0	0	0
87 INVENTORY VALUATION ADJ.	0	0	0	0	0	0	0	0	0
88 STATE TOTAL	46039	533294	35559	628727	459124	7809	928631	60977	147247

TABLE 8-6

STATE ESTIMATES OF 1960
NET INVENTORY CHANGE
(THOUSANDS OF 1958 DOLLARS)

INDUSTRY TITLE	37 PENNSYL- VANIA	38 RHODE ISLAND	39 SOUTH CAROLINA	40 SOUTH DAKOTA	41 TENNESSEE	42 TEXAS	43 UTAH	44 VERMONT	45 VIRGINIA
1 LIVESTOCK, PRDTS.	5907	53	1133	8459	2617	15836	1657	1379	2481
2 OTHER AGRICULTURE PRDTS.	11392	376	6056	68	10022	73522		881	7050
3 FORESTRY, FISHERIES	0	0	4429	0	0	6984	65	0	200
4 AGRI.,FORES.,FISH. SERV.	0	22	0	7	0	1514	0	0	256
5 IRON, FERRO. ORES MINING	2868	0	0		31	1504	3606	0	
6 NONFERROUS ORES MINING	243	0	20	24		349	82	0	
7 COAL MINING					109		371		1655
8 CRUDE PETRO.,NATURAL GAS	0	0	0	2	2	21	1570	0	9
9 STONE, CLAY MINING	0	175	1562	2	1002	9430	743	0	1250
10 CHEM.,FERT. MIN. MINING	0	0	0		0	3751	0		0
11 NEW CONSTRUCTION	0	0	0		0	0	0		0
12 MAINT., REPAIR CONSTR.	0	0	0		0	0	0		0
13 ORDNANCE, ACCESSORIES	0	4	0		3349	1534	4747		0
14 FOOD, KINDRED PRDTS.	10909	556	1367	881	4890	9220	1061	431	5250
15 TOBACCO MANUFACTURES	0	0	38		256		0		655
16 FABRICS	0	0	63180	0	5281	0	31	0	14093
17 TEXTILE PRDTS.			12296	17	9453	1576	182	3	9142
18 APPAREL	54046	7234	31655		73083	33780	44	0	14157
19 MISC. TEXTILE PRDTS.	1117	0	0		204	0		0	
20 LUMBER, WOOD PRDTS.	2141	62	749	154	1933	0	333	646	719
21 WOODEN CONTAINERS					0	0			
22 HOUSEHOLD FURNITURE	1683		174	43	6223	4612	237	272	6615
23 OTHER FURNITURE	6596	0		7	1271	1804	170		2074
24 PAPER, ALLIED PRDTS.	10369	301	5137	5	10576	8867	272	141	2693
25 PAPERBOARD CONTAINERS	1493	35	2582		1924	3489	113	450	1316
26 PRINTING, PUBLISHING	4670	425	519	152	2250	5330	501		1715
27 CHEMICALS,SELECT. PRDTS.	0	1226	11912	82	31550	113885	249		3565
28 PLASTICS, SYNTHETICS	11102	2169	22850		19389	27995		10	3054
29 DRUGS, COSMETICS	43942	43	5037	73	6853	4397	45	1	7000
30 PAINT, ALLIED PRDTS.	616		176		86	1542	5	38	135
31 PETROLEUM, RELATED INDS.	0	0	720		517	71324	3766		2216
32 RUBBER, MISC. PLASTICS	5377	3969	2774		4565	11204	913	122	3110
33 LEATHER TANNING, PRDTS.	0	0	97	137	1741	0	26	288	
34 FOOTWEAR, LEATHER PRDTS.		3558			13493	2486	89	824	1272
35 GLASS, GLASS PRDTS.	16361	1870	4271		6283	1046	7		
36 STONE, CLAY PRDTS.	0	187	794	153	856	8338	1099		2829
37 PRIMARY IRON, STEEL MFR.	52621		499		0	39641	18941		1873
38 PRIMARY NONFERROUS MFR.	9773	11372	409	0	21560	43001	11269	1212	9597

39 METAL CONTAINERS	5908	0	62	0	0	1928	0	0	168
40 FABRICATED METAL PRDTS.	20440	0	5188	553	5300	29311	6110	0	8497
41 SCREW MACH. PRDTS., ETC.	0	0	397	49	906	1116	42	7	112
42 OTHER FAB. METAL PRDTS.	1909	0	1684	0	7322	20494	243	243	4429
43 ENGINES, TURBINES	35422	13	0	137	0	2391	187	0	0
44 FARM MACH., EQUIP.	0	0	106	0	8317	493	1141	61	977
45 CONSTRUC. MACH., EQUIP.	2749	13	14	106	272	12153	0	84	67
46 MATERIAL HANDLING MACH.	10116	0	63	311	904	586	68	0	74
47 METALWORKING MACHINERY	2570	0	1612	0	989	2410	310	2267	221
48 SPECIAL MACH., EQUIP.	15612	0	6529	260	943	5519	1543	0	349
49 GENERAL MACH., EQUIP.	0	2058	1234	320	1391	9006	597	94	1531
50 MACHINE SHOP PRDTS.	43101	0	1230	0	0	5593	0	0	637
51 OFFICE, COMPUT. MACHINES	0	7	1087	0	2699	1400	1032	708	9356
52 SERVICE IND. MACHINES	0	104	0	0	5554	14591	320	386	877
53 ELECT. TRANSMISS. EQUIP.	16017	366	1559	0	9909	3995	0	173	6727
54 HOUSEHOLD APPLIANCES	52	0	462	0	2216	139	450	715	23
55 ELECTRIC LIGHTING EQUIP.	29947	960	54	0	0	934	1940	0	20
56 RADIO, TV, ETC., EQUIP.	1149	89	89	5	12829	19429	13	2488	17814
57 ELECTRONIC COMPONENTS	0	3201	7125	204	4568	10109	509	520	309
58 MISC. ELECTRICAL MACH.	8005	1624	207	0	949	709	7557	0	46699
59 MOTOR VEHICLES, EQUIP.	635	148	0	89	0	0	1140	1219	631
60 AIRCRAFT, PARTS	11194	635	322	542	1489	108319	77	32	8179
61 OTHER TRANSPORT. EQUIP.	1300	2216	2077	0	9319	8526	37	767	1111
62 PROFESS., SCIEN. INSTRU.	8316	164	801	0	1967	20782	487	234	1035
63 MEDICAL, PHOTO. EQUIP.	19189	3812	1980	48	20	8154	5773	10	3977
64 MISC. MANUFACTURING	26	3775	4733	3	4616	822	10	744	22478
65 TRANSPORT., WAREHOUSING	0	2	14	0	13736	3051	0	0	24
66 COMMUNICA.,EXC. BRDCAST.	0	0	0	0	27	0	0	0	0
67 RADIO, TV BROADCASTING	0	0	0	0	0	0	0	0	0
68 ELEC.,GAS,WATER,SAN.SER.	0	0	0	0	0	0	0	0	0
69 WHOLESALE, RETAIL TRADE	59848	3594	10968	1744	17966	89623	7751	1156	29255
70 FINANCE, INSURANCE	0	0	0	0	0	0	0	0	0
71 REAL ESTATE, RENTAL	0	0	0	0	0	0	0	0	0
72 HOTELS, PERSONAL SERV.	0	0	0	0	0	0	0	0	0
73 BUSINESS SERVICES	0	0	0	0	0	0	0	0	0
74 RESEARCH, DEVELOPMENT	0	0	0	0	0	0	0	0	0
75 AUTO. REPAIR, SERVICES	0	0	0	0	0	0	0	0	0
76 AMUSEMENTS	0	0	204	200	318	1397	313	180	76
77 MED.,EDUC. SERVICES	0	0	0	0	0	0	0	0	0
78 FEDERAL GOVT. ENTERPRISE	0	0	0	0	0	0	0	0	0
79 STATE, LOCAL GOVT. ENT.	0	0	0	0	0	0	0	0	0
80 IMPORTS	0	0	0	0	0	0	0	0	0
81 BUS.TRAVEL, ENT., GIFTS.	0	0	0	0	0	0	0	0	0
82 OFFICE SUPPLIES	0	0	0	0	0	0	0	0	0
83 SCRAP, USED GOODS	-50080	-6260	-12519	-4173	-25040	-138719	-8137	-2087	-26008
84 GOVERNMENT INDUSTRY	0	0	0	0	0	0	0	0	0
85 REST OF WORLD INDUSTRY	0	0	0	0	0	0	0	0	0
86 HOUSEHOLD INDUSTRY	0	0	0	0	0	0	0	0	0
87 INVENTORY VALUATION ADJ.	0	0	0	0	0	0	0	0	0
88 STATE TOTAL	493016	50158	217731	10664	330855	752324	81717	16184	247868

TABLE 8-6

STATE ESTIMATES OF 1980
NET INVENTORY CHANGE
(THOUSANDS OF 1958 DOLLARS)

INDUSTRY TITLE	46 WASHINGTON	47 WEST VIRGINIA	48 WISCONSIN	49 WYOMING	50 ALASKA	51 HAWAII	52 NO STATE ALLOCATION	53 NATIONAL TOTAL
1 LIVESTOCK, PRDTS.	2346	0	8986	2042	107	1100	0	257998
2 OTHER AGRICULTURE PRDTS.	11109	1437	16588	783	15	17036	0	729002
3 FORESTRY, FISHERIES	7377	0	0	67	6647	354	0	73000
4 AGRI.,FORES.+FISH. SERV.	0	60	0	0	1	741	0	12998
5 IRON, FERRO. ORES MINING	154	0	0	2386	71	0	0	52998
6 NONFERROUS ORES MINING	367	0	0	4530	299	0	0	31998
7 COAL MINING	0	2955	0	0	30	0	0	8999
8 CRUDE PETRO.,NATURAL GAS	83	0	0	3731	152	0	0	52999
9 STONE, CLAY MINING	0	0	0	1276	93	474	0	59996
10 CHEM.,FERT. MIN. MINING	0	0	0	0	0	0	0	0
11 NEW CONSTRUCTION	0	0	0	0	0	0	0	0
12 MAINT., REPAIR CONSTR.	0	0	0	0	0	0	0	0
13 ORDNANCE, ACCESSORIES	200	2505	5	0	0	0	0	99999
14 FOOD, KINDRED PRDTS.	3323	649	5105	56	603	2873	0	197001
15 TOBACCO MANUFACTURES	0	32	0	0	0	0	0	11999
16 FABRICS	260	14	3057	0	0	5	0	170999
17 TEXTILE PRDTS.	254	770	4933	0	0	38	0	170000
18 APPAREL	3409	51	0	0	33	3078	0	728999
19 MISC. TEXTILE PRDTS.	259	0	2943	3	0	58	0	45000
20 LUMBER, WOOD PRDTS.	5682	0	0	25	659	226	0	124001
21 WOODEN CONTAINERS	1590	0	0	0	20	0	0	18001
22 HOUSEHOLD FURNITURE	0	0	1720	3	4	356	0	72998
23 OTHER FURNITURE	255	155	20591	0	5	155	0	39998
24 PAPER, ALLIED PRDTS.	11476	0	2559	0	2030	284	0	202000
25 PAPERBOARD CONTAINERS	650	0	3039	0	0	153	0	97002
26 PRINTING, PUBLISHING	587	425	2180	59	112	509	0	125996
27 CHEMICALS,SELECT. PRDTS.	15172	19137	10149	0	77	853	0	355000
28 PLASTICS, SYNTHETICS	1331	16645	0	0	0	0	0	277000
29 DRUGS, COSMETICS	25	474	0	0	0	139	0	405000
30 PAINT, ALLIED PRDTS.	213	20	0	0	0	0	0	15000
31 PETROLEUM, RELATED INDS.	10216	0	0	1569	118	781	0	212001
32 RUBBER, MISC. PLASTICS	664	144	5613	5	6	42	0	227997
33 LEATHER TANNING, PRDTS.	45	0	2563	0	0	0	0	11999
34 FOOTWEAR, LEATHER PRDTS.	33	168	0	0	0	156	0	114998
35 GLASS, GLASS PRDTS.	21	0	0	0	0	27	0	65998
36 STONE, CLAY PRDTS.	1434	0	1478	175	106	458	0	75999
37 PRIMARY IRON, STEEL MFR.	2954	15085	10533	0	0	514	0	616002
38 PRIMARY NONFERROUS MFR.	36876	27962	0	0	0	0	0	479001

	C1	C2	C3	C4	C5	C6	C7	C8	C9
39 METAL CONTAINERS	3956	0	14078	0	0	0	2732	0	116999
40 FABRICATED METAL PRDTS.	5522	0	0	4	99	0	804	0	310000
41 SCREW MACH. PRDTs., ETC.	342	4857	4715	23	0	0	0	0	69999
42 OTHER FAB. METAL PRDTS.	977	730	1995	58	0	0	87	0	268002
43 ENGINES, TURBINES	265	0	16846	0	0	0	0	0	136999
44 FARM MACH., EQUIP.	0	79	18435	12	0	0	53	0	154000
45 CONSTRUC. MACH., EQUIP.	414	*0	0	0	0	0	0	0	72000
46 MATERIAL HANDLING MACH.	*0	1767	930	0	0	0	2	0	15998
47 METALWORKING MACHINERY	1620	0	10147	0	0	0	12	0	144997
48 SPECIAL MACH., EQUIP.	570	228	11394	0	0	0	254	0	109002
49 GENERAL MACH., EQUIP.	2326	661	0	7	0	0	10	0	209002
50 MACHINE SHOP PRDTS.	904	415	1076	74	35	0	69	0	67996
51 OFFICE, COMPUT. MACHINES	624	2751	10625	0	0	0	0	0	479000
52 SERVICE IND. MACHINES	1030	0	20302	0	0	0	15	0	137997
53 ELECT. TRANSMISS. EQUIP.	0	7503	5484	0	0	0	9	0	200997
54 HOUSEHOLD APPLIANCES	556	0	0	0	0	0	0	0	132000
55 ELECTRIC LIGHTING EQUIP.	3	1	10831	7	0	0	18	0	90996
56 RADIO, TV, ETC., EQUIP.	315	73	6970	0	7	0	12	0	384999
57 ELECTRONIC COMPONENTS	0	0	6806	0	8	0	8	0	370998
58 MISC. ELECTRICAL MACH.	73	0	0	0	0	0	0	0	56996
59 MOTOR VEHICLES, EQUIP.	3338	0	218697	0	0	0	92	0	2076003
60 AIRCRAFT, PARTS	30357	1690	0	8	2	0	0	0	164001
61 OTHER TRANSPORT. EQUIP.	49388	950	1594	14	109	0	130	0	299000
62 PROFESS., SCIEN. INSTRU.	42	133	0	97	8	0	0	0	175002
63 MEDICAL, PHOTO. EQUIP.	25	15	53	27	0	0	8	0	89998
64 MISC. MANUFACTURING	1314	2482	3806	2	23	0	122	0	169000
65 TRANSPORT., WAREHOUSING	7061	8	14492		4083	0	6688	0	675998
66 COMMUNICA.-EXC. BRDCAST.	14		3	2	1	0	7	0	995
67 RADIO, TV BROADCASTING			0						
68 ELEC.,GAS,WATER,SAN.SER.			0	0	0	0	0	0	
69 WHOLESALE, RETAIL TRADE	18537	85	20369	439	3248	0	9500	0	1571006
70 FINANCE, INSURANCE	0	0	0	0	0	0	0	0	0
71 REAL ESTATE, RENTAL	0	0	0	0	0	0	0	0	0
72 HOTELS, PERSONAL SERV.	0	0	0	0	0	0	0	0	0
73 BUSINESS SERVICES	0	0	0	0	0	0	0	0	0
74 RESEARCH, DEVELOPMENT	0	0	0	0	0	0	0	0	0
75 AUTO. REPAIR, SERVICES	0	0	0	0	0	0	0	0	0
76 AMUSEMENTS	53	206	411	51	153	0	520	0	83000
77 MED.,EDUC. SERVICES	0	0	0	0	0	0	0	0	0
78 FEDERAL GOVT. ENTERPRISE	0	0	0	0	0	0	0	0	0
79 STATE, LOCAL GOVT. ENT.	0	0	0	0	0	0	0	0	0
80 IMPORTS	0	0	0	0	0	0	0	0	0
81 BUS.,TRAVEL, ENT., GIFTS.	0	0	0	0	0	0	0	0	0
82 OFFICE SUPPLIES	0	0	0	0	0	0	0	0	0
83 SCRAP, USED GOODS	-13923	-4173	-28170	-2608	-2399	0	-13563	0	-1782000
84 GOVERNMENT INDUSTRY	0	0	0	0	0	0	0	0	0
85 REST OF WORLD INDUSTRY	0	0	0	0	0	0	0	0	0
86 HOUSEHOLD INDUSTRY	0	0	0	0	0	0	0	0	0
87 INVENTORY VALUATION ADJ.	0	0	0	0	0	0	0	0	0
88 STATE TOTAL	228716	109149	473931	14925	16565	0	37999	0	13290954

TABLE B-7

STATE ESTIMATES OF 1970
NET FOREIGN EXPORTS BY STATE OF EXIT
(THOUSANDS OF 1958 DOLLARS)

INDUSTRY TITLE	1 ALABAMA	2 ARIZONA	3 ARKANSAS	4 CALIFORNIA	5 COLORADO	6 CONNECTICUT	7 DELAWARE	8 DISTRICT OF COLUMBIA	9 FLORIDA
1 LIVESTOCK, PRDTS.	0	686	0	2565	0	0	0	0	439
2 OTHER AGRICULTURE PRDTS.	10539	11786	0	185660	0	0	0	0	4077
3 FORESTRY, FISHERIES	2822	41	0	33636	0	0	0	0	261
4 AGRI.,FORES.,FISH. SERV.	192	0	198	1615	115	140	49	10	768
5 IRON, FERRO. ORES MINING	0	60	0	83105	0	0	541	0	0
6 NONFERROUS ORES MINING	0	341	0	943	0	0	0	0	465
7 COAL MINING	1197	134	0	339	0	0	0	0	0
8 CRUDE PETRO.,NATURAL GAS	0	631	0	4332	0	0	0	0	5
9 STONE, CLAY MINING	184	479	0	1537	0	0	0	0	493
10 CHEM.,FERT. MIN. MINING	0	81	0	204	0	0	0	0	15461
11 NEW CONSTRUCTION	0	0	0	0	0	0	0	4000	0
12 MAINT., REPAIR CONSTR.	0	0	0	0	0	0	0	0	62
13 ORDNANCE, ACCESSORIES	123	0	0	10733	0	0	0	0	0
14 FOOD, KINDRED PRDTS.	136982	6770	0	284110	0	0	134	0	14322
15 TOBACCO MANUFACTURES	0	2009	0	10323	0	0	0	0	155664
16 FABRICS	136	84	0	3828	0	1	0	0	18
17 TEXTILE PRDTS.	10	185	0	16731	0	0	0	0	73
18 APPAREL	36	4730	0	33244	0	1	0	0	1381
19 MISC. TEXTILE PRDTS.	0	16	0	98	0	1	0	0	1
20 LUMBER, WOOD PRDTS.	5549	2752	0	20419	0	0	0	0	145
21 WOODEN CONTAINERS	33	50	0	133	0	0	0	0	168
22 HOUSEHOLD FURNITURE	3	61	0	219	0	0	0	0	82
23 OTHER FURNITURE	3	51	0	194	0	0	0	0	82
24 PAPER, ALLIED PRDTS.	16402	2441	0	27287	0	0	16	0	10497
25 PAPERBOARD CONTAINERS	1303	88	0	541	0	0	0	0	42
26 PRINTING, PUBLISHING	0	1396	0	3510	0	0	0	0	0
27 CHEMICALS,SELECT. PRDTS.	104268	0	0	299997	0	0	128	0	54909
28 PLASTICS, SYNTHETICS	957	3781	0	45187	0	0	126	0	2452
29 DRUGS, COSMETICS	23	8841	0	25600	0	0	0	0	2092
30 PAINT, ALLIED PRDTS.	61	51	0	469	0	1	0	0	1
31 PETROLEUM, RELATED INDS.	3320	1954	0	224631	0	0	4	0	27368
32 RUBBER, MISC. PLASTICS	1272	3553	0	18965	0	0	1	0	495
33 LEATHER TANNING, PRDTS.	403	80	0	505	0	0	0	0	34
34 FOOTWEAR, LEATHER PRDTS.	36	769	0	2784	0	0	0	0	217
35 GLASS, GLASS PRDTS.	30	243	0	676	0	0	0	0	105
36 STONE, CLAY PRDTS.	1620	1035	0	2790	0	0	0	0	177
37 PRIMARY IRON, STEEL MFR.	36405	989	0	75153	0	2381	1	0	10012
38 PRIMARY NONFERROUS MFR.	821	94	0	13141	0	0	0	0	218

#	Industry	(1)	(2)	(3)	(4)	(5)	(6)	(7)	(8)	(9)
39	METAL CONTAINERS	196	0	0	0	0	2182	0	354	392
40	FABRICATED METAL PRDTS.	1848	0	1	0	0	13982	0	244	3680
41	SCREW MACH. PRDTS., ETC.	1049	0	1	0	0	9532	0	1036	2137
42	OTHER FAB. METAL PRDTS.	123	0	0	0	0	8951	0	2704	82
43	ENGINES, TURBINES	7757	0	0	0	0	68238	0	17035	198
44	FARM MACH., EQUIP.	133	0	0	15	0	19014	0	4605	629
45	CONSTRUC. MACH., EQUIP.	1418	0	0	2	0	115115	0	9927	1475
46	MATERIAL HANDLING MACH.	63	0	0	0	0	13163	0	733	85
47	METALWORKING MACHINERY	542	0	0	36	0	39779	0	85	1778
48	SPECIAL MACH., EQUIP.	1142	0	0	0	0	21096	0	10628	1997
49	GENERAL MACH., EQUIP.	10460	1177	0	8701	0	44671	0	6831	2656
50	MACHINE SHOP PRDTS.	31	0	0	1	0	477	0	10497	42
51	OFFICE, COMPUT. MACHINES	4362	10	114	0	0	71594	0	32	150
52	SERVICE IND. MACHINES	7362	17	8	0	0	29974	0	14798	754
53	ELECT. TRANSMISS. EQUIP.	1826	3	73	0	0	52092	0	1885	330
54	HOUSEHOLD APPLIANCES	884	1	36	0	0	15237	0	13465	159
55	ELECTRIC LIGHTING EQUIP.	361	1	14	0	0	14069	0	2561	65
56	RADIO, TV, ETC., EQUIP.	1501	3	50	0	0	47097	0	4161	272
57	ELECTRONIC COMPONENTS	586	1	23	0	0	27855	0	9410	106
58	MISC. ELECTRICAL MACH.	166	0	7	0	0	8952	0	8766	30
59	MOTOR VEHICLES, EQUIP.	3075	0	288	0	0	64285	0	20128	485
60	AIRCRAFT, PARTS	90418	0	0	0	0	731982	0	81847	0
61	OTHER TRANSPORT. EQUIP.	11015	0	0	0	0	14967	0	5179	51
62	PROFESS., SCIEN. INSTRU.	672	0	0	0	0	77835	0	14719	112
63	MEDICAL, PHOTO. EQUIP.	299	0	0	0	0	24609	0	2636	50
64	MISC. MANUFACTURING	495	0	0	0	0	31260	0	4370	60
65	TRANSPORT., WAREHOUSING	124988	452	2139	14852	17800	273181	19162	5871	+6614
66	COMMUNICA.,EXC. BRDCAST.	3111	2158	7	919	993	12842	573	674	853
67	RADIO, TV BROADCASTING	1635	100	77	343	584	2373	661	460	1069
68	ELEC.,GAS+WATER+SAN.SER.	0	0	0	0	0	11734	0	1051	0
69	WHOLESALE, RETAIL TRADE	62323	17139	9073	28934	30158	294554	12869	14908	28260
70	FINANCE, INSURANCE	1932	272	155	1155	559	7457	478	404	703
71	REAL ESTATE, RENTAL	6934	715	2254	14596	3440	50339	3327	2187	8600
72	HOTELS, PERSONAL SERV.	16250	3122	696	4131	3849	38958	1905	3730	3196
73	BUSINESS SERVICES	8288	2918	872	3367	2808	42096	820	1754	2287
74	RESEARCH, DEVELOPMENT	0	0	0	0	0	0	0	0	0
75	AUTO. REPAIR, SERVICES	35	7	2	14	12	125	7	11	12
76	AMUSEMENTS	6928	4651	0	877	3039	250876	0	12	16
77	MED.,EDUC. SERVICES	52	121	184	162	93	417	12	271	12
78	FEDERAL GOVT. ENTERPRISE	1085	1126	94	608	443	4451	287	0	+459
79	STATE, LOCAL GOVT. ENT.	0	0	0	0	0	0	0	0	0
80	IMPORTS	0	0	0	0	0	0	0	0	0
81	BUS.TRAVEL, ENT., GIFTS.	0	0	0	0	0	0	0	0	0
82	OFFICE SUPPLIES	0	0	0	0	0	0	0	0	0
83	SCRAP, USED GOODS	1055	0	0	534	0	39597	0	492	4410
84	GOVERNMENT INDUSTRY	0	0	0	0	0	0	0	0	0
85	REST OF WORLD INDUSTRY	0	0	0	0	0	0	0	0	0
86	HOUSEHOLD INDUSTRY	0	0	0	0	0	0	0	0	0
87	INVENTORY VALUATION ADJ.	0	0	0	0	0	0	0	0	0
88	STATE TOTAL	684987	36791	17787	82402	63894	4031012	40299	339552	439015

TABLE 8-7

STATE ESTIMATES OF 1970
NET FOREIGN EXPORTS BY STATE OF EXIT
(THOUSANDS OF 1958 DOLLARS)

INDUSTRY TITLE	10 GEORGIA	11 IDAHO	12 ILLINOIS	13 INDIANA	14 IOWA	15 KANSAS	16 KENTUCKY	17 LOUISIANA	18 MAINE
1 LIVESTOCK, PRDTS.	227	0	5109	39	0	0	0	13700	38
2 OTHER AGRICULTURE PRDTS.	218	0	50098	0	0	0	0	270967	430
3 FORESTRY, FISHERIES	15	0	6	0	0	0	3	5015	81
4 AGRI.,FORES.,FISH. SERV.	349	0	359	188	0	0	0	162	38
5 IRON, FERRO. ORES MINING	0	57	47	0	234	0	155	0	51
6 NONFERROUS ORES MINING	117	0	20	0	0	0	0	473	95
7 COAL MINING	0	0	0	0	0	0	0	0	34
8 CRUDE PETRO.,NATURAL GAS	0	0	965	0	0	0	0	3413	3
9 STONE, CLAY MINING	1439	0	0	0	0	0	0	0	183
10 CHEM.,FERT. MIN. MINING	0	0	215	0	0	0	0	1524	199
11 NEW CONSTRUCTION	0	0	0	0	0	0	0	0	0
12 MAINT., REPAIR CONSTR.	0	0	0	0	0	0	0	13088	0
13 ORDNANCE, ACCESSORIES	1172	0	6662	0	0	0	0	9007	123
14 FOOD, KINDRED PRDTS.	23242	0	164337	290	0	0	0	642441	2108
15 TOBACCO MANUFACTURES	0	0	0	0	0	0	0	8548	28
16 FABRICS	3977	0	1408	0	0	0	0	4110	242
17 TEXTILE PRDTS.	2	0	2	0	0	0	0	5457	163
18 APPAREL	27877	0	6206	1	0	0	0	2763	13
19 MISC. TEXTILE PRDTS.	21	0	350	0	0	0	0	46	18
20 LUMBER, WOOD PRDTS.	5282	0	140	0	0	0	0	5046	4944
21 WOODEN CONTAINERS	0	0	5	0	0	0	0	1025	37
22 HOUSEHOLD FURNITURE	1555	0	108	0	0	0	0	188	20
23 OTHER FURNITURE	1500	0	104	0	0	0	0	181	16
24 PAPER, ALLIED PRDTS.	87642	0	207	0	0	0	0	148972	18984
25 PAPERBOARD CONTAINERS	424	0	10	0	0	0	0	5182	125
26 PRINTING, PUBLISHING	0	0	0	0	0	0	0	0	1054
27 CHEMICALS,SELECT. PRDTS.	4461	0	10155	1841	0	0	0	171056	10311
28 PLASTICS, SYNTHETICS	7756	0	2876	0	0	0	0	64094	1819
29 DRUGS, COSMETICS	24257	0	308	0	0	0	0	9354	163
30 PAINT, ALLIED PRDTS.	10	0	97	0	0	0	0	2107	68
31 PETROLEUM, RELATED INDS.	3445	0	14648	221	0	0	0	185712	191
32 RUBBER, MISC. PLASTICS	5502	0	784	0	0	0	0	12635	425
33 LEATHER TANNING, PRDTS.	1168	0	565	0	0	0	0	1366	80
34 FOOTWEAR, LEATHER PRDTS.	690	0	136	0	0	0	0	179	4
35 GLASS, GLASS PRDTS.	84	0	20	0	0	0	0	6077	340
36 STONE, CLAY PRDTS.	5719	0	51	0	0	0	0	2693	678
37 PRIMARY IRON, STEEL MFR.	432	0	4100	0	0	0	0	68321	122
38 PRIMARY NONFERROUS MFR.	0	0	748	0	0	0	0	46064	1001

Industry	(1)	(2)	(3)	(4)	(5)	(6)	(7)	(8)	(9)
39 METAL CONTAINERS	1438	0	82	0	0	0	0	1058	72
40 FABRICATED METAL PRDTS.	13810	0	1235	0	0	0	0	10234	1741
41 SCREW MACH. PRDTS., ETC.	7717	0	436	0	0	0	0	6813	1542
42 OTHER FAB. METAL PRDTS.	155	0	886	0	0	0	0	4975	2881
43 ENGINES, TURBINES	9344	0	1375	0	0	0	0	4143	4369
44 FARM MACH., EQUIP.	19598	0	5923	34	0	0	0	37613	373
45 CONSTRUC. MACH., EQUIP.	36864	0	53930	58	0	0	0	99164	1530
46 MATERIAL HANDLING MACH.	1525	0	6471	7	0	0	0	5777	242
47 METALWORKING MACHINERY	3449	0	20185	18	0	0	0	25574	798
48 SPECIAL MACH., EQUIP.	6313	0	716	56	0	0	0	47302	5059
49 GENERAL MACH., EQUIP.	9215	0	2452	0	0	0	0	33862	2176
50 MACHINE SHOP PRDTS.	27	0	134	0	0	0	0	532	16
51 OFFICE, COMPUT. MACHINES	3851	0	2068	0	0	0	0	2032	10969
52 SERVICE IND. MACHINES	6487	0	7609	0	0	0	0	9700	209
53 ELECT. TRANSMISS. EQUIP.	9391	0	1349	0	0	0	0	12903	1634
54 HOUSEHOLD APPLIANCES	4529	0	650	0	0	0	0	6224	1268
55 ELECTRIC LIGHTING EQUIP.	1859	0	266	0	0	0	0	2551	288
56 RADIO, TV, ETC., EQUIP.	10340	0	3641	1	0	0	0	11500	2867
57 ELECTRONIC COMPONENTS	2999	0	430	0	0	0	0	4118	1226
58 MISC. ELECTRICAL MACH.	851	0	122	0	0	0	0	1168	754
59 MOTOR VEHICLES, EQUIP.	30344	0	36348	0	0	0	0	23420	2037
60 AIRCRAFT, PARTS	4575	0	250	0	0	0	0	26636	21159
61 OTHER TRANSPORT. EQUIP.	6523	0	228	0	0	0	0	17813	455
62 PROFESS., SCIEN. INSTRU.	13057	0	18395	11	0	0	0	6719	193
63 MEDICAL, PHOTO. EQUIP.	5744	0	8099	5	0	0	0	2958	814
64 MISC. MANUFACTURING	9513	0	3765	2	0	0	0	3730	974
65 TRANSPORT., WAREHOUSING	29448	8639	252417	93746	29659	27924	60750	246989	5357
66 COMMUNICA.,EXC. BRDCAST.	357	7	6495	1559	592	526	674	1845	12
67 RADIO, TV BROADCASTING	1329	319	1340	959	655	526	921	785	301
68 ELEC.,GAS,WATER,SAN.SER.									468
69 WHOLESALE, RETAIL TRADE	67425	6485	242521	53707	39323	28219	26728	38274	8157
70 FINANCE, INSURANCE	1112	180	4123	1538	846	631	762	1155	278
71 REAL ESTATE, RENTAL	10781	1166	46856	23874	7151	4615	8180	5972	2314
72 HOTELS, PERSONAL SERV.	5569	1002	18610	6398	3459	2735	3591	3983	1556
73 BUSINESS SERVICES	4435	497	44835	4444	1873	1538	2050	3781	355
74 RESEARCH, DEVELOPMENT	0	0	0	0	0	0	0	0	0
75 AUTO. REPAIR, SERVICES	19	4	48	19	11	10	110	13	4
76 AMUSEMENTS	3269		20792	1648	1108	1125		5076	0
77 MED.,EDUC. SERVICES	195	3	524	149	40	17	25		7
78 FEDERAL GOVT. ENTERPRISE	791	115	2961	870	562	487	498	502	222
79 STATE, LOCAL GOVT. ENT.									
80 IMPORTS	0	0	0	0	0	0	0	0	0
81 BUS.TRAVEL, ENT., GIFTS.	0	0	0	0	0	0	0	0	0
82 OFFICE SUPPLIES	0	0	0	0	0	0	0	0	0
83 SCRAP, USED GOODS	629	0	1874	0	0	0	0	12608	211
84 GOVERNMENT INDUSTRY	0	0	0	0	0	0	0	0	0
85 REST OF WORLD INDUSTRY	0	0	0	0	0	0	0	0	0
86 HOUSEHOLD INDUSTRY	0	0	0	0	0	0	0	0	0
87 INVENTORY VALUATION ADJ.	0	0	0	0	0	0	0	0	0
88 STATE TOTAL	556880	18475	1091387	191753	85514	58353	104449	2440499	129112

191

STATE ESTIMATES OF 1970
NET FOREIGN EXPORTS BY STATE OF EXIT
(THOUSANDS OF 1958 DOLLARS)

INDUSTRY TITLE	19 MARYLAND	20 MASSA-CHUSETTS	21 MICHIGAN	22 MINNESOTA	23 MISSISSIPPI	24 MISSOURI	25 MONTANA	26 NEBRASKA	27 NEVADA
1 LIVESTOCK, PRDTS.	366	140	4715	835	0	0	375	0	0
2 OTHER AGRICULTURE PRDTS.	0	1736	53026	40443	38259	0	13487	0	0
3 FORESTRY, FISHERIES	76	164	4281	0	0	0	475	0	0
4 AGRI.,FORES.,FISH. SERV.	192	177	230	152	107	0	35	0	0
5 IRON, FERRO. ORES MINING	180	0	11572	27131	0	222	2621	111	0
6 NONFERROUS ORES MINING	605	26	838	0	1035	0	256	0	0
7 COAL MINING	164120	0	100335	0	0	0	360	0	0
8 CRUDE PETRO.,NATURAL GAS	0	0	2471	839	0	0	153	0	0
9 STONE, CLAY MINING	454	36	6515	12	0	0	372	0	0
10 CHEM.,FERT. MIN. MINING	3	0	9003	0	0	0	366	0	0
11 NEW CONSTRUCTION	0	0	0	0	0	0	0	0	0
12 MAINT., REPAIR CONSTR.	0	0	0	0	0	0	0	0	0
13 ORDNANCE, ACCESSORIES	10425	3763	4503	0	0	0	308	0	0
14 FOOD, KINDRED PRDTS.	28570	8770	116631	65038	11316	0	8801	0	0
15 TOBACCO MANUFACTURES	19543	954	100	234	0	0	441	0	0
16 FABRICS	5224	5045	4660	0	0	0	472	0	0
17 TEXTILE PRDTS.	649	19	4313	9	39	0	447	0	0
18 APPAREL	48549	880	2824	1	1	0	1645	0	0
19 MISC. TEXTILE PRDTS.	2436	444	481	0	0	0	50	0	0
20 LUMBER, WOOD PRDTS.	6962	729	30290	0	640	0	8492	0	0
21 WOODEN CONTAINERS	1258	30	228	0	0	0	63	0	0
22 HOUSEHOLD FURNITURE	36	29	1393	0	0	0	52	0	0
23 OTHER FURNITURE	35		1181	0	0	0	44	0	0
24 PAPER, ALLIED PRDTS.	2896	6979	36320	0	2168	0	2475	0	0
25 PAPERBOARD CONTAINERS	660	861	1638	0	0	0	112	0	0
26 PRINTING, PUBLISHING	0	0	29527	0	0	0	3959	0	0
27 CHEMICALS,SELECT. PRDTS.	81395	1838	24568	13	21802	0	3124	0	0
28 PLASTICS, SYNTHETICS	55326	8746	82178	59	2	0	6529	0	0
29 DRUGS, COSMETICS	3812	19	34595	0	0	0	149	0	0
30 PAINT, ALLIED PRDTS.	883	35	3674	0	0	0	861	0	0
31 PETROLEUM, RELATED INDS.	11574	179	18770	0	0	0	3813	0	0
32 RUBBER, MISC. PLASTICS	1702	4110	71177	0	0	0	787	0	0
33 LEATHER TANNING, PRDTS.	169	8863	7488	0	0	0	508	0	0
34 FOOTWEAR, LEATHER PRDTS.		508	890	0	0	0	694	0	0
35 GLASS, GLASS PRDTS.	6193	3	11672	0	0	0	1383	0	0
36 STONE, CLAY PRDTS.	9595	35	22475	0	0	0		0	0
37 PRIMARY IRON, STEEL MFR.	63208	4868	135888	13322	574	0	1140	0	0
38 PRIMARY NONFERROUS MFR.	102927	3334	36974	2081	0	0	3417	0	0

39 METAL CONTAINERS	850	144	2156	0	0	0	306	0	0
40 FABRICATED METAL PRDTS.	8078	1707	48262	0	0	0	7346	0	0
41 SCREW MACH. PRDTS., ETC.	4559	772	42039	0	0	0	6509	0	0
42 OTHER FAB. METAL PRDTS.	5010	1306	102972	4	0	0	7117	0	0
43 ENGINES, TURBINES	774	14579	29847	0	0	0	15822	0	0
44 FARM MACH., EQUIP.	9701	27	103912	2	44	0	8256	0	0
45 CONSTRUC. MACH., EQUIP.	50673	1555	118632	747	154	0	12721	0	0
46 MATERIAL HANDLING MACH.	7627	418	28321	89	9	0	939	0	0
47 METALWORKING MACHINERY	14561	4613	50777	0	0	0	9717	0	0
48 SPECIAL MACH., EQUIP.	11448	42501	33655	10	172	0	5625	0	0
49 GENERAL MACH., EQUIP.	6611	1045	79349	48	243	0	13551	0	0
50 MACHINE SHOP PRDTS.	502	58	646	2	4	0	39	0	0
51 OFFICE, COMPUT. MACHINES	4255	3298	106197	39	15	0	41273	0	0
52 SERVICE IND. MACHINES	5651	776	35883	147	69	0	2444	0	0
53 ELECT. TRANSMISS. EQUIP.	5001	2068	44040	0	1	0	9862	0	0
54 HOUSEHOLD APPLIANCES	2895	997	33238	0	0	0	7651	0	0
55 ELECTRIC LIGHTING EQUIP.	1186	409	7824	0	0	0	1736	0	0
56 RADIO, TV, ETC., EQUIP.	5141	3574	74072	1	1	0	17298	0	0
57 ELECTRONIC COMPONENTS	1915	661	30860	0	0	0	7392	0	0
58 MISC. ELECTRICAL MACH.	543	187	18910	0	0	0	4547	0	0
59 MOTOR VEHICLES, EQUIP.	6323	432	1068222	0	42	0	20701	0	0
60 AIRCRAFT, PARTS	6913	0	78473	0	0	0	147297	0	0
61 OTHER TRANSPORT. EQUIP.	1742	363	35742	3	0	0	3000	0	0
62 PROFESS., SCIEN. INSTRU.	2291	17134	5253	11	4	0	544	0	0
63 MEDICAL, PHOTO. EQUIP.	1009	7546	17834	5	1	0	2325	0	0
64 MISC. MANUFACTURING	1024	2013	35404	1	0	0	11787	0	0
65 TRANSPORT., WAREHOUSING	81134	28525	75793	204955	17487	25643	15334	14131	1072
66 COMMUNICA.+EXC. BRDCAST.	1559	2885	2882	1398	437	2438	7	475	4
67 RADIO, TV BROADCASTING	513	632	1222	703	714	862	313	419	195
68 ELEC.,GAS,WATER,SAN.SER.	0	1124	5150	1505	0	0	986	0	0
69 WHOLESALE, RETAIL TRADE	37242	86503	116995	69838	14875	102444	7026	28327	3246
70 FINANCE, INSURANCE	1078	2396	2973	1247	519	1367	200	456	141
71 REAL ESTATE, RENTAL	8466	19772	41603	9023	3512	13706	718	2343	269
72 HOTELS, PERSONAL SERV.	4639	8404	11161	5055	2044	6988	996	2055	4803
73 BUSINESS SERVICES	4101	7905	24206	7685	1076	9227	220	2117	560
74 RESEARCH, DEVELOPMENT	0	0	0	0	0	0	0	0	0
75 AUTO. REPAIR, SERVICES	21	24	40	2224	7	21	3	877	3
76 AMUSEMENTS	1081	4270	14936	204	0	7291	0	0	0
77 MED.,EDUC. SERVICES	66	237	620	853	221	0	1	34	41
78 FEDERAL GOVT. ENTERPRISE	527	1515	1516	0	276	1168	135	359	90
79 STATE, LOCAL GOVT. ENT.	0	0	0	0	0	0	0	0	0
80 IMPORTS	0	0	0	0	0	0	0	0	0
81 BUS.-TRAVEL, ENT., GIFTS.	0	0	0	0	0	0	0	0	0
82 OFFICE SUPPLIES	0	0	0	0	0	0	0	0	0
83 SCRAP, USED GOODS	29621	1704	66088	5976	69	0	1814	0	0
84 GOVERNMENT INDUSTRY	0	0	0	0	0	0	0	0	0
85 REST OF WORLD INDUSTRY	0	0	0	0	0	0	0	0	0
86 HOUSEHOLD INDUSTRY	0	0	0	0	0	0	0	0	0
87 INVENTORY VALUATION ADJ.	0	0	0	0	0	0	0	0	0
88 STATE TOTAL	969574	337402	3476129	461947	117953	171380	461827	51710	10424

TABLE 8-7

STATE ESTIMATES OF 1970
NET FOREIGN EXPORTS BY STATE OF EXIT
(THOUSANDS OF 1958 DOLLARS)

	INDUSTRY TITLE	28 NEW HAMPSHIRE	29 NEW JERSEY	30 NEW MEXICO	31 NEW YORK	32 NORTH CAROLINA	33 NORTH DAKOTA	34 OHIO	35 OKLAHOMA	36 OREGON
1	LIVESTOCK, PRDTS.	0	1013	0	3964	495	628	597	0	234
2	OTHER AGRICULTURE PRDTS.	0		0	6775	12249	4570	39	0	336409
3	FORESTRY, FISHERIES	0	828	0	5969	299	798	321	0	201
4	AGRI.,FORES.,FISH. SERV.	39	225	58	541	0	28	50	155	106
5	IRON, FERRO. ORES MINING	0	180	0	791	20	2150	4	0	24
6	NONFERROUS ORES MINING	0	88	0	5729	0	155	8588	0	48
7	COAL MINING	0	20	0	8563	0	2142	0	0	0
8	CRUDE PETRO.,NATURAL GAS	0		0	9157	14	460	176	0	9
9	STONE, CLAY MINING	0	545	0	20556	44	1112	0	0	0
10	CHEM.,FERT. MIN. MINING	0	11	0	31295	0	1677	0	0	0
11	NEW CONSTRUCTION	0	0	0	0	0	0		0	0
12	MAINT.,REPAIR CONSTR.		0		88952		740	740		246
13	ORDNANCE, ACCESSORIES		101227		150715	4358	14773	12969		
14	FOOD, KINDRED PRDTS.		46206		49602	1197	18	651		88640
15	TOBACCO MANUFACTURES		185300		101945	0	849	0		
16	FABRICS		11737		25324	167	804	357		339
17	TEXTILE PRDTS.		343		135105	215	501	14		2
18	APPAREL		21976		11408	157	89	86		816
19	MISC. TEXTILE PRDTS.		444		12136	10	5641	8		4
20	LUMBER, WOOD PRDTS.		336		786	11	43	11		113073
21	WOODEN CONTAINERS							11		252
22	HOUSEHOLD FURNITURE		179		4864	23896	257	3889		2
23	OTHER FURNITURE		172		4411	39	218	4839		2
24	PAPER, ALLIED PRDTS.		8091		158329	0	6722	2		24309
25	PAPERBOARD CONTAINERS		1050		21108	34	302	167		1045
26	PRINTING, PUBLISHING		0		131861	175	5499	1073		0
27	CHEMICALS,SELECT. PRDTS.		48657		401276	5735	0	9366		1276
28	PLASTICS, SYNTHETICS		40424		456686	0	14651	0		173
29	DRUGS, COSMETICS		8753		318163	67	6443	6		1288
30	PAINT, ALLIED PRDTS.		1338		26611	1106	684	367		2
31	PETROLEUM, RELATED INDS.		22141		87868	0	2599	134		1393
32	RUBBER, MISC. PLASTICS		8656		176934	29	13186			9
33	LEATHER TANNING, PRDTS.		1294		22230	31	1321			46
34	FOOTWEAR, LEATHER PRDTS.		1157		18232		155			53
35	GLASS, GLASS PRDTS.		11307		54820		2068			6
36	STONE, CLAY PRDTS.		1124		75594		4125			
37	PRIMARY IRON, STEEL MFR.		85263		294854	6216	10851	19603		7638
38	PRIMARY NONFERROUS MFR.		16267		321331	15	5893	1244		46195

194

#	Industry	(1)	(2)	(3)	(4)	(5)	(6)	(7)	(8)	(9)
39	METAL CONTAINERS	0	398	0	10517	82	354	142	0	80
40	FABRICATED METAL PRDTS.	0	4243	0	158129	773	8547	1379	0	780
41	SCREW MACH. PRDTS., ETC.	0	2133	0	109062	439	7572	761	0	466
42	OTHER FAB. METAL PRDTS.	0	12836	0	125911	3	18907	616	0	215
43	ENGINES, TURBINES	0	1007	0	428390	26102	5116	1520	0	1954
44	FARM MACH., EQUIP.	0	12088	0	95151	6	18859	978	0	2558
45	CONSTRUC. MACH., EQUIP.	0	38647	0	462349	359	17911	30431	0	40673
46	MATERIAL HANDLING MACH.	0	5795	0	76559	16	1265	3651	0	5074
47	METALWORKING MACHINERY	0	11636	0	280141	20367	5846	11255	0	735
48	SPECIAL MACH., EQUIP.	0	30400	0	518857	885	6205	466	0	235
49	GENERAL MACH., EQUIP.	0	11421	0	309151	2	14498	1741	0	1120
50	MACHINE SHOP PRDTS.	0	1344	0	3439	386	105	95	0	24
51	OFFICE, COMPUT. MACHINES	0	7135	0	794821	622	19544	1460	0	2128
52	SERVICE IND. MACHINES	0	11152	0	183021	12035	856	5400	0	1623
53	ELECT. TRANSMISS. EQUIP.	0	18750	0	332683	5803	7611	2304	0	957
54	HOUSEHOLD APPLIANCES	0	9044	0	185654	2380	5905	1111	0	462
55	ELECTRIC LIGHTING EQUIP.	0	3707	0	63564	8407	1341	455	0	189
56	RADIO, TV, ETC., EQUIP.	0	17859	0	397697	3826	13353	1887	0	993
57	ELECTRONIC COMPONENTS	0	5983	0	143003	1091	5705	736	0	304
58	MISC. ELECTRICAL MACH.	0	1698	0	61322	2960	3509	209	0	87
59	MOTOR VEHICLES, EQUIP.	0	65248	0	642466	0	145379	17865	0	1164
60	AIRCRAFT, PARTS	0	51211	0	630984	0	6561	415	0	5950
61	OTHER TRANSPORT. EQUIP.	0	10547	0	107904	67	757	1948	0	132
62	PROFESS., SCIEN. INSTRU.	0	11405	0	397953	23	3225	859	0	1225
63	MEDICAL, PHOTO. EQUIP.	0	5023	0	199873	40	6735	399	0	538
64	MISC. MANUFACTURING	0	5536	0	180228				0	608
65	TRANSPORT., WAREHOUSING	2413	51921	3135	407076	43920	17755	506631	16130	51100
66	COMMUNICA.,EXC. BRDCAST.	12	946	269	38231	1180	4	4249	911	853
67	RADIO, TV BROADCASTING	219	343	443	1529	1588	242	1393	608	614
68	ELEC.,GAS,WATER,SAN.SER.	325	0	966	8938	8938	579	7122	0	0
69	WHOLESALE, RETAIL TRADE	420	106289	6485	551118	58127	10155	151565	28843	37025
70	FINANCE, INSURANCE	243	2899	253	7504	1175	172	2829	760	666
71	REAL ESTATE, RENTAL	204	28900	350	58025	14473	238	47509	2931	4701
72	HOTELS, PERSONAL SERV.	121	10577	1702	38391	5940	700	13817	2967	2810
73	BUSINESS SERVICES	406	7350	568	158074	2385	0	15965	2046	1771
74	RESEARCH, DEVELOPMENT	0	0	0	0	0	0	0	0	0
75	AUTO. REPAIR, SERVICES	3	31	5	78	18	2	43	11	10
76	AMUSEMENTS	0	2959	0	138075	2153	0	5865	674	780
77	MED.,EDUC. SERVICES	12	263	146	7737	137	0	563	86	24
78	FEDERAL GOVT. ENTERPRISE	133	1509	0	5566	671	152	2071	492	361
79	STATE, LOCAL GOVT. ENT.	0	0	0	0	0	0	0	0	0
80	IMPORTS	0	0	0	0	0	0	0	0	0
81	BUS.TRAVEL, ENT., GIFTS.	0	0	0	0	0	0	0	0	0
82	OFFICE SUPPLIES	0	0	0	0	0	0	0	0	0
83	SCRAP, USED GOODS	0	19804	0	200522	645	6234	8202	0	20946
84	GOVERNMENT INDUSTRY	0	0	0	0	0	0	0	0	0
85	REST OF WORLD INDUSTRY	0	0	0	0	0	0	0	0	0
86	HOUSEHOLD INDUSTRY	0	0	0	0	0	0	0	0	0
87	INVENTORY VALUATION ADJ.	0	0	0	0	0	0	0	0	0
88	STATE TOTAL	11262	1216391	14382	11765177	275662	488659	921217	56613	815775

TABLE B-7

STATE ESTIMATES OF 1970
NET FOREIGN EXPORTS BY STATE OF EXIT
(THOUSANDS OF 1958 DOLLARS)

INDUSTRY TITLE	37 PENNSYL-VANIA	38 RHODE ISLAND	39 SOUTH CAROLINA	40 SOUTH DAKOTA	41 TENNESSEE	42 TEXAS	43 UTAH	44 VERMONT	45 VIRGINIA
1 LIVESTOCK, PRDTS.	849	0	833	0	7	4376	0	120	1
2 OTHER AGRICULTURE PRDTS.	0	0	18686	0	11	2241132	0	544	0
3 FORESTRY, FISHERIES	10	0	0	0	0	503	0	152	10
4 AGRI.,FORES.,FISH. SERV.	379	32	119	72	158	942	0	30	178
5 IRON. FERRO. ORES MINING	113	0	0	0	0	0	0	0	39
6 NONFERROUS ORES MINING	224	0	166	0	0	1144	0	153	236
7 COAL MINING	142888	0	0	0	0	17126	0	235	67775
8 CRUDE PETRO.,NATURAL GAS	0	0	0	0	0	10424	0	105	0
9 STONE, CLAY MINING	585	0	531	0	0	2679	0	570	359
10 CHEM.,FERT. MIN. MINING	0	0	25	0	0	18582	0	518	0
11 NEW CONSTRUCTION	0	0	0	0	0	0	0	0	0
12 MAINT., REPAIR CONSTR.	0	0	0	0	0	0	0	0	0
13 ORDNANCE, ACCESSORIES	23502	0	679	0	0	2097	0	371	432
14 FOOD, KINDRED PRDTS.	26632	0	14163	0	703	356686	0	2819	18068
15 TOBACCO MANUFACTURES	4410	0	0	0	0	1425	0	86	179015
16 FABRICS	3599	0	22402	0	0	2645	0	536	11989
17 TEXTILE PRDTS.	2171	0	0	0	0	3205	0	507	16
18 APPAREL	18717	0	24901	0	1	5704	0	40	303
19 MISC. TEXTILE PRDTS.	666	0	29	0	1	86	0	56	40
20 LUMBER, WOOD PRDTS.	467	0	4662	0	0	3180	0	15392	8278
21 WOODEN CONTAINERS	32	0	62	0	0	53	0	117	217
22 HOUSEHOLD FURNITURE	81	0	902	0	0	643	0	60	60
23 OTHER FURNITURE	78	0	870	0	0	548	0	51	1
24 PAPER, ALLIED PRDTS.	5655	0	57563	0	0	52652	0	4796	24069
25 PAPERBOARD CONTAINERS	369	0	296	0	0	1495	0	216	143
26 PRINTING, PUBLISHING	0	0	0	0	0	4062	0	3284	0
27 CHEMICALS,SELECT. PRDTS.	60086	0	749	0	193	811474	0	0	50640
28 PLASTICS, SYNTHETICS	50917	0	7300	0	22	175080	0	5667	9881
29 DRUGS, COSMETICS	2993	0	9842	0	1	7723	0	507	164
30 PAINT, ALLIED PRDTS.	1210	0	10	0	0	1557	0	212	12
31 PETROLEUM, RELATED INDS.	134479	0	0	0	3	352973	0	593	27
32 RUBBER, MISC. PLASTICS	1509	0	5100	0	3	12935	0	1323	335
33 LEATHER TANNING, PRDTS.	384	0	32	0	0	984	0	252	78
34 FOOTWEAR, LEATHER PRDTS.	420	0	516	0	0	791	0	12	45
35 GLASS, GLASS PRDTS.	6927	0	270	0	9	1501	0	1060	405
36 STONE, CLAY PRDTS.	2324	0	97	0	39	6318	0	2115	439
37 PRIMARY IRON, STEEL MFR.	26979	0	0	0	4	63774	0	108	6619
38 PRIMARY NONFERROUS MFR.	4483	0	6910	0	15	62415	0	3120	1753

		(1)	(2)	(3)	(4)	(5)	(6)	(7)	(8)	(9)
39	METAL CONTAINERS	398	98	0	0	6	0	3158	226	116
40	FABRICATED METAL PRDTS.	3966	1109	0	0	57	0	23411	5424	1095
41	SCREW MACH. PRDTS., ETC.	2134	532	0	0	33	0	15158	4805	664
42	OTHER FAB. METAL PRDTS.	7774	34	0	0	4	0	17367	8981	111
43	ENGINES, TURBINES	327	13241	0	0	0	0	22708	13616	64
44	FARM MACH., EQUIP.	2366	4286	0	0	45	0	134148	1164	2933
45	CONSTRUC. MACH., EQUIP.	3042	30298	0	0	3	0	6886	4771	5099
46	MATERIAL HANDLING MACH.	1206	1336	0	0	0	0	153094	754	764
47	METALWORKING MACHINERY	3305	5717	0	0	0	0	83112	2486	53
48	SPECIAL MACH., EQUIP.	22489	22442	0	0	0	0	70401	15768	3347
49	GENERAL MACH., EQUIP.	849	3191	0	0	0	0	1241	6779	258
50	MACHINE SHOP PRDTS.	571	9	0	0	0	0	22440	50	31
51	OFFICE, COMPUT. MACHINES	2027	1335	0	0	0	0	14882	34177	162
52	SERVICE IND. MACHINES	734	2246	0	0	0	0	34675	650	252
53	ELECT. TRANSMISS. EQUIP.	084	9293	0	0	31	0	8711	5092	166
54	HOUSEHOLD APPLIANCES	970	4484	0	0	15	0	9911	3951	80
55	ELECTRIC LIGHTING EQUIP.	808	1838	0	0	6	0	25356	896	33
56	RADIO, TV, ETC., EQUIP.	5037	9326	0	0	22	0	20168	8934	152
57	ELECTRONIC COMPONENTS	303	2964	0	0	10	0	6586	3817	530
58	MISC. ELECTRICAL MACH.	370	842	0	0	3	0	128736	2348	15
59	MOTOR VEHICLES, EQUIP.	1612	10965	0	0	88	0	50803	6347	1442
60	AIRCRAFT, PARTS	12583	9822	0	0	0	0	36191	65898	32750
61	OTHER TRANSPORT. EQUIP.	91	781	0	0	8	0	54684	1417	101
62	PROFESS., SCIEN. INSTRU.	591	7525	0	0	0	0	11603	600	89
63	MEDICAL, PHOTO. EQUIP.	286	3311	0	0	0	0	6766	2538	39
64	MISC. MANUFACTURING	222	5491	0	0	0	0	283457	3036	39
65	TRANSPORT., WAREHOUSING	224595	18112	3607	3600	23382	9028	5701	2232	358964
66	COMMUNICA., EXC. BRDCAST.	4649	553	16	4	2204	12	2574	7	973
67	RADIO, TV BROADCASTING	1689	809	136	236	1210	242	8307	112	1075
68	ELEC., GAS, WATER, SAN. SER.	0	0	0	0	0	0	69131	93	0
69	WHOLESALE, RETAIL TRADE	150199	15590	9981	8116	55580	12237	3459	2198	36426
70	FINANCE, INSURANCE	357	617	327	184	1089	200	22950	147	1058
71	REAL ESTATE, RENTAL	4453	7032	3197	392	10921	1650	15999	1213	9294
72	HOTELS, PERSONAL SERV.	1596	2531	1072	788	4693	1294	13079	750	6078
73	BUSINESS SERVICES	23839	1451	1759	320	4846	1223	0	0	2946
74	RESEARCH, DEVELOPMENT	0	0	0	3	0	0	52	2	0
75	AUTO. REPAIR, SERVICES	51	8	3	0	15	5	9027	0	17
76	AMUSEMENTS	5531	0	0	0	1922	841	502	841	0
77	MED., EDUC. SERVICES	6-5	37	21	154	48	0	1861	1	47
78	FEDERAL GOVT. ENTERPRISE	251	324	189	0	632	163	0	106	588
79	STATE, LOCAL GOVT. ENT.	0	0	0	0	0	0	0	0	0
80	IMPORTS	0	0	0	0	0	0	0	0	0
81	BUS. TRAVEL, ENT., GIFTS.	0	0	0	0	0	0	0	0	0
82	OFFICE SUPPLIES	0	585	0	0	0	0	0	0	0
83	SCRAP, USED GOODS	617	585	0	0	2	0	19292	597	1618
84	GOVERNMENT INDUSTRY	0	0	0	0	0	0	0	0	0
85	REST OF WORLD INDUSTRY	0	0	0	0	0	0	0	0	0
86	HOUSEHOLD INDUSTRY	0	0	0	0	0	0	0	0	0
87	INVENTORY VALUATION ADJ.	0	0	0	0	0	0	0	0	0
88	STATE TOTAL	1125972	378879	20337	18869	108043	26899	5663844	257711	851006

TABLE B-7

STATE ESTIMATES OF 1970
NET FOREIGN EXPORTS BY STATE OF EXIT
(THOUSANDS OF 1958 DOLLARS)

INDUSTRY TITLE	46 WASHINGTON	47 WEST VIRGINIA	48 WISCONSIN	49 WYOMING	50 ALASKA	51 HAWAII	52 NO STATE ALLOCATION	53 NATIONAL TOTAL
1 LIVESTOCK, PRDTS.	1550	0	979	0	2	117	0	45000
2 OTHER AGRICULTURE PRDTS.	450880	0	45586	0	0	398	0	3798000
3 FORESTRY, FISHERIES	7480	0	173	0	0	0	0	63000
4 AGRI.,FORES.,FISH. SERV.	188	38	190	12	0	31	0	10000
5 IRON, FERRO. ORES MINING	7791	0	27603	0	0	1	0	164000
6 NONFERROUS ORES MINING	805	0	34	0	23	1	0	14000
7 COAL MINING	1060	0	4643	0	0	0	0	524000
8 CRUDE PETRO.,NATURAL GAS	449	0	938	0	0	0	0	30000
9 STONE, CLAY MINING	1145	0	263	0	13	0	0	42000
10 CHEM.,FERT. MIN. MINING	1078	0	364	0	0	0	0	92000
11 NEW CONSTRUCTION	0	0	0	0	0	0	0	4000
12 MAINT., REPAIR CONSTR.	0	0	0	0	0	0	0	0
13 ORDNANCE, ACCESSORIES	2653	0	987	0	246	246	0	270000
14 FOOD, KINDRED PRDTS.	123686	0	45079	0	25	1618	0	2421000
15 TOBACCO MANUFACTURES	1297	0	4	0	0	0	0	619000
16 FABRICS	1426	0	467	0	0	3	0	189000
17 TEXTILE PRDTS.	1363	0	175	0	0	0	0	62000
18 APPAREL	8952	0	1126	0	1169	15	0	350000
19 MISC. TEXTILE PRDTS.	148	0	83	0	0	0	0	17000
20 LUMBER, WOOD PRDTS.	237720	0	1237	0	1187	0	0	495000
21 WOODEN CONTAINERS	260	0	13	0	0	0	0	5000
22 HOUSEHOLD FURNITURE	172	0	69	0	2	2	0	11000
23 OTHER FURNITURE	145	0	60	0	2	0	0	10000
24 PAPER, ALLIED PRDTS.	182043	0	1683	0	4843	62	0	918000
25 PAPERBOARD CONTAINERS	1831	0	117	0	0	3	0	39000
26 PRINTING, PUBLISHING	11654	0	1193	0	0	3	0	197000
27 CHEMICALS,SELECT. PRDTS.	74895	0	88	0	0	1	0	2239000
28 PLASTICS, SYNTHETICS	9329	0	3373	0	0	2	0	1057000
29 DRUGS, COSMETICS	19388	0	1405	0	0	0	0	498000
30 PAINT, ALLIED PRDTS.	442	0	150	0	0	0	0	40000
31 PETROLEUM, RELATED INDS.	3142	0	564	0	0	199	0	1100000
32 RUBBER, MISC. PLASTICS	11242	0	2861	0	0	0	0	369000
33 LEATHER TANNING, PRDTS.	2335	0	1627	0	0	0	0	51000
34 FOOTWEAR, LEATHER PRDTS.	1652	0	223	0	368	0	0	31000
35 GLASS, GLASS PRDTS.	2042	0	449	0	0	0	0	108000
36 STONE, CLAY PRDTS.	4128	0	899	0	9	1	0	140000
37 PRIMARY IRON, STEEL MFR.	10233	0	2539	0	49	65	0	957000
38 PRIMARY NONFERROUS MFR.	172716	0	2246	0	10	134	0	856000

No.	Industry	(1)	(2)	(3)	(4)	(5)	(6)	(7)	(8)
39	METAL CONTAINERS	932	0	264	0	0	0	0	26000
40	FABRICATED METAL PRDTS.	22232	0	3665	0	19	3	0	347000
41	SCREW MACH. PRDTS., ETC.	19371	0	2726	0	0	1	0	250000
42	OTHER FAB. METAL PRDTS.	21020	0	4186	0	0	0	0	355000
43	ENGINES, TURBINES	53973	0	4836	0	0	6	0	741000
44	FARM MACH., EQUIP.	24668	0	5355	0	0	17	0	403000
45	CONSTRUC. MACH., EQUIP.	47239	0	27695	0	46	67	0	1352000
46	MATERIAL HANDLING MACH.	3980	0	3131	0	0	8	0	176000
47	METALWORKING MACHINERY	31726	0	2143	0	0	6	0	691000
48	SPECIAL MACH., EQUIP.	16865	0	1635	0	0	8	0	936000
49	GENERAL MACH., EQUIP.	41358	0	4441	0	0	35	0	687000
50	MACHINE SHOP PRDTS.	149	0	94	0	0	0	0	10000
51	OFFICE, COMPUT. MACHINES	130958	0	5330	0	0	62	0	1288000
52	SERVICE IND. MACHINES	9248	0	5281	0	0	50	0	350000
53	ELECT. TRANSMISS. EQUIP.	29251	0	2545	0	0	285	0	615000
54	HOUSEHOLD APPLIANCES	22630	0	1712	0	0	138	0	328000
55	ELECTRIC LIGHTING EQUIP.	5156	0	468	0	0	56	0	126000
56	RADIO, TV, ETC., EQUIP.	55151	0	3841	0	0	214	0	735000
57	ELECTRONIC COMPONENTS	21832	0	1523	0	0	360	0	299000
58	MISC. ELECTRICAL MACH.	13405	0	843	0	0	26	0	132000
59	MOTOR VEHICLES, EQUIP.	61479	0	39212	0	0	7	0	2416000
60	AIRCRAFT, PARTS	433471	0	3224	0	0	146	0	2501000
61	OTHER TRANSPORT. EQUIP.	8891	0	2180	0	0	1	0	273000
62	PROFESS., SCIEN. INSTRU.	11234	0	2371	0	0	32	0	652000
63	MEDICAL, PHOTO. EQUIP.	11065	0	1672	0	0	14	0	316000
64	MISC. MANUFACTURING	39467	0	1913	0	0	19	0	358000
65	TRANSPORT., WAREHOUSING	79171	111908	222161	4127	4258	4258	0	4182000
66	COMMUNICA.,EXC. BRDCAST.	1083	506	1017	4	166	802	0	114000
67	RADIO, TV BROADCASTING	803	513	1004	206	93	224	0	38000
68	ELEC.,GAS,WATER,SAN.SER.	6565	11620	0	93	0	0	0	55000
69	WHOLESALE, RETAIL TRADE	43060	335	45799	2073	1507	6118	0	2900000
70	FINANCE, INSURANCE	909	5067	1304	83	106	157	0	64000
71	REAL ESTATE, RENTAL	7762	1629	16122	220	309	733	0	593000
72	HOTELS, PERSONAL SERV.	4255	907	5394	890	419	1596	0	310000
73	BUSINESS SERVICES	3711	0	5410	0	0	828	0	435000
74	RESEARCH, DEVELOPMENT	0	4	0	1	1	0	0	0
75	AUTO. REPAIR, SERVICES	15	0	16	0	0	4	0	1000
76	AMUSEMENTS	2791	3	2347	2	0	0	0	503000
77	MED.,EDUC. SERVICES	44	298	156	61	50	82	0	14000
78	FEDERAL GOVT. ENTERPRISE	643	0	782	0	0	112	26102	68000
79	STATE, LOCAL GOVT. ENT.	0	0	0	0	0	0	0	0
80	IMPORTS	0	0	0	0	0	0	-50000000	-50000000
81	BUS.TRAVEL, ENT., GIFTS.	0	0	0	0	0	0	0	0
82	OFFICE SUPPLIES	0	0	0	0	0	0	0	0
83	SCRAP, USED GOODS	69867	0	1741	0	0	0	0	523000
84	GOVERNMENT INDUSTRY	0	0	0	0	0	0	0	0
85	REST OF WORLD INDUSTRY	0	0	0	0	0	0	8500000	8500000
86	HOUSEHOLD INDUSTRY	0	0	0	0	0	0	2000	2000
87	INVENTORY VALUATION ADJ.	0	0	0	0	0	0	0	0
88	STATE TOTAL	2714759	132830	585024	7680	14948	19455	-41471898	2500000

199

TABLE 8-8

STATE ESTIMATES OF 1980
NET FOREIGN EXPORTS BY STATE OF EXIT
(THOUSANDS OF 1958 DOLLARS)

INDUSTRY TITLE	1 ALABAMA	2 ARIZONA	3 ARKANSAS	4 CALIFORNIA	5 COLORADO	6 CONNECTICUT	7 DELAWARE	8 DISTRICT OF COLUMBIA	9 FLORIDA
1 LIVESTOCK, PRDTS.	0	1068	0	3990	0	0	0	0	682
2 OTHER AGRICULTURE PRDTS.	14263	15950	0	251261	0	0	0	0	5517
3 FORESTRY, FISHERIES	4032	58	0	48052	0	0	0	13	373
4 AGRI.,FORES.,FISH. SERV.	250	0	258	2099	150	182	64	0	998
5 IRON, FERRO. ORES MINING	0	66	0	91212	0	0	593	0	0
6 NONFERROUS ORES MINING	0	634	0	1752	0	0	0	0	865
7 COAL MINING	1225	138	0	347	0	0	0	0	0
8 CRUDE PETRO.,NATURAL GAS	0	484	0	3321	0	0	0	0	1057
9 STONE, CLAY MINING	394	1027	0	3294	0	0	0	0	28906
10 CHEM.,FERT. MIN. MINING	0	152	0	381	0	0	0	0	0
11 NEW CONSTRUCTION	0	0	0	0	0	0	0	4000	0
12 MAINT., REPAIR CONSTR.	0	0	0	0	0	1	0	0	121
13 ORDNANCE, ACCESSORIES	242	0	0	21069	0	0	260	0	27720
14 FOOD, KINDRED PRDTS.	265137	13103	0	549913	0	0	0	0	165973
15 TOBACCO MANUFACTURES	0	2142	0	11006	0	0	0	0	17
16 FABRICS	135	82	0	3768	0	1	0	0	160
17 TEXTILE PRDTS.	22	404	0	36431	0	0	0	0	1696
18 APPAREL	43	5811	0	40842	0	2	0	0	8
19 MISC. TEXTILE PRDTS.	3	136	0	815	0	7	0	0	185
20 LUMBER, WOOD PRDTS.	7096	3520	0	26112	0	0	0	0	134
21 WOODEN CONTAINERS	27	40	0	107	0	0	0	0	238
22 HOUSEHOLD FURNITURE	9	176	0	638	0	0	0	0	57
23 OTHER FURNITURE	2	36	0	136	0	0	0	0	20055
24 PAPER, ALLIED PRDTS.	31338	4663	0	52135	0	0	30	0	20
25 PAPERBOARD CONTAINERS	635	43	0	264	0	0	0	0	0
26 PRINTING, PUBLISHING	0	4918	0	12365	0	0	0	0	76956
27 CHEMICALS,SELECT. PRDTS.	146134	0	0	419051	0	0	179	0	3639
28 PLASTICS, SYNTHETICS	1419	5612	0	67075	0	0	187	0	2370
29 DRUGS, COSMETICS	26	10013	0	28993	0	1	0	0	1
30 PAINT, ALLIED PRDTS.	99	82	0	763	0	0	0	0	0
31 PETROLEUM, RELATED INDS.	3257	1916	0	220343	0	0	3	0	26846
32 RUBBER, MISC. PLASTICS	2023	5654	0	30169	0	0	1	0	787
33 LEATHER TANNING, PRDTS.	419	84	0	525	0	0	0	0	36
34 FOOTWEAR, LEATHER PRDTS.	35	744	0	2694	0	0	0	0	210
35 GLASS, GLASS PRDTS.	69	554	0	1539	0	0	0	0	239
36 STONE, CLAY PRDTS.	4688	2995	0	8070	0	0	0	0	511
37 PRIMARY IRON, STEEL MFR.	34504	937	0	71227	0	2257	0	0	9489
38 PRIMARY NONFERROUS MFR.	906	104	0	14492	0	0	0	0	240

39 METAL CONTAINERS	377	341	0	2098	0	0	0	0	188
40 FABRICATED METAL PRDTS.	4306	284	0	16360	0	2	0	0	2162
41 SCREW MACH. PRDTS., ETC.	2838	1375	0	12658	0	2	0	0	1393
42 OTHER FAB. METAL PRDTS.	129	4251	0	14069	0	0	0	0	194
43 ENGINES, TURBINES	313	26898	0	107746	0	0	0	0	12248
44 FARM MACH., EQUIP.	1328	9724	0	40152	0	0	0	0	282
45 CONSTRUC. MACH., EQUIP.	2214	14906	0	172842	0	23	3	0	2129
46 MATERIAL HANDLING MACH.	99	842	0	15108	0	3	3	0	72
47 METALWORKING MACHINERY	1806	10797	0	40412	0	37	1	0	552
48 SPECIAL MACH., EQUIP.	3068	10495	0	32409	0	13368	1809	0	1754
49 GENERAL MACH., EQUIP.	3078	12117	0	51333	0	12	0	0	12074
50 MACHINE SHOP PRDTS.	84	64	0	955	0	1	0	0	62
51 OFFICE, COMPUT. MACHINES	258	23874	0	115506	0	4	17	0	7039
52 SERVICE IND. MACHINES	1888	4660	0	74076	0	183	40	0	18196
53 ELECT. TRANSMISS. EQUIP.	593	24193	0	93596	0	19	5	0	3280
54 HOUSEHOLD APPLIANCES	167	2678	0	15933	0	132	2	0	925
55 ELECTRIC LIGHTING EQUIP.	205	13079	0	44217	0	37	2	0	1133
56 RADIO, TV, ETC., EQUIP.	370	12840	0	64268	0	46	3	0	2049
57 ELECTRONIC COMPONENTS	239	19934	0	63350	0	68	1	0	1333
58 MISC. ELECTRICAL MACH.	81	7893	0	24279	0	52	0	0	448
59 MOTOR VEHICLES, EQUIP.	560	23218	0	74156	0	18	0	0	3547
60 AIRCRAFT, PARTS	0	93138	0	832956	0	332	0	0	102890
61 OTHER TRANSPORT. EQUIP.	54	5464	0	15789	0	0	0	0	11620
62 PROFESS., SCIEN. INSTRU.	219	28806	0	152328	0	0	0	0	1315
63 MEDICAL, PHOTO. EQUIP.	108	5748	0	53656	0	0	0	0	651
64 MISC. MANUFACTURING	100	7227	0	51693	0	0	0	0	819
65 TRANSPORT., WAREHOUSING	75506	9510	31039	442500	28832	24058	3465	733	202455
66 COMMUNICA.,EXC. BRDCAST.	1122	886	753	16898	1307	1209	10	2839	4094
67 RADIO, TV BROADCASTING	3150	1357	1949	6996	1723	1009	226	296	4820
68 ELEC.,GAS,WATER,SAN.SER.	0	1357	0	15147	0	0	0	0	0
69 WHOLESALE, RETAIL TRADE	49952	26352	22747	520651	53307	51144	16038	30295	110160
70 FINANCE, INSURANCE	1405	808	957	14912	1118	2310	310	545	3864
71 REAL ESTATE, RENTAL	14053	3573	5437	82256	5622	23850	3685	1168	11331
72 HOTELS, PERSONAL SERV.	4403	5139	2624	53662	5302	5690	958	4300	22384
73 BUSINESS SERVICES	4043	3102	1450	74417	4963	5953	1540	5158	14652
74 RESEARCH, DEVELOPMENT	24	0	14	249	24	28	5	0	70
75 AUTO. REPAIR, SERVICES	0	21	0	337161	4084	1179	0	15	0
76 AMUSEMENTS	30	22	22	774	173	302	342	6251	9310
77 MED.,EDUC. SERVICES	0	675	22	11062	1101	1510	234	225	96
78 FEDERAL GOVT. ENTERPRISE	1139	614	713	1411	0	0	0	2799	2697
79 STATE, LOCAL GOVT. ENT.	0	0	0	0	0	0	0	0	0
80 IMPORTS	0	0	0	0	0	0	0	0	0
81 BUS.,TRAVEL, ENT., GIFTS.	0	0	0	0	0	0	0	0	0
82 OFFICE SUPPLIES	0	0	0	0	0	0	0	0	0
83 SCRAP, USED GOODS	764	849	0	68367	0	923	0	0	1821
84 GOVERNMENT INDUSTRY	0	0	0	0	0	0	0	0	0
85 REST OF WORLD INDUSTRY	0	0	0	0	0	0	0	0	0
86 HOUSEHOLD INDUSTRY	0	0	0	0	0	0	0	0	0
87 INVENTORY VALUATION ADJ.	0	0	0	0	0	0	0	0	0
88 STATE TOTAL	705355	502457	67963	5854559	107706	135952	30041	58637	952219

TABLE 8-8

STATE ESTIMATES OF 1940

NET FOREIGN EXPORTS BY STATE OF EXIT

(THOUSANDS OF 1958 DOLLARS)

INDUSTRY TITLE	10 GEORGIA	11 IDAHO	12 ILLINOIS	13 INDIANA	14 IOWA	15 KANSAS	16 KENTUCKY	17 LOUISIANA	18 MAINE
1 LIVESTOCK, PRDTS.	353	0	7948	60	0	0	0	21311	60
2 OTHER AGRICULTURE PRDTS.	295	0	67800	0	0	0	0	36711	581
3 FORESTRY, FISHERIES	21	0	8	0	0	0	4	7164	115
4 AGRI.,FORES.,FISH. SERV.	454	74	466	245	304	0	202	210	50
5 IRON, FERRO. ORES MINING	0	0	51	0	0	0	0	0	0
6 NONFERROUS ORES MINING	217	0	38	0	0	0	0	878	95
7 COAL MINING	0	0	987	0	0	0	0	3491	97
8 CRUDE PETRO.,NATURAL GAS	0	0	0	0	0	0	0	2	26
9 STONE, CLAY MINING	3084	0	461	0	0	0	0	3265	392
10 CHEM.,FERT. MIN. MINING	0	0	0	0	0	0	0	24468	373
11 NEW CONSTRUCTION	0	0	0	0	0	0	0	0	0
12 MAINT., REPAIR CONSTR.	0	0	0	0	0	0	0	0	0
13 ORDNANCE, ACCESSORIES	2301	0	13077	0	0	0	0	17679	242
14 FOOD, KINDRED PRDTS.	44986	0	318085	562	0	0	0	1243487	4080
15 TOBACCO MANUFACTURES	0	0	0	0	0	0	0	9115	30
16 FABRICS	3914	0	1386	0	0	0	0	4045	239
17 TEXTILE PRDTS.	4	0	4	0	0	0	0	11881	354
18 APPAREL	34250	0	7625	2	0	0	0	3395	16
19 MISC. TEXTILE PRDTS.	173	0	2905	0	0	0	0	381	150
20 LUMBER, WOOD PRDTS.	6754	0	180	0	0	0	0	6454	6323
21 WOODEN CONTAINERS	0	0	4	0	0	0	0	820	30
22 HOUSEHOLD FURNITURE	4525	0	313	0	0	0	0	547	56
23 OTHER FURNITURE	1050	0	73	0	0	0	0	127	11
24 PAPER, ALLIED PRDTS.	167455	0	395	0	0	0	0	284635	36273
25 PAPERBOARD CONTAINERS	207	0	6	0	0	0	0	2524	61
26 PRINTING, PUBLISHING	0	0	0	0	0	0	0	0	3712
27 CHEMICALS,SELECT. PRDTS.	6253	0	14232	2580	0	0	0	239739	14450
28 PLASTICS, SYNTHETICS	11513	0	4269	0	0	0	0	95140	2699
29 DRUGS, COSMETICS	27471	0	349	0	0	0	0	10594	184
30 PAINT, ALLIED PRDTS.	16	0	157	1	0	0	0	3425	110
31 PETROLEUM, RELATED INDS.	3379	0	14369	216	0	0	0	182166	187
32 RUBBER, MISC. PLASTICS	8752	0	1247	0	0	0	0	20101	675
33 LEATHER TANNING, PRDTS.	114	0	587	0	0	0	0	1419	84
34 FOOTWEAR, LEATHER PRDTS.	1131	0	132	0	0	0	0	173	4
35 GLASS, GLASS PRDTS.	1571	0	46	0	0	0	0	13844	775
36 STONE, CLAY PRDTS.	243	0	149	0	0	0	0	7791	1962
37 PRIMARY IRON, STEEL MFR.	5420	0	3885	0	0	0	0	64752	116
38 PRIMARY NONFERROUS MFR.	477	0	825	0	0	0	0	50799	1104

No.	Industry	C1	C2	C3	C4	C5	C6	C7	C8	C9
39	METAL CONTAINERS	1383	0	78	0	0	0	0	1018	70
40	FABRICATED METAL PRDTS.	16158	0	1444	0	0	0	0	11975	2036
41	SCREW MACH. PRDTS., ETC.	10248	0	578	0	0	0	0	9049	2048
42	OTHER FAB. METAL PRDTS.	243	0	1393	0	0	0	0	7819	4530
43	ENGINES, TURBINES	14753	0	2172	0	0	0	0	6542	6898
44	FARM MACH., EQUIP.	41383	0	12507	73	0	0	0	79424	788
45	CONSTRUC. MACH., EQUIP.	55351	0	80975	87	0	0	0	148893	2298
46	MATERIAL HANDLING MACH.	1364	0	7427	8	0	0	0	6629	278
47	METALWORKING MACHINERY	3504	0	20506	19	0	0	0	25981	811
48	SPECIAL MACH., EQUIP.	9598	0	1100	87	0	0	0	72672	7774
49	GENERAL MACH., EQUIP.	10536	0	2830	0	0	0	0	39087	2511
50	MACHINE SHOP PRDTS.	55	0	268	0	0	0	0	1064	32
51	OFFICE, COMPUT. MACHINES	6211	0	3335	0	0	0	0	3279	17696
52	SERVICE IND. MACHINES	16331	0	18806	0	0	0	0	23972	516
53	ELECT. TRANSMISS. EQUIP.	16874	0	2423	0	0	0	0	23183	2936
54	HOUSEHOLD APPLIANCES	4736	0	680	0	0	0	0	6509	1325
55	ELECTRIC LIGHTING EQUIP.	5843	0	838	0	0	0	0	8017	904
56	RADIO, TV, ETC., EQUIP.	14110	0	4970	2	0	0	0	15693	3912
57	ELECTRONIC COMPONENTS	6820	0	978	0	0	0	0	9366	2787
58	MISC. ELECTRICAL MACH.	2308	0	331	0	0	0	0	3170	2043
59	MOTOR VEHICLES, EQUIP.	35003	0	41930	0	0	0	0	27016	2349
60	AIRCRAFT, PARTS	5206	0	284	0	0	0	0	30309	24078
61	OTHER TRANSPORT. EQUIP.	6881	0	240	0	0	0	0	18792	480
62	PROFESS., SCIEN. INSTRU.	25552	0	36000	22	0	0	0	13149	379
63	MEDICAL, PHOTO. EQUIP.	12524	0	17658	10	0	0	0	6451	1775
64	MISC. MANUFACTURING	15731	0	6225	4	0	0	0	6168	1611
65	TRANSPORT., WAREHOUSING	47697	13993	408864	151850	48042	45231	98403	400073	8677
66	COMMUNICA.-EXC. BRDCAST.	4698	140	8546	2065	779	692	886	2429	15
67	RADIO, TV BROADCASTING	3915	940	3950	2854	1932	1549	2715	2314	888
68	ELEC.,GAS,WATER,SAN.SER.	0	0	0	0	0	0	0	0	603
69	WHOLESALE, RETAIL TRADE	119179	11462	428677	94931	69506	49879	47245	67653	14419
70	FINANCE, INSURANCE	2224	361	8244	3176	1691	1261	1525	2310	556
71	REAL ESTATE, RENTAL	17618	1906	76565	39012	11686	7541	13366	9759	3780
72	HOTELS, PERSONAL SERV.	7670	1380	25634	8812	4764	3767	4947	5486	2142
73	BUSINESS SERVICES	7842	878	79262	7856	3311	2718	3625	6685	627
74	RESEARCH, DEVELOPMENT	0	0	0	0	0	0	0	0	0
75	AUTO. REPAIR, SERVICES	39	7	96	38	22	19	221	26	8
76	AMUSEMENTS	4393	0	27943	2214	1488	1512	6822	0	0
77	MED.,EDUC. SERVICES	352	6	1160	277	74	32	46	54	12
78	FEDERAL GOVT. ENTERPRISE	1956	286	7358	2163	1396	1211	1238	1247	551
79	STATE, LOCAL GOVT. ENT.	0	0	0	0	0	0	0	0	5
80	IMPORTS	0	0	0	0	0	0	0	0	0
81	BUS.TRAVEL, ENT., GIFTS.	0	0	0	0	0	0	0	0	0
82	OFFICE SUPPLIES	0	0	0	0	0	0	0	0	0
83	SCRAP, USED GOODS	1085	0	3236	0	0	0	0	21770	365
84	GOVERNMENT INDUSTRY	0	0	0	0	0	0	0	0	0
85	REST OF WORLD INDUSTRY	0	0	0	0	0	0	0	0	0
86	HOUSEHOLD INDUSTRY	0	0	0	0	0	0	0	0	0
87	INVENTORY VALUATION ADJ.	0	0	0	0	0	0	0	0	0
88	STATE TOTAL	834177	31303	1807570	319226	144995	115412	174423	3834388	201229

203

TABLE 8-8

STATE ESTIMATES OF 1980
NET FOREIGN EXPORTS BY STATE OF EXIT
(THOUSANDS OF 1958 DOLLARS)

INDUSTRY TITLE	19 MARYLAND	20 MASSA-CHUSETTS	21 MICHIGAN	22 MINNESOTA	23 MISSISSIPPI	24 MISSOURI	25 MONTANA	26 NEBRASKA	27 NEVADA
1 LIVESTOCK, PRDTS.	570	218	7334	1299	0	0	582	0	0
2 OTHER AGRICULTURE PRDTS.	0	2350	71762	54733	51777	0	18252	0	0
3 FORESTRY, FISHERIES	108	235	6116		0	0	679	0	0
4 AGRI.,FORES.,FISH. SERV.	250	230	299	198	139	289	46	144	0
5 IRON, FERRO. ORES MINING	198	0	12700	29778	0	0	2877	0	0
6 NONFERROUS ORES MINING	1123	49	1555		1922	0	475	0	0
7 COAL MINING	167878	0	102632	0	0	0	368	0	0
8 CRUDE PETRO.,NATURAL GAS	0	0	1894	643	0	0	117	0	0
9 STONE, CLAY MINING	974	79	13960	27	0	0	799	0	0
10 CHEM.,FERT. MIN. MINING	6	0	16832		0	0	685	0	0
11 NEW CONSTRUCTION	0	0	0		0	0	0	0	0
12 MAINT.,REPAIR CONSTR.	0	0	0		0	0	0	0	0
13 ORDNANCE, ACCESSORIES	20464	7386	8839		21904	0	605	0	0
14 FOOD, KINDRED PRDTS.	55299	16974	225746	125885	0	0	17035	0	0
15 TOBACCO MANUFACTURES	20837	1017	106	249	9	0	471	0	0
16 FABRICS	5141	4965	4586			0	465	0	0
17 TEXTILE PRDTS.	1414	42	9393	0	85	0	973	0	0
18 APPAREL	59646	1081	3469	1	1	0	2021	0	0
19 MISC. TEXTILE PRDTS.	20206	3681	3986	0		0	411	0	0
20 LUMBER, WOOD PRDTS.	8904	932	38735	0	817	0	10860	0	0
21 WOODEN CONTAINERS	1007	0	183		0	0	51	0	0
22 HOUSEHOLD FURNITURE	105	87	4053		0	0	152	0	0
23 OTHER FURNITURE	24	20	826		0	0	31	0	0
24 PAPER, ALLIED PRDTS.	5534	13334	69395		4144	0	4728	0	0
25 PAPERBOARD CONTAINERS	321	420	797		0	0	54	0	0
26 PRINTING, PUBLISHING	0	0	104018	18	30557	0	13948	0	0
27 CHEMICALS,SELECT. PRDTS.	114077	2576	34434	88	4	0	0	0	0
28 PLASTICS, SYNTHETICS	82126	12983	121985			0	4638	0	0
29 DRUGS, COSMETICS	4317	21	39180			0	7394	0	0
30 PAINT, ALLIED PRDTS.	1435	57	5971			0	243	0	0
31 PETROLEUM, RELATED INDS.	11353	176	18412			0	845	0	0
32 RUBBER, MISC. PLASTICS	2707	6538	113228			0	6066	0	0
33 LEATHER TANNING, PRDTS.	142	9210	7782			0	817	0	0
34 FOOTWEAR, LEATHER PRDTS.	163	492	861			0	491	0	0
35 GLASS, GLASS PRDTS.	14106	6	26587			0	1580	0	0
36 STONE, CLAY PRDTS.	27758	103	65016			0	4001	0	0
37 PRIMARY IRON, STEEL MFR.	59906	4613	128788	12625	544	0	1080	0	0
38 PRIMARY NONFERROUS MFR.	113508	3677	40775	2295	0	0	3769	0	0

Code	Industry	1	2	3	4	5	6	7	8	9
39	METAL CONTAINERS	0	0	293	0	0	0	2072	138	817
40	FABRICATED METAL PRDTS.	0	0	8595	0	0	0	56468	1998	9451
41	SCREW MACH. PRDTS., ETC.	0	0	8643	0	0	0	55828	1025	6055
42	OTHER FAB. METAL PRDTS.	0	0	11187	0	6	0	161853	2052	7875
43	ENGINES. TURBINES	0	0	24983	0	0	0	47127	23019	1221
44	FARM MACH., EQUIP.	0	0	17434	0	95	4	279427	58	20484
45	CONSTRUC. MACH., EQUIP.	0	0	19099	0	231	-121	178124	2335	76384
46	MATERIAL HANDLING MACH.	0	0	1079	0	10	103	32504	480	8754
47	METALWORKING MACHINERY	0	0	9872	0	0	0	51585	4686	15199
48	SPECIAL MACH., EQUIP.	0	0	8642	0	264	16	51704	65295	17589
49	GENERAL MACH., EQUIP.	0	0	15641	0	280	55	91591	1207	7863
50	MACHINE SHOP PRDTS.	0	0	79	0	8	5	1293	116	1603
51	OFFICE, COMPUT. MACHINES	0	0	66588	0	24	63	171332	5321	6865
52	SERVICE IND. MACHINES	0	0	6040	0	171	363	88683	1918	16437
53	ELECT. TRANSMISS. EQUIP.	0	0	17719	0	2	0	79129	3715	10783
54	HOUSEHOLD APPLIANCES	0	0	8001	0	0	0	34758	1043	3027
55	ELECTRIC LIGHTING EQUIP.	0	0	5458	0	0	0	24590	1285	3729
56	RADIO, TV, ETC., EQUIP.	0	0	23606	0	2	2	101080	4878	7016
57	ELECTRONIC COMPONENTS	0	0	16810	0	2	0	70183	1504	4355
58	MISC. ELECTRICAL MACH.	0	0	12333	0	0	0	51285	508	1474
59	MOTOR VEHICLES, EQUIP.	0	0	23880	0	0	0	1232256	499	7295
60	AIRCRAFT, PARTS	0	0	167615	0	49	0	89298	0	7868
61	OTHER TRANSPORT. EQUIP.	0	0	3165	0	0	3	37706	383	1838
62	PROFESS., SCIEN. INSTRU.	0	0	1063	0	3	22	10280	33532	4484
63	MEDICAL, PHOTO. EQUIP.	0	0	5069	0	6	10	33884	16455	2200
64	MISC. MANUFACTURING	0	0	19490	0	3	2	60200	3328	1695
65	TRANSPORT., WAREHOUSING	1737	22889	24837	41536	28326	331986	122768	46206	131420
66	COMMUNICA.,EXC. BRDCAST.	5	625	10	3207	574	1839	3792	3797	2065
67	RADIO, TV BROADCASTING	574	1236	922	2541	2106	2071	3602	1862	1514
68	ELEC.,GAS,WATER,SAN.SER.	0	0	1273	0	0	1943	6648	1450	0
69	WHOLESALE, RETAIL TRADE	5738	50070	12418	181079	26293	123446	206798	152902	65828
70	FINANCE, INSURANCE	281	912	401	2735	1038	2494	5945	4793	2156
71	REAL ESTATE, RENTAL	441	3829	1173	22396	5740	14745	67981	32308	13835
72	HOTELS, PERSONAL SERV.	6616	2831	1372	9626	2816	6964	15374	11576	6349
73	BUSINESS SERVICES	990	3743	390	16311	1903	13586	42792	13976	7249
74	RESEARCH, DEVELOPMENT	0	13	5	41	13	0	0	0	0
75	AUTO. REPAIR, SERVICES	7	13	13	9798	0	29	80	48	42
76	AMUSEMENTS	0	1179	1179	0	410	2988	20073	5739	1453
77	MED.,EDUC. SERVICES	76	0	62	0	688	380	1152	440	123
78	FEDERAL GOVT. ENTERPRISE	224	62	337	2903	0	2121	3768	3765	1309
79	STATE, LOCAL GOVT. ENT.	0	892	179	0	0	130	227	0	0
80	IMPORTS	0	0	0	0	0	0	0	0	0
81	BUS.TRAVEL, ENT., GIFTS.	0	0	0	0	118	0	0	0	0
82	OFFICE SUPPLIES	0	0	0	0	0	0	0	0	0
83	SCRAP, USED GOODS	0	0	3132	0	0	10318	114106	2943	51143
84	GOVERNMENT INDUSTRY	0	0	0	0	0	0	0	0	0
85	REST OF WORLD INDUSTRY	0	0	0	0	0	0	0	0	0
86	HOUSEHOLD INDUSTRY	0	0	0	0	0	0	0	0	0
87	INVENTORY VALUATION ADJ.	0	0	0	0	0	0	0	0	0
88	STATE TOTAL	16689	88425	656445	292470	183081	744649	4966581	552135	1338454

TABLE 8-8

STATE ESTIMATES OF 1980
NET FOREIGN EXPORTS BY STATE OF EXIT
(THOUSANDS OF 1958 DOLLARS)

INDUSTRY TITLE	28 NEW HAMPSHIRE	29 NEW JERSEY	30 NEW MEXICO	31 NEW YORK	32 NORTH CAROLINA	33 NORTH DAKOTA	34 OHIO	35 OKLAHOMA	36 OREGON
1 LIVESTOCK, PRDTS.	0	1577	0	6167	770	978	929	0	363
2 OTHER AGRICULTURE PRDTS.	0	0	0	9169	16576	6184	53	0	455276
3 FORESTRY, FISHERIES	0	1183	0	8528	0	1139	0	0	287
4 AGRI.,FORES.,FISH. SERV.	51	292	76	703	389	36	417	202	138
5 IRON, FERRO. ORES MINING	0	198	0	868	0	2361	54	0	26
6 NONFERROUS ORES MINING	0	163	0	10639	37	289	0	0	89
7 COAL MINING	0	20	0	8759	0	2191	8785	0	0
8 CRUDE PETRO.,NATURAL GAS	0	0	0	7020	0	353	0	0	0
9 STONE, CLAY MINING	0	1167	0	44049	30	2382	378	0	19
10 CHEM.,FERT. MIN. MINING	0	20	0	58508	83	3135	1	0	0
11 NEW CONSTRUCTION	0	0	0	0	0	0	0	0	0
12 MAINT.,REPAIR CONSTR.	0	0	0	0	0	0	0	0	0
13 ORDNANCE, ACCESSORIES	0	198705	0	174608	0	1453	1453	0	484
14 FOOD, KINDRED PRDTS.	0	89435	0	291718	8434	28595	25102	0	171568
15 TOBACCO MANUFACTURES	0	197573	0	52887	20	20	0	0	0
16 FABRICS	0	11551	0	100326	1177	836	641	0	334
17 TEXTILE PRDTS.	0	745	0	55142	0	1749	0	0	4
18 APPAREL	0	26999	0	165986	205	616	438	0	1002
19 MISC. TEXTILE PRDTS.	0	3686	0	94624	1	740	115	0	33
20 LUMBER, WOOD PRDTS.	0	430	0	15519	275	7213	110	0	144595
21 WOODEN CONTAINERS	0	0	0	629	126	34	0	0	202
22 HOUSEHOLD FURNITURE	0	520	0	14150	27	748	33	0	6
23 OTHER FURNITURE	0	121	0	3088	8	152	8	0	1
24 PAPER, ALLIED PRDTS.	0	15461	0	302515	45659	12845	0	0	46446
25 PAPERBOARD CONTAINERS	0	512	0	10283	19	147	0	0	510
26 PRINTING, PUBLISHING	0	0	0	464526	0	19372	0	0	0
27 CHEMICALS,SELECT. PRDTS.	0	68194	0	562396	48	21747	5451	0	1788
28 PLASTICS, SYNTHETICS	0	60004	0	677899	260	7297	7183	0	257
29 DRUGS, COSMETICS	0	9913	0	360329	6495	1112	0	0	1458
30 PAINT, ALLIED PRDTS.	0	2173	0	43243	0	2549	271	0	3
31 PETROLEUM, RELATED INDS.	0	21718	0	86190	66	20977	1052	0	1367
32 RUBBER, MISC. PLASTICS	0	13771	0	281465	1759	1373	14899	0	14
33 LEATHER TANNING, PRDTS.	0	1345	0	23101	0	150	0	0	48
34 FOOTWEAR, LEATHER PRDTS.	0	1120	0	17644	0	0	6	0	52
35 GLASS, GLASS PRDTS.	0	25755	0	124682	65	4711	837	0	0
36 STONE, CLAY PRDTS.	0	3253	0	218682	90	11932	386	0	17
37 PRIMARY IRON, STEEL MFR.	0	80808	0	279450	5891	10284	18579	0	7238
38 PRIMARY NONFERROUS MFR.	0	17939	0	354365	17	6498	1371	0	50944

#	Industry	(1)	(2)	(3)	(4)	(5)	(6)	(7)	(8)	(9)
39	METAL CONTAINERS	0	382	0	10114	79	341	136	0	76
40	FABRICATED METAL PRDTS.	0	4965	0	-85015	904	10000	1614	0	912
41	SCREW MACH. PRDTS., ETC.	0	2832	0	-44833	584	10057	1010	0	619
42	OTHER FAB. METAL PRDTS.	0	20176	0	-97753	4	29718	968	0	338
43	ENGINES, TURBINES	0	1589	0	76406	41214	8078	2400	0	3086
44	FARM MACH., EQUIP.	0	25526	0	200927	13	39824	2065	0	5401
45	CONSTRUC. MACH., EQUIP.	0	58027	0	94208	538	26893	45691	0	61071
46	MATERIAL HANDLING MACH.	0	6650	0	87867	18	1452	4191	0	5823
47	METALWORKING MACHINERY	0	11821	0	284601	31290	5939	11434	0	747
48	SPECIAL MACH., EQUIP.	0	46705	0	-97132	1021	9533	716	0	360
49	GENERAL MACH., EQUIP.	0	13184	0	356850	621	16735	2009	0	1294
50	MACHINE SHOP PRDTS.	0	2688	0	6877	1538	210	190	0	49
51	OFFICE, COMPUT. MACHINES	0	11513	0	1282330	21624	31531	2356	0	3432
52	SERVICE IND. MACHINES	0	27561	0	452322	6068	2116	13347	0	4010
53	ELECT. TRANSMISS. EQUIP.	0	33689	0	59807	7481	13675	4138	0	1719
54	HOUSEHOLD APPLIANCES	0	9458	0	-94145	11473	6175	1162	0	482
55	ELECTRIC LIGHTING EQUIP.	0	11650	0	201032	8701	4212	1430	0	595
56	RADIO, TV, ETC., EQUIP.	0	24372	0	542706	2958	18221	2576	0	1355
57	ELECTRONIC COMPONENTS	0	13607	0	-25227	3415	12974	1674	0	691
58	MISC. ELECTRICAL MACH.	0	4606	0	167668	0	9518	566	0	235
59	MOTOR VEHICLES, EQUIP.	0	75267	0	-41123	131	167703	20609	0	1343
60	AIRCRAFT, PARTS	0	58276	0	118025	49	6921	0	0	6771
61	OTHER TRANSPORT. EQUIP.	0	11126	0	113633	66	1481	437	0	139
62	PROFESS., SCIEN. INSTRU.	0	22320	0	-78820	0	7032	3811	0	2397
63	MEDICAL, PHOTO. EQUIP.	0	10952	0	435795	131	11138	1873	0	1174
64	MISC. MANUFACTURING	0	9155	0	298029	49	28760	659	0	1006
65	TRANSPORT., WAREHOUSING	3910	84103	5077	659380	71141	5	820641	26127	82770
66	COMMUNIC.,EXC. BRDCAST.	15	1245	354	50304	1552	713	5590	1199	1122
67	RADIO, TV BROADCASTING	644	1009	1305	4507	4681	747	4107	1792	1810
68	ELEC.,GAS,WATER,SAN.SER.	413	0	1248	11538	0	17950	9194	0	65446
69	WHOLESALE, RETAIL TRADE	7430	187876	11462	674150	102744	344	267903	50982	1330
70	FINANCE, INSURANCE	487	5796	505	15010	2351	5659	5659	1519	7683
71	REAL ESTATE, RENTAL	3340	47224	571	94816	23650	389	77633	4789	3870
72	HOTELS, PERSONAL SERV.	1671	14568	2344	52880	8182	965	19031	4086	3130
73	BUSINESS SERVICES	713	12993	1004	279448	4217	0	28224	3618	0
74	RESEARCH, DEVELOPMENT	0	0	10	157	36	0	0	0	0
75	AUTO. REPAIR, SERVICES	5	61	0	185564	2893	5	86	22	20
76	AMUSEMENTS	2	3977	0	14368	253	0	7882	905	1048
77	MED.,EDUC. SERVICES	22	489	364	13833	1668	378	1045	159	44
78	FEDERAL GOVT. ENTERPRISE	330	3751	55	769	0	210	5147	1222	896
79	STATE, LOCAL GOVT. ENT.	1	0	0	0	0	0	175	0	0
80	IMPORTS	0	0	0	0	0	0	0	0	0
81	BUS.TRAVEL, ENT., GIFTS.	0	0	0	0	0	0	0	0	0
82	OFFICE SUPPLIES	0	0	0	0	0	0	0	0	0
83	SCRAP, USED GOODS	0	34193	0	346214	1113	10764	14162	0	36164
84	GOVERNMENT INDUSTRY	0	0	0	0	0	0	0	0	0
85	REST OF WORLD INDUSTRY	0	0	0	0	0	0	0	0	0
86	HOUSEHOLD INDUSTRY	0	0	0	0	0	0	0	0	0
87	INVENTORY VALUATION ADJ.	0	0	0	0	0	0	0	0	0
88	STATE TOTAL	19038	1771733	24379	18124726	452783	711527	1482108	96622	1195034

TABLE 8-8

STATE ESTIMATES OF 1980
NET FOREIGN EXPORTS BY STATE OF EXIT
(THOUSANDS OF 1958 DOLLARS)

INDUSTRY TITLE	37 PENNSYL- VANIA	38 RHODE ISLAND	39 SOUTH CAROLINA	40 SOUTH DAKOTA	41 TENNESSEE	42 TEXAS	43 UTAH	44 VERMONT	45 VIRGINIA
1 LIVESTOCK, PRDTS.	1321	0	1296	0	10	6808	0	187	2
2 OTHER AGRICULTURE PRDTS.	0	0	25289	0	14	3033022	0	736	0
3 FORESTRY, FISHERIES	14	0	0	0	0	719	0	217	14
4 AGRI.,FORES.,FISH. SERV.	492	41	155	94	205	1225	0	39	231
5 IRON, FERRO. ORES MINING	124	0	0	0	0	0	0	0	44
6 NONFERROUS ORES MINING	415	0	308	0	0	2125	0	284	438
7 COAL MINING	146161	0	0	0	0	17519	0	240	69328
8 CRUDE PETRO.,NATURAL GAS	0	0	0	0	0	7991	0	81	0
9 STONE, CLAY MINING	1252	0	1138	0	0	5740	0	1221	768
10 CHEM.,FERT. MIN. MINING	0	0	46	0	0	34740	0	969	0
11 NEW CONSTRUCTION	0	0	0	0	0	0	0	0	0
12 MAINT., REPAIR CONSTR.	0	0	0	0	0	0	0	0	0
13 ORDNANCE, ACCESSORIES	46134	0	1332	0	0	4117	0	727	848
14 FOOD, KINDRED PRDTS.	51548	0	27413	0	1360	690390	0	5457	34971
15 TOBACCO MANUFACTURES	4702	0	0	0	0	1519	0	93	190871
16 FABRICS	3542	0	22046	0	0	2603	0	527	11799
17 TEXTILE PRDTS.	4728	0	0	0	1	6979	0	1104	34
18 APPAREL	22996	0	30594	0	1	7007	0	49	371
19 MISC. TEXTILE PRDTS.	5522	0	244	0	0	711	0	467	87
20 LUMBER, WOOD PRDTS.	598	0	5962	0	0	4068	0	19684	10585
21 WOODEN CONTAINERS	25	0	50	0	0	42	0	93	173
22 HOUSEHOLD FURNITURE	237	0	2624	0	0	1870	0	176	1
23 OTHER FURNITURE	55	0	609	0	0	384	0	36	1
24 PAPER, ALLIED PRDTS.	10805	0	109985	0	270	100601	0	9163	45989
25 PAPERBOARD CONTAINERS	180	0	145	0	0	728	0	105	70
26 PRINTING, PUBLISHING	0	0	0	0	0	14312	0	11570	0
27 CHEMICALS,SELECT. PRDTS.	84211	0	1050	0	270	1137296	0	0	70973
28 PLASTICS, SYNTHETICS	75579	0	10835	0	34	259886	0	8413	14668
29 DRUGS, COSMETICS	3390	0	11146	0	1	8747	0	575	185
30 PAINT, ALLIED PRDTS.	1966	0	16	0	0	2531	0	344	20
31 PETROLEUM, RELATED INDS.	131912	0	0	0	2	346235	0	582	27
32 RUBBER, MISC. PLASTICS	2401	0	8113	0	5	20576	0	2104	532
33 LEATHER TANNING, PRDTS.	399	0	32	0	0	1023	0	262	81
34 FOOTWEAR, LEATHER PRDTS.	407	0	500	0	0	766	0	12	43
35 GLASS, GLASS PRDTS.	15777	0	616	0	21	3418	0	2415	922
36 STONE, CLAY PRDTS.	6723	0	280	0	114	18276	0	6116	1270
37 PRIMARY IRON, STEEL MFR.	25570	0	0	0	4	60442	0	102	6272
38 PRIMARY NONFERROUS MFR.	4943	0	7621	0	17	68831	0	3441	1933

#	Sector	(1)	(2)	(3)	(4)	(5)	(6)	(7)	(8)	(9)
39	METAL CONTAINERS	112	217	0	3037	6	0	95		382
40	FABRICATED METAL PRDTS.	1281	6346	0	27392	66	0	1297		4640
41	SCREW MACH. PRDTS., ETC.	882	6382	41	20130	43	0	705		2834
42	OTHER FAB. METAL PRDTS.	175	14117	0	27251	6	0	53		12220
43	ENGINES, TURBINES	102	21499	0	27422	1	0	20906		515
44	FARM MACH., EQUIP.	6193	2456	0	47953	0	0	9049		4995
45	CONSTRJC. MACH., EQUIP.	7656	7163	0	201420	69	0	45492		12074
46	MATERIAL HANDLING MACH.	877	865	0	7903	3	0	1533		1384
47	METALWORKING MACHINERY	54	2526	0	155532	0	0	5808		3353
48	SPECIAL MACH., EQUIP.	5143	24226	0	127687	0	0	34478		34552
49	GENERAL MACH., EQUIP.	298	7825	0	51264	0	0	3583		5597
50	MACHINE SHOP PRDTS.	61	100	0	2482	0	0	19		1141
51	OFFICE, COMPUT. MACHINES	262	55140	0	36203	0	0	2153		4885
52	SERVICE IND. MACHINES	623	1607	0	36778	0	0	5550		11700
53	ELECT. TRANSMISS. EQUIP.	298	9150	0	62303	56	0	16697		7337
54	HOUSEHOLD APPLIANCES	84	4132	0	9108	16	0	4689		2060
55	ELECTRIC LIGHTING EQUIP.	103	2818	0	31149	19	0	5775		2531
56	RADIO, TV, ETC., EQUIP.	208	12192	0	34602	29	0	12728		6874
57	ELECTRONIC COMPONENTS	1205	8681	0	45867	23	0	6742		2962
58	MISC. ELECTRICAL MACH.	41	6369	0	17861	8	0	2282		1003
59	MOTOR VEHICLES, EQUIP.	1664	7322	0	148505	101	0	12648		1904
60	AIRCRAFT, PARTS	37267	74989	0	57812	0	0	11177		14315
61	OTHER TRANSPORT. EQUIP.	107	1494	0	38180	9	0	824		834
62	PROFESS., SCIEN. INSTRU.	174	1172	0	107022	0	0	14726		10159
63	MEDICAL, PHOTO. EQUIP.	85	5534	0	25299	0	0	7219		4985
64	MISC. MANUFACTURING	65	5020	0	11188	0	0	9081		38398
65	TRANSPORT., WAREHOUSING	581449	3615	14625	459145	37874	13930	29338	5841	363798
66	COMMUNICA.,EXC. BROCAST.	1281	10	15	7501	2900	5	728	20	6512
67	RADIO, TV BROADCASTING	3167	331	713	7587	3567	696	2384	400	4977
68	ELEC.,GAS,WATER,SAN.SER.	0	119	0	10723	0	0	0	17641	
69	WHOLESALE, RETAIL TRADE	64386	3884	21629	122195	98242	14346	29324	654	265696
70	FINANCE, INSURANCE	2116	292	401	6920	2179	367	1233	5225	6714
71	REAL ESTATE, RENTAL	15187	1983	2697	37503	17846	641	11490	1477	72312
72	HOTELS, PERSONAL SERV.	8372	1034	1783	22038	6465	1086	3487	3109	21482
73	BUSINESS SERVICES	5207	0	2161	23121	8567	565	2565		42144
74	RESEARCH, DEVELOPMENT	33	0	0	0	0	0	16	6	102
75	AUTO. REPAIR, SERVICES	0	3	10	105	29	5	68		7394
76	AMUSEMENTS	86	0	1131	12132	2584	0	805	38	1198
77	MED.,EDUC. SERVICES	1462	2	0	931	88	0			6364
78	FEDERAL GOVT. ENTERPRISE	0	262	405	4627	1571	382		471	
79	STATE, LOCAL GOVT. ENT.	0	3	0	754	0	0			
80	IMPORTS	0	0	0	0	0	0	0		
81	BUS.TRAVEL, ENT., GIFTS.	0	0	0	0	0	0	0		
82	OFFICE SUPPLIES	0	0	0	0	0	0	0		
83	SCRAP, USED GOODS	2793	1031	0	33310	3	0	1010		10631
84	GOVERNMENT INDUSTRY	0	0	0	0	0	0	0		
85	REST OF WORLD INDUSTRY	0	0	0	0	0	0	0		
86	HOUSEHOLD INDUSTRY	0	0	0	0	0	0	0		
87	INVENTORY VALUATION ADJ.	0	0	0	0	0	0	0		
88	STATE TOTAL	1214113	379502	45576	8013189	184429	3217	587302	34923	1634482

TABLE B-8

STATE ESTIMATES OF 1990
NET FOREIGN EXPORTS BY STATE OF EXIT
(THOUSANDS OF 1958 DOLLARS)

INDUSTRY TITLE	46 WASHINGTON	47 WEST VIRGINIA	48 WISCONSIN	49 WYOMING	50 ALASKA	51 HAWAII	52 NO STATE ALLOCATION	53 NATIONAL TOTAL
1 LIVESTOCK, PRDTS.	2411	0	1523	0	2	181	0	70000
2 OTHER AGRICULTURE PRDTS.	610196	0	61694	0	0	538	0	5139999
3 FORESTRY, FISHERIES	10687	0	247	0	0	0	0	90000
4 AGRI.,FORES.,FISH. SERV.	245	50	247	16	0	40	0	12998
5 IRON, FERRO. ORES MINING	8551	0	30296	0	0	1	0	179998
6 NONFERROUS ORES MINING	1496	0	63	0	42	0	0	26000
7 COAL MINING	1084	0	4749	0	0	0	0	535999
8 CRUDE PETRO.,NATURAL GAS	344	0	720	0	0	0	0	23000
9 STONE, CLAY MINING	2453	0	564	0	28	0	0	90002
10 CHEM.,FERT. MIN. MINING	2016	0	680	0	0	0	0	172001
11 NEW CONSTRUCTION	0	0	0	0	0	0	0	4000
12 MAINT.,REPAIR CONSTR.	0	0	0	0	0	0	0	0
13 ORDNANCE, ACCESSORIES	5207	0	1937	0	484	484	0	529998
14 FOOD, KINDRED PRDTS.	239401	0	87253	0	47	3132	0	4686000
15 TOBACCO MANUFACTURES	1383	0	4	0	0	0	0	659998
16 FABRICS	1403	0	459	0	0	0	0	186000
17 TEXTILE PRDTS.	2968	0	379	0	0	3	0	135000
18 APPAREL	10997	0	1384	0	1436	0	0	430000
19 MISC. TEXTILE PRDTS.	1223	0	684	0	0	18	0	140999
20 LUMBER, WOOD PRDTS.	303991	0	1581	0	1518	0	0	633001
21 WOODEN CONTAINERS	208	0	10	0	0	0	0	4001
22 HOUSEHOLD FURNITURE	499	0	200	0	0	0	0	31999
23 OTHER FURNITURE	102	0	42	0	6	0	0	7001
24 PAPER, ALLIED PRDTS.	347826	0	3217	0	1	119	0	1753998
25 PAPERBOARD CONTAINERS	891	0	57	0	9253	1	0	19000
26 PRINTING, PUBLISHING	41056	0	4203	0	0	0	0	694000
27 CHEMICALS,SELECT. PRDTS.	104967	0	122	0	0	1	0	3138003
28 PLASTICS, SYNTHETICS	13848	0	5006	0	0	3	0	1568999
29 DRUGS, COSMETICS	21958	0	1591	0	0	0	0	564000
30 PAINT, ALLIED PRDTS.	719	0	244	0	0	0	0	65002
31 PETROLEUM, RELATED INDS.	3083	0	553	0	0	196	0	1079000
32 RUBBER, MISC. PLASTICS	17884	0	4551	0	0	0	0	586999
33 LEATHER TANNING, PRDTS.	2426	0	1691	0	0	0	0	53000
34 FOOTWEAR, LEATHER PRDTS.	1598	0	216	0	356	0	0	30000
35 GLASS, GLASS PRDTS.	4650	0	1023	0	0	0	0	246001
36 STONE, CLAY PRDTS.	11943	0	2601	0	25	3	0	404998
37 PRIMARY IRON, STEEL MFR.	9699	0	2407	0	47	62	0	906999
38 PRIMARY NONFERROUS MFR.	190471	0	2477	0	11	148	0	943998

39 METAL CONTAINERS	896	0	254	0	0	0	0	25000
40 FABRICATED METAL PRDTS.	26013	0	4288	0	22	4	0	405998
41 SCREW MACH. PRDTS., ETC.	25725	0	3621	0	0	1	0	331998
42 OTHER FAB. METAL PRDTS.	33040	0	6580	0	0	0	0	558000
43 ENGINES, TURBINES	85219	0	7635	0	0	8	0	1170000
44 FARM MACH., EQUIP.	52090	0	11308	0	0	34	0	850998
45 CONSTRUC. MACH., EQUIP.	70930	0	41583	0	69	101	0	2030000
46 MATERIAL HANDLING MACH.	4568	0	3594	0	0	10	0	202000
47 METALWORKING MACHINERY	32231	0	2176	0	0	6	0	702001
48 SPECIAL MACH., EQUIP.	25911	0	2513	0	0	12	0	1438002
49 GENERAL MACH., EQUIP.	47738	0	5126	0	0	41	0	792999
50 MACHINE SHOP PRDTS.	298	0	187	0	0	0	0	20000
51 OFFICE, COMPUT. MACHINES	211281	0	8600	0	0	102	0	2078000
52 SERVICE IND. MACHINES	22857	0	13050	0	0	124	0	864999
53 ELECT. TRANSMISS. EQUIP.	52556	0	4572	0	0	512	0	1104996
54 HOUSEHOLD APPLIANCES	23664	0	1790	0	0	145	0	342999
55 ELECTRIC LIGHTING EQUIP.	16205	0	1469	0	0	178	0	395999
56 RADIO, TV, ETC., EQUIP.	75260	0	5242	0	0	293	0	1003000
57 ELECTRONIC COMPONENTS	49650	0	3463	0	0	819	0	680000
58 MISC. ELECTRICAL MACH.	36358	0	2284	0	0	70	0	357999
59 MOTOR VEHICLES, EQUIP.	70920	0	45233	0	0	8	0	2787000
60 AIRCRAFT, PARTS	493267	0	3668	0	0	165	0	2845999
61 OTHER TRANSPORT. EQUIP.	9379	0	2300	0	0	1	0	287999
62 PROFESS., SCIEN. INSTRU.	21928	0	4639	0	0	63	0	1276000
63 MEDICAL, PHOTO. EQUIP.	24125	0	3645	0	0	32	0	689001
64 MISC. MANUFACTURING	65263	0	3163	0	0	32	0	592000
65 TRANSPORT., WAREHOUSING	128242	181269	359856	6684	6896	6896	0	6773999
66 COMMUNICA.,EXC. BRDCAST.	1424	666	1337	5	487	1055	0	149997
67 RADIO, TV BROADCASTING	2367	1514	2958	609	120	661	0	111997
68 ELEC.,GAS,WATER,SAN.SER.	8475	0	0	0	0	0	0	70998
69 WHOLESALE, RETAIL TRADE	76113	20540	80954	3664	2663	10814	0	5125997
70 FINANCE, INSURANCE	1817	671	2609	166	212	315	0	127999
71 REAL ESTATE, RENTAL	12684	8279	26344	359	505	1198	0	969004
72 HOTELS, PERSONAL SERV.	5916	2244	7429	1226	577	2198	0	426999
73 BUSINESS SERVICES	6559	1603	9564	0	0	1464	0	769003
74 RESEARCH, DEVELOPMENT	30	8	0	3	0	0	0	0
75 AUTO. REPAIR, SERVICES	0	0	32	2	0	8	0	2000
76 AMUSEMENTS	3750	0	3155	3	0	0	0	676002
77 MED.,EDUC. SERVICES	82	0	289	4	0	151	0	25995
78 FEDERAL GOVT. ENTERPRISE	1600	740	1943	153	124	279	64872	169000
79 STATE, LOCAL GOVT. ENT.	2412	0	0	54	54	0	0	6999
80 IMPORTS	0	0	0	0	0	0	-68339000	-68339000
81 BUS.TRAVEL, ENT., GIFTS.	0	0	0	0	0	0	0	0
82 OFFICE SUPPLIES	0	0	0	0	0	0	0	0
83 SCRAP, USED GOODS	120631	0	3007	0	46	139	0	903002
84 GOVERNMENT INDUSTRY	0	0	0	0	0	0	0	0
85 REST OF WORLD INDUSTRY	0	0	0	0	0	0	11852000	11852000
86 HOUSEHOLD INDUSTRY	0	0	0	0	0	0	3000	3000
87 INVENTORY VALUATION ADJ.	0	0	0	0	0	0	0	0
88 STATE TOTAL	3929357	217590	916135	12889	25033	32871	-56419128	9499969

TABLE B-9

STATE ESTIMATES OF 1970
STATE AND LOCAL GOVERNMENT NET PURCHASES OF GOODS AND SERVICES
(THOUSANDS OF 1958 DOLLARS)

INDUSTRY TITLE	1 ALABAMA	2 ARIZONA	3 ARKANSAS	4 CALIFORNIA	5 COLORADO	6 CONNECTICUT	7 DELAWARE	8 DISTRICT OF COLUMBIA	9 FLORIDA
1 LIVESTOCK, PRDTS.	303	200	163	5052	271	362	84	205	761
2 OTHER AGRICULTURE PRDTS.	2326	1318	1269	29188	1967	2277	455	1785	7025
3 FORESTRY, FISHERIES	85	64	43	1067	85	96	21	43	192
4 AGRI.,FORES.,FISH. SERV.	-508	-667	-431	-19270	-675	-481	-69	-149	-2579
5 IRON, FERRO. ORES MINING	0	0	0	0	0	0	0	0	0
6 NONFERROUS ORES MINING	0	0	0	0	0	0	0	0	0
7 COAL MINING	372	266	199	4852	348	431	105	202	865
8 CRUDE PETRO.,NATURAL GAS	0	0	0	0	0	0	0	0	0
9 STONE, CLAY MINING	-1095	-696	-598	-6037	-628	-974	-308	-282	-1535
10 CHEM.,FERT. MIN. MINING	867	552	474	4788	498	771	246	225	1215
11 NEW CONSTRUCTION	231548	170088	127147	2108147	166656	239791	60097	181328	456614
12 MAINT., REPAIR CONSTR.	77290	53271	41659	594819	54525	74613	21392	24240	131320
13 ORDNANCE, ACCESSORIES	52	40	29	886	49	74	18	34	120
14 FOOD, KINDRED PRDTS.	11914	7764	6251	132139	10730	12286	2865	6742	29034
15 TOBACCO MANUFACTURES	25	12	2	275	22	25	6	6	69
16 FABRICS	352	267	202	6029	335	450	106	225	927
17 TEXTILE PRDTS.	41	21	21	395	33	36	7	30	119
18 APPAREL	3044	2089	1699	45374	2771	3542	806	2035	8236
19 MISC. TEXTILE PRDTS.	204	163	122	3034	204	244	61	102	468
20 LUMBER, WOOD PRDTS.	83	66	50	1474	83	110	28	55	226
21 WOODEN CONTAINERS	0	0	0	0	0	0	0	0	0
22 HOUSEHOLD FURNITURE	458	337	251	6362	406	576	147	254	985
23 OTHER FURNITURE	5257	4010	2871	64920	4552	6112	1414	4562	12121
24 PAPER, ALLIED PRDTS.	1470	1142	749	12632	1461	1320	346	318	2847
25 PAPERBOARD CONTAINERS	1085	1085	1085	23876	1085	2171	1085	1085	3256
26 PRINTING, PUBLISHING	11421	9094	6233	152767	11291	12663	3170	4489	25600
27 CHEMICALS,SELECT. PRDTS.	9214	7925	5723	171575	9103	9744	2209	4079	27239
28 PLASTICS, SYNTHETICS	0	0	0	0	0	0	0	0	0
29 DRUGS, COSMETICS	11042	5780	5641	98593	9037	10078	2127	7754	29541
30 PAINT, ALLIED PRDTS.	61	73	48	1981	77	59	10	19	274
31 PETROLEUM, RELATED INDS.	15090	11138	8319	215977	13483	19227	4887	8413	32979
32 RUBBER, MISC. PLASTICS	2453	1854	1360	39583	2309	3365	836	1534	5652
33 LEATHER TANNING, PRDTS.	0	0	0	0	0	0	0	0	0
34 FOOTWEAR, LEATHER PRDTS.	22	16	12	340	20	29	7	14	52
35 GLASS, GLASS PRDTS.	896	547	438	9799	839	1075	166	472	2019
36 STONE, CLAY PRDTS.	282	220	160	4591	271	368	90	164	680
37 PRIMARY IRON, STEEL MFR.	71	60	43	1149	67	76	19	29	181
38 PRIMARY NONFERROUS MFR.	0	0	0	0	0	0	0	0	0

39 METAL CONTAINERS	0	0	0	0	0	0	0	0	0
40 FABRICATED METAL PRDTS.	0	0	0	0	0	0	0	0	0
41 SCREW MACH. PRDTS., ETC.	380	253	209	3114	253	386	112	132	618
42 OTHER FAB. METAL PRDTS.	808	592	433	8526	688	852	200	612	1813
43 ENGINES, TURBINES	0	0	0	0	0	0	0	0	0
44 FARM MACH., EQUIP.	399	332	233	5893	395	376	88	134	1056
45 CONSTRUC. MACH., EQUIP.	982	681	546	8105	613	1008	275	653	1716
46 MATERIAL HANDLING MACH.	1885	1414	1007	20650	1832	1735	418	665	4412
47 METALWORKING MACHINERY	250	230	153	3839	160	354	56	670	763
48 SPECIAL MACH., EQUIP.	162	124	89	2229	145	200	46	141	385
49 GENERAL MACH., EQUIP.	281	226	156	3731	242	343	74	315	679
50 MACHINE SHOP PRDTS.	1285	988	661	11859	1248	1218	318	349	2505
51 OFFICE, COMPUT. MACHINES	4274	3267	2207	41537	4154	4165	1077	1300	8536
52 SERVICE IND. MACHINES	1787	1385	994	25344	1551	2268	503	1908	4420
53 ELECT. TRANSMISS. EQUIP.	334	305	202	5146	220	472	76	855	1004
54 HOUSEHOLD APPLIANCES	314	279	192	4782	209	436	70	785	942
55 ELECTRIC LIGHTING EQUIP.	325	251	168	3052	321	309	81	84	640
56 RADIO, TV, ETC., EQUIP.	3851	2670	2125	38551	2753	4235	1179	1822	6890
57 ELECTRONIC COMPONENTS	80	120	80	3091	120	80	0	40	442
58 MISC. ELECTRICAL MACH.	435	337	223	3851	427	400	104	116	849
59 MOTOR VEHICLES, EQUIP.	15290	11471	8319	184038	13199	17603	4310	10555	33191
60 AIRCRAFT, PARTS	0	0	0	0	0	0	0	0	0
61 OTHER TRANSPORT. EQUIP.	504	560	370	9272	378	856	131	1661	1853
62 PROFESS., SCIEN. INSTRU.	3577	2694	2027	39640	2781	4023	847	4435	8984
63 MEDICAL, PHOTO. EQUIP.	2026	1489	1073	21352	1802	2135	552	866	4086
64 MISC. MANUFACTURING	2595	1997	1387	31758	2448	2946	729	1403	5600
65 TRANSPORT., WAREHOUSING	18313	14124	9806	217168	17824	18958	4752	6740	40314
66 COMMUNICA.,EXC. BRDCAST.	8365	6902	4885	129355	8628	10622	2620	4349	20602
67 RADIO, TV BROADCASTING	452	328	208	4672	461	467	95	114	837
68 ELEC.,GAS,WATER,SAN.SER.	24836	18688	12497	222536	24097	24974	6614	7254	45853
69 WHOLESALE, RETAIL TRADE	2899	2193	1738	53690	2576	3803	901	1976	7920
70 FINANCE, INSURANCE	6621	5305	3628	89577	6572	7299	1822	2570	14994
71 REAL ESTATE, RENTAL	13578	10461	7605	222258	13048	18518	4573	8346	31975
72 HOTELS, PERSONAL SERV.	1783	845	1212	56049	1260	3455	660	3274	8084
73 BUSINESS SERVICES	23805	18020	13432	371256	23015	27707	6458	13419	62506
74 RESEARCH, DEVELOPMENT	0	0	0	0	0	0	0	0	0
75 AUTO. REPAIR, SERVICES	2074	1675	1215	38198	2039	2715	645	1244	5503
76 AMUSEMENTS	-1726	-1309	-856	-12601	-1697	-1505	-404	-332	-3129
77 MED.,EDUC. SERVICES	6857	3160	3496	59789	5375	6026	1167	5536	19836
78 FEDERAL GOVT. ENTERPRISE	4290	3228	2367	66935	4061	5664	1395	2581	9992
79 STATE, LOCAL GOVT. ENT.	466	359	261	7977	443	666	165	303	1081
80 IMPORTS	53	63	41	1699	66	51	8	17	235
81 BUS.TRAVEL, ENT., GIFTS.	0	0	0	0	0	0	0	0	0
82 OFFICE SUPPLIES	5736	4404	3184	90122	5486	7469	1844	3287	13402
83 SCRAP, USED GOODS	7617	5672	4335	70950	4619	8276	1930	9214	15793
84 GOVERNMENT INDUSTRY	452092	336104	235615	4745153	435417	452476	113346	166255	968892
85 REST OF WORLD INDUSTRY	0	0	0	0	0	0	0	0	0
86 HOUSEHOLD INDUSTRY	0	0	0	0	0	0	0	0	0
87 INVENTORY VALUATION ADJ.	0	0	0	0	0	0	0	0	0
88 STATE TOTAL	1006459	739989	538766	10630514	880502	1044562	261184	515673	2132578

TABLE 8-9

STATE ESTIMATES OF 1970
STATE AND LOCAL GOVERNMENT NET PURCHASES OF GOODS AND SERVICES
(THOUSANDS OF 1958 DOLLARS)

INDUSTRY TITLE	10 GEORGIA	11 IDAHO	12 ILLINOIS	13 INDIANA	14 IOWA	15 KANSAS	16 KENTUCKY	17 LOUISIANA	18 MAINE
1 LIVESTOCK, PRDTS.	467	83	1265	410	295	209	335	377	86
2 OTHER AGRICULTURE PRDTS.	4688	686	9509	3376	2131	1676	2277	3115	565
3 FORESTRY, FISHERIES	117	21	341	139	96	64	96	107	32
4 AGRI.,FORES.,FISH. SERV.	-1028	-527	-2009	-768	-652	-661	-660	-1377	-315
5 IRON,FERRO. ORES MINING	0	0	0	0	0	0	0	0	0
6 NONFERROUS ORES MINING	0	0	0	0	0	0	0	0	0
7 COAL MINING	527	100	1502	547	381	268	410	452	111
8 CRUDE PETRO.,NATURAL GAS									
9 STONE, CLAY MINING	-1166	-305	-2498	-1396	-1177	-767	-1057	-1343	-357
10 CHEM.,FERT. MIN. MINING	927	240	1977	1110	933	609	840	1068	282
11 NEW CONSTRUCTION	301789	57581	709114	326227	228591	167680	254092	295989	68610
12 MAINT., REPAIR CONSTR.	88656	21543	218316	107301	83977	56544	76902	95565	24951
13 ORDNANCE, ACCESSORIES	62	16	226	61	53	35	65	66	-18
14 FOOD, KINDRED PRDTS.	19311	2961	46996	18635	11835	8618	12159	14245	3163
15 TOBACCO MANUFACTURES	47	6	106	37	22	19	25	31	6
16 FABRICS	502	123	1490	450	360	258	417	483	119
17 TEXTILE PRDTS.	86	10	162	64	36	30	36	51	8
18 APPAREL	4923	965	12630	4145	3001	2210	3361	4066	911
19 MISC. TEXTILE PRDTS.	265	61	835	305	224	163	244	265	61
20 LUMBER, WOOD PRDTS.	121	28	359	110	88	61	99	116	28
21 WOODEN CONTAINERS	0	0	0	0	0	0	0	0	0
22 HOUSEHOLD FURNITURE	560	132	1788	592	474	320	532	569	150
23 OTHER FURNITURE	7422	1303	19891	7673	5104	3807	6098	6647	1528
24 PAPER, ALLIED PRDTS.	1948	337	5216	2819	1639	1180	1461	1620	431
25 PAPERBOARD CONTAINERS	2171	0	6512	2171	1085	1085	2171	2171	0
26 PRINTING, PUBLISHING	14938	3422	44249	18236	12408	8888	12653	14272	3760
27 CHEMICALS+SELECT. PRDTS.	14291	4390	34755	13441	10119	8063	10430	14936	3566
28 PLASTICS, SYNTHETICS	0	0	0	0	0	0	0	0	0
29 DRUGS, COSMETICS	21572	2389	43405	17315	10089	7637	10181	13006	2310
30 PAINT, ALLIED PRDTS.	116	54	241	95	76	73	77	147	34
31 PETROLEUM, RELATED INDS.	18543	4429	59692	19281	15635	10547	17651	18911	4986
32 RUBBER, MISC. PLASTICS	3011	731	10454	3024	2519	1691	2993	3092	822
33 LEATHER TANNING, PRDTS.	29	7	93	27	22	15	26	27	7
34 FOOTWEAR, LEATHER PRDTS.									
35 GLASS, GLASS PRDTS.	1266	243	4253	1840	1121	905	735	1227	286
36 STONE, CLAY PRDTS.	366	90	1180	370	294	206	338	370	97
37 PRIMARY IRON, STEEL MFR.	98	31	253	100	79	60	81	107	26
38 PRIMARY NONFERROUS MFR.	0	0	0	0	0	0	0	0	0

	C1	C2	C3	C4	C5	C6	C7	C8	C9
39 METAL CONTAINERS	0	0	0	0	0	0	0	0	0
40 FABRICATED METAL PRDTS.	0	0	0	0	0	0	0	0	0
41 SCREW MACH. PRDTS., ETC.	124	471	392	265	406	480	1054	109	418
42 OTHER FAB. METAL PRDTS.	225	994	882	594	794	1257	2924	191	1183
43 ENGINES, TURBINES	141	0	0	0	0	0	0	0	0
44 FARM MACH., EQUIP.	141	582	422	346	442	667	1441	159	609
45 CONSTRUC. MACH., EQUIP.	307	1266	1059	685	985	1225	2668	263	1160
46 MATERIAL HANDLING MACH.	558	2325	1890	1518	2024	3353	6964	533	2869
47 METALWORKING MACHINERY	58	401	378	172	157	290	924	49	439
48 SPECIAL MACH., EQUIP.	48	205	192	115	157	226	647	42	226
49 GENERAL MACH., EQUIP.	81	368	345	205	262	405	1082	67	403
50 MACHINE SHOP PRDTS.	383	1439	1305	1010	1415	2341	4591	303	1578
51 OFFICE, COMPUT. MACHINES	1271	4821	4388	3327	4667	7634	15578	1018	5640
52 SERVICE IND. MACHINES	521	2341	2193	1261	1666	2414	7157	453	2580
53 ELECT. TRANSMISS. EQUIP.	80	528	497	231	218	389	1245	66	575
54 HOUSEHOLD APPLIANCES	70	489	471	209	209	366	1187	70	558
55 ELECTRIC LIGHTING EQUIP.	97	363	331	257	359	598	1178	76	427
56 RADIO, TV, ETC., EQUIP.	1266	4838	4182	2681	4025	4787	11863	1096	4371
57 ELECTRONIC COMPONENTS	40	241	120	120	120	161	361	80	201
58 MISC. ELECTRICAL MACH.	128	484	437	346	480	816	1548	100	576
59 MOTOR VEHICLES, EQUIP.	4645	19012	17371	11048	15409	22004	56549	3962	20289
60 AIRCRAFT, PARTS	0	0	0	0	0	0	0	0	0
61 OTHER TRANSPORT. EQUIP.	138	974	917	416	370	696	2216	114	1065
62 PROFESS.. SCIEN. INSTRU.	942	4842	4235	2622	3251	5275	12979	820	5870
63 MEDICA_, PHOTO. EQUIP.	619	2398	2155	1501	2143	3170	7248	517	2617
64 MISC. MANUFACTURING	797	3110	2904	1927	2711	4050	10016	665	3399
65 TRANSPORT., WAREHOUSING	5724	22239	19460	14286	19804	30604	69088	5119	24953
66 COMMUNICA..EXC. BROCAST.	2926	11245	10156	6641	9400	12993	35789	2702	11655
67 RADIO, TV BROADCASTING	154	572	440	480	602	1010	1967	111	494
68 ELEC.,GAS,WATER,SAN.SER.	7205	26272	25616	18748	27103	44292	91441	5137	31028
69 WHOLESALE, RETAIL TRADE	1046	4319	3509	2127	2944	3195	11828	1164	4113
70 FINANCE, INSURANCE	2193	8351	7331	5192	7210	10613	25617	2025	8713
71 REAL ESTATE, RENTAL	4606	17396	16621	9591	14122	17291	58266	4162	17031
72 HOTELS, PERSONAL SERV.	579	3388	2572	907	1188	-202	10298	941	3969
73 BUSINESS SERVICES	7724	32165	26850	18165	24621	34331	97826	8012	35705
74 RESEARCH, DEVELOPMENT	0	0	0	0	0	0	0	0	0
75 AUTO. REPAIR, SERVICES	748	2949	2526	1571	2174	2646	8797	784	2817
76 AMUSEMENTS	-485	-1798	-1673	-1365	-1919	-3377	-6026	-345	-2255
77 MED.,EDUC. SERVICES	1261	8213	6082	4632	5937	10516	27494	1460	14744
78 FEDERAL GOVT. ENTERPRISE	1412	5397	5123	3012	4414	5551	18094	1271	5471
79 STATE, LOCAL GOVT. ENT.	161	593	585	317	478	549	2029	142	553
80 IMPORTS	29	126	65	63	65	32	206	46	99
81 BUS.TRAVEL, ENT., GIFTS.	0	0	0	0	0	0	0	0	0
82 OFFICE SUPPLIES	1921	7309	6837	4110	5969	7533	23962	1755	7285
83 SCRAP, USED GOODS	2169	10438	8930	5328	6836	9528	21823	1837	10367
84 GOVERNMENT INDUSTRY	132810	524012	466156	347622	484361	778459	1698982	112508	630427
85 REST OF WORLD INDUSTRY	0	0	0	0	0	0	0	0	0
86 HOUSEHOLD INDUSTRY	0	0	0	0	0	0	0	0	0
87 INVENTORY VALUATION ADJ.									0
88 STATE TOTAL	301005	1226053	1069320	753776	1048439	1576024	3581209	260736	1370947

STATE ESTIMATES OF 1970

STATE AND LOCAL GOVERNMENT NET PURCHASES OF GOODS AND SERVICES

(THOUSANDS OF 1958 DOLLARS)

INDUSTRY TITLE	19 MARYLAND	20 MASSA-CHUSETTS	21 MICHIGAN	22 MINNESOTA	23 MISSISSIPPI	24 MISSOURI	25 MONTANA	26 NEBRASKA	27 NEVADA
1 LIVESTOCK, PRDTS.	486	836	1144	475	224	416	67	144	109
2 OTHER AGRICULTURE PRDTS.	3904	5580	8446	3680	1870	3346	474	1129	783
3 FORESTRY, FISHERIES	128	192	320	139	64	117	21	43	32
4 AGRI.,FORES.,FISH. SERV.	-937	-459	-1781	-973	-505	-802	-350	-574	-216
5 IRON, FERRO. ORES MINING	0	0	0	0	0	0	0	0	0
6 NONFERROUS ORES MINING	0	0	0	0	0	0	0	0	0
7 COAL MINING	572	928	1388	576	262	509	90	180	124
8 CRUDE PETRO.,NATURAL GAS	0	0	0	0	0	0	0	0	0
9 STONE, CLAY MINING	-895	-1095	-2039	-1459	-786	-1343	-466	-602	-339
10 CHEM.,FERT. MIN. MINING	708	864	1617	1158	624	1068	369	477	270
11 NEW CONSTRUCTION	340073	370107	633652	327630	153872	308920	78179	145129	70772
12 MAINT.,REPAIR CONSTR.	81197	100961	185205	108660	54260	99884	29755	41942	23950
13 ORDNANCE, ACCESSORIES	82	165	205	83	38	68	13	26	21
14 FOOD, KINDRED PRDTS.	18442	27044	43346	18274	8510	16637	2626	5552	3681
15 TOBACCO MANUFACTURES	41	66	94	41	19	37	3	12	9
16 FABRICS	569	990	1348	565	265	481	96	190	135
17 TEXTILE PRDTS.	68	89	145	63	31	59	7	18	13
18 APPAREL	4932	8002	11377	4836	2328	4228	750	1560	1100
19 MISC. TEXTILE PRDTS.	326	509	774	326	143	285	61	102	61
20 LUMBER, WOOD PRDTS.	138	237	326	138	66	116	22	44	33
21 WOODEN CONTAINERS	0	0	0	0	0	0	0	0	0
22 HOUSEHOLD FURNITURE	665	1151	1621	703	326	605	129	233	167
23 OTHER FURNITURE	9075	11949	18430	7903	3485	7247	1386	3100	1687
24 PAPER, ALLIED PRDTS.	2023	2201	5132	2172	899	2051	393	712	346
25 PAPERBOARD CONTAINERS	2171	4341	5426	2171	1085	2171	0	1085	1085
26 PRINTING, PUBLISHING	16905	24379	41763	17623	7717	15688	3264	5980	3554
27 CHEMICALS,SELECT. PRDTS.	14055	17068	31417	14911	7242	12980	3558	6142	3264
28 PLASTICS, SYNTHETICS	0	0	0	0	0	0	0	0	0
29 DRUGS, COSMETICS	17644	24669	39167	16838	8345	15757	1912	4726	3315
30 PAINT, ALLIED PRDTS.	108	70	217	113	57	95	37	61	24
31 PETROLEUM, RELATED INDS.	22043	40196	54033	23315	10828	19945	4233	7669	5578
32 RUBBER, MISC. PLASTICS	3847	7436	9508	3883	1770	3261	632	1230	954
33 LEATHER TANNING, PRDTS.	0	0	0	0	0	0	0	0	0
34 FOOTWEAR, LEATHER PRDTS.	35	66	84	34	16	29	5	10	9
35 GLASS, GLASS PRDTS.	1332	2418	3899	1579	687	1225	252	399	145
36 STONE, CLAY PRDTS.	442	789	1076	449	206	382	79	148	106
37 PRIMARY IRON, STEEL MFR.	100	131	226	112	55	98	29	45	24
38 PRIMARY NONFERROUS MFR.	0	0	0	0	0	0	0	0	0

#	Industry	C1	C2	C3	C4	C5	C6	C7	C8	C9
39	METAL CONTAINERS	0	0	0	0	0	0	0	0	0
40	FABRICATED METAL PRDTS.	0	0	0	0	0	0	0	0	0
41	SCREW MACH. PRDTS., ETC.	127	206	147	477	274	530	898	571	380
42	OTHER FAB. METAL PRDTS.	240	458	214	1119	534	1197	2721	1606	1321
43	ENGINES, TURBINES	0	0	0	0	0	0	0	0	0
44	FARM MACH., EQUIP.	120	244	141	565	290	624	1345	618	583
45	CONSTRUC. MACH., EQUIP.	320	606	376	1252	685	1354	2272	1441	1202
46	MATERIAL HANDLING MACH.	506	969	514	2661	1271	2865	6635	3188	2770
47	METALWORKING MACHINERY	87	258	65	369	144	362	634	634	743
48	SPECIAL MACH., EQUIP.	55	93	40	222	109	248	597	415	284
49	GENERAL MACH., EQUIP.	92	184	72	392	180	422	1007	665	543
50	MACHINE SHOP PRDTS.	324	629	350	1776	799	1301	4460	2107	1779
51	OFFICE, COMPUT. MACHINES	1116	2082	1137	5905	2693	6363	15057	7492	6028
52	SERVICE IND. MACHINES	622	1103	446	2475	1203	2736	6580	4687	3371
53	ELECT. TRANSMISS. EQUIP.	117	334	87	490	196	486	1133	857	954
54	HOUSEHOLD APPLIANCES	105	314	87	471	192	454	1082	803	890
55	ELECTRIC LIGHTING EQUIP.	82	157	87	451	202	484	1147	543	454
56	RADIO, TV, ETC., EQUIP.	1328	2110	1382	4898	2757	5521	10301	7086	4492
57	ELECTRONIC COMPONENTS	40	80	40	161	80	161	321	120	151
58	MISC. ELECTRICAL MACH.	105	214	117	605	266	542	1515	678	510
59	MOTOR VEHICLES, EQUIP.	4970	8526	4283	20703	10316	22913	52090	33891	23921
60	AIRCRAFT, PARTS	0	0	0	0	0	0	0	0	0
61	OTHER TRANSPORT. EQUIP.	209	633	158	893	346	870	2016	1519	1820
62	PROFESS., SCIEN. INSTRU.	1136	2442	970	5152	2427	5369	11840	7478	6967
63	MEDICAL, PHOTO. EQUIP.	607	1026	576	2735	1352	3009	6762	3949	2813
64	MISC. MANUFACTURING	804	1351	682	3550	1709	3941	9435	5803	4014
65	TRANSPORT., WAREHOUSING	5333	9338	5073	25308	12217	27894	65550	35805	26655
66	COMMUNICA.-EXC. BRDCAST.	3019	4597	2431	12087	6195	13862	33250	21854	13551
67	RADIO- TV BROADCASTING	50	233	149	671	330	772	1756	839	606
68	ELEC.-GAS,WATER,SAN.SER.	6438	11362	6168	33984	15205	36674	88813	46300	34562
69	WHOLESALE, RETAIL TRADE	1212	1697	934	3892	2331	4677	10333	8103	4508
70	FINANCE, INSURANCE	2056	3502	1916	9112	4484	10232	24183	13962	9813
71	REAL ESTATE, RENTAL	5250	6938	3559	18282	9849	21701	53173	40671	21555
72	HOTELS, PERSONAL SERV.	1248	1031	333	2414	2048	3357	7951	10241	3991
73	BUSINESS SERVICES	8326	12784	6489	33073	17573	37878	69721	58905	38016
74	RESEARCH, DEVELOPMENT	0	0	0	0	0	0	0	0	0
75	AUTO. REPAIR, SERVICES	810	1178	621	2828	1566	3563	7979	5782	3345
76	AMUSEMENTS	-381	-795	-441	-2399	-1021	-2510	-5974	-2486	-2329
77	MED.,EDUC. SERVICES	2102	2846	1010	9913	5412	10536	24438	15931	11362
78	FEDERAL GOVT. ENTERPRISE	1611	2151	1098	5753	3077	6470	16536	12419	6723
79	STATE, LOCAL GOVT. ENT.	188	236	121	616	338	743	1841	1489	741
80	IMPORTS	21	52	32	81	49	96	186	60	93
81	BUS.,TRAVEL, ENT., GIFTS.	0	0	0	0	0	0	0	0	0
82	OFFICE SUPPLIES	2126	2938	1527	7714	4102	9056	21963	16075	8953
83	SCRAP, USED GOODS	2453	5591	2702	10145	5043	10523	18953	12223	12768
84	GOVERNMENT INDUSTRY	125330	219400	116371	627508	296177	682006	1617134	863326	657225
85	REST OF WORLD INDUSTRY	0	0	0	0	0	0	0	0	0
86	HOUSEHOLD INDUSTRY	0	0	0	0	0	0	0	0	0
87	INVENTORY VALUATION ADJ.	0	0	0	0	0	0	0	0	0
88	STATE TOTAL	301100	536012	289689	1373858	677003	1496097	3315527	1899570	1458526

TABLE B-9

STATE ESTIMATES OF 1970

STATE AND LOCAL GOVERNMENT NET PURCHASES OF GOODS AND SERVICES

(THOUSANDS OF 1958 DOLLARS)

INDUSTRY TITLE	28 NEW HAMPSHIRE	29 NEW JERSEY	30 NEW MEXICO	31 NEW YORK	32 NORTH CAROLINA	33 NORTH DAKOTA	34 OHIO	35 OKLAHOMA	36 OREGON
1 LIVESTOCK, PRDTS.	62	810	118	3949	392	96	856	351	233
2 OTHER AGRICULTURE PRDTS.	425	5525	850	29813	3103	510	6114	2077	1609
3 FORESTRY, FISHERIES	21		43	928	117	32	256	96	85
4 AGRI.,FORES.,FISH. SERV.	-122	-1184	-441	-3550	-797	-351	-1356	-540	-1010
5 IRON, FERRO. ORES MINING	0	0	0	0	0	0	0	0	0
6 NONFERROUS ORES MINING	0	0	0	0	0	0		0	0
7 COAL MINING	78	956	161	4381	495	123	1078	418	314
8 CRUDE PETRO.,NATURAL GAS	0	0	0	0	0	0	0	0	0
9 STONE, CLAY MINING	-267	-1441	-440	-4442	-1136	-323	-2983	-737	-828
10 CHEM.,FERT. MIN. MINING	213	1140	348	3522	900	258	2364	585	657
11 NEW CONSTRUCTION	52608	452357	98456	1571304	286508	65094	667730	178354	204580
12 MAINT., REPAIR CONSTR.	18270	128370	33095	453027	87627	24503	218633	59700	63159
13 ORDNANCE, ACCESSORIES	12	157	21	712	22	22	154	75	46
14 FOOD, KINDRED PRDTS.	2338	28293	4924	136439	16104	3124	33536	11441	9223
15 TOBACCO MANUFACTURES	6	63	9	334	34	6	69	25	16
16 FABRICS	77	989	154	4543	456	140	1010	450	321
17 TEXTILE PRDTS.	7	89	15	500	56	7	107	31	25
18 APPAREL	622	7993	1246	38631	3987	997	8510	3434	2510
19 MISC. TEXTILE PRDTS.	41	550	102	2342	285	81	611	244	204
20 LUMBER, WOOD PRDTS.	17	237	39	1082	110	33	243	110	77
21 WOODEN CONTAINERS	0	0	0	0	0	0	0	0	0
22 HOUSEHOLD FURNITURE	102	1195	193	5239	570	174	1335	559	392
23 OTHER FURNITURE	1126	13087	2281	53253	7063	1600	15499	5208	4789
24 PAPER, ALLIED PRDTS.	300	2997	777	11724	2135	412	4401	1208	1405
25 PAPERBOARD CONTAINERS	0	4341	1085	19535	2171	1085	4341	2171	1085
26 PRINTING, PUBLISHING	2450	27873	5666	116391	15598	4107	33793	12310	11095
27 CHEMICALS,SELECT. PRDTS.	2038	21411	4999	86995	12489	3851	25844	9537	10450
28 PLASTICS, SYNTHETICS	0	0	0	0	0	0	0	0	0
29 DRUGS, COSMETICS	1972	24519	3851	133547	14806	1836	29386	8798	6763
30 PAINT, ALLIED PRDTS.	14	143	48	467	94	38	168	64	108
31 PETROLEUM, RELATED INDS.	3381	39998	6332	176874	18773	5846	43990	18787	12952
32 RUBBER, MISC. PLASTICS	547	7171	1021	32478	3097	1014	7240	3381	2136
33 LEATHER TANNING, PRDTS.	5	0	0	0	0	0	0	0	0
34 FOOTWEAR, LEATHER PRDTS.	200	63	9	294	27	9	63	29	18
35 GLASS, GLASS PRDTS.	62	2336	426	10137	1384	254	3591	905	842
36 STONE, CLAY PRDTS.	17	791	125	3531	366	116	831	368	259
37 PRIMARY IRON, STEEL MFR.	0	160	36	622	93	29	203	74	76
38 PRIMARY NONFERROUS MFR.		0	0	0	0	0	0	0	0

	C1	C2	C3	C4	C5	C6	C7	C8	C9
39 METAL CONTAINERS	0	0	0	0	0	0	0	0	0
40 FABRICATED METAL PRDTS.	0	0	0	0	0	0	0	0	0
41 SCREW MACH. PRDTS., ETC.	91	654	153	2405	415	124	1060	324	300
42 OTHER FAB. METAL PRDTS.	169	1837	354	7505	1092	218	2351	707	711
43 ENGINES, TURBINES	0	0	0	0	0	0	0	0	0
44 FARM MACH., EQUIP.	85	845	219	3345	560	142	1136	356	433
45 CONSTRUC. MACH., EQUIP.	235	1711	392	5706	1098	293	2756	754	810
46 MATERIAL HANDLING MACH.	379	4025	946	17161	2687	535	5437	1602	1766
47 METALWORKING MACHINERY	56	731	94	2190	357	53	774	185	282
48 SPECIAL MACH., EQUIP.	35	433	69	1838	216	53	478	179	146
49 GENERAL MACH., EQUIP.	60	737	124	2851	387	85	845	277	272
50 MACHINE SHOP PRDTS.	267	2708	654	10745	1822	374	3827	1116	1204
51 OFFICE, COMPUT. MACHINES	886	9295	2140	37749	6035	1264	12699	3856	3962
52 SERVICE IND. MACHINES	385	4889	743	20300	2396	574	5296	1946	1641
53 ELECT. TRANSMISS. EQUIP.	74	977	126	3015	474	76	1032	258	373
54 HOUSEHOLD APPLIANCES	70	908	122	2932	454	70	977	244	349
55 ELECTRIC LIGHTING EQUIP.	68	696	166	2786	465	95	971	287	306
56 RADIO, TV, ETC., EQUIP.	911	7662	1565	29763	4353	1324	10888	3684	3132
57 ELECTRONIC COMPONENTS	40	241	80	723	161	120	281	120	161
58 MISC. ELECTRICAL MACH.	89	902	225	3529	627	122	1300	362	413
59 MOTOR VEHICLES, EQUIP.	3336	36859	6672	151403	19964	4946	44810	15594	13633
60 AIRCRAFT, PARTS	0	0	0	0	0	0	0	0	0
61 OTHER TRANSPORT. EQUIP.	134	1766	226	5182	864	125	1873	432	688
62 PROFESS., SCIEN. INSTRU.	772	8494	1477	32955	4925	859	10634	2884	3250
63 MEDICAL, PHOTO. EQUIP.	435	4498	929	18594	2668	639	5908	1951	1779
64 MISC. MANUFACTURING	554	6417	1206	26861	3531	862	7707	2747	2383
65 TRANSPORT., WAREHOUSING	3841	42204	9035	176957	25419	5954	53807	18023	17256
66 COMMUNICA.,EXC. BRDCAST.	1917	23229	4134	101183	11861	3336	26094	10473	8288
67 RADIO, TV BROADCASTING	93	1111	236	3544	770	154	1689	438	431
68 ELEC.,GAS,WATER,SAN.SER.	5154	55321	12129	226915	34868	7285	74583	23322	22174
69 WHOLESALE, RETAIL TRADE	657	7974	1222	36306	3523	1245	8131	3773	2668
70 FINANCE, INSURANCE	1421	16096	3313	66966	9125	2391	19574	7100	6498
71 REAL ESTATE, RENTAL	3035	39725	5829	179102	17480	5640	40375	18623	12159
72 HOTELS, PERSONAL SERV.	379	7615	190	45022	1655	862	4212	3615	891
73 BUSINESS SERVICES	5001	62267	10908	283071	32044	8609	68237	27257	22054
74 RESEARCH, DEVELOPMENT	0	0	0	0	0	0	0	0	0
75 AUTO. REPAIR, SERVICES	461	5906	960	26213	2703	900	6027	2748	2041
76 AMUSEMENTS	-349	-3424	-896	-13358	-2510	-446	-5173	-1351	-1590
77 MED.,EDUC. SERVICES	1160	15200	2145	88481	9144	867	17644	5142	3671
78 FEDERAL GOVT. ENTERPRISE	942	12203	1822	55253	5510	1701	12614	5657	3756
79 STATE, LOCAL GOVT. ENT.	104	1415	192	6411	585	203	1382	676	411
80 IMPORTS	12	122	41	400	81	32	144	55	92
81 BUS.TRAVEL, ENT., GIFTS.	0	0	0	0	0	0	0	0	0
82 OFFICE SUPPLIES	1264	16088	2514	71309	7425	2297	16893	7460	5176
83 SCRAP, USED GOODS	1775	14872	2985	45846	9156	1963	21862	5269	6848
84 GOVERNMENT INDUSTRY	92754	1018851	217784	4346883	631471	133760	1327566	422165	406377
85 REST OF WORLD INDUSTRY	0	0	0	0	0	0	0	0	0
86 HOUSE-HOLD INDUSTRY	0	0	0	0	0	0	0	0	0
87 INVENTORY VALUATION ADJ.	0	0	0	0	0	0	0	0	0
88 STATE TOTAL	215358	2205264	458777	9032948	1332934	304346	2926317	919821	890785

TABLE B-9

STATE ESTIMATES OF 1970
STATE AND LOCAL GOVERNMENT NET PURCHASES OF GOODS AND SERVICES
(THOUSANDS OF 1958 DOLLARS)

INDUSTRY TITLE	37 PENNSYL-VANIA	38 RHODE ISLAND	39 SOUTH CAROLINA	40 SOUTH DAKOTA	41 TENNESSEE	42 TEXAS	43 UTAH	44 VERMONT	45 VIRGINIA
1 LIVESTOCK, PRDTS.	1057	133	222	54	388	1513	112	45	404
2 OTHER AGRICULTURE PRDTS.	7116	814	1797	334	3334	6649	680	267	2975
3 FORESTRY, FISHERIES	309	32	64	21	96	331	43	11	128
4 AGRI.,FORES.,FISH. SERV.	-1919	-207	-344	-264	-693	-5526	-355	-153	-868
5 IRON, FERRO. ORES MINING	0	0	0	0	0	0	0	0	0
6 NONFERROUS ORES MINING	0	0	0	0	0	0	0	0	0
7 COAL MINING	1320	155	262	80	447	1691	160	59	509
8 CRUDE PETRO.,NATURAL GAS	0	0	0	0	0	0	0	0	0
9 STONE, CLAY MINING	-3073	-290	-538	-425	-1328	-1396	-459	-293	-1768
10 CHEM.,FERT. MIN. MINING	2433	228	429	336	1056	1107	366	234	1404
11 NEW CONSTRUCTION	738740	69639	135902	68379	319882	822308	9611	47850	372663
12 MAINT., REPAIR CONSTR.	236989	22743	41898	27207	92634	187066	34769	18494	121655
13 ORDNANCE, ACCESSORIES	203	28	37	11	62	411	22	9	73
14 FOOD, KINDRED PRDTS.	39361	4266	8552	2252	14939	34490	4697	1660	15847
15 TOBACCO MANUFACTURES	81	9	19	3	34	66	6	3	31
16 FABRICS	1300	171	254	79	440	2387	146	62	488
17 TEXTILE PRDTS.	119	12	31	5	58	46	12	3	51
18 APPAREL	10533	1311	2237	597	3980	15611	1143	468	4117
19 MISC. TEXTILE PRDTS.	774	81	143	61	244	1120	102	41	285
20 LUMBER, WOOD PRDTS.	315	39	61	22	105	585	39	17	121
21 WOODEN CONTAINERS	0	0	0	0	0	0	0	0	0
22 HOUSEHOLD FURNITURE	1663	210	308	113	549	2662	197	87	654
23 OTHER FURNITURE	18461	1983	3541	1186	7130	26245	2211	873	7875
24 PAPER, ALLIED PRDTS.	4991	412	946	393	1536	1704	815	243	2069
25 PAPERBOARD CONTAINERS	5426	1085	1085	1085	2171	10853	1085	2051	2171
26 PRINTING, PUBLISHING	41200	4472	7661	2988	12827	49267	5780	1947	16174
27 CHEMICALS,SELECT. PRDTS.	32154	3596	6172	2923	11551	52584	4577		13734
28 PLASTICS, SYNTHETICS	32704	3383	8340	1457	15266	13553	3274	1158	13915
29 DRUGS, COSMETICS	229	24	42	28	81	566	40	17	101
30 PAINT, ALLIED PRDTS.									
31 PETROLEUM, RELATED INDS.	55167	7083	10233	3699	18094	90888	6468	2865	21484
32 RUBBER, MISC. PLASTICS	9400	1275	1741	544	2943	17662	1043	441	3424
33 LEATHER TANNING, PRDTS.	81	11	16	0	0	0	0	0	0
34 FOOTWEAR, LEATHER PRDTS.		250	646	5	27	146	9	4	29
35 GLASS, GLASS PRDTS.	3736	139	199	218	1032	3080	377	127	1161
36 STONE, CLAY PRDTS.	1065	29	45	67	340	1891	125	51	398
37 PRIMARY IRON, STEEL MFR.	248			24	88	374	36	17	107
38 PRIMARY NONFERROUS MFR.	0	0	0	0	0	0	0	0	0

220

		1	2	3	4	5	6	7	8	9
39	METAL CONTAINERS	0	0	0	0	0	0	0	0	0
40	FABRICATED METAL PRDTS.	0	0	0	0	0	0	0	0	0
41	SCREW MACH. PRDTS.,ETC.	1166	124	209	132	462	1057	162	94	595
42	OTHER FAB. METAL PRDTS.	2708	267	536	187	1074	2860	343	131	1195
43	ENGINES, TURBINES	0	0	0	0	0	0	0	0	0
44	FARM MACH., EQUIP.	1348	130	262	123	473	1424	208	78	584
45	CONSTRUC. MACH., EQUIP.	2994	300	535	328	1336	3280	390	235	1610
46	MATERIAL HANDLING MACH.	6271	571	1269	471	2169	3884	933	303	2615
47	METALWORKING MACHINERY	905	85	171	40	551	2543	65	35	483
48	SPECIAL MACH., EQUIP.	586	68	112	34	217	948	67	26	237
49	GENERAL MACH., EQUIP.	1013	108	191	60	410	1688	117	46	438
50	MACHINE SHOP PRDTS.	4368	390	825	343	1374	2331	686	219	1814
51	OFFICE, COMPUT. MACHINES	14699	1357	2784	1104	4627	9196	2232	717	5999
52	SERVICE IND. MACHINES	6495	753	1249	362	2565	11532	700	284	2696
53	ELECT. TRANSMISS. EQUIP.	1212	117	227	54	715	3338	91	47	633
54	HOUSEHOLD APPLIANCES	1134	105	209	52	663	3037	87	35	593
55	ELECTRIC LIGHTING EQUIP.	1119	100	210	86	345	597	175	55	457
56	RADIO, TV, ETC., EQUIP.	12464	1418	2233	1230	4771	15170	1610	895	5954
57	ELECTRONIC COMPONENTS	361	361	80	40	120	883	80	40	161
58	MISC. ELECTRICAL MACH.	1479	125	279	116	464	645	236	73	615
59	MOTOR VEHICLES, EQUIP.	53402	5884	10066	3766	19545	71635	6653	2748	22645
60	AIRCRAFT, PARTS	2180	202	409	0	0	0	0	0	0
61	OTHER TRANSPORT. EQUIP.	2180	202	409	95	1350	6223	155	82	1177
62	PROFESS., SCIEN. INSTRU.	12038	1155	2443	775	5739	16506	1315	574	5791
63	MEDICAL, PHOTO. EQUIP.	6907	717	1305	533	2351	6551	952	372	2915
64	MISC. MANUFACTURING	9300	1009	1746	624	3067	11224	1232	442	3706
65	TRANSPORT., WAREHOUSING	53946	6496	12215	4701	20593	59906	9193	3154	25730
66	COMMUNICA.,EXC. BRDCAST.	32580	3872	6119	2159	10313	47546	4178	1570	12444
67	RADIO, TV BROADCASTING	1851	124	332	143	480	1756	255	78	599
68	ELEC.,GAS,WATER,SAN.SER.	36575	8176	16177	6182	26152	52699	12979	4079	34511
69	WHOLESALE, RETAIL TRADE	10544	1462	2038	737	3819	22189	1130	582	4188
70	FINANCE, INSURANCE	23866	2578	4439	1750	7440	28563	3371	1195	9393
71	REAL ESTATE, RENTAL	52352	7003	9710	3066	16351	96846	5927	2451	19088
72	HOTELS, PERSONAL SERV.	6758	1526	1736	26	3486	28697	-117	231	2203
73	BUSINESS SERVICES	8523	10217	17009	5438	29413	127553	10425	3989	32965
74	RESEARCH, DEVELOPMENT	0	0	0	0	0	0	0	0	0
75	AUTO. REPAIR, SERVICES	7872	1038	1476	514	2550	15393	929	391	2946
76	AMUSEMENTS	-5783	-455	-1096	-453	-1768	-989	-953	-278	-2404
77	MED.,EDUC. SERVICES	19330	2029	5386	663	10048	5730	1633	587	8355
78	FEDERAL GOVT. ENTERPRISE	16186	2126	3042	949	5140	28379	1846	752	5961
79	STATE, LOCAL GOVT. ENT.	1827	21	334	102	559	3704	198	86	651
80	IMPORTS	196	21	35	24	69	485	35	14	87
81	BUS.,TRAVEL, ENT., GIFTS.	0	0	0	0	0	0	0	0	0
82	OFFICE SUPPLIES	21628	2794	4030	1327	6815	37409	2547	1028	8030
83	SCRAP, USED GOODS	23761	2206	4356	2225	12207	35340	2723	1616	13175
84	GOVERNMENT INDUSTRY	1550999	151181	302880	109693	508190	1162165	222860	73061	626718
85	REST OF WORLD INDUSTRY	0	0	0	0	0	0	0	0	0
86	HOUSEHOLD INDUSTRY	0	0	0	0	0	0	0	0	0
87	INVENTORY VALUATION ADJ.	0	0	0	0	0	0	0	0	0
88	STATE TOTAL	3386056	340791	649570	262200	1225557	3269857	461776	180771	1468968

TABLE B-9

STATE ESTIMATES OF 1970
STATE AND LOCAL GOVERNMENT NET PURCHASES OF GOODS AND SERVICES
(THOUSANDS OF 1958 DOLLARS)

INDUSTRY TITLE	46 WASHINGTON	47 WEST VIRGINIA	48 WISCONSIN	49 WYOMING	50 ALASKA	51 HAWAII	52 NO STATE ALLOCATION	53 NATIONAL TOTAL
1 LIVESTOCK, PRDTS.	373	152	555	43	92	160	0	27000
2 OTHER AGRICULTURE PRDTS.	2398	1063	3789	419	425	1069	0	188000
3 FORESTRY, FISHERIES	117	43	171	11	21	43	0	7000
4 AGRI.,FORES.,FISH. SERV.	-1221	-361	-1313	-258	-206	-539	0	-63000
5 IRON, FERRO. ORES MINING	0	0	0	0	0	0	0	0
6 NONFERROUS ORES MINING	0	0	0	0	0	0	0	0
7 COAL MINING	490	192	710	56	109	188	0	31000
8 CRUDE PETRO.,NATURAL GAS	0	0	0	0	0	0	0	0
9 STONE, CLAY MINING	-1204	-786	-1508	-350	-527	-214	0	-58000
10 CHEM.,FERT. MIN. MINING	954	624	1194	279	420	171	0	46000
11 NEW CONSTRUCTION	385519	128645	367476	51500	84387	82083	0	15928000
12 MAINT., REPAIR CONSTR.	92417	51358	123341	21621	32766	22837	0	4787000
13 ORDNANCE, ACCESSORIES	76	29	106	6	23	34	0	5000
14 FOOD, KINDRED PRDTS.	14034	5776	21281	1897	2582	5185	0	924000
15 TOBACCO MANUFACTURES	25	12	41	3	6	9	0	2000
16 FABRICS	502	190	696	58	131	221	0	33000
17 TEXTILE PRDTS.	38	18	63	7	5	15	0	3000
18 APPAREL	3877	1561	5617	506	915	1677	0	267000
19 MISC. TEXTILE PRDTS.	305	122	428	41	61	122	0	18000
20 LUMBER, WOOD PRDTS.	121	44	171	17	33	55	0	8000
21 WOODEN CONTAINERS	0	0	0	0	0	0	0	0
22 HOUSEHOLD FURNITURE	633	261	868	75	184	244	0	39000
23 OTHER FURNITURE	9049	2542	9504	797	1588	2553	0	429000
24 PAPER, ALLIED PRDTS.	1995	749	2884	272	253	515	0	100000
25 PAPERBOARD CONTAINERS	2171	1085	3256	380	1085	1085	0	140000
26 PRINTING, PUBLISHING	16533	6160	23003	2012	3305	5755	0	935000
27 CHEMICALS,SELECT. PRDTS.	14453	5473	18500	2492	3179	5613	0	828000
28 PLASTICS, SYNTHETICS	0	0	0	0	0	0	0	0
29 DRUGS, COSMETICS	10263	4837	17252	1768	1512	3971	0	798000
30 PAINT, ALLIED PRDTS.	134	41	151	27	23	57	0	7000
31 PETROLEUM, RELATED INDS.	20786	8630	28811	2431	6135	8259	0	1305000
32 RUBBER, MISC. PLASTICS	3512	1359	4910	322	1017	1520	0	229000
33 LEATHER TANNING, PRDTS.	0	0	0	0	0	0	0	2000
34 FOOTWEAR, LEATHER PRDTS.	29	12	42	3	9	13	0	2000
35 GLASS, GLASS PRDTS.	1438	513	1651	202	127	304	0	75000
36 STONE, CLAY PRDTS.	410	157	567	44	111	171	0	26000
37 PRIMARY IRON, STEEL MFR.	107	45	138	19	29	38	0	6000
38 PRIMARY NONFERROUS MFR.	0	0	0	0	0	0	0	0

39	METAL CONTAINERS	0	0	0	0	0	0	0	0	0
40	FABRICATED METAL PRDTS.	0	0	0	0	0	0	0	0	0
41	SCREW MACH. PRDTS.. ETC.	450	259	583	103	180	0	115	0	24000
42	OTHER FAB. METAL PRDTS.	1284	392	1416	136	210	0	338	0	61000
43	ENGINES. TURBINES	0	0	0	0	0	0	0	0	0
44	FARM MACH. EQUIP.	592	224	787	101	103	0	199	0	32000
45	CONSTRUC. MACH.. EQUIP.	1469	620	1435	258	448	0	304	0	63000
46	MATERIAL HANDLING MACH.	2502	953	3598	371	347	0	773	0	139000
47	METALWORKING MACHINERY	869	64	365	21	82	0	154	0	24000
48	SPECIAL MACH.. EQUIP.	274	78	302	22	52	0	87	0	14000
49	GENERAL MACH.. EQUIP.	567	125	511	37	85	0	147	0	24000
50	MACHINE SHOP PRDTS.	1760	666	2496	232	262	0	477	0	90000
51	OFFICE. COMPUT. MACHINES	5841	2201	8313	745	903	0	1667	0	307000
52	SERVICE IND. MACHINES	3325	826	3265	229	587	0	992	0	158000
53	ELECT. TRANSMISS. EQUIP.	1119	91	499	27	113	0	206	0	32000
54	HOUSEHOLD APPLIANCES	1030	87	471	35	105	0	192	0	30000
55	ELECTRIC LIGHTING EQUIP.	443	168	638	57	64	0	124	0	23000
56	RADIO. TV. ETC.. EQUIP.	5028	2483	6244	929	1775	0	1444	0	270000
57	ELECTRONIC COMPONENTS	201	80	241	40	40	0	90	0	11000
58	MISC. ELECTRICAL MACH.	605	221	847	78	79	0	156	0	30000
59	MOTOR VEHICLES. EQUIP.	23920	8027	27799	2569	5066	0	7178	0	1218000
60	AIRCRAFT. PARTS	0	0	0	0	0	0	0	0	0
61	OTHER TRANSPORT. EQUIP.	2141	148	871	48	199	0	371	0	58000
62	PROFESS.. SCIEN. INSTRU.	7052	1611	5851	593	1008	0	1576	0	284000
63	MEDICAL. PHOTO. EQUIP.	2758	1109	3734	376	603	0	838	0	150000
64	MISC. MANUFACTURING	3894	1335	5030	401	747	0	1249	0	209000
65	TRANSPORT.. WAREHOUSING	25389	9652	35910	3303	4576	0	8292	0	1418000
66	COMMUNICA..EXC. BRDCAST.	12736	4793	17777	1430	2912	0	4883	0	767000
67	RADIO. TV BROADCASTING	721	265	753	97	53	0	158	0	35000
68	ELEC..GAS.WATER.SAN.SER.	33227	12694	48490	3848	5347	0	9416	0	1766000
69	WHOLESALE. RETAIL TRADE	4151	1724	5513	582	1324	0	1890	0	277000
70	FINANCE. INSURANCE	9638	3576	13368	1189	1905	0	3353	0	543000
71	REAL ESTATE. RENTAL	19764	7534	27575	1846	5505	0	8488	0	1276000
72	HOTELS. PERSONAL SERV.	1967	957	2853	193	1219	0	1950	0	251000
73	BUSINESS SERVICES	33279	12557	46705	4154	7284	0	13568	0	2107000
74	RESEARCH. DEVELOPMENT	0	0	0	0	0	0	0	0	0
75	AUTO. REPAIR. SERVICES	3151	1168	4257	358	829	0	1376	0	200000
76	AMUSEMENTS	-2277	-863	-3342	-302	-258	0	-541	0	-112000
77	MED.*EDUC. SERVICES	5553	2825	10027	1082	712	0	2396	0	495000
78	FEDERAL GOVT. ENTERPRISE	6074	2337	8539	588	1647	0	2566	0	392000
79	STATE. LOCAL GOVT. ENT.	685	261	950	58	205	0	305	0	45000
80	IMPORTS	115	35	130	23	20	0	49	0	6000
81	BUS.TRAVEL. ENT.. GIFTS.	0	0	0	0	0	0	0	0	0
82	OFFICE SUPPLIES	8257	3149	11511	833	2183	0	3424	0	522000
83	SCRAP. USED GOODS	15395	4025	10770	1702	3118	0	2735	0	532000
84	GOVERNMENT INDUSTRY	599352	230686	870568	77548	98554	0	187961	0	33857000
85	REST OF WORLD INDUSTRY	0	0	0	0	0	0	0	0	0
86	HOUSEHOLD INDUSTRY	0	0	0	0	0	0	0	0	0
87	INVENTORY VALUATION ADJ.	0	0	0	0	0	0	0	0	0
88	STATE TOTAL	1424677	539695	1822002	192260	289990	0	414151	0	74500000

TABLE B-10

STATE ESTIMATES OF 1980
STATE AND LOCAL GOVERNMENT NET PURCHASES OF GOODS AND SERVICES
(THOUSANDS OF 1958 DOLLARS)

INDUSTRY TITLE	1 ALABAMA	2 ARIZONA	3 ARKANSAS	4 CALIFORNIA	5 COLORADO	6 CONNECTICUT	7 DELAWARE	8 DISTRICT OF COLUMBIA	9 FLORIDA
1 LIVESTOCK, PRDTS.	900	725	533	9615	805	813	275	609	2032
2 OTHER AGRICULTURE PRDTS.	1124	907	667	12020	1006	1016	343	761	2541
3 FORESTRY, FISHERIES	43	34	26	451	38	38	13	28	95
4 AGRI.,FORES.,FISH. SERV.	-6510	-5249	-3857	-69563	-5823	-5879	-1985	-4405	-14701
5 IRON, FERRO. ORES MINING	0	0	0	0	0	0	0	0	0
6 NONFERROUS ORES MINING	0	0	0	0	0	0	0	0	0
7 COAL MINING	3951	3186	2341	42218	3535	3568	1205	2673	8922
8 CRUDE PETRO.,NATURAL GAS	0	0	0	0	0	0	0	0	0
9 STONE, CLAY MINING	-591	-476	-350	-6311	-529	-534	-180	-399	-1333
10 CHEM.,FERT. MIN. MINING	591	476	350	6311	529	534	180	399	1333
11 NEW CONSTRUCTION	501101	404058	296906	5354688	448247	452580	152785	339073	1131594
12 MAINT., REPAIR CONSTR.	107278	86503	63564	1146364	95963	96891	32709	72591	242258
13 ORDNANCE, ACCESSORIES	408	329	241	4357	365	368	125	276	921
14 FOOD, KINDRED PRDTS.	19262	15532	11413	205835	17231	17397	5873	13034	43498
15 TOBACCO MANUFACTURES	43	34	26	451	38	38	13	13	95
16 FABRICS	591	476	350	6311	529	534	180	399	1333
17 TEXTILE PRDTS.	85	68	50	901	76	76	25	57	191
18 APPAREL	7199	5805	4265	76925	6440	6501	2195	4871	16256
19 MISC. TEXTILE PRDTS.	43	34	26	451	38	38	13	28	95
20 LUMBER, WOOD PRDTS.	85	68	50	901	76	76	25	57	191
21 WOODEN CONTAINERS	43	34	26	451	38	38	13	28	95
22 HOUSEHOLD FURNITURE	5554	4478	3291	59347	4968	5016	1693	3758	12541
23 OTHER FURNITURE	11374	9171	6740	121547	10174	10273	3468	7696	25686
24 PAPER, ALLIED PRDTS.	324	261	191	3456	289	292	99	219	730
25 PAPERBOARD CONTAINERS	0	0	0	0	0	0	0	0	0
26 PRINTING, PUBLISHING	15818	12754	9372	169025	14150	14286	4823	10703	35720
27 CHEMICALS,SELECT. PRDTS.	20176	16268	11955	215601	18048	18223	6152	13652	45562
28 PLASTICS, SYNTHETICS	0	0	0	0	0	0	0	0	0
29 DRUGS, COSMETICS	10882	8775	6448	116289	9735	9829	3318	7364	24575
30 PAINT, ALLIED PRDTS.	0	0	0	0	0	0	0	0	0
31 PETROLEUM, RELATED INDS.	35277	28445	20902	376962	31556	31861	10756	23870	79662
32 RUBBER, MISC. PLASTICS	8070	6507	4782	86240	7220	7289	2461	5461	18225
33 LEATHER TANNING, PRDTS.	85	68	50	901	76	76	25	57	191
34 FOOTWEAR, LEATHER PRDTS.	0	0	0	0	0	0	0	0	0
35 GLASS, GLASS PRDTS.	0	0	0	0	0	0	0	0	0
36 STONE, CLAY PRDTS.	365	295	217	3906	327	330	111	248	826
37 PRIMARY IRON, STEEL MFR.	85	68	50	901	76	76	25	57	191
38 PRIMARY NONFERROUS MFR.	0	0	0	0	0	0	0	0	0

39 METAL CONTAINERS	0	0	0	0	0	0	0	0	0
40 FABRICATED METAL PRDTS.	0	0	0	0	0	0	0	0	0
41 SCREW MACH. PRDTS., ETC.	324	261	191	3456	289	292	99	219	730
42 OTHER FAB. METAL PRDTS.	3529	2846	2091	3771	3157	3187	1076	2387	7969
43 ENGINES, TURBINES	365	295	217	3906	327	330	111	248	826
44 FARM MACH., EQUIP.	1420	1145	842	15174	1270	1282	432	961	3207
45 CONSTRUC. HANDLING EQUIP.	1322	1065	783	14123	1183	1194	403	894	2985
46 MATERIAL HANDLING MACH.	3571	2880	2116	38162	3194	3226	1089	2417	8065
47 METALWORKING MACHINERY	633	511	375	6761	566	571	192	428	1428
48 SPECIAL MACH., EQUIP.	3065	2471	1816	32753	2742	2768	935	2074	6921
49 GENERAL MACH., EQUIP.	450	363	266	4807	403	406	138	304	1016
50 MACHINE SHOP PRDTS.	2516	2030	1491	26894	2251	2273	768	1703	5683
51 OFFICE, COMPUT. MACHINES	7987	6439	4732	85338	7144	7213	2435	5403	18034
52 SERVICE IND. MACHINES	2109	1701	1250	22537	1886	1904	643	1427	4763
53 ELECT. TRANSMISS. EQUIP.	591	476	350	6311	529	534	180	399	1333
54 HOUSEHOLD APPLIANCES	85	68	50	901	76	76	25	57	191
55 ELECTRIC LIGHTING EQUIP.	591	476	350	6311	529	534	180	399	1333
56 RADIO, TV, ETC., EQUIP.	4302	3470	2549	45974	3849	3886	1311	2911	9715
57 ELECTRONIC COMPONENTS	0	0	0	0	0	0	0	0	0
58 MISC. ELECTRICAL MACH.	2292	1848	1358	24490	2050	2070	699	1551	5176
59 MOTOR VEHICLES, EQUIP.	36556	29477	21659	390635	32700	33016	11146	24736	82552
60 AIRCRAFT, PARTS	0	0	0	0	0	0	0	0	0
61 OTHER TRANSPORT. EQUIP.	4486	3616	2658	47928	4012	4051	1367	3034	10128
62 PROFESS., SCIEN. INSTRU.	6735	5430	3991	71967	6024	6083	2054	4557	15208
63 MEDICAL, PHOTO. EQUIP.	1280	1031	758	13672	1145	1156	390	866	2889
64 MISC. MANUFACTURING	15410	12425	9130	164668	13785	13918	4698	10427	34798
65 TRANSPORT., WAREHOUSING	27474	22153	16228	293577	24575	24814	8377	18590	62041
66 COMMUNICA.,EXC. BRDCAST.	16422	13242	9730	175486	14690	14832	5007	11112	37085
67 RADIO, TV BROADCASTING	0	0	0	0	0	0	0	0	0
68 ELEC.,GAS,WATER,SAN.SER.	31194	25395	18660	336547	28173	28445	9602	21311	71122
69 WHOLESALE, RETAIL TRADE	20050	16167	11880	214249	17935	18108	6113	13566	45276
70 FINANCE, INSURANCE	14848	11973	8797	158658	13281	13410	4527	10047	33529
71 REAL ESTATE, RENTAL	24718	19931	14645	264129	22111	22324	7536	16725	55818
72 HOTELS, PERSONAL SERV.	4245	3424	2516	45374	3798	3835	1294	2873	9589
73 BUSINESS SERVICES	44570	35938	26408	476274	39869	40254	13590	30159	100650
74 RESEARCH, DEVELOPMENT	0	0	0	0	0	0	0	0	0
75 AUTO. REPAIR, SERVICES	8493	6848	5032	90748	7596	7670	2590	5746	19177
76 AMUSEMENTS	-2601	-2098	-1541	-27796	-2326	-2349	-793	-1760	-5874
77 MED.,EDUC. SERVICES	14271	11507	8455	152498	12766	12889	4351	9656	32227
78 FEDERAL GOVT. ENTERPRISE	6144	4954	3640	65656	5497	5549	1874	4158	13875
79 STATE, LOCAL GOVT. ENT.	675	545	400	7212	603	609	205	457	1524
80 IMPORTS	282	227	166	3004	251	254	86	190	635
81 BUS.TRAVEL, ENT., GIFTS.	0	0	0	0	0	0	0	0	0
82 OFFICE SUPPLIES	12697	10238	7523	135671	11357	11467	3871	8591	28670
83 SCRAP, USED GOODS	20879	16836	12371	223113	18677	18858	6366	14128	47150
84 GOVERNMENT INDUSTRY	663953	535376	393401	7094973	593927	599667	202441	449273	1499361
85 REST OF WORLD INDUSTRY	0	0	0	0	0	0	0	0	0
86 HOUSEHOLD INDUSTRY	0	0	0	0	0	0	0	0	0
87 INVENTORY VALUATION ADJ.	0	0	0	0	0	0	0	0	0
88 STATE TOTAL	1751895	1412614	1038009	18720403	1567112	1582250	534146	1185417	3956130

225

TABLE B-10

STATE ESTIMATES OF 1960

STATE AND LOCAL GOVERNMENT NET PURCHASES OF GOODS AND SERVICES

(THOUSANDS OF 1958 DOLLARS)

INDUSTRY TITLE	10 GEORGIA	11 IDAHO	12 ILLINOIS	13 INDIANA	14 IOWA	15 KANSAS	16 KENTUCKY	17 LOUISIANA	18 MAINE
1 LIVESTOCK, PRDTS.	1239	230	2976	1106	796	511	1118	970	216
2 OTHER AGRICULTURE PRDTS.	1549	288	3720	1383	995	638	1397	1213	269
3 FORESTRY, FISHERIES	58	11	140	52	38	24	52	52	10
4 AGRI.,FORES.,FISH. SERV.	-8964	-1662	-21526	-8003	-5759	-3696	-8086	-7016	-1557
5 IRON, FERRO. ORES MINING	0	0	0	0	0	0	0	0	0
6 NONFERROUS ORES MINING	0	0	0	0	0	0	0	0	0
7 COAL MINING	5440	1009	13065	4858	3495	2243	4907	4258	945
8 CRUDE PETRO.,NATURAL GAS	0	0	0	0	0	0	0	0	0
9 STONE, CLAY MINING	-813	-151	-1953	-726	-523	-335	-734	-637	-141
10 CHEM.,FERT. MIN. MINING	813	151	1953	726	523	335	734	637	141
11 NEW CONSTRUCTION	689990	127947	1656957	616051	443337	284487	622405	540092	119860
12 MAINT.,REPAIR CONSTR.	147716	27391	354729	131888	94912	60904	133248	115626	25661
13 ORDNANCE, ACCESSORIES	561	104	1349	502	361	232	507	439	97
14 FOOD, KINDRED PRDTS.	26523	4918	63693	23681	17042	10936	23925	20761	4607
15 TOBACCO MANUFACTURES	58	11	52	52	38	24	52	45	10
16 FABRICS	813	151	1953	726	523	335	734	637	141
17 TEXTILE PRDTS.	116	21	279	104	75	48	105	90	20
18 APPAREL	9913	1838	23804	8851	6369	4087	8941	7759	1722
19 MISC. TEXTILE PRDTS.	58	11	140	52	38	24	52	45	10
20 LUMBER, WOOD PRDTS.	116	21	279	104	75	48	105	90	20
21 WOODEN CONTAINERS	58	11	140	52	38	24	52	45	10
22 HOUSEHOLD FURNITURE	7647	1418	18364	6828	4914	3153	6898	5986	1329
23 OTHER FURNITURE	15663	2904	37611	13984	10063	6458	14128	12259	2720
24 PAPER, ALLIED PRDTS.	445	82	1069	397	286	183	401	348	77
25 PAPERBOARD CONTAINERS	0	0	0	0	0	0	0	0	0
26 PRINTING, PUBLISHING	21780	4038	52303	19446	13994	8980	19647	17048	3783
27 CHEMICALS+SELECT. PRDTS.	27781	5151	66715	24804	17850	11454	25061	21746	4826
28 PLASTICS, SYNTHETICS	0	0	0	0	0	0	0	0	0
29 DRUGS, COSMETICS	14985	2779	35985	13379	9628	6178	13517	11730	2603
30 PAINT, ALLIED PRDTS.	0	0	0	0	0	0	0	0	0
31 PETROLEUM, RELATED INDS.	48574	9007	116647	43369	31210	20028	43817	38022	8438
32 RUBBER, MISC. PLASTICS	11112	2060	26687	9922	7140	4582	10025	8699	1930
33 LEATHER TANNING, PRDTS.	0	0	0	0	0	0	0	0	0
34 FOOTWEAR, LEATHER PRDTS.	116	21	279	104	75	48	105	90	20
35 GLASS, GLASS PRDTS.	0	0	0	0	0	0	0	0	0
36 STONE, CLAY PRDTS.	504	93	1209	449	323	208	455	394	87
37 PRIMARY IRON, STEEL MFR.	116	21	279	104	75	48	105	90	20
38 PRIMARY NONFERROUS MFR.	0	0	0	0	0	0	0	0	0

39 METAL CONTAINERS	0	0	0	0	0	0	0	0	0
40 FABRICATED METAL PRDTS.	0	82	1069	397	286	183	401	348	77
41 SCREW MACH. PRDTS., ETC.	445	901	11670	4339	3123	2004	4383	3803	844
42 OTHER FAB. METAL PRDTS.	4860	93	1209	449	323	208	455	394	87
43 ENGINES, TURBINES	504	363	4696	1746	1256	806	1764	1531	340
44 FARM MACH., EQUIP.	1955	338	4370	1625	1170	751	1642	1424	316
45 CONSTRUC. MACH., EQUIP.	1820	912	11308	4390	3159	2027	4436	3849	855
46 MATERIAL HANDLING MACH.	4913	782	2092	778	560	360	786	682	151
47 METALWORKING MACHINERY	871	115	10135	3758	2712	1740	3807	3303	733
48 SPECIAL MACH., EQUIP.	4221	643	1488	554	398	255	559	485	108
49 GENERAL MACH., EQUIP.	619	1157	8322	398	2226	1428	3126	2713	602
50 MACHINE SHOP PRDTS.	3465	643	26407	3035	7066	4534	9920	8607	1910
51 OFFICE, COMPUT. MACHINES	10997	8322	6973	9818	1866	1197	2620	2273	504
52 SERVICE IND. MACHINES	2904	2039	1953	2593	523	335	734	637	141
53 ELECT. TRANSMISS. EQUIP.	313	539	279	726	75	48	105	105	20
54 HOUSEHOLD APPLIANCES	116	151	1953	104	335	335	734	90	90
55 ELECTRIC LIGHTING EQUIP.	313	21	726	726	523	335	734	637	141
56 RADIO, TV, ETC., EQUIP.	5924	1099	14226	5289	3806	2442	5344	4637	637
57 ELECTRONIC COMPONENTS	0	0	0	0	0	0	0	0	0
58 MISC. ELECTRICAL MACH.	3156	585	7578	2817	2028	1301	2847	2470	549
59 MOTOR VEHICLES, EQUIP.	50336	9334	120878	44942	32342	20754	45406	39401	8744
60 AIRCRAFT, PARTS	6176	0	14831	0	0	0	0	0	0
61 OTHER TRANSPORT. EQUIP.	9274	1145	22269	5514	3969	2547	5571	4834	1072
62 PROFESS., SCIEN. INSTRU.	1762	1720	4231	8280	5959	3823	8365	7258	1611
63 MEDICAL, PHOTO. EQUIP.	21218	326	50955	1573	1132	726	1589	1379	306
64 MISC. MANUFACTURING	37829	3934	90844	18944	13634	8749	19140	16609	3686
65 TRANSPORT., WAREHOUSING	22612	7015	54302	33775	24307	15597	34124	29611	6571
66 COMMUNICA., EXC. BRDCAST.	43366	4193	104141	20189	14529	9323	20397	17700	3929
67 RADIO, TV BROADCASTING	27607	8041	66297	38719	27864	17880	39119	33946	7534
68 ELEC., GAS, WATER, SAN. SER.	20444	5119	49095	24649	17739	11392	24903	21609	4796
69 WHOLESALE, RETAIL TRADE	34035	3791	81732	18254	13136	8429	18441	16003	3551
70 FINANCE, INSURANCE	5846	6311	14041	30388	21868	14032	30701	26641	5913
71 REAL ESTATE, RENTAL	51371	1084	147378	5220	3757	2411	5274	4576	1015
72 HOTELS, PERSONAL SERV.	0	11380	0	54794	39432	25303	55360	48039	10661
73 BUSINESS SERVICES	11694	2169	28080	10440	7514	4821	10548	9153	2032
74 RESEARCH, DEVELOPMENT	-3582	-664	-8601	-3198	-2301	-1477	-3231	-2803	-622
75 AUTO. REPAIR, SERVICES	19650	3643	47189	17545	12626	8102	17725	15381	3413
76 AMUSEMENTS	8460	1569	20317	7554	5436	3488	7632	6623	1470
77 MED., EDUC. SERVICES	930	173	2231	830	597	383	838	727	162
78 FEDERAL GOVT. ENTERPRISE	387	72	930	345	249	160	349	303	67
79 STATE, LOCAL GOVT. ENT.	173	0	345	0	0	0	0	0	0
80 IMPORTS	72	0	0	0	0	0	0	0	0
81 BUS. TRAVEL, ENT., GIFTS.	0	0	0	0	0	0	0	0	0
82 OFFICE SUPPLIES	17482	3242	41982	15608	11233	7208	15770	13684	3037
83 SCRAP, USED GOODS	28750	5332	69040	25668	18472	11853	25934	22503	4994
84 GOVERNMENT INDUSTRY	914235	169530	2195466	816267	587421	376945	824686	715621	158815
85 REST OF WORLD INDUSTRY	0	0	0	0	0	0	0	0	0
86 HOUSEHOLD INDUSTRY	0	0	0	0	0	0	0	0	0
87 INVENTORY VALUATION ADJ.	0	0	0	0	0	0	0	0	0
88 STATE TOTAL	2412250	447308	5792842	2153759	1549946	994582	2175977	1888192	419038

227

TABLE 8-10

STATE ESTIMATES OF 1960

STATE AND LOCAL GOVERNMENT NET PURCHASES OF GOODS AND SERVICES

(THOUSANDS OF 1958 DOLLARS)

INDUSTRY TITLE	19 MARYLAND	20 MASSA-CHUSETTS	21 MICHIGAN	22 MINNESOTA	23 MISSISSIPPI	24 MISSOURI	25 MONTANA	26 NEBRASKA	27 NEVADA
1 LIVESTOCK, PRDTS.	1454	1522	2746	1183	629	1168	216	420	298
2 OTHER AGRICULTURE PRDTS.	1818	1902	3432	1479	786	1460	269	525	372
3 FORESTRY, FISHERIES	68	72	129	56	29	55	10	19	13
4 AGRI.,FORES.,FISH. SERV.	-10521	-11012	-19864	-8558	-4551	-8449	-1557	-3039	-2153
5 IRON, FERRO. ORES MINING	0	0	0	0	0	0	0	0	0
6 NONFERROUS ORES MINING	0	0	0	0	0	0	0	0	0
7 COAL MINING	6385	6683	12055	5194	2762	5129	945	1845	1307
8 CRUDE PETRO.,NATURAL GAS	0	0	0	0	0	0	0	0	0
9 STONE, CLAY MINING	-954	-999	-1802	-777	-412	-767	-141	-275	-195
10 CHEM.,FERT. MIN. MINING	954	999	1802	777	412	767	141	275	195
11 NEW CONSTRUCTION	809849	847684	1529010	658796	350337	650421	119860	233944	165783
12 MAINT., REPAIR CONSTR.	173377	181477	327338	141038	75002	139245	25661	50084	35492
13 ORDNANCE, ACCESSORIES	659	690	1245	536	285	529	97	190	135
14 FOOD, KINDRED PRDTS.	31131	32585	58775	25324	13467	25002	4607	8993	6373
15 TOBACCO MANUFACTURES	68	72	129	56	29	55	10	19	13
16 FABRICS	954	999	1802	777	412	767	141	275	195
17 TEXTILE PRDTS.	136	143	258	111	59	110	20	39	28
18 APPAREL	11634	12178	21965	9464	5032	9344	1722	3361	2381
19 MISC. TEXTILE PRDTS.	68	72	129	56	29	55	10	19	13
20 LUMBER, WOOD PRDTS.	136	143	258	111	59	110	20	39	28
21 WOODEN CONTAINERS	68	72	129	56	29	55	10	19	13
22 HOUSEHOLD FURNITURE	8976	9395	16946	7302	3883	7209	1329	2593	1838
23 OTHER FURNITURE	18383	19242	34707	14954	7952	14764	2720	5310	3763
24 PAPER, ALLIED PRDTS.	523	547	987	425	-226	420	77	151	107
25 PAPERBOARD CONTAINERS	0	0	0	0	0	0	0	0	0
26 PRINTING, PUBLISHING	25563	26758	48264	20795	11058	20531	3783	7384	5233
27 CHEMICALS,SELECT. PRDTS.	32607	34131	61564	26525	14106	26188	4826	9419	6675
28 PLASTICS, SYNTHETICS	0	0	0	0	0	0	0	0	0
29 DRUGS, COSMETICS	17588	18409	33206	14307	7609	14125	2603	5080	3601
30 PAINT, ALLIED PRDTS.	0	0	0	0	0	0	0	0	0
31 PETROLEUM, RELATED INDS.	57013	59676	107640	46378	24663	45788	8438	16469	11670
32 RUBBER, MISC. PLASTICS	13043	13652	24625	10610	5642	10476	1930	3768	2670
33 LEATHER TANNING, PRDTS.	0	0	0	0	0	0	0	0	0
34 FOOTWEAR, LEATHER PRDTS.	136	143	258	111	59	110	20	39	28
35 GLASS, GLASS PRDTS.	0	0	0	0	0	0	0	0	0
36 STONE, CLAY PRDTS.	591	618	1116	481	256	475	87	171	121
37 PRIMARY IRON, STEEL MFR.	136	143	258	111	59	110	20	39	28
38 PRIMARY NONFERROUS MFR.	0	0	0	0	0	0	0	0	0

39 METAL CONTAINERS	0	0	0	0	0	0	0	0	0
40 FABRICATED METAL PRDTS.	523	547	987	425	226	420	77	151	107
41 SCREW MACH. PRDTS., ETC.	5703	5970	10768	4640	2467	4581	844	1647	1167
42 OTHER FAB. METAL PRDTS.	551	618	1116	481	256	475	87	171	121
43 ENGINES, TURBINES	2295	2402	4333	1867	993	1843	340	663	470
44 FARM MACH., EQUIP.	2136	2236	4032	1738	924	1716	316	617	437
45 CONSTRUC. MACH., EQUIP.	5771	6041	10897	4695	2497	4635	855	1667	1182
46 MATERIAL HANDLING MACH.	1022	1071	1931	832	443	822	151	296	210
47 METALWORKING MACHINERY	4954	5185	9352	4030	2143	3978	733	1430	1014
48 SPECIAL MACH., EQUIP.	727	761	1372	591	314	584	108	210	149
49 GENERAL MACH., EQUIP.	4068	4257	7679	3309	1760	3267	602	1175	833
50 MACHINE SHOP PRDTS.	12906	13510	24368	10499	5583	10366	1910	3729	2642
51 OFFICE, COMPUT. MACHINES	3409	3568	6435	2773	1475	2737	504	985	698
52 SERVICE IND. MACHINES	954	999	1802	777	412	767	141	275	195
53 ELECT. TRANSMISS. EQUIP.	136	143	258	111	59	110	20	39	28
54 HOUSEHOLD APPLIANCES	954	999	1802	777	412	767	141	275	195
55 ELECTRIC LIGHTING EQUIP.	6953	7278	13128	5656	3008	5585	1029	2009	1423
56 RADIO, TV, ETC., EQUIP.									
57 ELECTRONIC COMPONENTS									
58 MISC. ELECTRICAL MACH.	3704	3877	6993	3013	1602	2975	549	1070	758
59 MOTOR VEHICLES, EQUIP.	58079	61840	111544	48060	25557	47449	8744	17067	12094
60 AIRCRAFT, PARTS	0	0	0	0	0	0	0	0	0
61 OTHER TRANSPORT. EQUIP.	7248	7588	13686	5896	3135	5822	1072	2094	1483
62 PROFESS., SCIEN. INSTRU.	10884	11353	20550	8854	4708	8741	1611	3144	2228
63 MEDICAL, PHOTO. EQUIP.	2068	2165	3904	1682	894	1661	306	597	423
64 MISC. MANUFACTURING	24904	26068	47020	20260	10773	20002	3686	7194	5098
65 TRANSPORT., WAREHOUSING	44401	46475	83830	36119	19208	35660	6571	12826	9089
66 COMMUNICA.,EXC. BRDCAST.	26540	27780	50109	21590	11482	21315	3929	7667	5433
67 RADIO, TV BROADCASTING	0	0	0	0	0	0	0	0	0
68 ELEC.,GAS,WATER,SAN.SER.	50900	53277	96099	41405	22019	40880	7534	14704	10420
69 WHOLESALE, RETAIL TRADE	32403	33917	61177	26359	14018	26024	4796	9360	6633
70 FINANCE, INSURANCE	23996	25117	45304	19520	10380	19272	3551	6932	4913
71 REAL ESTATE, RENTAL	39947	41814	75420	32496	17281	32043	5913	11540	8177
72 HOTELS, PERSONAL SERV.	6863	7183	12956	5582	2968	5512	1015	1982	1405
73 BUSINESS SERVICES	72032	75397	135997	58597	31161	57852	10661	20808	14746
74 RESEARCH, DEVELOPMENT	0	0	0	0	0	0	0	0	0
75 AUTO. REPAIR, SERVICES	13724	14366	25913	11165	5937	11023	2032	3964	2810
76 AMUSEMENTS	-4234	-4400	-7937	-3420	-1818	-3376	-622	-1214	-860
77 MED.,EDUC. SERVICES	23064	24141	43545	18762	9977	18524	3413	6662	4721
78 FEDERAL GOVT. ENTERPRISE	9930	10394	18748	8078	4296	7976	1470	2868	2033
79 STATE, LOCAL GOVT. ENT.	1091	1142	2060	888	472	876	167	315	223
80 IMPORTS	455	476	858	370	197	365	62	132	93
81 BUS.TRAVEL, ENT., GIFTS.	0	0	0	0	0	0	0	0	0
82 OFFICE SUPPLIES	20519	21478	38740	16591	8876	16480	3037	5927	4200
83 SCRAP, USED GOODS	35744	35320	63708	27449	14597	27101	4994	9747	6908
84 GOVERNMENT INDUSTRY	1073050	1123181	2025936	872306	464196	861808	158815	309975	219662
85 REST OF WORLD INDUSTRY	0	0	0	0	0	0	0	0	0
86 HOUSEHOLD INDUSTRY	0	0	0	0	0	0	0	0	0
87 INVENTORY VALUATION ADJ.	0	0	0	0	0	0	0	0	0
88 STATE TOTAL	2831287	2963570	5345527	2303201	1224796	2273930	419038	817875	579586

STATE ESTIMATES OF 1980
STATE AND LOCAL GOVERNMENT NET PURCHASES OF GOODS AND SERVICES
(THOUSANDS OF 1958 DOLLARS)

INDUSTRY TITLE	28 NEW HAMPSHIRE	29 NEW JERSEY	30 NEW MEXICO	31 NEW YORK	32 NORTH CAROLINA	33 NORTH DAKOTA	34 OHIO	35 OKLAHOMA	36 OREGON
1 LIVESTOCK, PRDTS.	162	1658	404	8138	1093	256	2081	850	744
2 OTHER AGRICULTURE PRDTS.	203	2072	504	10172	1367	321	2601	1064	931
3 FORESTRY, FISHERIES	7	78	19	382	51	12	97	97	35
4 AGRI.,FORES.,FISH. SERV.	-1171	-11991	-2919	-58870	-7910	-1857	-15054	-6154	-5388
5 IRON, FERRO. ORES MINING	0	0	0	0	0	0	0	0	0
6 NONFERROUS ORES MINING	0	0	0	0	0	0	0	0	0
7 COAL MINING	710	7278	1771	35728	4800	1128	9136	3734	3270
8 CRUDE PETRO.,NATURAL GAS	0	0	0	0	0	0	0	0	0
9 STONE, CLAY MINING	-106	-1088	-265	-5341	-718	-168	-1365	-559	-489
10 CHEM.,FERT. MIN. MINING	106	1088	265	5341	718	168	1365	559	489
11 NEW CONSTRUCTION	90111	923067	224702	4531563	608831	142966	1158743	473664	414744
12 MAINT., REPAIR CONSTR.	19292	197615	48106	970144	130342	30607	248070	101405	88791
13 ORDNANCE, ACCESSORIES	74	751	183	3688	496	116	943	385	337
14 FOOD, KINDRED PRDTS.	3464	35483	8638	174193	23403	5496	44542	18208	15943
15 TOBACCO MANUFACTURES	7	78	19	382	51	12	97	40	35
16 FABRICS	106	1088	265	5341	718	168	1365	559	489
17 TEXTILE PRDTS.	16	156	38	762	102	24	195	80	70
18 APPAREL	1294	13261	3228	65100	8747	2053	16646	6804	5958
19 MISC. TEXTILE PRDTS.	7	78	19	382	51	12	97	40	35
20 LUMBER, WOOD PRDTS.	16	156	38	762	102	24	195	80	70
21 WOODEN CONTAINERS	7	78	19	382	51	12	97	40	35
22 HOUSEHOLD FURNITURE	999	10230	2490	50223	6747	1584	12842	5250	4597
23 OTHER FURNITURE	2046	20953	5100	102863	13820	3246	26303	10752	9415
24 PAPER, ALLIED PRDTS.	58	595	145	2924	393	92	748	306	268
25 PAPERBOARD CONTAINERS	0	0	0	0	0	0	0	0	0
26 PRINTING, PUBLISHING	2844	29137	7093	143042	19218	4513	36576	14951	13092
27 CHEMICALS,SELECT. PRDTS.	3628	37166	9048	182458	24514	5756	46655	19072	16699
28 PLASTICS, SYNTHETICS									
29 DRUGS, COSMETICS	1957	20046	4879	98413	13222	3105	25165	10286	9008
30 PAINT, ALLIED PRDTS.	0	0	0	0	0	0	0	0	0
31 PETROLEUM, RELATED INDS.	6344	64982	15819	319015	42861	10064	81574	33346	29197
32 RUBBER, MISC. PLASTICS	1451	14867	3619	72983	9806	2303	18662	7628	6680
33 LEATHER TANNING, PRDTS.	0	0	0	0	0	0	0	0	0
34 FOOTWEAR, LEATHER PRDTS.	16	156	38	762	102	24	195	80	70
35 GLASS, GLASS PRDTS.	0	0	0	0	0	0	0	0	0
36 STONE, CLAY PRDTS.	66	673	164	3306	444	104	846	345	303
37 PRIMARY IRON, STEEL MFR.	16	156	38	762	102	24	195	80	70
38 PRIMARY NONFERROUS MFR.	0	0	0	0	0	0	0	0	0

39	METAL CONTAINERS	0	0	0	0	0	0	0	0	0
40	FABRICATED METAL PRDTS.	0	0	0	0	0	0	0	0	0
41	SCREW MACH. PRDTS., ETC.	58	595	145	2924	393	92	748	306	268
42	OTHER FAB. METAL PRDTS.	634	6501	1583	31914	4288	1007	8160	3336	2921
43	ENGINES, TURBINES	66	673	164	3306	444	104	846	345	303
44	FARM MACH., EQUIP.	256	2616	637	12842	1725	405	3284	1342	1175
45	CONSTRUC. MACH., EQUIP.	238	2435	592	11952	1606	377	3056	1249	1094
46	MATERIAL HANDLING MACH.	642	6579	1601	32296	4339	1019	8258	3376	2955
47	METALWORKING MACHINERY	113	1166	284	5721	769	180	1463	598	524
48	SPECIAL MACH., EQUIP.	551	5646	1374	27718	3724	874	7088	2897	2537
49	GENERAL MACH., EQUIP.	81	829	201	4068	547	129	1040	425	372
50	MACHINE SHOP PRDTS.	452	4636	1128	22760	3058	718	5819	2379	2083
51	OFFICE, COMPUT. MACHINES	1436	14711	3581	72220	9703	2278	18467	7548	6610
52	SERVICE IND. MACHINES	379	3885	946	19072	2563	602	4876	1994	1745
53	ELECT. TRANSMISS. EQUIP.	106	1088	265	5341	718	168	1365	559	489
54	HOUSEHOLD APPLIANCES	16	156	38	762	102	24	195	80	70
55	ELECTRIC LIGHTING EQUIP.	106	1088	265	5341	718	168	1365	559	489
56	RADIO, TV, ETC., EQUIP.	774	7925	1929	38907	5228	1228	9949	4066	3561
57	ELECTRONIC COMPONENTS	0	0	0	0	0	0	0	0	0
58	MISC. ELECTRICAL MACH.	412	4222	1027	20725	2784	653	5300	2166	1897
59	MOTOR VEHICLES, EQUIP.	6573	67339	16393	330586	44415	10430	84532	34555	30256
60	AIRCRAFT, PARTS	0	0	0	0	0	0	0	0	0
61	OTHER TRANSPORT. EQUIP.	807	8262	2012	40560	5449	1279	10372	4239	3712
62	PROFESS., SCIEN. INSTRU.	1211	12406	3020	60904	8183	1922	15573	6366	5575
63	MEDICAL, PHOTO. EQUIP.	230	2357	574	11571	1555	365	2959	1209	1059
64	MISC. MANUFACTURING	2772	28386	6910	139355	18722	4396	35634	14566	12754
65	TRANSPORT., WAREHOUSING	4940	50608	12319	248448	33379	7839	63529	25969	22738
66	COMMUNICA., EXC. BRDCAST.	2953	30251	7364	148509	19953	4685	37974	15523	13592
67	RADIO, TV BROADCASTING	0	0	0	0	0	0	0	0	0
68	ELEC., GAS, WATER, SAN. SER.	5664	58015	14122	284813	38266	8985	72828	29770	26067
69	WHOLESALE, RETAIL TRADE	3605	36933	8990	181313	24360	5720	46362	18952	16594
70	FINANCE, INSURANCE	2673	27350	6657	134269	18040	4236	34333	14034	12288
71	REAL ESTATE, RENTAL	4445	45532	11084	223527	30032	7052	57157	23364	20458
72	HOTELS, PERSONAL SERV.	764	7821	1904	38399	5159	1212	9819	4014	3514
73	BUSINESS SERVICES	8015	82102	19986	403060	54152	12716	103064	42130	36890
74	RESEARCH, DEVELOPMENT	0	0	0	0	0	0	0	0	0
75	AUTO. REPAIR, SERVICES	1527	15644	3808	76797	10318	2423	19637	8027	7029
76	AMUSEMENTS	-468	-4791	-1166	-23522	-3160	-743	-6015	-2459	-2153
77	MED., EDUC. SERVICES	2567	26288	6400	129055	17339	4071	33000	13490	11811
78	FEDERAL GOVT. ENTERPRISE	1105	11318	2755	55564	7465	1753	14208	5807	5085
79	STATE, LOCAL GOVT. ENT.	122	1243	302	6103	820	192	1561	638	559
80	IMPORTS	51	518	126	2543	341	80	650	265	233
81	BUS., TRAVEL, ENT., GIFTS.	0	0	0	0	0	0	0	0	0
82	OFFICE SUPPLIES	2283	23387	5693	114815	15426	3623	29359	12001	10508
83	SCRAP, USED GOODS	3755	38461	9363	188816	25368	5956	48281	19736	17281
84	GOVERNMENT INDUSTRY	119398	1223062	297729	6004313	806700	189429	1535334	627604	549535
85	REST OF WORLD INDUSTRY	0	0	0	0	0	0	0	0	0
86	HOUSEHOLD INDUSTRY	0	0	0	0	0	0	0	0	0
87	INVENTORY VALUATION ADJ.	0	0	0	0	0	0	0	0	0
88	STATE TOTAL	315039	3227110	785572	15842667	2128515	499812	4051042	1655960	1449976

STATE ESTIMATES OF 1980
STATE AND LOCAL GOVERNMENT NET PURCHASES OF GOODS AND SERVICES
(THOUSANDS OF 1958 DOLLARS)

INDUSTRY TITLE	37 PENNSYL-VANIA	38 RHODE ISLAND	39 SOUTH CAROLINA	40 SOUTH DAKOTA	41 TENNESSEE	42 TEXAS	43 UTAH	44 VERMONT	45 VIRGINIA
1 LIVESTOCK, PRDTS.	2393	305	542	179	1162	2563	437	165	1268
2 OTHER AGRICULTURE PRDTS.	2990	381	678	224	1453	3203	547	207	1585
3 FORESTRY, FISHERIES	112	15	26	9	55	120	21	7	60
4 AGRI.,FORES.,FISH. SERV.	-17308	-2206	-3920	-1298	-8409	-18539	-3163	-1193	-9173
5 IRON, FERRO. ORES MINING	0	0	0	0	0	0	0	0	0
6 NONFERROUS ORES MINING	0	0	0	0	0	0	0	0	0
7 COAL MINING	10504	1339	2380	788	5103	11252	1919	724	5568
8 CRUDE PETRO.,NATURAL GAS	0	0	0	0	0	0	0	0	0
9 STONE, CLAY MINING	-1570	-200	-355	-118	-763	-1682	-287	-108	-832
10 CHEM.,FERT. MIN. MINING	1570	200	355	118	763	1682	287	108	832
11 NEW CONSTRUCTION	1332324	169825	301816	99932	647244	1427056	243474	91845	706163
12 MAINT., REPAIR CONSTR.	285231	36357	64615	21394	138566	305512	52124	19662	151180
13 ORDNANCE, ACCESSORIES	1084	138	245	82	526	1161	198	75	574
14 FOOD, KINDRED PRDTS.	51214	6528	11602	3841	24880	54856	9359	3530	27145
15 TOBACCO MANUFACTURES	112	15	26	9	55	120	21	21	60
16 FABRICS	1570	200	355	118	763	1682	287	108	832
17 TEXTILE PRDTS.	225	28	51	17	109	240	41	16	119
18 APPAREL	19140	2440	4336	1436	9299	20500	3498	1319	10145
19 MISC. TEXTILE PRDTS.	112	15	26	9	55	120	21	7	60
20 LUMBER, WOOD PRDTS.	225	28	51	17	109	240	41	16	119
21 WOODEN CONTAINERS	112	15	26	9	55	120	21	7	60
22 HOUSEHOLD FURNITURE	14766	1882	3345	1108	7173	15816	2698	1018	7827
23 OTHER FURNITURE	30242	3855	6851	2269	14692	32393	5527	2085	16029
24 PAPER, ALLIED PRDTS.	859	110	195	65	418	921	157	59	456
25 PAPERBOARD CONTAINERS	0	0	0	0	0	0	0	0	0
26 PRINTING, PUBLISHING	42055	5361	9527	3154	20430	45046	7685	2900	22290
27 CHEMICALS,SELECT. PRDTS.	53645	6838	12152	4024	26060	57458	9803	3698	28432
28 PLASTICS, SYNTHETICS	0	0	0	0	0	0	0	0	0
29 DRUGS, COSMETICS	28935	3688	6554	2171	14057	30992	5288	1995	15335
30 PAINT, ALLIED PRDTS.	0	0	0	0	0	0	0	0	0
31 PETROLEUM, RELATED INDS.	93794	11955	21247	7035	45565	100463	17140	6466	49712
32 RUBBER, MISC. PLASTICS	21458	2735	4860	1609	10424	22983	3921	1479	11373
33 LEATHER TANNING, PRDTS.	0	0	0	0	0	0	0	0	0
34 FOOTWEAR, LEATHER PRDTS.	225	28	51	17	109	240	41	16	119
35 GLASS, GLASS PRDTS.	0	0	0	0	0	0	0	0	0
36 STONE, CLAY PRDTS.	972	123	220	73	473	1041	178	67	515
37 PRIMARY IRON, STEEL MFR.	225	28	51	17	109	240	41	16	119
38 PRIMARY NONFERROUS MFR.	0	0	0	0	0	0	0	0	0

#	Industry	1	2	3	4	5	6	7	8	9
39	METAL CONTAINERS	0	0	0	0	0	0	0	0	0
40	FABRICATED METAL PRDTS.	0	0	0	0	0	0	0	0	0
41	SCREW MACH. PRDTS., ETC.	859	110	195	65	418	921	157	59	456
42	OTHER FAB. METAL PRDTS.	9383	1196	2126	704	4558	10050	1715	646	4973
43	ENGINES, TURBINES	972	123	220	73	473	1041	178	67	515
44	FARM MACH., EQUIP.	3776	481	855	283	1834	4044	690	261	2001
45	CONSTRUC. MACH., EQUIP.	3514	448	796	264	1707	3764	642	243	1862
46	MATERIAL HANDLING MACH.	9496	1211	2151	712	4613	10171	1735	655	5033
47	METALWORKING MACHINERY	1583	215	381	127	817	1802	307	115	891
48	SPECIAL MACH., EQUIP.	8150	1039	1846	611	3959	8729	1489	561	4320
49	GENERAL MACH., EQUIP.	1196	153	271	90	581	1282	218	83	634
50	MACHINE SHOP PRDTS.	6692	853	1516	502	3251	7167	1223	461	3547
51	OFFICE, COMPUT. MACHINES	21233	2706	4810	1593	10315	22743	3880	1464	11254
52	SERVICE IND. MACHINES	5608	715	1270	420	2724	6006	1025	387	2972
53	ELECT. TRANSMISS. EQUIP.	1570	200	355	118	763	1682	287	108	832
54	HOUSEHOLD APPLIANCES	225	28	51	17	109	240	41	16	119
55	ELECTRIC LIGHTING EQUIP.	1570	200	355	118	763	1682	287	108	832
56	RADIO, TV, ETC., EQUIP.	11439	1458	2592	858	5557	12253	2091	788	6063
57	ELECTRONIC COMPONENTS	0	0	0	0	0	0	0	0	0
58	MISC. ELECTRICAL MACH.	6093	776	1380	457	2960	6527	1113	420	3230
59	MOTOR VEHICLES, EQUIP.	97195	12390	22018	7290	47218	104107	17761	6701	51516
60	AIRCRAFT, PARTS									
61	OTHER TRANSPORT. EQUIP.	11925	1520	2701	895	5793	12773	2179	822	6320
62	PROFESS., SCIEN. INSTRU.	17906	2283	4056	1343	8699	19180	3273	1234	9491
63	MEDICAL, PHOTO. EQUIP.	3401	433	771	256	1653	3644	621	234	1803
64	MISC. MANUFACTURING	40971	5222	9281	3073	19904	43885	7487	2824	21716
65	TRANSPORT., WAREHOUSING	73046	9311	16548	5479	35486	78240	13349	5035	38717
66	COMMUNICA., EXC. BRDCAST.	43663	5566	9892	3275	21211	46768	7979	3010	23143
67	RADIO, TV BROADCASTING	0								
68	ELEC., GAS, WATER, SAN. SER.	83738	10673	18969	6281	40680	89691	15302	5773	44383
69	WHOLESALE, RETAIL TRADE	53306	6795	12076	3999	25897	57098	9741	3675	28254
70	FINANCE, INSURANCE	39476	5032	8943	2961	19178	42283	7214	2722	20924
71	REAL ESTATE, RENTAL	65719	8377	14888	4929	31926	70391	12010	4530	34833
72	HOTELS, PERSONAL SERV.	113504	15105	26845	8888	57569	126930	21656	8169	62810
73	BUSINESS SERVICES	22579	2878	5115	1693	10969	24185	4127	1556	11967
74	RESEARCH, DEVELOPMENT									
75	AUTO. REPAIR, SERVICES	-5915	-881	-1567	-519	-3360	-7407	-1264	-477	-3666
76	AMUSEMENTS	37944	4836	8596	2846	18433	40641	6934	2616	20111
77	MED., EDUC. SERVICES	16337	2082	3701	1225	7936	17498	2985	1126	8659
78	FEDERAL GOVT. ENTERPRISE	1794	228	407	135	872	1922	328	124	952
79	STATE, LOCAL GOVT. ENT.	743	95	169	56	364	801	137	52	396
80	IMPORTS	0	0	0	0	0	0	0	0	0
81	BUS. TRAVEL, ENT., GIFTS.	33755	4303	7547	2531	16399	36157	6169	2327	17892
82	OFFICE SUPPLIES	55513	7076	12575	4163	26969	59461	10145	3827	29423
83	SCRAP, USED GOODS									
84	GOVERNMENT INDUSTRY	1765328	225019	399905	132409	857598	1890848	322604	121694	935665
85	REST OF WORLD INDUSTRY	0	0	0	0	0	0	0	0	0
86	HOUSEHOLD INDUSTRY	0	0	0	0	0	0	0	0	0
87	INVENTORY VALUATION ADJ.	0	0	0	0	0	0	0	0	0
88	STATE TOTAL	4657900	593720	1055172	349374	2262815	4989091	851203	321096	2468799

TABLE 8-10

STATE ESTIMATES OF 1940

STATE AND LOCAL GOVERNMENT NET PURCHASES OF GOODS AND SERVICES
(THOUSANDS OF 1958 DOLLARS)

INDUSTRY TITLE	46 WASHINGTON	47 WEST VIRGINIA	48 WISCONSIN	49 WYOMING	50 ALASKA	51 HAWAII	52 NO STATE ALLOCATION	53 NATIONAL TOTAL
1 LIVESTOCK, PRDTS.	1312	453	1816	153	299	465	0	64003
2 OTHER AGRICULTURE PRDTS.	1640	565	2270	190	374	580	0	80002
3 FORESTRY, FISHERIES	62	21	85	7	15	22	0	3005
4 AGRI.,FORES.,FISH. SERV.	-9493	-3272	-13136	-1103	-2164	-3362	0	-462998
5 IRON, FERRO. ORES MINING	0	0	0	0	0	0	0	0
6 NONFERROUS ORES MINING	0	0	0	0	0	0	0	0
7 COAL MINING	5761	1986	7972	669	1314	2040	0	280998
8 CRUDE PETRO.,NATURAL GAS	0	0	0	0	0	0	0	0
9 STONE, CLAY MINING	-861	-296	-1191	-100	-196	-305	0	-42001
10 CHEM.,FERT. MIN. MINING	861	296	1191	100	196	305	0	42001
11 NEW CONSTRUCTION	730712	251851	1011156	84913	166649	258782	0	35639975
12 MAINT., REPAIR CONSTR.	156435	53917	216474	18179	35677	55401	0	7630006
13 ORDNANCE, ACCESSORIES	595	205	823	69	136	210	0	29002
14 FOOD, KINDRED PRDTS.	28089	9681	38869	3264	6406	9948	0	1370000
15 TOBACCO MANUFACTURES	62	21	85	7	15	22	0	3005
16 FABRICS	861	296	1191	100	196	305	0	42001
17 TEXTILE PRDTS.	123	43	170	15	28	44	0	6003
18 APPAREL	10497	3618	14526	1220	2394	3718	0	511999
19 MISC. TEXTILE PRDTS.	62	21	85	7	15	22	0	3005
20 LUMBER, WOOD PRDTS.	123	43	170	15	28	44	0	6003
21 WOODEN CONTAINERS	62	21	85	7	15	22	0	3005
22 HOUSEHOLD FURNITURE	8098	2791	11207	941	1847	2868	0	395001
23 OTHER FURNITURE	16587	5717	22952	1927	3783	5874	0	808995
24 PAPER, ALLIED PRDTS.	472	163	652	55	108	167	0	22998
25 PAPERBOARD CONTAINERS	0	0	0	0	0	0	0	0
26 PRINTING, PUBLISHING	23066	7950	31918	2681	5260	8169	0	1124997
27 CHEMICALS,SELECT. PRDTS.	29422	10140	40712	3419	6710	10420	0	1434995
28 PLASTICS, SYNTHETICS	0	0	0	0	0	0	0	0
29 DRUGS, COSMETICS	15869	5469	21959	1844	3619	5620	0	774003
30 PAINT, ALLIED PRDTS.	0	0	0	0	0	0	0	0
31 PETROLEUM, RELATED INDS.	51441	17730	71184	5978	11732	18217	0	2508999
32 RUBBER, MISC. PLASTICS	11768	4056	16286	1367	2684	4168	0	573998
33 LEATHER TANNING, PRDTS.	0	0	0	0	0	0	0	0
34 FOOTWEAR, LEATHER PRDTS.	123	43	170	15	28	44	0	6003
35 GLASS, GLASS PRDTS.	0	0	0	0	0	0	0	0
36 STONE, CLAY PRDTS.	533	184	737	62	121	189	0	26002
37 PRIMARY IRON, STEEL MFR.	123	43	170	15	28	44	0	6003
38 PRIMARY NONFERROUS MFR.	0	0	0	0	0	0	0	0

234

	C1	C2	C3	C4	C5	C6	C7
39 METAL CONTAINERS	0	0	0	0	0	0	0
40 FABRICATED METAL PRDTS.	0	0	0	0	0	0	0
41 SCREW MACH. PRDTS., ETC.	472	163	652	55	108	167	22998
42 OTHER FAB. METAL PRDTS.	5147	1773	7121	598	1174	1823	250998
43 ENGINES, TURBINES	533	184	737	62	121	189	26002
44 FARM MACH. EQUIP.	2070	713	2866	240	472	734	100998
45 CONSTRUC. MACH., EQUIP.	1527	565	2667	224	440	683	94005
46 MATERIAL HANDLING MACH.	5207	1795	7206	605	1188	1844	254001
47 METALWORKING MACHINERY	923	318	1276	107	211	327	45002
48 SPECIAL MACH., EQUIP.	4469	1540	6185	519	1020	1583	217994
49 GENERAL MACH., EQUIP.	656	226	908	76	150	232	31998
50 MACHINE SHOP PRDTS.	3670	1265	5078	426	837	1299	178999
51 OFFICE, COMPUT. MACHINES	11646	4013	16115	1354	2656	4124	567996
52 SERVICE IND. MACHINES	3075	1060	4255	358	701	1089	150000
53 ELECT. TRANSMISS. EQUIP.	861	296	1191	100	196	305	42001
54 HOUSEHOLD APPLIANCES	123	43	170	15	28	44	6003
55 ELECTRIC LIGHTING EQUIP.	861	296	1191	100	196	305	42001
56 RADIO, TV, ETC., EQUIP.	6274	2162	8681	729	1430	2222	305996
57 ELECTRONIC COMPONENTS	0	0	0	0	0	0	0
58 MISC. ELECTRICAL MACH.	3342	1152	4624	386	762	1184	163000
59 MOTOR VEHICLES, EQUIP.	53307	18373	73766	6195	12157	18878	2599999
60 AIRCRAFT, PARTS	0	0	0	0	0	0	0
61 OTHER TRANSPORT. EQUIP.	6541	2254	9051	760	1491	2317	318997
62 PROFESS., SCIEN. INSTRU.	9820	3385	13590	1141	2239	3478	478999
63 MEDICAL, PHOTO. EQUIP.	1866	643	2582	217	425	661	91000
64 MISC. MANUFACTURING	22471	7745	31095	2615	5125	7958	1095996
65 TRANSPORT., WAREHOUSING	40062	13808	55438	4656	9136	14188	1953999
66 COMMUNICA.,EXC. BRDCAST.	23947	8254	33137	2783	5461	8481	1167999
67 RADIO, TV BROADCASTING	0	0	0	0	0	0	0
68 ELEC.,GAS,WATER,SAN.SER.	45925	15829	63552	5337	10474	16265	2239999
69 WHOLESALE, RETAIL TRADE	29236	10076	40457	3397	6668	10354	1425992
70 FINANCE, INSURANCE	21650	7463	29960	2516	4938	7668	1056004
71 REAL ESTATE, RENTAL	36043	12423	49877	4188	8220	12765	1757999
72 HOTELS, PERSONAL SERV.	6192	2134	8568	719	1412	2192	301996
73 BUSINESS SERVICES	64993	22401	89937	7552	14823	23017	3169995
74 RESEARCH, DEVELOPMENT	0	0	0	0	0	0	0
75 AUTO. REPAIR, SERVICES	12383	4268	17136	1439	2324	4386	604000
76 AMUSEMENTS	-3793	-1307	-5248	-441	-365	-1343	-184998
77 MED.,EDUC. SERVICES	20810	7173	28797	2418	4746	7370	1014995
78 FEDERAL GOVT. ENTERPRISE	8959	3088	12390	1041	2043	3173	437001
79 STATE, LOCAL GOVT. ENT.	984	339	1361	115	224	348	48003
80 IMPORTS	410	142	567	48	93	145	20000
81 BUS.TRAVEL, ENT., GIFTS.	0	0	0	0	0	0	0
82 OFFICE SUPPLIES	18513	6381	25619	2151	4222	6557	902998
83 SCRAP, USED GOODS	30447	10494	42132	3538	6944	10782	1484998
84 GOVERNMENT INDUSTRY	968193	333702	1339781	112510	220810	342886	47222948
85 REST OF WORLD INDUSTRY	0	0	0	0	0	0	0
86 HOUSEHOLD INDUSTRY	0	0	0	0	0	0	0
87 INVENTORY VALUATION ADJ.	0	0	0	0	0	0	0
88 STATE TOTAL	2554620	880488	3535065	296863	582617	904723	124599919

STATE ESTIMATES OF 1970
FEDERAL GOVERNMENT PURCHASES
(THOUSANDS OF 1958 DOLLARS)

INDUSTRY TITLE	1 ALABAMA	2 ARIZONA	3 ARKANSAS	4 CALIFORNIA	5 COLORADO	6 CONNECTICUT	7 DELAWARE	0 DISTRICT OF COLUMBIA	9 FLORIDA
1 LIVESTOCK, PRDTS.	1086	1028	1109	4395	2625	181	40	0	815
2 OTHER AGRICULTURE PRDTS.	-423	-933	-6133	-2892	-709	-4	-12	0	-101
3 FORESTRY, FISHERIES	-1569	-3739	-4759	-59700	-2290	0	0	0	-2401
4 AGRI.,FORES.,FISH. SERV.	127	75	50	637	-107	63	12	911	167
5 IRON, FERRO. ORES MINING		-620		-53	-5755				
6 NONFERROUS ORES MINING	772	2710	18517	2737	1641				3753
7 COAL MINING	1355		26		394				
8 CRUDE PETRO.,NATURAL GAS									
9 STONE, CLAY MINING	-249	1524	-390	1608	-11	-155	-155		-605
10 CHEM.,FERT. MIN. MINING									
11 NEW CONSTRUCTION	72156	30240	34830	189021	91726	9544	6803	13043	78689
12 MAINT., REPAIR CONSTR.	26143	15076	8737	155640	24485	9777	2968	126232	38631
13 ORDNANCE, ACCESSORIES	171433	27550	31709	1561786	49469	180976	4939	50105	274135
14 FOOD, KINDRED PRDTS.	16856	4305	15184	100135	11742	9193	5925	3159	34526
15 TOBACCO MANUFACTURES	-14					-10			-79
16 FABRICS	7401		233	275	7	2211	303		107
17 TEXTILE PRDTS.	1157		692	1849	68	993	149		1964
18 APPAREL	5553	548	1775	7615	148	1856	464	1	1479
19 MISC. TEXTILE PRDTS.	935	166	36	6692	313	1112	206	57	-32
20 LUMBER, WOOD PRDTS.	-208	143	-47	2283	82	-21	-8	-2	730
21 WOODEN CONTAINERS	509		550	847	154	167			655
22 HOUSEHOLD FURNITURE	316	60	812	1830	90	201		9	1243
23 OTHER FURNITURE	847	372	756	5903	560	1003	47	3765	2014
24 PAPER, ALLIED PRDTS.	2115	354	862	4368	505	857	88	3892	486
25 PAPERBOARD CONTAINERS	173	85	176	1719	135	388	77	731	290
26 PRINTING, PUBLISHING	127	83	86	1156	139	228	21	492	
27 CHEMICALS, SELECT. PRDTS.	59514	4226	2372	9201	4037	12548	8167	345	32858
28 PLASTICS, SYNTHETICS	786	135		843	355	381	1329	77	1501
29 DRUGS, COSMETICS	66	6	533	9838	333	4556	579		1069
30 PAINT, ALLIED PRDTS.	16		6	333	12	12	77		52
31 PETROLEUM, RELATED INDS.	7899	318	6785	213396	2959	1232	10005	1052	6673
32 RUBBER, MISC. PLASTICS	232	1	5476	3677	10	3115	1148		1145
33 LEATHER TANNING, PRDTS.	0					0			406
34 FOOTWEAR, LEATHER PRDTS.	238		1294	792	149	454	109		198
35 GLASS, GLASS PRDTS.	56	25	62	1162		156			101
36 STONE, CLAY PRDTS.	77		33	327	39	52		112	67
37 PRIMARY IRON, STEEL MFR.	997	65	62	6004	317	2968	54		
38 PRIMARY NONFERROUS MFR.	-321	-74	-1066	-8262	-15	-9652	-120		-172

236

	1	2	3	4	5	6	7	8
39 METAL CONTAINERS	605	0	0	0	37	1639	0	47
40 FABRICATED METAL PRDTS.	3619	155	227	1879	753	11783	593	3280
41 SCREW MACH. PRDTS., ETC.	348	0	156	660	0	7403	277	409
42 OTHER FAB. METAL PRDTS.	1351	0	197	1962	698	16920	209	842
43 ENGINES, TURBINES	4696	2555	121	1896	1457	27243	68	2309
44 FARM MACH., EQUIP.	83	344		24	62	233	43	90
45 CONSTRUC. MACH., EQUIP.	96	38	0	44	575	4263		149
46 MATERIAL HANDLING MACH.	357	798	222	692	477	5027	2409	755
47 METALWORKING MACHINERY	530	79	112	9114	102	6905	694	374
48 SPECIAL MACH., EQUIP.	281	51		2446	53	2403	218	265
49 GENERAL MACH., EQUIP.	99			10058	297	9563	291	1182
50 MACHINE SHOP PRDTS.	615	102	319	6751	277	8910	670	457
51 OFFICE, COMPUT. MACHINES	9929	32710	414	16560	11431	56324	2498	4632
52 SERVICE IND. MACHINES	516		108	593	124	4151	697	1122
53 ELECT. TRANSMISS. EQUIP.	6490	0	0	12084	18137	65743	258	94
54 HOUSEHOLD APPLIANCES	13	8	24	436	0	301	176	0
55 ELECTRIC LIGHTING EQUIP.	482	0	0	616	459	4346	15	19
56 RADIO, TV, ETC., EQUIP.	103267		0	81459	14900	1069471	38533	16503
57 ELECTRONIC COMPONENTS	4733	0	134	20844	311	131443	0	800
58 MISC. ELECTRICAL MACH.	7225	0	779	2903	7790	28144	66	381
59 MOTOR VEHICLES, EQUIP.	2827	1319	1560	3868	731	23721	2157	16966
60 AIRCRAFT, PARTS	165864	36794	3619	981332	36860	1295969	1713	90357
61 OTHER TRANSPORT. EQUIP.	27490	40377	5565	177038	1088	125857	4795	25131
62 PROFESS., SCIEN. INSTRU.	4761		1849	41027	5377	51457	1262	640
63 MEDICAL, PHOTO. EQUIP.	765	504	121	4929	311	31981	0	0
64 MISC. MANUFACTURING	122	640	13	86	78	542	45	96
65 TRANSPORT., WAREHOUSING	93339	21558	6913	30255	29256	278906	18250	36031
66 COMMUNICA.,EXC. BRDCAST.	12016	33595	931	2724	7599	48994	2523	7914
67 RADIO, TV BROADCASTING								0
68 ELEC.,GAS,WATER,SAN.SER.	6083	21939	464	1655	3861	24254	1447	-195
69 WHOLESALE, RETAIL TRADE	25003	5742	2315	16263	10008	89305	9768	13122
70 FINANCE, INSURANCE	1742	493	168	1531	779	7174	795	1045
71 REAL ESTATE, RENTAL	7187	29093	475	2378	3524	23068	1769	-111
72 HOTELS, PERSONAL SERV.	17636	38299	856	4859	6395	44141	3567	7638
73 BUSINESS SERVICES	52082	61730	3383	7324	26677	226114	6355	32733
74 RESEARCH, DEVELOPMENT								0
75 AUTO. REPAIR, SERVICES	619	3025	47	252	369	2320	181	442
76 AMUSEMENTS	3977	594	191	1070	1081	17838	559	623
77 MED.,EDUC. SERVICES	50572	104423	3358	29159	24892	184477	12062	25387
78 FEDERAL GOVT. ENTERPRISE	2996	2662	252	1188	1458	12503	653	1431
79 STATE, LOCAL GOVT. ENT.	7247	40518	534	2778	4642	27467	2218	5549
80 IMPORTS								0
81 BUS.TRAVEL, ENT., GIFTS.								
82 OFFICE SUPPLIES	6284	18833	485	1495	3978	25493	1363	4187
83 SCRAP, USED GOODS	2341	13509	172	921	1501	8831	731	1809
84 GOVERNMENT INDUSTRY	653349	1188014	51462	112263	411302	2729275	115202	405792
85 REST OF WORLD INDUSTRY	0	0	0	0	0	0	0	0
86 HOUSEHOLD INDUSTRY	0	0	0	0	0	0	0	0
87 INVENTORY VALUATION ADJ.								0
88 STATE TOTAL	1770005	1904491	130697	1829793	823297	8967124	355495	1096072

TABLE 8-11

STATE ESTIMATES OF 1970
FEDERAL GOVERNMENT PURCHASES
(THOUSANDS OF 1958 DOLLARS)

INDUSTRY TITLE	10 GEORGIA	11 IDAHO	12 ILLINOIS	13 INDIANA	14 IOWA	15 KANSAS	16 KENTUCKY	17 LOUISIANA	18 MAINE
1 LIVESTOCK, PRDTS.	1473	755	4412	2484	9582	3781	1277	591	222
2 OTHER AGRICULTURE PRDTS.	-2436	-793	-8731	-2872	-12899	-5217	-1307	-1758	-14
3 FORESTRY, FISHERIES	-2157	-12960	-236	-131	0	0	-653	-4440	-55
4 AGRI.,FORES.,FISH. SERV.	154	30	353	105	70	72	91	89	27
5 IRON, FERRO. ORES MINING							0		
6 NONFERROUS ORES MINING	379	5495	298				95	0	0
7 COAL MINING	0	0	3287	0	0	80	6308	0	0
8 CRUDE PETRO.,NATURAL GAS	0	0	0	810	50	82	0	0	0
9 STONE, CLAY MINING	-1158	-37	-877	-588	241	-302	-588	-134	-57
10 CHEM.,FERT. MIN. MINING							0		
11 NEW CONSTRUCTION	20240	71014	83033	14974	11576	14181	96919	11867	1735
12 MAINT., REPAIR CONSTR.	42500	4794	60035	18821	9369	15841	22542	18536	4899
13 ORDNANCE, ACCESSORIES	23728	2018	214124	198321	83612	39437	2432	246961	22350
14 FOOD, KINDRED PRDTS.	31902	9242	82816	28435	35295	13791	16790	19862	8298
15 TOBACCO MANUFACTURES	-14	0	-7	-9	48	0	-157	18	
16 FABRICS	17809	0	403	165	0	411	296	110	2507
17 TEXTILE PRDTS.	9170	3	1310	291	339	487	0	720	322
18 APPAREL	8441	0	4162	1564	832	-12	3400	964	466
19 MISC. TEXTILE PRDTS.	3830	481	4227	1205	-42	128	1405	203	228
20 LUMBER, WOOD PRDTS.	-167	0	-135	-118	128	74	-77	108	-168
21 WOODEN CONTAINERS	893	12	391	197	169	509	351	430	36
22 HOUSEHOLD FURNITURE	695	137	1357	1916	771	394	393	1825	45
23 OTHER FURNITURE	968	255	5269	1894	482	190	630	228	169
24 PAPER, ALLIED PRDTS.	2349	23	3429	1194	237	141	599	104	2081
25 PAPERBOARD CONTAINERS	660	27	2292	694	180	1141	265		61
26 PRINTING, PUBLISHING	196	13620	1304	338	3177	1133	149		39
27 CHEMICALS,SELECT. PRDTS.	25390	0	60306	12597	396	1232	55012	10060	1933
28 PLASTICS, SYNTHETICS	259	0	392	289	1636	12	852	439	0
29 DRUGS, COSMETICS	2077	0	16584	12603	682		132	164	124
30 PAINT, ALLIED PRDTS.	63	0	471	64	164		70	13	0
31 PETROLEUM, RELATED INDS.	3326	21	42793	43418	71	17121	5864	112341	901
32 RUBBER, MISC. PLASTICS	1526	0	24964	19915	20	110	108	642	514
33 LEATHER TANNING, PRDTS.	0	0	0	0		28	0	0	0
34 FOOTWEAR, LEATHER PRDTS.	668	0	2085	385		0	444	134	4440
35 GLASS, GLASS PRDTS.	112	0	1438	1056		62	124	57	0
36 STONE, CLAY PRDTS.	115	9	207	126	49	102	54	143	10
37 PRIMARY IRON, STEEL MFR.	111	2	3760	3920	208		268		122
38 PRIMARY NONFERROUS MFR.	-308	-18	-6974	-5446	-224	-81	-112	-377	-98

39 METAL CONTAINERS	133	0	2019	59	0	33	0	301	62
40 FABRICATED METAL PRDTS.	3011	177	9553	6463	1851	1855	1890	1816	266
41 SCREW MACH. PRDTS., ETC.	991	473	2904	776	129	32	513	54	0
42 OTHER FAB. METAL PRDTS.	643	10	7057	2237	328	114	1234	205	10
43 ENGINES, TURBINES	388	638	15156	15106	1961	132	172	2624	57
44 FARM MACH., EQUIP.	116	29	1114	266	953	134	183	54	10
45 CONSTRUC. MACH., EQUIP.	1047	44	40202	3000	4972	631	180	334	0
46 MATERIAL HANDLING MACH.	344	4	22026	1347	668	504	763	224	0
47 METALWORKING MACHINERY	603	2	9610	5374	530	165	308	0	35
48 SPECIAL MACH., EQUIP.	459		2000	1638	198	111	104	42	55
49 GENERAL MACH., EQUIP.	3C		20813	15624	723	1440	3537	192	0
50 MACHINE SHOP PRDTS.	733	22	4027	5002	196	263	374	250	112
51 OFFICE, COMPUT. MACHINES	5224	1045	25948	3814	2486	2438	10463	3029	946
52 SERVICE IND. MACHINES	1286		7152	3649	958	440	2258	212	46
53 ELECT. TRANSMISS. EQUIP.	13379	0	32152	20015	3048	331	1245	0	219
54 HOUSEHOLD APPLIANCES	49	0	1618	845	357	0	893	0	0
55 ELECTRIC LIGHTING EQUIP.	618	0	3012	1062	0	36	37	29	40
56 RADIO, TV, ETC., EQUIP.	1250	0	204325	94432	37057	4453	9606	1187	3430
57 ELECTRONIC COMPONENTS	0	249	16302	7418	4588	1374	4365	0	4152
58 MISC. ELECTRICAL MACH.	2882	0	6351	19568	1220	1301	410	0	357
59 MOTOR VEHICLES, EQUIP.	5305	0	20487	145179	1927	2758	3297	593	243
60 AIRCRAFT, PARTS	391904	9141	70708	171020	12098	176332	3118	56397	3795
61 OTHER TRANSPORT. EQUIP.	31066	1999	36407	28233	4010	8039	3546	29944	21798
62 PROFESS., SCIEN. INSTRU.	5150	0	34517	3308	2386	831	915	266	906
63 MEDICAL, PHOTO. EQUIP.	753	0	24782	879	206	918	266	359	33
64 MISC. MANUFACTURING	119	22	321	101	56	54	69	78	20
65 TRANSPORT., WAREHOUSING	61830	6574	193261	53342	30903	23799	27245	67098	8535
66 COMMUNICA.,EXC. BRDCAST.	13688	1352	17229	5486	2462	4874	7110	5633	1430
67 RADIO, TV BROADCASTING	0	0	0	0	0	0	0	0	0
68 ELEC.,GAS,WATER,SAN.SER.	6521	805	9978	3097	1640	2513	3514	2967	805
69 WHOLESALE, RETAIL TRADE	19220	4457	60153	24990	13891	8236	13226	11568	3954
70 FINANCE, INSURANCE	1523	344	4867	1958	1032	579	1035	840	299
71 REAL ESTATE, RENTAL	5078	980	14398	3881	2482	2357	2932	3224	923
72 HOTELS, PERSONAL SERV.	9883	1815	24949	8014	5030	4657	5806	6424	1797
73 BUSINESS SERVICES	48579	5011	46470	14829	4664	15254	23797	24897	3817
74 RESEARCH, DEVELOPMENT	0	0	0	0	0	0	0	0	0
75 AUTO. REPAIR, SERVICES	529	103	1282	397	260	249	314	320	98
76 AMUSEMENTS	1321	232	4684	1440	992	793	894	1160	199
77 MED.,EDUC. SERVICES	29383	5633	111158	29794	18719	17144	19760	23135	6778
78 FEDERAL GOVT. ENTERPRISE	2815	267	6182	1879	1027	1277	1560	1337	482
79 STATE, LOCAL GOVT. ENT.	6580	1314	15552	4624	3100	3130	3938	3873	1198
80 IMPORTS	0	0	0	0	0	0	0	0	0
81 BUS.,TRAVEL, ENT., GIFTS.	0	0	0	0	0	0	0	0	0
82 OFFICE SUPPLIES	7055	739	9333	2952	1389	2561	3696	2975	768
83 SCRAP, USED GOODS	2091	435	5131	1521	1035	1015	1265	1261	394
84 GOVERNMENT INDUSTRY	757080	57717	774072	256833	82944	259008	397584	291226	67151
85 REST OF WORLD INDUSTRY	0	0	0	0	0	0	0	0	0
86 HOUSEHOLD INDUSTRY	0	0	0	0	0	0	0	0	0
87 INVENTORY VALUATION ADJ.	0	0	0	0	0	0	0	0	0
88 STATE TOTAL	1674456	195760	2527797	1330059	400728	666008	777108	966039	186356

TABLE B-11

STATE ESTIMATES OF 1970
FEDERAL GOVERNMENT PURCHASES
(THOUSANDS OF 1958 DOLLARS)

INDUSTRY TITLE	19 MARYLAND	20 MASSA-CHUSETTS	21 MICHIGAN	22 MINNESOTA	23 MISSISSIPPI	24 MISSOURI	25 MONTANA	26 NEBRASKA	27 NEVADA
1 LIVESTOCK, PRDTS.	204	137	818	3391	1131	3289	1227	4972	159
2 OTHER AGRICULTURE PRDTS.	-51	0	-682	-7549	-3482	-3537	-1874	-6025	-19
3 FORESTRY, FISHERIES	0	0	-1679	-847	-9200	-1367	-12100	-125	-430
4 AGRI.,FORES.,FISH. SERV.	153	187	171	110	54	182	38	49	23
5 IRON, FERRO. ORES MINING	0	0	0	0	0	0	-1497	0	0
6 NONFERROUS ORES MINING	0	0	228	0	142	3893	556	0	735
7 COAL MINING	90	0	0	0	0	171	22	0	0
8 CRUDE PETRO.,NATURAL GAS	0	0	0	0	0	0	0	0	0
9 STONE, CLAY MINING	-423	-228	234	-175	-114	-786	-107	-97	918
10 CHEM.,FERT. MIN. MINING	0	0	0	0	0	0	0	0	0
11 NEW CONSTRUCTION	50112	33711	13336	4596	17000	26581	48104	12534	23317
12 MAINT., REPAIR CONSTR.	38628	32277	26767	15334	12204	33691	6057	8837	5162
13 ORDNANCE, ACCESSORIES	98722	165093	158113	252736	6589	250138	142	38657	1340
14 FOOD, KINDRED PRDTS.	23164	26765	34605	33435	11274	33070	2593	17729	755
15 TOBACCO MANUFACTURES	0	-4	0	0	-5	0	0	0	
16 FABRICS	583	4972	70	233	342	304	0	46	0
17 TEXTILE PRDTS.	0	3384	1017	186	691	230	0	0	0
18 APPAREL	2847	6618	721	859	4799	4048	0	197	0
19 MISC. TEXTILE PRDTS.	1256	5130	7705	1876	1043	2236	0	182	0
20 LUMBER, WOOD PRDTS.	-50	-65	-89	-45	175	-34	454	-6	17
21 WOODEN CONTAINERS	313	273	195	101	789	200	0	0	0
22 HOUSEHOLD FURNITURE	235	783	750	149	877	282	0	52	14
23 OTHER FURNITURE	1451	1563	4580	895	451	1728	152	448	98
24 PAPER, ALLIED PRDTS.	1006	3562	2619	1770	697	1290	198	246	93
25 PAPERBOARD CONTAINERS	660	1089	1061	307	124	756	29	89	17
26 PRINTING, PUBLISHING	243	567	423	279	49	437	36	90	23
27 CHEMICALS,SELECT. PRDTS.	17287	20588	49365	4628	27291	18965	991	1849	1964
28 PLASTICS, SYNTHETICS	679	1412	1120	106	83	33			
29 DRUGS, COSMETICS	3506	2850	9052	1934	606	5248		945	
30 PAINT, ALLIED PRDTS.	88	78	160	24		127			
31 PETROLEUM, RELATED INDS.	7153	5543	11435	7251	6982	6796	4547	872	126
32 RUBBER, MISC. PLASTICS	4182	7695	16384	155	103	188		58	
33 LEATHER TANNING, PRDTS.	0	0	0	0	0	0			0
34 FOOTWEAR, LEATHER PRDTS.	433	6826	513	223	474	4572		21	0
35 GLASS, GLASS PRDTS.	480	18	738	86	70	246			
36 STONE, CLAY PRDTS.	63	112	127	74	40	109	9	22	11
37 PRIMARY IRON, STEEL MFR.	1274	3820	3194	280	18	445	19	11	9
38 PRIMARY NONFERROUS MFR.	-975	-6242	-4860	-197	-30	-295	-84	-155	-27

39 METAL CONTAINERS	573	105	35	176	0	633	0	59	0
40 FABRICATED METAL PRDTS.	1827	3124	6391	2426	1013	4026	75	1135	48
41 SCREW MACH. PRDTS., ETC.	727	1098	2693	344	268	321	33	14	0
42 OTHER FAB. METAL PRDTS.	1053	1795	5672	558	291	878	0	51	0
43 ENGINES, TURBINES	4731	12745	21663	1172	160	789	75	110	1768
44 FARM MACH., EQUIP.	54	73	239	228	71	170	14	118	8
45 CONSTRUC. MACH., EQUIP.	197	845	20043	2159	2400	523	0	143	21
46 MATERIAL HANDLING MACH.	1975	819	6553	1523	633	614	0	35	8
47 METALWORKING MACHINERY	1345	6546	13960	2275	32	1198	0	64	10
48 SPECIA_ MACH., EQUIP.	413	3009	771	839	64	309	0	0	5
49 GENERA_ MACH., EQUIP.	167	5241	16391	1185	143	899	0	548	0
50 MACHINE SHOP PRDTS.	763	4400	3041	2690	105	1345	7	37	13
51 OFFICE, COMPUT. MACHINES	7555	22278	20778	35860	1806	8529	1324	1707	786
52 SERVICE IND. MACHINES	1207	2060	6930	3515	435	4918	0	53	0
53 ELECT. TRANSMISS. EQUIP.	4985	14804	12067	9097	648	16829	0	590	0
54 HOUSEHOLD APPLIANCES	15	113	630	133	220	209	0	0	0
55 ELECTRIC LIGHTING EQUIP.	75	722	325	341	32	1341	0	0	0
56 RADIO, TV, ETC., EQUIP.	229109	447397	10499	78970	9903	78455	0	15357	1519
57 ELECTRONIC COMPONENTS	2283	47605	1204	5134	860	926	0	2307	0
58 MISC. ELECTRICAL MACH.	2494	6868	6277	2452	572	4296	0	209	0
59 MOTOR VEHICLES, EQUIP.	18926	4784	209732	2183	3815	24853	143	916	32
60 AIRCRAFT, PARTS	129281	176808	68920	18950	21231	481725	1074	2342	25319
61 OTHER TRANSPORT. EQUIP.	34351	53418	34748	5698	121296	9485	0	2551	26
62 PROFESS., SCIEN. INSTRU.	3314	55768	16746	5033	173	3841	0	1553	0
63 MEDICAL, PHOTO. EQUIP.	2056	20545	1076	3614	0	1765	0	0	0
64 MISC. MANUFACTURING	121	174	163	102	41	171	27	36	19
65 TRANSPORT., WAREHOUSING	48438	79462	83073	50314	15482	84054	6945	18277	5340
66 COMMUNICA.,EXC. BRDCAST.	12236	9301	7469	4095	3784	9924	1707	2579	1591
67 RADIO, TV BROADCASTING	0	0	0	0	0	0	0	0	0
68 ELEC.,GAS,WATER,SAN.SER.	6001	5351	4526	2660	1926	5507	1019	1453	817
69 WHOLESALE, RETAIL TRADE	14996	32067	38163	15436	7430	20869	3058	6211	1722
70 FINANCE, INSURANCE	1088	2790	2851	1152	568	1659	221	501	123
71 REAL ESTATE, RENTAL	5608	6903	6509	4084	1759	6615	1229	1746	866
72 HOTELS, PERSONAL SERV.	8824	12562	13808	7593	3633	11838	2077	3329	3411
73 BUSINESS SERVICES	55663	30190	18278	8746	12296	28087	3969	6899	10547
74 RESEARCH, DEVELOPMENT	0	0	0	0	0	0	0	0	0
75 AUTO. REPAIR, SERVICES	520	691	684	412	189	648	128	175	82
76 AMUSEMENTS	1762	2101	3166	1452	370	1965	221	654	2919
77 MED.,EDUC. SERVICES	32204	59839	55858	33881	10936	41755	7033	12968	3460
78 FEDERL GOVT. ENTERPRISE	2120	3207	2996	1597	824	2725	319	795	296
79 STATE, LOCAL GOVT. ENT.	6591	8250	7564	4879	2324	7971	1665	2162	1009
80 IMPORTS	0	0	0	0	0	0	0	0	0
81 BUS.,TRAVEL, ENT., GIFTS.	6350	5030	4098	2293	1981	5315	932	1386	835
82 OFFICE SUPPLIES	2113	2720	2507	1626	752	2616	551	711	327
83 SCRAP, USED GOODS	690103	422391	309678	146745	204381	476975	72724	121104	84977
84 GOVERNMENT INDUSTRY	0	0	0	0	0	0	0	0	0
85 REST OF WORLD INDUSTRY	0	0	0	0	0	0	0	0	0
86 HOUSEHOLD INDUSTRY	0	0	0	0	0	0	0	0	0
87 INVENTORY VALUATION ADJ.	0	0	0	0	0	0	0	0	0
88 STATE TOTAL	1597536	1904515	1386963	795936	516118	1750801	156084	292381	182212

241

TABLE B-11

STATE ESTIMATES OF 1970
FEDERAL GOVERNMENT PURCHASES
(THOUSANDS OF 1958 DOLLARS)

INDUSTRY TITLE	28 NEW HAMPSHIRE	29 NEW JERSEY	30 NEW MEXICO	31 NEW YORK	32 NORTH CAROLINA	33 NORTH DAKOTA	34 OHIO	35 OKLAHOMA	36 OREGON
1 LIVESTOCK, PRDTS.	80	187	822	701	1123	938	1822	2073	715
2 OTHER AGRICULTURE PRDTS.	0	-29	-570	-99	-4107	-5736	-2431	-1894	-470
3 FORESTRY, FISHERIES	-756	0	-1784	0	-1083	0	-63	-701	-156477
4 AGRI.,FORES.,FISH. SERV.	18	166	63	633	106	26	257	96	83
5 IRON, FERRO. ORES MINING	0	0	-1925	0	-18	0	0	0	0
6 NONFERROUS ORES MINING	0	392	903	2548	0	0	0	559	274
7 COAL MINING	0	0	145	0	0	23	2622	67	0
8 CRUDE PETRO.,NATURAL GAS	0	0	0	0	0	229	0	0	0
9 STONE, CLAY MINING	-27	-420	116	-48	1255	664	-1189	289	-380
10 CHEM.,FERT. MIN. MINING	0	0	0	0	0	0	0	0	0
11 NEW CONSTRUCTION	2789	13571	38280	100257	35616	11271	47461	40218	103688
12 MAINT., REPAIR CONSTR.	5179	35506	12739	91318	30820	5299	44838	25094	11979
13 ORDNANCE, ACCESSORIES	5593	108824	18459	302956	33452	8	185019	12438	3013
14 FOOD, KINDRED PRDTS.	1957	40935	2509	78938	75019	2226	52293	9745	11346
15 TOBACCO MANUFACTURES	0	-12	0	-5	-330	-9	-9	0	-7
16 FABRICS	1624	3047	0	3549	38874	0	2184	106	150
17 TEXTILE PRDTS.	310	2157	0	4040	3508	0	2555	155	73
18 APPAREL	478	9504	89	38325	16476	0	1913	809	375
19 MISC. TEXTILE PRDTS.	239	7254	110	19513	5639	0	-105	308	593
20 LUMBER, WOOD PRDTS.	-21	-52	57	-188	-308	-2	339	5	6476
21 WOODEN CONTAINERS	145	343	0	396	401	0	762	0	183
22 HOUSEHOLD FURNITURE	130	534	11	1605	4863	0	4081	86	208
23 OTHER FURNITURE	216	1896	262	7929	2007	104	3695	518	466
24 PAPER, ALLIED PRDTS.	609	2404	254	6611	1546	107	1542	416	1097
25 PAPERBOARD CONTAINERS	49	1481	47	2514	469	20	839	121	142
26 PRINTING, PUBLISHING	51	498	41	2217	181	27	1649	112	96
27 CHEMICALS,SELECT. PRDTS.	677	8138	969	4387	15296	0	69967	601	556
28 PLASTICS, SYNTHETICS	41	1744	0	1452	2499	0	6616	77	25
29 DRUGS, COSMETICS	0	29707	0	27495	1267	0	289	111	343
30 PAINT, ALLIED PRDTS.	0	297	0	169	36	0	9	9	36
31 PETROLEUM, RELATED INDS.	217	40554	3272	35992	900	7246	31985	39567	1320
32 RUBBER, MISC. PLASTICS	1120	7835	0	8654	2310	0	56481	6072	74
33 LEATHER TANNING, PRDTS.	0	0	0	7637	526	0	1342	0	0
34 FOOTWEAR, LEATHER PRDTS.	3020	1613	24	1506	360	0	2288	67	49
35 GLASS, GLASS PRDTS.	0	1670	0	287	83	0	335	428	42
36 STONE, CLAY PRDTS.	15	174	15	1468	79	5	6286	37	26
37 PRIMARY IRON, STEEL MFR.	484	455	0			0		220	644
38 PRIMARY NONFERROUS MFR.	-691	-4927	-3	-6331	-513	0	-7147	-674	-1108

	C1	C2	C3	C4	C5	C6	C7	C8	C9
39 METAL CONTAINERS	0	1258	0	545	0	0	610	34	119
40 FABRICATED METAL PRDTS.	303	5213	62	10371	1841	81	13564	3411	971
41 SCREW MACH. PRDTS., ETC.	27	1525	0	2594	502	0	2649	160	79
42 OTHER FAB. METAL PRDTS.	88	3940	0	5567	1520	0	5973	172	618
43 ENGINES, TURBINES	116	1292	2207	24285	486	57	6009	157	319
44 FARM MACH., EQUIP.	6	69	23	291	87	27	273	57	46
45 CONSTRUC. MACH., EQUIP.	217	754	0	1684	210	111	12947	1860	217
46 MATERIAL HANDLING MACH.	96	2520	41	4741	1760	0	17417	22	1888
47 METALWORKING MACHINERY	278	2913	17	5679	370	0	3555	209	59
48 SPECIAL MACH., EQUIP.	303	1182		1938	949	0	28760	1778	187
49 GENERAL MACH., EQUIP.	1577	5528		8712	105	0	8008	469	140
50 MACHINE SHOP PRDTS.	154	1560	118	3565	447	0	51463	3149	292
51 OFFICE, COMPUT. MACHINES	1227	16982	2147	103025	4144	13	9523	384	2956
52 SERVICE IND. MACHINES	0	4956	0	8549	856	906	41926	78	124
53 ELECT. TRANSMISS. EQUIP.	4311	24717	0	50397	17061	0	2473		13663
54 HOUSEHOLD APPLIANCES	0	103	0	484	257	0	2843	0	16
55 ELECTRIC LIGHTING EQUIP.	74	2416	0	3446	1239	0			
56 RADIO, TV, ETC., EQUIP.	38245	502091	3546	728364	119135	0	32211	82242	8870
57 ELECTRONIC COMPONENTS	10193	35645	197	58793	6421	0	5311	2629	1782
58 MISC. ELECTRICAL MACH.	753	10945	0	22299	9208	0	10009	52	1099
59 MOTOR VEHICLES, EQUIP.	40	9124	2264	24617	2060	295	104249	2005	11181
60 AIRCRAFT, PARTS	2865	117297	33175	618260	12364	813	527471	38169	14741
61 OTHER TRANSPORT. EQUIP.	369	26955	69	110034	5901	0	24592	1621	1295
62 PROFESS., SCIEN. INSTRU.	1338	46021	2721	84835	10435	0	12751	312	647
63 MEDICAL, PHOTO. EQUIP.	327	7308	0	117280	1642	0	13827	22	86
64 MISC. MANUFACTURING	14	190	48	596	101	18	249	75	27769
65 TRANSPORT., WAREHOUSING	5382	118445	9137	389923	61783	6805	121236	33426	3238
66 COMMUNICA., EXC. BRDCAST.	1682	10859	3845	24704	10012	1594	12971	8008	
67 RADIO, TV BROADCASTING	0		0						
68 ELEC., GAS, WATER, SAN. SER.	789	5658	2049	15725	4698	854	7415	3877	2064
69 WHOLESALE, RETAIL TRADE	3678	31925	3382	85736	21622	2376	51312	8659	12243
70 FINANCE, INSURANCE	307	2510	232	8332	1712	155	3867	635	979
71 REAL ESTATE, RENTAL	584	6457	1965	30089	3603	824	9701	3133	2921
72 HOTELS, PERSONAL SERV.	1349	12344	3424	45348	8349	1523	18714	5610	5255
73 BUSINESS SERVICES	6315	36578	18083	69347	36936	4697	37206	27541	6712
74 RESEARCH, DEVELOPMENT	0	0							
75 AUTO. REPAIR, SERVICES	61	617	210	2336	383	89	978	320	304
76 AMUSEMENTS	372	2312	367	15833	1262	178	4099	880	870
77 MED., EDUC. SERVICES	5300	45302	10589	167899	26949	5962	86913	23015	20087
78 FEDERAL GOVT. ENTERPRISE	415	3565	555	10525	2260	390	4421	1671	726
79 STATE, LOCAL GOVT. ENT.	759	7210	2740	28123	4517	1154	11310	4104	3699
80 IMPORTS	0	0		0	0	0			0
81 BUS. TRAVEL, ENT., GIFTS.	0	0		0	0	0			0
82 OFFICE SUPPLIES	864	5721	2037	13745	5142	847	7001	4143	1803
83 SCRAP, USED GOODS	240	2343	894	9359	1428	377	3726	1311	1231
84 GOVERNMENT INDUSTRY	95491	569549	195736	926275	592279	80590	595301	458296	120989
85 REST OF WORLD INDUSTRY	0	0	0	0	0	0	0	0	0
86 HOUSEHOLD INDUSTRY	0	0	0	0	0	0	0	0	0
87 INVENTORY VALUATION ADJ.	0	0	0	0	0	0	0	0	0
88 STATE TOTAL	214630	2009344	376787	4590679	1200391	133191	2450764	860954	257915

TABLE 8-11

STATE ESTIMATES OF 1970
FEDERAL GOVERNMENT PURCHASES
(THOUSANDS OF 1958 DOLLARS)

INDUSTRY TITLE	37 PENNSYLVANIA	38 RHODE ISLAND	39 SOUTH CAROLINA	40 SOUTH DAKOTA	41 TENNESSEE	42 TEXAS	43 UTAH	44 VERMONT	45 VIRGINIA
1 LIVESTOCK, PRDTS.	995	20	417	2817	1000	4634	416	70	655
2 OTHER AGRICULTURE PRDTS.	-38	0	-379	-2968	-499	-7875	-44	0	-257
3 FORESTRY, FISHERIES	-1825	0	-3836	-520	-666	-3115	-881	-1194	-756
4 AGRI.,FORES.,FISH. SERV.	319	22	52	35	139	326	53	14	130
5 IRON, FERRO. ORES MINING	-35	0	0	0	0	-1097	0	0	0
6 NONFERROUS ORES MINING	859	0	0	33	1426	1205	2581	0	721
7 COAL MINING	7672	0	0	0	549	355	355	0	2905
8 CRUDE PETRO.,NATURAL GAS	0	0	0	0	0	35	0	0	0
9 STONE, CLAY MINING	-1367	-13	-152	-114	-672	-3539	1642	-574	-729
10 CHEM.,FERT. MIN. MINING	0	0	0	0	0	0	0	0	0
11 NEW CONSTRUCTION	53826	5652	43013	8912	189662	78442	14273	3019	99166
12 MAINT., REPAIR CONSTR.	58128	6413	18929	5536	22129	83259	13601	2025	52983
13 ORDNANCE, ACCESSORIES	293958	4158	926	3602	169017	429113	31549	43862	86810
14 FOOD, KINDRED PRDTS.	74290	3587	9038	5373	22567	56918	5325	1626	22015
15 TOBACCO MANUFACTURES	-140	0	-14	0	-15		0	0	-161
16 FABRICS	5861	3649	29698	0	2576	1597	0	140	6355
17 TEXTILE PRDTS.	3784	1438	3425	0	958	429	0	0	1385
18 APPAREL	25731	618	5442	0	10441	6298	279	161	4843
19 MISC. TEXTILE PRDTS.	5580	429	2038	0	2511	2882	317	106	1378
20 LUMBER, WOOD PRDTS.	-84	-8	-5	18	-179	-88	29	14	-232
21 WOODEN CONTAINERS	312	0	302	0	580	673	0	85	698
22 HOUSEHOLD FURNITURE	1390	7	329	0	1745	660	40	190	1843
23 OTHER FURNITURE	4620	293	338	140	1249	2943	275	72	1102
24 PAPER, ALLIED PRDTS.	4084	165	839	144	1386	2338	228	202	1631
25 PAPERBOARD CONTAINERS	1887	163	335	27	433	613	57	52	294
26 PRINTING, PUBLISHING	919	58	63	31	242	518	52	40	171
27 CHEMICALS,SELECT. PRDTS.	2936	3924	22992	0	200829	23701	2283	422	38934
28 PLASTICS, SYNTHETICS	3059	247	2167	0	4598	1087	0	36	5364
29 DRUGS, COSMETICS	11619	314	1009	0	2615	2845	36	0	1954
30 PAINT, ALLIED PRDTS.	228	0	10	0	36	126	0	4	22
31 PETROLEUM, RELATED INDS.	80928	944	1073	7	8250	338220	7167	64	4736
32 RUBBER, MISC. PLASTICS	7499	1493	970	22	281	15127	0	347	2130
33 LEATHER TANNING, PRDTS.	0	0	0	0	0	0	0	0	0
34 FOOTWEAR, LEATHER PRDTS.	4723	294	368	0	2765	619	0	68	695
35 GLASS, GLASS PRDTS.	2488	136	368	0	516	272	0	0	134
36 STONE, CLAY PRDTS.	314	9	57	9	83	212	21	21	79
37 PRIMARY IRON, STEEL MFR.	6791	977	43	0	308	1931	209	135	193
38 PRIMARY NONFERROUS MFR.	-6092	-3956	-75	0	-404	-3987	-50	-659	-246

39 METAL CONTAINERS	748	0	0	0	26	414	0	0	67
40 FABRICATED METAL PRDTS.	16349	414	1238	124	3021	8480	797	82	2642
41 SCREW MACH. PRDTS., ETC.	2760	226	382	0	342	572	0	7	112
42 OTHER FAB. METAL PRDTS.	5353	400	551	0	1208	1503	41	38	854
43 ENGINES, TURBINES	19946	125	163	47	1319	4750	180	45	1600
44 FARM MACH., EQUIP.	226	8	23	20	150	178	25	5	56
45 CONSTRUC. MACH., EQUIP.	5065	4	97	15	194	7654	608	0	79
46 MATERIAL HANDLING MACH.	7781	69	109	0	3567	2313	88	0	980
47 METALWORKING MACHINERY	6601	1545	709	16	559	1646	44	1384	433
48 SPECIAL MACH., EQUIP.	2290	471	658	7	174	841	29	139	288
49 GENERAL MACH., EQUIP.	7724	407	221	21	2523	3114	359	0	128
50 MACHINE SHOP PRDTS.	3665	780	574	73	478	2403	157	380	675
51 OFFICE, COMPUT. MACHINES	20623	728	3894	1220	4892	13041	1761	2278	7430
52 SERVICE IND. MACHINES	6701	0	192	0	714	4284	558	218	462
53 ELECT. TRANSMISS. EQUIP.	69879	288	4153	231	825	497	0	0	23482
54 HOUSEHOLD APPLIANCES	299	7	119	0	555	93	0	0	9
55 ELECTRIC LIGHTING EQUIP.	2277	226	149	0	31	22	0	37	149
56 RADIO, TV, ETC., EQUIP.	159418	15995	1750	0	97212	162114	8101	0	76912
57 ELECTRONIC COMPONENTS	51896	2551	9226	602	1025	16071	746	6151	6148
58 MISC. ELECTRICAL MACH.	15436	1128	1870	0	440	380	0	859	0
59 MOTOR VEHICLES, EQUIP.	27437	69	549	81	4624	6360	340	0	1870
60 AIRCRAFT, PARTS	318931	3493	14402	675	36017	1375744	17873	14035	27620
61 OTHER TRANSPORT. EQUIP.	102902	3342	5930	0	7666	27425	1392	278	131674
62 PROFESS., SCIEN. INSTRU.	91125	8779	4005	0	2662	7186	839	1941	2594
63 MEDICAL, PHOTO. EQUIP.	3047	693	1021	0	0	5740	193	319	4799
64 MISC. MANUFACTURING	311	55	37	25	115	245	42	11	91
65 TRANSPORT., WAREHOUSING	161137	10628	18122	6764	42185	162206	10943	3867	56602
66 COMMUNICA.,EXC. BRDCAST.	17031	2078	6363	1556	6210	26433	4318	553	18037
67 RADIO, TV BROADCASTING	0	0	0	0	0	0	0	0	0
68 ELEC.,GAS,WATER,SAN.SER.	9535	979	2808	933	3729	12914	2109	347	7776
69 WHOLESALE, RETAIL TRADE	53884	4618	10689	2354	20672	42106	3950	1765	18110
70 FINANCE, INSURANCE	4297	379	864	157	1675	3096	272	136	1344
71 REAL ESTATE, RENTAL	11829	838	1655	1116	4814	11504	1701	453	4433
72 HOTELS, PERSONAL SERV.	22012	1583	3789	1880	9262	24164	2837	1100	8839
73 BUSINESS SERVICES	51886	7691	24875	3507	17567	100783	14963	1179	75279
74 RESEARCH, DEVELOPMENT	0	0	0	0	0	0	0	0	0
75 AUTO. REPAIR, SERVICES	1206	82	172	119	503	1158	177	49	407
76 AMUSEMENTS	4016	411	570	221	1035	3876	541	416	1319
77 MED.,EDUC. SERVICES	111580	7891	11899	6272	29404	81894	11199	3873	26320
78 FEDERAL GOVT. ENTERPRISE	5620	555	1339	343	1396	5883	712	205	3301
79 STATE, LOCAL GOVT. ENT.	14023	957	2142	1535	6151	14026	2289	607	5318
80 IMPORTS	0	0	0	0	0	0	0	0	0
81 BUS.TRAVEL, ENT., GIFTS.	0	0	0	0	0	0	0	0	0
82 OFFICE SUPPLIES	9141	1068	3222	849	3398	13706	2239	306	9086
83 SCRAP, USED GOODS	4607	303	657	508	2037	4492	733	202	1603
84 GOVERNMENT INDUSTRY	807680	122291	399335	65762	261786	1497507	244754	21447	1155862
85 REST OF WORLD INDUSTRY	0	0	0	0	0	0	0	0	0
86 HOUSEHOLD INDUSTRY	0	0	0	0	0	0	0	0	0
87 INVENTORY VALUATION ADJ.	0	0	0	0	0	0	0	0	0
88 STATE TOTAL	2893564	235189	679937	120136	1228620	4696140	417725	115059	2021735

TABLE 8-11

STATE ESTIMATES OF 1970
FEDERAL GOVERNMENT PURCHASES
(THOUSANDS OF 1958 DOLLARS)

INDUSTRY TITLE	46 WASHINGTON	47 WEST VIRGINIA	48 WISCONSIN	49 WYOMING	50 ALASKA	51 HAWAII	52 NO STATE ALLOCATION	53 NATIONAL TOTAL
1 LIVESTOCK, PRDTS.	648	181	1586	813	4	99	0	74000
2 OTHER AGRICULTURE PRDTS.	-1604	-0	-422	-125	-1	0	0	-100000
3 FORESTRY, FISHERIES	-61435	-1506	-819	-1152	-3594	0	0	-363000
4 AGRI.,FORES.,FISH. SERV.	131	49	94	18	36	26	0	-7000
5 IRON, FERRO. ORES MINING	0	0	0	0	0	0	0	-11000
6 NONFERROUS ORES MINING	426	0	384	547	89	0	0	55000
7 COAL MINING	1	11639	0	132	56	0	0	39000
8 CRUDE PETRO.,NATURAL GAS	0	0	0	0	0	0	0	0
9 STONE, CLAY MINING	-255	-259	-292	-225	0	0	0	-9000
10 CHEM.,FERT. MIN. MINING	0	0	0	0	0	0	0	0
11 NEW CONSTRUCTION	86553	43122	15510	17097	31310	11408	0	2175000
12 MAINT., REPAIR CONSTR.	31136	6745	13073	3115	10195	12978	0	1387000
13 ORDNANCE, ACCESSORIES	12543	49759	136379	42	129	1774	0	6090000
14 FOOD, KINDRED PRDTS.	18135	4770	38808	901	1246	10589	0	1131000
15 TOBACCO MANUFACTURES	0	-7	0	0	0	0	0	-1000
16 FABRICS	113	141	184	0	0	0	0	136000
17 TEXTILE PRDTS.	0	0	536	0	0	0	0	46000
18 APPAREL	520	749	1502	0	0	287	0	185000
19 MISC. TEXTILE PRDTS.	631	283	541	0	0	130	0	96000
20 LUMBER, WOOD PRDTS.	2343	-15	-161	43	153	-9	0	10000
21 WOODEN CONTAINERS	93	46	376	0	0	0	0	12000
22 HOUSEHOLD FURNITURE	221	66	377	0	0	53	0	27000
23 OTHER FURNITURE	766	323	1439	74	135	110	0	68000
24 PAPER, ALLIED PRDTS.	2394	291	3986	75	246	105	0	74000
25 PAPERBOARD CONTAINERS	239	96	581	14	26	46	0	24000
26 PRINTING, PUBLISHING	161	60	312	15	17	32	0	14000
27 CHEMICALS,SELECT. PRDTS.	2870	39317	12606	1074	0	51	0	922000
28 PLASTICS, SYNTHETICS	57	1616	247	0	0	0	0	37000
29 DRUGS, COSMETICS	220	134	1812	0	0	0	0	164000
30 PAINT, ALLIED PRDTS.	27	0	64	0	0	0	0	3000
31 PETROLEUM, RELATED INDS.	8837	6563	2187	10425	3897	1155	0	1163000
32 RUBBER, MISC. PLASTICS	83	262	6725	0	0	0	0	209000
33 LEATHER TANNING, PRDTS.	0	0	0	0	0	0	0	0
34 FOOTWEAR, LEATHER PRDTS.	33	110	1762	0	0	24	0	50000
35 GLASS, GLASS PRDTS.	54	1566	18	0	0	0	0	18000
36 STONE, CLAY PRDTS.	53	49	69	5	4	11	0	4000
37 PRIMARY IRON, STEEL MFR.	582	692	1187	30	0	46	0	51000
38 PRIMARY NONFERROUS MFR.	-3640	-761	-1530	0	0	-19	0	-89000

246

#	Industry	1	2	3	4	5	6	7	8
39	METAL CONTAINERS	131	128	370	0	0	33	0	11000
40	FABRICATED METAL PRDTS.	1830	910	5266	33	0	79	0	147000
41	SCREW MACH. PRDTS., ETC.	33	389	1019	0	0	5	0	34000
42	OTHER FAB. METAL PRDTS.	414	1064	1118	0	564	14	0	75000
43	ENGINES, TURBINES	1230	137	30925	62	13	177	0	222000
44	FARM MACH., EQUIP.	66	30	550	7	0	8	0	7000
45	CONSTRUC. MACH., EQUIP.	522	326	6455	0	17	0	0	121000
46	MATERIAL HANDLING MACH.	5466	79	2399	0	4	17	0	100000
47	METALWORKING MACHINERY	297	179	4208	0	2	190	0	105000
48	SPECIAL MACH., EQUIP.	303	0	1526	0	0	98	0	31000
49	GENERAL MACH., EQUIP.	246	12	12035	14	6	254	0	162000
50	MACHINE SHOP PRDTS.	565	127	2489	12	0	702	0	69000
51	OFFICE, COMPUT. MACHINES	4629	1736	6132	641	1175	0	0	560000
52	SERVICE IND. MACHINES	297	122	4084	0	0	0	0	85000
53	ELECT. TRANSMISS. EQUIP.	3758	4585	28101	0	0	0	0	522000
54	HOUSEHOLD APPLIANCES	26	0	437	0	0	0	0	11000
55	ELECTRIC LIGHTING EQUIP.	207	1470	257	0	0	0	0	29000
56	RADIO, TV, ETC., EQUIP.	24889	0	18758	0	0	1588	0	4723000
57	ELECTRONIC COMPONENTS	265	1414	1405	0	0	0	0	486000
58	MISC. ELECTRICAL MACH.	558	0	3725	0	0	0	0	182000
59	MOTOR VEHICLES, EQUIP.	1840	581	20641	48	323	64	0	711000
60	AIRCRAFT, PARTS	317375	2711	26096	1794	8208	3277	0	8001000
61	OTHER TRANSPORT. EQUIP.	24652	2402	22043	0	0	3430	0	1352000
62	PROFESS., SCIEN. INSTRU.	479	1530	8480	0	0	0	0	534000
63	MEDICAL, PHOTO. EQUIP.	194	467	442	0	0	33	0	256000
64	MISC. MANUFACTURING	111	41	95	13	23	16	0	6000
65	TRANSPORT., WAREHOUSING	45840	15282	44396	3703	5818	16974	0	2771000
66	COMMUNICA.,EXC. BRDCAST.	9743	1794	3485	894	3296	4515	0	416000
67	RADIO, TV BROADCASTING	0	0	0	0	0	0	0	
68	ELEC.,GAS,WATER,SAN.SER.	4881	1173	2270	518	1560	1869	0	224000
69	WHOLESALE, RETAIL TRADE	13234	8383	20339	1409	902	2297	0	903000
70	FINANCE, INSURANCE	985	643	1499	96	72	144	0	72000
71	REAL ESTATE, RENTAL	4630	1761	3544	589	1039	970	0	256000
72	HOTELS, PERSONAL SERV.	7476	3297	7147	1145	1497	2220	0	464000
73	BUSINESS SERVICES	35099	3284	8486	2310	13312	19154	0	1415000
74	RESEARCH, DEVELOPMENT	0	0	0	0	0	0	900000	900000
75	AUTO. REPAIR, SERVICES	450	177	350	62	110	81	0	25000
76	AMUSEMENTS	1548	505	1468	163	75	558	0	96000
77	MED.,EDUC. SERVICES	31278	11223	33609	2845	3535	5999	0	1742000
78	FEDERAL GOVT. ENTERPRISE	2036	562	1455	157	435	801	0	105000
79	STATE, LOCAL GOVT. ENT.	5668	2169	4179	809	1542	1013	0	306000
80	IMPORTS	0	0	0	0	0	0	3344000	3344000
81	BUS.TRAVEL, ENT., GIFTS.	5082	1005	1952	483	1696	2255	0	0
82	OFFICE SUPPLIES	1827	723	1393	267	489	292	0	221000
83	SCRAP, USED GOODS							0	100000
84	GOVERNMENT INDUSTRY	536235	63290	124008	40058	193231	299369	2320000	23200000
85	REST OF WORLD INDUSTRY	0	0	0	0	0		0	
86	REST OF WORLD INDUSTRY	0	0	0	0	0		0	
87	INVENTORY VALUATION ADJ.								
88	STATE TOTAL	1199336	301792	707789	91049	282878	407394	6564000	68800000

TABLE B-12

STATE ESTIMATES OF 1980
FEDERAL GOVERNMENT PURCHASES
(THOUSANDS OF 1958 DOLLARS)

INDUSTRY TITLE	1 ALABAMA	2 ARIZONA	3 ARKANSAS	4 CALIFORNIA	5 COLORADO	6 CONNECTICUT	7 DELAWARE	8 DISTRICT OF COLUMBIA	9 FLORIDA
1 LIVESTOCK, PRDTS.	318	305	287	1272	746	43	10	0	252
2 OTHER AGRICULTURE PRDTS.	143	489	2650	1311	214	1	6	0	53
3 FORESTRY, FISHERIES	-1206	-4343	-4084	-37932	-1122				-1389
4 AGRI.,FORES.,FISH. SERV.	6470	3579	2350	26994	2473	1553	387	36384	7596
5 IRON, FERRO. ORES MINING									0
6 NONFERROUS ORES MINING	3982	21740	188586	11110	15668				27838
7 COAL MINING	527	0	26	0	242	0	0	0	0
8 CRUDE PETRO.,NATURAL GAS	0	0	0	0	0	0	0	0	0
9 STONE, CLAY MINING	0	0	0	0	0	0	0	0	0
10 CHEM.,FERT. MIN. MINING	0	0	0	0	0	0	0	0	0
11 NEW CONSTRUCTION	166022	131985	121485	705902	325912	37974	31664	45525	313599
12 MAINT., REPAIR CONSTR.	67599	38237	15219	177970	62167	17965	5790	283896	83810
13 ORDNANCE, ACCESSORIES	302328	25014	35324	1069562	61221	163550	7680	41963	361020
14 FOOD, KINDRED PRDTS.	6764	1685	9813	76714	7746	3579	3853	1064	20242
15 TOBACCO MANUFACTURES	37	0	0	0	0	41	265	0	290
16 FABRICS	3219		184	215	5	1734	47	0	
17 TEXTILE PRDTS.	205		221	338	15	225			52
18 APPAREL	2569	334	1478	6342	130	1322	438		1714
19 MISC. TEXTILE PRDTS.	1480	449	104	19071	893	3895	761	136	5224
20 LUMBER, WOOD PRDTS.	416	-318	426	-4799	-123	65	17		262
21 WOODEN CONTAINERS	418	0	1118	1252	150	343			1228
22 HOUSEHOLD FURNITURE	69	14	318	715	35	78	0	4	254
23 OTHER FURNITURE	1417	681	1963	21972	1693	1802	132	8760	2770
24 PAPER, ALLIED PRDTS.	3654	806	1791	15450	1467	2213	268	11755	4636
25 PAPERBOARD CONTAINERS	438	227	369	3667	321	776	215	1971	644
26 PRINTING, PUBLISHING	1222	856	1906	10509	2290	4352	333	7517	4822
27 CHEMICALS,SELECT. PRDTS.	75960	5394	5344	7992	4154	13274	10875	472	39245
28 PLASTICS, SYNTHETICS	551	0	0	1413	0	659	2223	223	1464
29 DRUGS, COSMETICS	150	449	1887	39514	1397	22907	2453		5166
30 PAINT, ALLIED PRDTS.	59	22	37	2174	77	79			403
31 PETROLEUM, RELATED INDS.	4413	191	5151	121442	3014	1257	8819	1171	6510
32 RUBBER, MISC. PLASTICS	150	2	3502	2204	15	1849	693		657
33 LEATHER TANNING, PRDTS.	6	0	32	9	3	9			6
34 FOOTWEAR, LEATHER PRDTS.	173	71	956	266	88	266	71		191
35 GLASS, GLASS PRDTS.	0	0	0	0	0	0	0	0	0
36 STONE, CLAY PRDTS.	136	62	102	1463	181	91	14	1000	320
37 PRIMARY IRON, STEEL MFR.	2134	152	290	14793	751	12849	222	0	237
38 PRIMARY NONFERROUS MFR.	916	158	3012	22123	34	23877	170	0	282

TABLE B-12

STATE ESTIMATES OF 1980
FEDERAL GOVERNMENT PURCHASES
(THOUSANDS OF 1958 DOLLARS)

INDUSTRY TITLE	19 MARYLAND	20 MASSA-CHUSETTS	21 MICHIGAN	22 MINNESOTA	23 MISSISSIPPI	24 MISSOURI	25 MONTANA	26 NEBRASKA	27 NEVADA
1 LIVESTOCK, PRDTS.	52	25	153	786	324	618	313	1254	36
2 OTHER AGRICULTURE PRDTS.	19	0	300	2761	1392	1684	703	2029	7
3 FORESTRY, FISHERIES	0	0	-822	-533	-8699	-669	-10648	-61	-221
4 AGRI.,FORES.,FISH. SERV.	5567	4453	4096	3415	2231	4288	1154	1165	751
5 IRON, FERRO. ORES MINING	0	0	0	0	0	0	0	0	0
6 NONFERROUS ORES MINING	0	0	0	0	0	0	0	0	0
7 COAL MINING	39	0	2023	0	1019	15806	3386	5369	5369
8 CRUDE PETRO.,NATURAL GAS	0	0	0	0	0	103	9	0	0
9 STONE, CLAY MINING	0	0	0	0	0	0	0	0	0
10 CHEM.,FERT. MIN. MINING	0	0	0	0	0	0	0	0	0
11 NEW CONSTRUCTION	206543	118060	35172	14828	39199	95563	156725	34601	102467
12 MAINT., REPAIR CONSTR.	79204	60877	44273	28595	25873	63689	11762	16786	12013
13 ORDNANCE, ACCESSORIES	127763	88768	166220	104671	8961	242353	229	3698	1346
14 FOOD, KINDRED PRDTS.	15148	16519	24098	16386	8626	18732	1338	10512	509
15 TOBACCO MANUFACTURES	0	0	10	0	0	0	0	0	0
16 FABRICS	528	2209	31	104	152	14	0	20	0
17 TEXTILE PRDTS.	0	649	234	60	286	292	0	0	0
18 APPAREL	1963	5995	373	445	5028	71	0	216	0
19 MISC. TEXTILE PRDTS.	3555	15088	290	3098	4014	2427	0	299	0
20 LUMBER, WOOD PRDTS.	191	197	167	220	-9	3692	-902	37	-28
21 WOODEN CONTAINERS	513	235	176	119	1390	178	0	0	0
22 HOUSEHOLD FURNITURE	53	276	15037	35	465	236	284	12	8
23 OTHER FURNITURE	2535	2823	5878	2896	1613	87	785	1219	0
24 PAPER, ALLIED PRDTS.	2164	5130	2546	4671	1076	3306	79	832	414
25 PAPERBOARD CONTAINERS	1513	2984	4235	411	348	3837	615	220	161
26 PRINTING, PUBLISHING	3142	6918	29206	4839	839	1533	2067	1462	47
27 CHEMICALS,SELECT. PRDTS.	22231	15144	1277	5395	34876	7478	42	2001	516
28 PLASTICS, SYNTHETICS	496	1067	49593	154	115	15551	944	0	3993
29 DRUGS, COSMETICS	13797	15379	1384	4349	2387	42	2067	3717	0
30 PAINT, ALLIED PRDTS.	338	508	13049	147	42	9944	0	0	0
31 PETROLEUM, RELATED INDS.	6506	5475	9957	7361	9944	26442	3139	523	124
32 RUBBER, MISC. PLASTICS	1094	2157	12	74	944	8156	0	28	0
33 LEATHER TANNING, PRDTS.	7	148	360	130	68	108	0	0	0
34 FOOTWEAR, LEATHER PRDTS.	214	4468	0	0	11	104	0	16	0
35 GLASS, GLASS PRDTS.	0	0	0	210	330	3131	0	0	0
36 STONE, CLAY PRDTS.	135	245	232	1403	0	0	43	71	0
37 PRIMARY IRON, STEEL MFR.	5265	18219	8182	437	93	310	90	56	30
38 PRIMARY NONFERROUS MFR.	2420	7457	6012	437	58	1687	194	404	37
39 METAL CONTAINERS	63	0	0	5216	66	0	0	0	900
40 FABRICATED METAL PRDTS.	5199	1985	1692	33630	2148	5362	791	442	8068
41 SCREW MACH. PRDTS., ETC.	2731	572	1726	48506	0	3783	1113	0	1773
42 OTHER FAB. METAL PRDTS.	4277	6093	1365	52690	4272	11012	545	5806	5784
43 ENGINES, TURBINES	6018	231	235	34163	3205	4383	262	905	9930
44 FARM MACH., EQUIP.	866	69	438	1683	610	103	26	52	372
45 CONSTRUC. MACH., EQUIP.	331	146	4576	4778	1307	90	0	1545	199
46 MATERIAL HANDLING MACH.	922	368	3539	9247	879	1296	861	363	702
47 METALWORKING MACHINERY	843	30	356	13222	415	40547	79	143	1641
48 SPECIAL MACH., EQUIP.	539	163	582	3943	61	4210	0	6	454
49 GENERAL MACH., EQUIP.	1304	145	438	19827	639	12349	210	101	131
50 MACHINE SHOP PRDTS.	257	0	4347	5040	267	6935	689	583	583
51 OFFICE, COMPUT. MACHINES	7783	13400	1046	124992	12109	36265	159	54815	17311
52 SERVICE IND. MACHINES	1543	802	176	5785	184	859	0	765	765
53 ELECT. TRANSMISS. EQUIP.	74	1252	1026	50333	13662	9106	136	0	6427
54 HOUSEHOLD APPLIANCES	0	0	0	1597	0	1172	0	45	82
55 ELECTRIC LIGHTING EQUIP.	0	25	183	183	14	14	205	0	23
56 RADIO, TV, ETC., EQUIP.	12831	162459	65540	1751214	11132	61267	945	0	169551
57 ELECTRONIC COMPONENTS	1442	14635	0	204954	410	26447	2184	0	8051
58 MISC. ELECTRICAL MACH.	793	0	156	3285	1446	3303	4515	3054	9286
59 MOTOR VEHICLES, EQUIP.	24642	692	3115	41740	51683	5335	2147	36767	1993
60 AIRCRAFT, PARTS	136859	62101	2315	894491	528	737977	4269	39191	235619
61 OTHER TRANSPORT. EQUIP.	14033	373	5214	95820	14273	171130	117	418	25510
62 PROFESS., SCIEN. INSTRU.	1011	9977	3292	130004	727	44655	182	9549	10032
63 MEDICAL, PHOTO. EQUIP.	1978	2937	1096	46408	1313	10305	3141	45190	2549
64 MISC. MANUFACTURING	23055	2170	26290	12746	28073	1365	1795	48980	2698
65 TRANSPORT., WAREHOUSING	17432	14496	6057	232190	16424	35677	1778	49550	84398
66 COMMUNICA.,EXC. BRDCAST.	16103	10844	2490	93786	17976	3679	4736	8328	27231
67 RADIO, TV BROADCASTING	23039	10898	1673	91905	18573	3920	60	247	25903
68 ELEC.,GAS,WATER,SAN.SER.	435	12779	7628	174016	476	28397	1407	55962	54286
69 WHOLESALE, RETAIL TRADE	9621	316	1474	4324	9330	574	1564	81479	1300
70 FINANCE, INSURANCE	14151	7794	239	62491	13301	6204	2717	50929	23998
71 REAL ESTATE, RENTAL	27672	11171	20490	86329	26563	8051	445	27474	31245
72 HOTELS, PERSONAL SERV.	3931	15598	1673	225206	3603	6943	117	376	56799
73 BUSINESS SERVICES	215	3000	7628	23570	876	2335	6774	207095	6961
74 RESEARCH, DEVELOPMENT	49807	566	1599	9338	53968	409	759	7770	2735
75 AUTO. REPAIR, SERVICES	4093	43150	724	359666	3871	59440	1884	60682	125535
76 AMUSEMENTS	0	2529	0	34518	13966	3203	0	0	9304
77 MED.,EDUC. SERVICES	14375	10832	0	47761	0	9260	444	26940	21754
78 FEDERAL GOVT. ENTERPRISE	0	0	0	0	3769	0	170	13374	0
79 STATE, LOCAL GOVT. ENT.	4293	2512	0	23036	1486	1924	0	0	5912
80 IMPORTS	1791	1060	0	8743	0	912	0	0	2318
81 BUS.TRAVEL, ENT., GIFTS.	0	0	0	0	0	0	0	0	0
82 OFFICE SUPPLIES	0	0	0	0	0	0	0	0	0
83 SCRAP, USED GOODS	0	0	0	0	0	0	0	0	0
84 GOVERNMENT INDUSTRY	435812	270618	116034	2808930	437134	116164	62905	700899	694484
85 REST OF WORLD INDUSTRY	0	0	0	0	0	0	0	0	0
86 HOUSEHOLD INDUSTRY	0	0	0	0	0	0	0	0	0
87 INVENTORY VALUATION ADJ.	0	0	0	0	0	0	0	0	0
88 STATE TOTAL	1524954	926958	721141	10230544	1275081	1796780	187539	1980323	2583995

TABLE B-12

STATE ESTIMATES OF 1980
FEDERAL GOVERNMENT PURCHASES
(THOUSANDS OF 1958 DOLLARS)

	INDUSTRY TITLE	10 GEORGIA	11 IDAHO	12 ILLINOIS	13 INDIANA	14 IOWA	15 KANSAS	16 KENTUCKY	17 LOUISIANA	18 MAINE
1	LIVESTOCK, PRDTS.	445	198	1029	508	2195	934	277	151	65
2	OTHER AGRICULTURE PRDTS.	970	316	2219	1182	4281	1900	522	749	5
3	FORESTRY, FISHERIES.	-2505	-15049	-129	-71			-319	-2174	-27
4	AGRI.,FORES.,FISH. SERV.	7432	1046	8396	2491	1687	1670	2524	3247	1456
5	IRON, FERRO. ORES MINING	1531	22311	2525	0	0	0	676	0	0
6	NONFERROUS ORES MINING	0	0	2100	391	27	328	4389	0	0
7	COAL MINING	0	0	0	0	0	0	0	0	0
8	CRUDE PETRO.,NATURAL GAS	0	0	0	0	0	39	0	0	0
9	STONE, CLAY MINING	0	0	0	0	0	0	0	0	0
10	CHEM.,FERT. MIN. MINING	81180	226721	264162	45222	25179	34294	354152	52687	6825
11	NEW CONSTRUCTION	91683	8214	105395	33200	14728	31861	46524	35688	9087
12	MAINT., REPAIR CONSTR.	18796	762	83326	115212	89317	31236	2440	345345	26503
13	ORDNANCE, ACCESSORIES	19242	2874	39794	18148	22019	5546	9514	7986	6503
14	FOOD, KINDRED PRDTS.	57	0	305	129	30	0	862	14	1113
15	TOBACCO MANUFACTURES	12496	0	260	93	0	0	131	20	0
16	FABRICS	2960	2	3040	1663	160	200	3296	567	471
17	TEXTILE PRDTS.	7159		7493	2062	2372	810	3787	1591	376
18	APPAREL	10679	-921	535	381	76	23	344	131	614
19	MISC. TEXTILE PRDTS.	638	0	586	401	220	17	430	306	62
20	LUMBER, WOOD PRDTS.	1330	501	507	450	37	1106	168	44	16
21	WOODEN CONTAINERS	271	321	16948	3394	1310	1119	1179	1682	385
22	HOUSEHOLD FURNITURE	2622	62	6670	3002	742	528	1008	2515	5336
23	OTHER FURNITURE	5971	579	5454	1394	282	2160	704	660	84
24	PAPER, ALLIED PRDTS.	1435	22409	17485	3134	3460	9402	1734	1021	600
25	PAPERBOARD CONTAINERS	3203	0	46435	12144	2671	167	70300	21384	2023
26	PRINTING, PUBLISHING	33899	0	452	364	284	4847	1404	318	0
27	CHEMICALS,SELECT. PRDTS.	325	10	68102	49588	6439	43	733	671	467
28	PLASTICS, SYNTHETICS	9555	0	3312	418	126	10213	556	51	549
29	DRUGS, COSMETICS	400	0	49300	26461	399	53	6349	122108	234
30	PAINT, ALLIED PRDTS.	743	0	14019	9026	103	315	3321	384	79
31	PETROLEUM, RELATED INDS.	3308	51	51	213	2	13	11	0	2360
32	RUBBER, MISC. PLASTICS	732	1545	1545	46	46	210	323	100	2
33	LEATHER TANNING, PRDTS.	14	0	688	198	85	237	140	111	37
34	FOOTWEAR, LEATHER PRDTS.	409	43	9811	16441	1106	227	1327	715	348
35	GLASS, GLASS PRDTS.	0	9	14965	11023	611		286	941	223
36	STONE, CLAY PRDTS.	349	39							
37	PRIMARY IRON, STEEL MFR.	456								
38	PRIMARY NONFERROUS MFR.	649								
39	METAL CONTAINERS	300	0	4884	99	0	0	0	648	143
40	FABRICATED METAL PRDTS.	7813	589	29146	9219	2991	3045	6875	3002	728
41	SCREW MACH. PRDTS., ETC.	6403	2740	17984	4162	768	165	3493	194	44
42	OTHER FAB. METAL PRDTS.	2871	41	27728	9507	1355	472	5053	1107	136
43	ENGINES, TURBINES	959	1891	24617	29920	3533	435	532	5353	31
44	FARM MACH., EQUIP.	826	265	10877	1512	10147	718	2058	226	0
45	CONSTRUC. MACH., EQUIP.	1373	90	58131	4195	4075	1445	268	822	88
46	MATERIAL HANDLING MACH.	583	9	40662	2441	662	608	812	228	0
47	METALWORKING MACHINERY	2052	2	28223	16058	1462	435	767	102	88
48	SPECIAL MACH., EQUIP.	915	20	4009	2260	582	304	269	452	110
49	GENERAL MACH., EQUIP.	62	1376	44224	30398	827	3570	6325	136	108
50	MACHINE SHOP PRDTS.	743		3663	3071	108	272	337	5452	1000
51	OFFICE, COMPUT. MACHINES	8043	331	35091	5112	3275	3211	17885	247	68
52	SERVICE IND. MACHINES	2233	2069	10586	4257	1118	514	3321	0	207
53	ELECT. TRANSMISS. EQUIP.	15538	462	31586	15563	2895	1051	1051	100	2
54	HOUSEHOLD APPLIANCES	133	7146	6087	3635	1662	315	5610	1	
55	ELECTRIC LIGHTING EQUIP.	29	2710	89	33	1	1		2167	6104
56	RADIO, TV, ETC., EQUIP.	943	3317	154416	101566	62038	4935	17637		6549
57	ELECTRONIC COMPONENTS	0	7134	11634	5294	5784	1963	3330	0	571
58	MISC. ELECTRICAL MACH.	2140	132	5364	21013	873	1538	439	1377	338
59	MOTOR VEHICLES, EQUIP.	15108	2352	30325	99204	2471	5568	7237	74443	6015
60	AIRCRAFT, PARTS	642017	11371	109586	122033	8092	289026	4472	25488	19920
61	OTHER TRANSPORT. EQUIP.	30731	2069	17696	25601	3208	6914	3684	601	984
62	PROFESS., SCIEN. INSTRU.	12184	462	64255	6319	5838	931	1637	684	195
63	MEDICAL, PHOTO. EQUIP.	1021	2905	21459	1747	316	1359	1359	2029	7131
64	MISC. MANUFACTURING	2905	462	6400	2039	851	952	23202	49996	1783
65	TRANSPORT., WAREHOUSING	55067	7146	169172	43986	36256	16877	14372	12551	1874
66	COMMUNICA.,EXC. BROCAST.	26895	2710	23430	7657	5782	9988			
67	RADIO, TV BROADCASTING	25219	3317	37554	11890	5380	8055	12360	11481	6168
68	ELEC.,GAS,WATER,SAN.SER.	38238	7134	102303	40609	20371	11738	21992	20956	130
69	WHOLESALE, RETAIL TRADE	798	132	2163	942	442	346	403	535	1442
70	FINANCE, INSURANCE	12532	2352	35536	10016	6505	6669	6948	9107	3424
71	REAL ESTATE, RENTAL	18611	3567	38172	13092	8478	8261	10369	11738	2218
72	HOTELS, PERSONAL SERV.	43680	2866	44381	12111	2647	8907	20259	20505	
73	BUSINESS SERVICES	5071	864	10787	3114	1686	1780	2741	3054	813
74	RESEARCH, DEVELOPMENT	796	82	2562	609	370	364	478	702	91
75	AUTO. REPAIR, SERVICES	66158	7566	252162	48861	25452	29248	38497	40501	10305
76	AMUSEMENTS	7511	728	12593	4421	1960	3074	4193	3573	1213
77	MED.,EDUC. SERVICES	21831	3257	50207	15059	7630	10978	12823	12792	2395
78	FEDERAL GOVT. ENTERPRISE	0	0	0	0	0	0	0	0	0
79	STATE, LOCAL GOVT. ENT.	0	0	0	0	0	0	0	0	0
80	IMPORTS	-5874	922	11129	3376	2042	2496	3318	3016	876
81	BUS.TRAVEL, ENT., GIFTS	2070	431	5080	1506	1025	1005	1252	1248	390
82	OFFICE SUPPLIES									
83	SCRAP, USED GOODS									
84	GOVERNMENT INDUSTRY	855232	56345	641105	247931	76864	272056	399955	304443	66025
85	REST OF WORLD INDUSTRY	0	0	0	0	0	0	0	0	0
86	HOUSEHOLD INDUSTRY	0	0	0	0	0	0	0	0	0
	TOTAL		391126	3013866	1349671	507814	859807	1183421	1229969	215493

39	METAL CONTAINERS	797	247	104	402	0	1323	0	115	0
40	FABRICATED METAL PRDTS.	3640	5355	19948	4326	2048	11353	238	3669	83
41	SCREW MACH. PRDTS., ETC.	4681	6741	18011	1953	1647	1857	173	100	100
42	OTHER FAB. METAL PRDTS.	2762	10745	33485	3074	746	3663	222	209	0
43	ENGINES, TURBINES	11747	23620	40701	2970	438	1925	91	244	4780
44	FARM MACH., EQUIP.	269	472	2432	2715	732	1575		1211	39
45	CONSTRUC. MACH., EQUIP.	152	1144	30071	4917	3411	889		198	18
46	MATERIAL HANDLING MACH.	2210	1558	7169	1755	1048	1327		37	9
47	METALWORKING MACHINERY	3985	21864	43447	7143	94	3617		81	51
48	SPECIAL MACH., EQUIP.	1310	3398	1628	1275	124	519			3
49	GENERAL MACH., EQUIP.	206	6420	38504	1492	177	1865		1142	
50	MACHINE SHOP PRDTS.	566	2695	3585	2896	92	1318	5	45	15
51	OFFICE, COMPUT. MACHINES	11322	22194	49563	64891	2379	12269	1046	2249	1035
52	SERVICE IND. MACHINES	1714	2957	10080	5215	507	8545		62	0
53	ELECT. TRANSMISS. EQUIP.	3863	13844	11721	9076	548	19679		462	0
54	HOUSEHOLD APPLIANCES	75	303	1697	928	1379	563		0	0
55	ELECTRIC LIGHTING EQUIP.	2	14	7	15	1	45		0	0
56	RADIO, TV, ETC., EQUIP.	406314	692582	7933	59094	17886	112145	0	21535	2683
57	ELECTRONIC COMPONENTS	1645	66524	1232	7300	1548	1214	0	3338	0
58	MISC. ELECTRICAL MACH.	3051	7841	8248	1329	1272	4522		148	0
59	MOTOR VEHICLES, EQUIP.	26870	6144	205066	4626	6241	40046	76	1862	26
60	AIRCRAFT, PARTS	84896	122726	90704	12522	34255	784269	1072	3057	32859
61	OTHER TRANSPORT. EQUIP.	30817	43184	31068	2695	113021	8139		2982	22
62	PROFESS., SCIEN. INSTRU.	6682	103270	38353	12939	393	8177		3332	0
63	MEDICAL, PHOTO. EQUIP.	3878	40534	978	6559	0	1811		0	
64	MISC. MANUFACTURING	1970	2683	3473	2235	902	2759	500	696	443
65	TRANSPORT., WAREHOUSING	40578	65816	72500	50781	17275	70712	6437	22589	4696
66	COMMUNICA.,EXC. BRDCAST.	21976	12935	17988	9890	7858	20806	4359	3524	2125
67	RADIO, TV BROADCASTING	0	0	0	0	0			0	0
68	ELEC.,GAS,WATER,SAN.SER.	21040	11850	16696	10455	7953	20446	3428	5584	3705
69	WHOLESALE, RETAIL TRADE	27928	51165	66719	24341	11611	34118	4718	9701	3573
70	FINANCE, INSURANCE	537	1288	1364	687	271	947	102	324	86
71	REAL ESTATE, RENTAL	16787	12001	15820	10329	4090	16389	3063	5259	2803
72	HOTELS, PERSONAL SERV.	17315	20347	21714	13742	6430	20006	4051	5782	5888
73	BUSINESS SERVICES	52051	24266	18210	9156	7183	25508	2354	5678	11421
74	RESEARCH, DEVELOPMENT	0	0	0	0	0	0		0	0
75	AUTO. REPAIR, SERVICES	5656	6093	5680	3036	1515	5412	943	1142	873
76	AMUSEMENTS	1057	781	1690	715	147	950	84	381	2171
77	MED.,EDUC. SERVICES	72846	114405	106514	65284	14405	79151	11564	21701	8925
78	FEDERAL GOVT. ENTERPRISE	5403	7238	7284	4670	1914	5625	925	1864	906
79	STATE, LOCAL GOVT. ENT.	19589	12476	11386	15611	8173	16630	5697	7495	3542
80	IMPORTS	0	0	0	0	0	0		0	0
81	BUS.TRAVEL, ENT., GIFTS.	5615	5934	5248	3253	1883	5903	1166	1580	808
82	OFFICE SUPPLIES	2092	2693	2482	1610	744	2590	545	704	324
83	SCRAP, USED GOODS									
84	GOVERNMENT INDUSTRY	765528	374728	314140	132089	186980	442430	72474	103760	103182
85	REST OF WORLD INDUSTRY	0	0	0	0	0	0	0	0	0
86	HOUSEHOLD INDUSTRY	0	0	0	0	0	0	0	0	0
87	INVENTORY VALUATION ADJ.	0	0	0	0	0	0	0	0	0
88	STATE TOTAL	2237548	2334548	1837760	787263	607927	2325423	296698	357960	324710

TABLE B-12

STATE ESTIMATES OF 1960
FEDERAL GOVERNMENT PURCHASES
(THOUSANDS OF 1958 DOLLARS)

INDUSTRY TITLE	28 NEW HAMPSHIRE	29 NEW JERSEY	30 NEW MEXICO	31 NEW YORK	32 NORTH CAROLINA	33 NORTH DAKOTA	34 OHIO	35 OKLAHOMA	36 OREGON
1 LIVESTOCK, PRDTS.	17	42	234	158	320	202	309	470	165
2 OTHER AGRICULTURE PRDTS.	0	12	256	39	1862	1437	1046	681	164
3 FORESTRY, FISHERIES	-370	0	-1947	0	-1187	0	-31	-343	-181701
4 AGRI.,FORES.,FISH. SERV.	399	3853	2397	15271	4530	644	6100	2205	3179
5 IRON, FERRO. ORES MINING	0	0	0	0	0	0	0	0	0
6 NONFERROUS ORES MINING	0	1591	7959	17189	0	0	0	0	2617
7 COAL MINING	0	0	0	0	0	212	2012	0	0
8 CRUDE PETRO.,NATURAL GAS	0	0	78	0	0	178	0	2267	0
9 STONE, CLAY MINING	0	0	0	0	0	0	0	29	0
10 CHEM.,FERT. MIN. MINING	0	0	0	0	0	0	0	0	0
11 NEW CONSTRUCTION	11523	47748	172096	406521	102726	49136	166657	121575	290994
12 MAINT., REPAIR CONSTR.	10430	68165	26537	164686	66955	10197	88476	50853	22177
13 ORDNANCE, ACCESSORIES	7762	62562	25343	205246	32829	14	183664	11776	2773
14 FOOD, KINDRED PRDTS.	1363	29747	2010	42589	20450	896	34710	3918	7773
15 TOBACCO MANUFACTURES	0	30	0	13	1331	0	24	0	29
16 FABRICS	746	1353	0	1576	34043	0	0	-110	155
17 TEXTILE PRDTS.	57	401	0	751	909	0	830	29	32
18 APPAREL	481	8440	48	25511	17058	0	1737	866	367
19 MISC. TEXTILE PRDTS.	395	22368	417	49728	9310	0	3382	939	2123
20 LUMBER, WOOD PRDTS.	110	102	-74	617	943	7	315	14	-12941
21 WOODEN CONTAINERS	125	456	0	341	500	0	292	0	330
22 HOUSEHOLD FURNITURE	50	203	2	377	2124	0	203	34	49
23 OTHER FURNITURE	848	6331	1066	16157	7159	194	7443	956	862
24 PAPER, ALLIED PRDTS.	1340	5838	770	10752	3729	325	8248	1539	2908
25 PAPERBOARD CONTAINERS	124	2682	161	3245	1138	76	2482	242	419
26 PRINTING, PUBLISHING	905	9037	931	31479	3404	465	11518	1789	1580
27 CHEMICALS,SELECT. PRDTS.	340	3336	952	1573	17739	0	65545	1210	590
28 PLASTICS, SYNTHETICS	45	1283	0	1609	3865	0	1853	118	38
29 DRUGS, COSMETICS	0	116426	0	107023	5780	0	19997	459	825
30 PAINT, ALLIED PRDTS.	0	1766	0	667	295	0	1616	47	192
31 PETROLEUM, RELATED INDS.	197	28738	4172	22398	1299	9973	35062	39391	843
32 RUBBER, MISC. PLASTICS	693	4509	1	4064	1298	0	22344	2712	41
33 LEATHER TANNING, PRDTS.	74	44	1	92	14	0	16	16	0
34 FOOTWEAR, LEATHER PRDTS.	2215	1332	18	2754	416	0	492	52	28
35 GLASS, GLASS PRDTS.	0	0	64	0	0	0	0	28	0
36 STONE, CLAY PRDTS.	36	503	0	816	150	31	627	159	137
37 PRIMARY IRON, STEEL MFR.	1761	1984	0	6497	438	0	30107	645	1754
38 PRIMARY NONFERROUS MFR.	1101	6120	9	16811	974	0	17484	837	2691

	C1	C2	C3	C4	C5	C6	C7	C8	C9
39 METAL CONTAINERS	0	2108	0	800	0	0	890	75	227
40 FABRICATED METAL PRDTS.	643	9251	190	18186	7418	321	49271	6101	3145
41 SCREW MACH. PRDTS., ETC.	192	11021	0	20283	3068	0	16688	1004	455
42 OTHER FAB. METAL PRDTS.	381	10790	0	23953	6847	0	26912	393	2362
43 ENGINES, TURBINES	274	3760	5092	55005	1385	178	9256	242	956
44 FARM MACH., EQUIP.	38	411	157	1392	868	251	2827	555	383
45 CONSTRUC. MACH., EQUIP.	361	1447	0	2907	347	222	22882	4208	422
46 MATERIAL HANDLING MACH.	231	2531	209	11738	4536	0	19722	26	4711
47 METALWORKING MACHINERY	765	9719	28	11863	1072	0	58249	805	261
48 SPECIAL MACH., EQUIP.	832	3544	0	5240	2037	0	6754	221	534
49 GENERAL MACH., EQUIP.	3961	6925	0	10795	238	0	35251	3619	387
50 MACHINE SHOP PRDTS.	91	944	132	3982	376	8	8399	468	168
51 OFFICE, COMPUT. MACHINES	1975	27337	3699	160210	5854	1193	102790	4148	3895
52 SERVICE IND. MACHINES	0	7329	0	9973	1000	0	13947	448	144
53 ELECT. TRANSMISS. EQUIP.	3624	24362	0	39153	16944	0	40759	67	10461
54 HOUSEHOLD APPLIANCES	0	279	0	1303	1612	0	12097	0	45
55 ELECTRIC LIGHTING EQUIP.	2	75	0	88	60	0	85	0	0
56 RADIO, TV, ETC., EQUIP.	67959	394972	6253	992335	211282	0	27794	137673	9485
57 ELECTRONIC COMPONENTS	16926	25025	294	49728	8820	0	6918	3767	0
58 MISC. ELECTRICAL MACH.	574	6613	0	14262	12415	0	6231	107	1734
59 MOTOR VEHICLES, EQUIP.	31	14883	1352	33896	3501	343	167102	1604	2486
60 AIRCRAFT, PARTS	3086	81925	44550	675927	17016	812	603279	62079	17162
61 OTHER TRANSPORT. EQUIP.	400	16809	71	44372	5728	0	11471	1872	13253
62 PROFESS., SCIEN. INSTRU.	1456	94613	7932	98858	24690	0	22984	570	2850
63 MEDICAL, PHOTO. EQUIP.	737	8560	0	130528	3167	0	8465	13	1760
64 MISC. MANUFACTURING	231	3088	493	11377	2734	371	3696	1550	1870
65 TRANSPORT., WAREHOUSING	4394	107752	8758	236351	67052	14330	96154	17365	26681
66 COMMUNICA.,EXC. BRODCAST.	1722	18839	9253	47739	19607	3378	24476	15088	7573
67 RADIO, TV BROADCASTING	0	0	0	0	0	0	0	0	0
68 ELEC.,GAS,WATER,SAN.SER.	2726	16495	8102	35384	18844	2481	26297	12867	6152
69 WHOLESALE, RETAIL TRADE	6178	61287	6588	141983	40966	3571	84032	13688	19924
70 FINANCE, INSURANCE	128	963	156	5162	803	85	1620	439	411
71 REAL ESTATE, RENTAL	1353	16475	5030	54917	9844	2063	24283	8296	6802
72 HOTELS, PERSONAL SERV.	2298	19115	7785	72013	14084	2964	30365	9672	9150
73 BUSINESS SERVICES	5449	36028	18727	63154	31318	2736	34865	16127	4976
74 RESEARCH, DEVELOPMENT	0	0	0	0	0	0	0	0	0
75 AUTO. REPAIR, SERVICES	576	5792	2206	20575	3652	513	8415	2488	2284
76 AMUSEMENTS	169	1213	225	12818	588	62	2270	375	395
77 MED.,EDUC. SERVICES	9533	81358	25344	327545	61193	10019	173439	47617	37056
78 FEDERAL GOVT. ENTERPRISE	964	9320	1590	21852	5902	879	10317	3886	2342
79 STATE, LOCAL GOVT. ENT.	1919	22372	9565	42184	14786	4027	22488	13454	7926
80 IMPORTS	0	0	0	0	0	0	0	0	0
81 BUS.TRAVEL, ENT., GIFTS.	0	0	0	0	0	0	0	0	0
82 OFFICE SUPPLIES	696	5682	2108	18951	4144	884	8174	3567	2490
83 SCRAP, USED GOODS	238	2320	885	9265	1414	373	3689	1298	1219
84 GOVERNMENT INDUSTRY	100490	560605	232062	744412	589327	77424	534371	487524	115414
85 REST OF WORLD INDUSTRY	0	0	0	0	0	0	0	0	0
86 HOUSEHOLD INDUSTRY	0	0	0	0	0	0	0	0	0
87 INVENTORY VALUATION ADJ.	0	0	0	0	0	0	0	0	0
88 STATE TOTAL	286370	2170934	652337	5459009	1565040	203475	3084535	1130947	481145

TABLE B-12

STATE ESTIMATES OF 1980
FEDERAL GOVERNMENT PURCHASES
(THOUSANDS OF 1958 DOLLARS)

INDUSTRY TITLE	37 PENNSYL- VANIA	38 RHODE ISLAND	39 SOUTH CAROLINA	40 SOUTH DAKOTA	41 TENNESSEE	42 TEXAS	43 UTAH	44 VERMONT	45 VIRGINIA
1 LIVESTOCK, PRDTS.	229	4	96	731	224	1161	102	17	147
2 OTHER AGRICULTURE PRDTS.	15	0	137	743	190	3568	11	0	98
3 FORESTRY, FISHERIES	-893	0	-4441	-568	-449	-3462	-983	-699	-417
4 AGRI.,FORES.,FISH. SERV.	8586	879	1275	830	4556	12991	1633	331	4851
5 IRON,FERRO.ORES MINING	0	0	0	0	0	0	0	0	0
6 NONFERROUS ORES MINING	8198	0	0	181	5790	11419	13904	0	2929
7 COAL MINING	4089	0	0	0	398	39	315	0	2519
8 CRUDE PETRO.,NATURAL GAS	0	0	0	0	0	0	0	0	0
9 STONE, CLAY MINING	0	0	0	0	0	0	0	0	0
10 CHEM.,FERT. MIN. MINING	0	0	0	0	0	0	0	0	0
11 NEW CONSTRUCTION	119350	16334	131739	29654	581587	199537	63710	11283	369954
12 MAINT.,.REPAIR CONSTR.	105369	12080	42678	10144	41115	154082	28114	3645	108142
13 ORDNANCE, ACCESSORIES	221566	4353	795	2890	160730	501320	29154	35692	42192
14 FOOD, KINDRED PRDTS.	48729	2479	6567	3211	15435	37313	3547	1030	16729
15 TOBACCO MANUFACTURES	423	0	60	0	87	0	0	0	609
16 FABRICS	2744	1621	26709	0	2284	1321	0	62	5785
17 TEXTILE PRDTS.	703	267	1094	0	410	80	0	0	507
18 APPAREL	19999	656	6077	0	10960	6321	190	83	4316
19 MISC. TEXTILE PRDTS.	14363	708	3365	0	5948	4758	1221	174	2275
20 LUMBER, WOOD PRDTS.	363	25	148	-24	584	286	-50	16	738
21 WOODEN CONTAINERS	269	0	470	0	867	986	0	74	1159
22 HOUSEHOLD FURNITURE	535	2	137	0	784	316	18	83	789
23 OTHER FURNITURE	17008	958	1234	593	4835	10144	1035	132	4601
24 PAPER, ALLIED PRDTS.	9717	273	2204	583	4523	7969	925	310	3403
25 PAPERBOARD CONTAINERS	2868	231	809	45	1023	1575	165	100	687
26 PRINTING, PUBLISHING	12501	886	1156	560	4262	9490	1007	755	3152
27 CHEMICALS,SELECT. PRDTS.	1053	3684	38955	0	309116	48114	3191	214	41102
28 PLASTICS, SYNTHETICS	3132	351	3646	0	5241	1488	111	27	3947
29 DRUGS, COSMETICS	52201	756	5146	0	11335	10356	0	0	9207
30 PAINT, ALLIED PRDTS.	1363	89	89	0	225	1001	0	38	161
31 PETROLEUM, RELATED INDS.	57810	592	1415	5	9814	358914	9059	38	6423
32 RUBBER, MISC. PLASTICS	2616	738	555	15	138	9263	3	106	1135
33 LEATHER TANNING, PRDTS.	102	8	0	0	63	15	0	2	14
34 FOOTWEAR, LEATHER PRDTS.	3069	243	0	0	1881	452	0	53	426
35 GLASS, GLASS PRDTS.	0	0	0	46	0	0	0	0	0
36 STONE, CLAY PRDTS.	528	43	168	0	242	799	100	32	292
37 PRIMARY IRON, STEEL MFR.	27835	2835	178	0	742	11947	1005	391	804
38 PRIMARY NONFERROUS MFR.	9767	8922	210	0	1067	9969	133	1810	692

39 METAL CONTAINERS	1681	0	0	0	44	817	0	0	135
40 FABRICATED METAL PRDTS.	46643	729	4874	376	8081	29406	3156	145	8741
41 SCREW MACH. PRDTS., ETC.	19631	1790	3027	0	1984	4683	214	44	863
42 OTHER FAB. METAL PRDTS.	23036	1855	2482	0	6649	9577	442	102	4640
43 ENGINES, TURBINES	21286	287	457	155	1810	12797		110	3658
44 FARM MACH., EQUIP.	1411	47	200	203	1490	1052		35	436
45 CONSTRUC. MACH., EQUIP.	4644	6	216	21	328	17283			124
46 MATERIAL HANDLING MACH.	13959	82	194	0	6643	5802		0	1889
47 METALWORKING MACHINERY	14822	5005	2757	82	1483	7148		3682	2498
48 SPECIAL MACH., EQUIP.	5273	1037	1931	8	192	1328		218	380
49 GENERAL MACH., EQUIP.	9426	512	291	53	5015	7196		28	383
50 MACHINE SHOP PRDTS.	5057	488	624	59	425	2570		440	552
51 OFFICE, COMPUT. MACHINES	32444	710	8137	2153	6445	18419		241	11767
52 SERVICE IND. MACHINES	7817	0	0	0	833	4998		3990	23323
53 ELECT. TRANSMISS. EQUIP.	67723	274	3235	231	549	417		254	22
54 HOUSEHOLD APPLIANCES	806	20	745	0	3392	299		0	4
55 ELECTRIC LIGHTING EQUIP.	90	6	5	0	1			2	
56 RADIO, TV, ETC., EQUIP.	119152	14308	3116	778	178433	283575	11943	9347	57735
57 ELECTRONIC COMPONENTS	54158	3695	15266	0	1825	23042	1112	1472	10457
58 MISC. ELECTRICAL MACH.	12034	859	2016	91	874	602	531		
59 MOTOR VEHICLES, EQUIP.	21206	155	780	674	4246	13186		20681	3668
60 AIRCRAFT, PARTS	410092	5259	16659	0	48590	1705229	26154	297	37674
61 OTHER TRANSPORT. EQUIP.	45632	3306	4102	0	8543	29454	1425	4784	95449
62 PROFESS., SCIEN. INSTRU.	152728	18128	8950	0	5558	19190	1816	980	5709
63 MEDICAL, PHOTO. EQUIP.	3855	905	3539	353	2570	8502	246	112	6464
64 MISC. MANUFACTURING	5517	1318	781	7476	39574	4811	894	2924	2216
65 TRANSPORT., WAREHOUSING	103748	9733	16974	3660	14463	80784	10101	773	49003
66 COMMUNICA.,EXC. BRDCAST.	26913	2716	11802	0		51729	8922		29445
67 RADIO, TV BROADCASTING									
68 ELEC.,GAS,WATER,SAN.SER.	27356	2090	10479	3089	17148	47492	8876	778	29382
69 WHOLESALE, RETAIL TRADE	84308	6760	18005	3255	32019	76970	7130	2533	32938
70 FINANCE, INSURANCE	1593	170	352	93	680	2228	164	55	631
71 REAL ESTATE, RENTAL	27158	1891	4348	2989	11112	33009	4426	811	12112
72 HOTELS, PERSONAL SERV.	34342	2034	6339	3812	16653	41988	5594	2034	15569
73 BUSINESS SERVICES	44288	4500	21468	2025	17023	63243	15856	988	77456
74 RESEARCH, DEVELOPMENT	0	0	0	0	0	0	0	0	0
75 AUTO. REPAIR, SERVICES	10536	559	1506	748	4369	10724	1720	369	3803
76 AMUSEMENTS	1454	146	290	125	498	2048	327	240	504
77 MED.,EDUC. SERVICES	193468	13372	21927	12347	59170	177500	26409	7265	44685
78 FEDERAL GOVT. ENTERPRISE	14763	1244	3690	607	4349	15436	1843	377	4710
79 STATE, LOCAL GOVT. ENT.	32069	1497	7619	5288	11901	38859	5462	1830	10902
80 IMPORTS	0	0	0	0	0	0	0	0	0
81 BUS.TRAVEL, ENT., GIFTS.	10308	870	2259	1071	4291	12022	1963	413	6017
82 OFFICE SUPPLIES	4562	300	650	503	2017	4447	726	200	1587
83 SCRAP, USED GOODS									
84 GOVERNMENT INDUSTRY	551373	100058	383377	62841	252243	1585291	236975	17833	996628
85 REST OF WORLD INDUSTRY	0	0	0	0	0	0	0	0	0
86 HOUSEHOLD INDUSTRY	0	0	0	0	0	0	0	0	0
87 INVENTORY VALUATION ADJ.	0	0	0	0	0	0	0	0	0
88 STATE TOTAL	3025231	268650	868367	164809	1969519	5868685	547611	141717	2234068

TABLE B-12

STATE ESTIMATES OF 1960
FEDERAL GOVERNMENT PURCHASES
(THOUSANDS OF 1958 DOLLARS)

INDUSTRY TITLE	46 WASHINGTON	47 WEST VIRGINIA	48 WISCONSIN	49 WYOMING	50 ALASKA	51 HAWAII	52 NO STATE ALLOCATION	53 NATIONAL TOTAL
1 LIVESTOCK, PRDTS.	152	28	363	205	1	31	0	18004
2 OTHER AGRICULTURE PRDTS.	615	0	174	42	0	0	0	36996
3 FORESTRY, FISHERIES	-59378	-737	-401	-1262	-3729	0	0	-355001
4 AGRI.,FORES.,FISH. SERV.	4152	2061	2272	437	1685	1031	0	231003
5 IRON, FERRO. ORES MINING	0	0	0	0	0	0	0	0
6 NONFERROUS ORES MINING	3307	0	1557	5221	763	0	0	409002
7 COAL MINING	0	8358	0	46	47	0	0	26000
8 CRUDE PETRO.,NATURAL GAS	0	0	0	0	0	0	0	0
9 STONE, CLAY MINING	0	0	0	0	0	0	0	0
10 CHEM.,FERT. MIN. MINING	0	0	0	0	0	0	0	0
11 NEW CONSTRUCTION	248697	93502	52172	66670	143654	55556	0	7326023
12 MAINT., REPAIR CONSTR.	66502	11671	23275	6740	31421	42456	0	2668015
13 ORDNANCE, ACCESSORIES	16269	42162	119272	64	219	2987	0	5314043
14 FOOD, KINDRED PRDTS.	11936	3271	23155	490	1021	8679	0	702002
15 TOBACCO MANUFACTURES	0	27	0	0	0	0	0	3998
16 FABRICS	118	62	82	0	0	0	0	101999
17 TEXTILE PRDTS.	0	0	187	0	0	0	0	12001
18 APPAREL	505	562	1187	0	0	304	0	153000
19 MISC. TEXTILE PRDTS.	1834	958	894	0	0	449	0	245000
20 LUMBER, WOOD PRDTS.	-3414	92	564	-54	-345	37	0	-13994
21 WOODEN CONTAINERS	169	40	417	0	0	0	0	16999
22 HOUSEHOLD FURNITURE	52	16	88	0	0	26	0	9999
23 OTHER FURNITURE	2304	1141	5311	313	513	420	0	192002
24 PAPER, ALLIED PRDTS.	5826	508	9703	230	837	383	0	177001
25 PAPERBOARD CONTAINERS	461	134	1083	38	70	128	0	48998
26 PRINTING, PUBLISHING	2416	1046	4879	266	512	776	0	201999
27 CHEMICALS,SELECT. PRDTS.	3919	48366	7241	1061	512	63	0	1111005
28 PLASTICS, SYNTHETICS	83	2097	400	0	0	0	0	41998
29 DRUGS, COSMETICS	530	558	8080	0	0	0	0	679002
30 PAINT, ALLIED PRDTS.	212	0	253	0	0	0	0	19003
31 PETROLEUM, RELATED INDS.	12406	4100	1402	10104	4902	1499	0	1042010
32 RUBBER, MISC. PLASTICS	56	115	3450	0	0	0	0	100997
33 LEATHER TANNING, PRDTS.	0	2	30	0	0	1	0	1000
34 FOOTWEAR, LEATHER PRDTS.	18	68	897	0	0	17	0	30000
35 GLASS, GLASS PRDTS.	0	0	0	0	0	0	0	0
36 STONE, CLAY PRDTS.	222	83	215	26	40	46	0	12004
37 PRIMARY IRON, STEEL MFR.	2861	2925	5050	115	0	254	0	197003
38 PRIMARY NONFERROUS MFR.	9266	2059	1870	0	0	38	0	189004

39	METAL CONTAINERS	364	186	1223	0	0	99	0	24002
40	FABRICATED METAL PRDTS.	6209	1606	9328	70	0	286	0	387001
41	SCREW MACH. PRDTS., ETC.	196	1475	6046	0	0	22	0	223003
42	OTHER FAB. METAL PRDTS.	1722	6098	3957	0	0	69	0	315001
43	ENGINES, TURBINES	1701	335	40728	151	1383	435	0	386001
44	FARM MACH., EQUIP.	406	243	5823	34	63	46	0	59994
45	CONSTRUC. MACH., EQUIP.	571	355	7443	0	0	0	0	183003
46	MATERIAL HANDLING MACH.	12331	170	2732	0	0	42	0	168000
47	METALWORKING MACHINERY	848	551	9773	0	19	1045	0	324000
48	SPECIAL MACH., EQUIP.	752	0	3171	0	2	164	0	59999
49	GENERAL MACH., EQUIP.	315	35	24463	35	0	0	0	280005
50	MACHINE SHOP PRDTS.	617	122	1582	0	7	317	0	60999
51	OFFICE, COMPUT. MACHINES	6230	2745	12979	0	15	924	0	962001
52	SERVICE IND. MACHINES	347	141	5786	0	845	0	0	117000
53	ELECT. TRANSMISS. EQUIP.	3627	4573	26344	0	1547	0	0	473004
54	HOUSEHOLD APPLIANCES	69	0	2076	0	0	0	0	48998
55	ELECTRIC LIGHTING EQUIP.	9	71	5	0	0	0	0	1002
56	RADIO, TV, ETC., EQUIP.	18565	0	30473	0	0	0	0	6469025
57	ELECTRONIC COMPONENTS	363	1020	2366	0	0	2262	0	610999
58	MISC. ELECTRICAL MACH.	383	0	5326	0	0	0	0	183004
59	MOTOR VEHICLES, EQUIP.	2389	628	34697	46	310	80	0	843997
60	AIRCRAFT, PARTS	488161	1900	17296	1707	10961	3410	0	8896025
61	OTHER TRANSPORT. EQUIP.	22946	1850	13974	0	0	2870	0	1045003
62	PROFESS., SCIEN. INSTRU.	1280	3352	10151	0	0	0	0	968997
63	MEDICAL, PHOTO. EQUIP.	695	1258	461	0	0	0	0	323999
64	MISC. MANUFACTURING	2595	451	1980	256	431	355	0	116000
65	TRANSPORT., WAREHOUSING	33405	11117	38198	2045	6019	14457	0	2249011
66	COMMUNICA.,EXC. BRDCAST.	16215	4348	5067	2234	6945	8239	0	774005
67	RADIO, TV BROADCASTING							0	0
68	ELEC.,GAS,WATER,SAN.SER.	10543	4051	8203	2342	6785	7887	0	758006
69	WHOLESALE, RETAIL TRADE	21245	9022	31756	1751	1981	5254	0	1555002
70	FINANCE, INSURANCE	498	177	678	49	38	148	0	37004
71	REAL ESTATE, RENTAL	11665	4069	8534	1479	3393	4148	0	619004
72	HOTELS, PERSONAL SERV.	13493	4675	11997	2373	5110	4776	0	823001
73	BUSINESS SERVICES	29315	2581	7920	1337	15782	22874	0	1270000
74	RESEARCH, DEVELOPMENT	0	0	0	0	0	0	931000	931000
75	AUTO. REPAIR, SERVICES	3763	1008	2740	384	1273	939	0	224000
76	AMUSEMENTS	803	224	692	76	58	402	0	55003
77	MED.,EDUC. SERVICES	52580	14128	51779	3905	10467	15442	0	3417020
78	FEDERAL GOVT. ENTERPRISE	3789	1101	2456	260	1225	2281	0	258000
79	STATE, LOCAL GOVT. ENT.	13507	3247	12374	2569	4953	3492	0	720003
80	IMPORTS	0	0	0	0	0	0	4228000	4228000
81	BUS.TRAVEL, ENT., GIFTS.	0	0	0	0	0	0	0	0
82	OFFICE SUPPLIES	4687	1441	2783	578	1393	1343	0	233003
83	SCRAP, USED GOODS	1809	716	1379	264	484	289	0	99003
84	GOVERNMENT INDUSTRY	374667	41986	114998	38536	236736	367896	2206700	22067000
85	REST OF WORLD INDUSTRY	0	0	0	0	0	0	-495000	-495000
86	HOUSEHOLD INDUSTRY	0	0	0	0	0	0	0	0
87	INVENTORY VALUATION ADJ.	0	0	0	0	0	0	0	0
88	STATE TOTAL	1497779	358331	856869	154093	498976	587514	6870700	84300242

Bibliography*

1. American Petroleum Institute. *Petroleum Facts and Figures, 1967.* New York: 1967.
2. Anderson, Carolyn W., and McMillan, Douglas W. "State Estimates of Gross Private Domestic Investment, 1947, 1958, 1963." EDA Report No. 11 (Harvard Economic Research Project), August 1968.
3. Association of American Railroads. Bureau of Railway Economics. *Yearbook of Railroad Facts, 1966.* Washington, D.C.: 1966.
4. ———. Bureau of Railway Economics. *Yearbook of Railroad Facts, 1967.* Washington, D.C.: 1967.
5. Berner, Richard B. "State Estimates of Net Purchases of Goods and Services by State and Local Governments, 1947, 1958, 1963." EDA Report No. 12 (Harvard Economic Research Project), August 1968.
6. Bretzfelder, Robert B., Dallavalle, Q. Francis, and Hirschberg, David A. "Personal Income, 1968, and Disposable Income, 1929–68, by States and Regions." *Survey of Current Business* 49, no. 4 (April 1969): 16–32.
7. Buechner, William R. "State Estimates of Exports from the United States, 1947, 1958, 1963." EDA Report No. 9 (Harvard Economic Research Project), August 1968.
8. Carlsson, Bo, and Grubb, Norton. "State Estimates of Federal Government Purchases, 1947, 1958, 1963." EDA Report No. 13 (Harvard Economic Research Project), August 1968.
9. Dominion Bureau of Statistics. *Travel Between Canada and Other Countries.* Ottawa, Ontario: 1969.
10. [Jack] Faucett Associates, Inc. "Capital Flow and Capital Expenditure Matrices—1963." Unpublished worksheets.
11. ———. "Capital Stocks Series, by 3-Digit SIC for Manufacturing Sectors, and by IO for Non-Manufacturing Sectors, in Constant and Current Dollars." Data prepared for the Executive Office of the President, Office of Emergency Planning, National Resource Analysis Center, Resource Evaluation Division. Unpublished, 1969.
12. ———. "Development of a Matrix of Interindustry Transactions in Capital Goods in 1963." Appendix D. Prepared for the Bureau of Labor Statistics, U.S. Department of Labor. Unpublished, 1966.
13. ———. "Measures of 1947, 1958, and 1963 Output, Organized by Input-Output Sector and Within Input-Output Sector by State, in Current Dollars for Input-Output Sectors 1–79, 84, and 86." Unpublished worksheets.

---

*Material published by the U.S. Government Printing Office, Washington, D.C. 20402, is cited as: GPO, [date].

14. [Jack] Faucett Associates, Inc. "Output and Employment Estimates for IO Sectors, 1958–1966, by Quarters." Prepared for the U.S. Department of the Army, Corps of Engineers. Unpublished, June 1967 (revised December 1967).

15. ——. "Private Residential Construction—1958 (based on data on the value of construction contracts from F. W. Dodge Co., McGraw-Hill, Inc., New York) Unpublished worksheets.

16. ——. "Projections of State Output by Input-Output Industry." Unpublished worksheets.

17. ——. "Total Construction by State—1958, based on data on the value of construction contracts from F. W. Dodge Co., McGraw-Hill, Inc., New York." Unpublished worksheets

18. ——. "Total Construction by State—1963 (based on data on construction permits from U.S. Department of Commerce, Bureau of the Census)." Unpublished worksheets.

19. Federal Communications Commission. *Common Carrier Statistics, 1967.* GPO, 1969.

20. Federal Deposit Insurance Corporation. *Summary of Accounts and Deposits in All Commercial Banks, June 29, 1968.* Washington, D.C.: 1969.

21. ——. *Summary of Accounts and Deposits in All Mutual Savings Banks, June 29, 1968.* Washington, D.C.: 1969.

22. Federal Home Loan Bank Board. *Combined Financial Statements, 1968.* Washington, D.C.: 1969.

23. Frumkin, Norman. "Construction Activity in the 1958 Input-Output Study." *Survey of Current Business,* 45, no. 5 (May 1965): 13–24.

24. ——. "Direct Requirements Per Dollar of Selected Type of New Construction and Maintenance and Repair Construction, 1958 (producers' prices)." Washington, D.C. Unpublished table, 1969.

25. General Services Administration. "Construction Expenditure Data." Unpublished worksheets.

26. ——.*Statistical Supplement, Stockpile Report to the Congress, January–June 1969, July–December 1969.* Prepared for the Executive Office of Emergency Planning, Washington, D.C.: 1970.

27. Henson, Mary F. "Trends in the Income of Families and Persons in the United States, 1947–1964." Technical Paper No. 17. Prepared for the Population Division, Bureau of the Census, U.S. Department of Commerce. GPO, 1967.

28. "Hospital Statistics, Statistical Tables." *Hospitals, Journal of the American Hospital Association,* Guide Issue—Part 2, Vol. 41, no. 15 (August 1, 1967): 452–480.

29. Hutchins, Clayton D., and Barr, Richard H. *Statistics of State School Systems, 1965–66.* Prepared for the National Center for Educational Statistics, Office of Education, U.S. Department of Health, Education, and Welfare. GPO, 1968.

—— Jack Faucett Associates, Inc. See entries 10 through 18.

30. King, Pamela M. "State Estimates of Purchases by the New Construction Industry, 1947, 1958, 1963." EDA Report No. 10 (Harvard Economic Research Project), August 1968.

31. L'Esperance, W. L. and others. "Gross State Product and an Econometric Model of a State." *Journal of the American Statistical Association,* 64, no. 327 (September 1969).

32. Miller, Etienne H. "Foreign Earnings from U.S. Travelers in 1968 Decline Slightly to $3.9 Billion." *Survey of Current Business* 49, no. 6 (June 1969): 17–20.

33. ——. "Foreign Travel Boom Continued in 1963." *Survey of Current Business* 44, no. 6 (June 1964): 22–26.

34. ——. "Foreign Travel Payments Continue to Rise in 1965." *Survey of Current Business* 46, no. 6 (June 1966): 15–17.

35. ——. "Foreign Travel Payments Hit New High in 1964." *Survey of Current Business* 45, no. 6 (June 1965): 25–29.

36. ——. "Foreign Travel Spending Up Sharply in 1962 After Pause in 1961." *Survey of Current Business* 43, no. 6 (June 1963): 27–32.

37. ——. "U.S. Residents Spent $4 Billion on Foreign Travel Last Year." *Survey of Current Business* 47, no. 6 (June 1967): 13–16.

38. ——. "U.S. Spending for Foreign Travel Totaled $4-3/4 Billion in 1967." *Survey of Current Business* 48, no. 6 (June 1968): 14–17.

39. Mushkin, Selma J. *Health and Hospital Expenditures of State and Local Governments: 1970 Projections.* Chicago: The Council of State Governments, 1966.

40. Mushkin, Selma J., and Harris, Robert. *Financing Public Welfare: 1970 Projections.* Chicago: The Council of State Governments, 1965.

41. ——. *Transportation Outlays of States and Localities: Projections to 1970.* Chicago: The Council of State Governments, 1965.

42. Mushkin, Selma J., and McLoone, Eugene P. *Local School Expenditures: 1970 Projections.* Chicago: The Council of State Governments, 1965.

43. ——. *Public Spending for Higher Education, 1970.* Chicago: The Council of State Governments, 1965.

44. Myers, Edward T. "Transit—City by City." *Modern Railroads* 23, no. 4 (April 1968): 83–84.

45. National Aeronautics and Space Administration. Staff Operations Division. Procurement Office. *Annual Procurement Report, Fiscal Year 1967.* Washington, D.C.: 1967.

46. ——. *Annual Procurement Report, Fiscal Year 1968.* Washington, D.C.: 1968.

47. ——. "Construction Expenditure Data." Unpublished worksheets.

48. National Planning Association. Center for Economic Projections. *NPA Methodology for Long-Term National Economic Projections.* National Economic Projections Services, Report No. 69-N-1. Washington, D.C.: 1969.

49. ——. *Projections to 1975, 1980, and 1985 of Population, Income, and Industry Employment.* Regional Economic Projections Series, Report No. 68-R-1. Washington, D.C.: 1969.

50. National Science Foundation. Office of Economic and Manpower Studies. *Federal Funds for Research, Development, and Other Scientific Activities, Fiscal Years 1968, 1969, and 1970.* Surveys of Science Resources Series, Vol. XVIII, NSF 69–31. Washington, D.C.: 1969.

51. ——. *Geographic Distribution of Federal Funds for Research and Develop-*

ment, Fiscal Year 1965. Surveys of Science Resources Series, NSF 67–8. Washington, D.C.: 1967.

52. Niemi, Albert William, Jr. "Gross State Product and Productivity, 1948–1965." Unpublished Ph.D. dissertation, University of Connecticut, 1969.

53. Ono, Mitsuo. "A Graphic Technique for Projecting Family Income Size Distribution." American Statistical Association Proceedings of the Social Statistics Section (August 1969): 298–301.

54. Polenske, Karen R. "A Multiregional Input-Output Model for the United States." EDA Report No. 21 (Harvard Economic Research Project), December 1970.

55. Polenske, Karen R.; Anderson, Carolyn W.; and Shirley, Mary M. "A Guide for Users of the U.S. Multiregional Input-Output Model." Prepared for the Office of Economics and Systems Analysis, U.S. Department of Transportation, June 1972.

56. Polenske, Karen R., and Smith, James F. "Alignment of 1960 BLS Consumer Expenditure Categories with the 80-Order OBE Input-Output Industrial Classification." EDA Report No. 5 (Harvard Economic Research Project), February 1968.

57. Polenske, Karen R., and Whiston, Isabelle B. "State Estimates of Personal Consumption Expenditures, 1947, 1958, 1963, Scheme II." EDA Report No. 14 (Harvard Economic Research Project), August 1968.

58. Polenske, Karen R., and others. *State Estimates of the Gross National Product, 1947, 1958, 1963.* Lexington: Lexington Books, D.C. Heath and Company, 1972.

59. Rafuse, Robert W., Jr. *Water Supply and Sanitation Expenditures of State and Local Governments: Projections to 1970.* Chicago: The Council of State Governments, 1966.

60. Rodgers, John M. *State Estimates of Outputs, Employment, and Payrolls, 1947, 1958, 1963.* Lexington: Lexington Books, D.C. Heath and Company, 1972.

61. Schecter, Henry B. "Estimates of Housing Requirements for the Coming Decade." Paper prepared for the Annual Meeting of the Federal Statistics Users' Conference, Washington, D.C.: November 20, 1969.

62. Tennessee Valley Authority. "Construction Data for 1970." Unpublished worksheets.

63. Texas Eastern Transmission Corporation. *Competition and Growth in American Energy Markets, 1947-1985.* Houston: 1968.

64. U.S. Atomic Energy Commission. *1969 Financial Report.* GPO, 1969.

65. U.S. Bureau of the Budget, Executive Office of the President. *The Budget of the United States Government, 1970–Appendix.* GPO, 1969.

66. U.S. Department of Agriculture. *Agricultural Statistics, 1969.* GPO, 1969.

67. ——. Economic Research Service. *Farm Income Situation.* Washington, D.C.: 1969.

68. U.S. Department of the Army. Corps of Engineers. *Waterborne Commerce of the United States, 1963.* Washington, D.C.: 1965.

69. U.S. Department of Commerce. Bureau of the Census. *Annual Survey of Manufactures, 1966.* GPO, 1969.

70. U.S. Department of Commerce. Bureau of the Census. *Census of Business, 1963*, Vol. I, *Retail Trade–Summary Statistics;* Vol. II, *Retail Trade–Area Statistics;* Vol. VI, *Selected Services–Summary Statistics;* Vol. VII, *Selected Services–Area Statistics.* GPO, 1965.

71. ——. *Census of Governments, 1957*, Vol. III, no. 5, *Compendium of Government Finances.* GPO, 1959.

72. ——. *Census of Governments, 1962*, Vol. IV, no. 4. *Compendium of Government Finances;* Vol. VI, *Historical Statistics of Governmental Finances and Employment.* GPO, 1964.

73. ——. *Census of Governments, 1967*, Vol. IV, *Compendium of Government Finances;* Vol. VI, *Historical Statistics on Governmental Finances and Employment.* GPO, 1969.

74. ——. *Census of Transportation, 1967.* Vol. I, *National Travel Survey.* GPO, 1969.

75. ——. *Compendium of State Government Finances in 1957* (State Finances, 1957, no. 2). GPO, 1958.

76. ——. *Compendium of State Government Finances in 1958* (State Finances, 1958, no. 2). GPO, 1960.

77. ——. *Compendium of State Government Finances in 1959* (State Finances, 1959, no. 2). GPO, 1960.

78. ——. *Compendium of State Government Finances in 1960* (State Finances, 1960, no. 2). GPO, 1961.

79. ——. *Compendium of State Government Finances in 1961* (State Finances, 1961, no. 2). GPO, 1962.

80. ——. *Compendium of State Government Finances in 1962* (State Finances, 1962, no. 2). GPO, 1963.

81. ——. *Compendium of State Government Finances in 1963* (State Finances, 1963, no. 2). GPO, 1964.

82. ——. *Compendium of State Government Finances in 1964* (State Finances, 1964, no. 2). GPO, 1965.

83. ——. *Compendium of State Government Finances in 1965.* Series GF, no. 4. GPO, 1966.

84. ——. *County Business Patterns, 1967.* GPO, 1968.

85. ——. "Estimates of the Civilian Population of States by Broad Age Groups, Hawaii and Puerto Rico, July 1, 1957." *Current Population Reports.* Series P–25, no. 172. GPO, 1958.

86. ——. "Estimates of the Civilian Population of States by Broad Age Groups, and Selected Outlying Areas, July 1, 1958." *Current Population Reports.* Series P–25, no. 214. GPO, 1959.

87. ——. "Estimates of the Population of States by Age, 1960 to 1966, with Provisional Estimates for July 1, 1967." *Current Population Reports.* Series P–25, no. 384. GPO, 1968.

88. ——. "Estimates of the Population of States, by Age, 1965 to 1967, with Provisional Estimates for July 1, 1968." *Current Population Reports.* Series P–25, no. 420. GPO, 1969.

89. ——. "Estimates of the Population of States, July 1, 1968 and 1969." *Current Population Reports.* Series P–25, no. 436. GPO, 1970.

90. U.S. Department of Commerce. Bureau of the Census. "Estimates of the Population of States, July 1, 1966, with Provisional Estimates for July 1, 1967." *Current Population Reports.* Series P–25, no. 380. GPO, 1967.

91. ——. "Estimates of the Population of States, July 1, 1967, with Provisional Estimates for July 1, 1968." *Current Population Reports.* Series P–25, no. 414. GPO, 1969.

92. ——. *Governmental Finances in 1958.* Governmental Finances Series G-GF58, no. 2. GPO, 1959.

93. ——. *Governmental Finances in 1959.* Governmental Finances Series G-GF59, no. 2. GPO, 1960.

94. ——. *Governmental Finances in 1960.* Governmental Finances Series G-GF60, No. 2. GPO, 1961.

95. ——. *Governmental Finances in 1961.* Governmental Finances Series G-GF61, no. 2. GPO, 1962.

96. ——. *Governmental Finances in 1963.* Governmental Finances Series G-GF63, no. 2. GPO, 1964.

97. ——. *Governmental Finances in 1963–1964.* Governmental Finances Series G-GF64, no. 1. GPO, 1965.

98. ——. *Governmental Finances in 1964–1965.* Governmental Finances Series GF, no. 6. GPO, 1966.

99. ——. *Governmental Finances in 1965–1966.* Governmental Finances Series GF, no. 13. GPO, 1967.

100. ——. *Governmental Finances in 1967–1968.* Governmental Finances Series GF68, no. 6. GPO, 1969.

101. ——. *Highlights of the U.S. Export and Import Trade.* Report FT-990. GPO, December 1969.

102. ——. *Housing Construction Statistics 1889–1964.* GPO, 1966.

103. ——. "Projections of the Number of Households and Families: 1967 to 1985." *Current Population Reports.* Series P–25, no. 394. GPO, 1968.

104. ——. "Projections of the Number of Households, by States: July 1, 1970, and 1975." *Current Population Reports.* Series P–25, no. 387. GPO, 1968.

105. ——. "Projections of the United States, by Age, Sex, and Color, to 1990, with Extensions of Population by Age and Sex to 2015." *Current Population Reports.* Series P–25, no. 381. GPO, 1967.

106. ——. *Public Employment in 1966.* Government Employment Series GE, no. 4. GPO, 1967.

107. ——. "Revised Estimates of the Population of States and Components of Population Change, 1950 to 1960." *Current Population Reports.* Series P–25, no. 304. GPO, 1965.

108. ——. "Revised Projections of the Population of States, 1970 to 1985." *Current Population Reports.* Series P–25, no. 375. GPO, 1967.

109. ——. "Shipments of Defense-Oriented Industries, 1966." In *Current Industrial Reports* MA–173(66)–1. GPO, 1968.

110. ——. "Shipments of Defense-Oriented Industries in Large Standard Metropolitan Statistical Areas, 1966 and 1967 (Preliminary)." In *Current Industrial Reports* MA–175(67)–1. GPO, 1968.

111. ——. "Shipments of Defense-Oriented Industries, 1967." In *Current Industrial Reports* MA–175(67)–2. GPO, 1969.

112. U.S. Department of Commerce, Bureau of the Census. *State Government Finances in 1966.* Governmental Finances Series GF, no. 11. GPO, 1967.

113. ——. *State Government Finances in 1967.* Governmental Finances Series GF67, no. 1. GPO, 1968.

114. ——. *State Government Finances in 1968.* Governmental Finances Series GF68, no. 3. GPO, 1969.

115. ——. *Statistical Abstract of the United States, 1962.* GPO, 1962.

116. ——. *Statistical Abstract of the United States, 1963.* GPO, 1963.

117. ——. *Statistical Abstract of the United States, 1964.* GPO, 1964.

118. ——. *Statistical Abstract of the United States, 1965.* GPO, 1965.

119. ——. *Statistical Abstract of the United States, 1966.* GPO, 1966.

120. ——. *Statistical Abstract of the United States, 1967.* GPO, 1967.

121. ——. *Statistical Abstract of the United States, 1968.* GPO, 1968.

122. ——. *Statistical Abstract of the United States, 1969.* GPO, 1969.

123. ——. *U.S. Census of Population, 1960.* Vol. I, *Characteristics of the Population.* GPO, 1963.

124. ——. *U.S. Exports—World Area, Country Schedule By Commodity Groupings, and Method of Transportation.* (Revised through December 1968 Statistics.) Report FT–455. 1968 Annual. GPO, July 1969.

125. ——. "Value of New Construction Put in Place, 1946–1963, Revised." *Construction Reports—*Series C30. GPO, 1964.

126. ——. "Value of New Construction Put in Place, 1962–1966." *Construction Reports—*Series C30–66S. GPO, 1967.

127. U.S. Department of Commerce. Business and Defense Services Administration. *Construction Statistics 1915–1964, A Supplement to Construction Review.* GPO, 1966.

128. ——. "Statistical Series." *Construction Review* 15, no. 11 (November 1969): 14–59.

129. U.S. Department of Commerce, Office of Business Economics. "Breakdown of Imputations for Food, Clothing, and Housing Furnished in Kind, 1968, by Type and by Occupational Group." Unpublished worksheets, 1969.

130. ——. "Breakdown of Imputations for Services Provided Without Financial Intermediaries, 1968, by Type of Financial Institutions." Unpublished worksheets, 1969.

131. ——. "Consumer Expenditures Data for 1968." Unpublished worksheets.

132. ——. "Input-Output Structure of the U.S. Economy: 1963." *Survey of Current Business* 49, no. 11 (November 1969): 16–47.

133. ——. *National Income, 1954 Edition. A Supplement to the Survey of Current Business.* GPO, 1954.

134. ——. *The National Income and Product Accounts of the United States, 1929–1965· Statistical Tables.* GPO, 1966.

135. ——. *Survey of Current Business* 48, no. 9 (September 1968).

136. ——. *Survey of Current Business* 49, no. 11 (September 1969).

137. ——. *Survey of Current Business* 50, no. 3 (March 1970).

138. ——. "U.S. National Income and Product Accounts, 1963–66." *Survey of Current Business* 47, no. 7 (July 1967): 9–44.

139. U.S. Department of Commerce. Office of Business Economics. "U.S. National Income and Product Accounts, 1964–67." *Survey of Current Business* 48, no. 7 (July 1968): 15–51.

140. ——. "U.S. National Income and Product Accounts, 1965–68." *Survey of Current Business* 49, no. 7 (July 1969): 13–49.

141. U.S. Department of Defense. "Construction Data by State for 1970." Unpublished worksheets.

142. ——. Office of the Secretary of Defense. Directorate for Information Operations. "Defense Personnel and Total Population in the United States by State, as of 30 June 1969." Unpublished, 1969.

143. ——. "Military and Civilian Personnel in the Washington, D.C. Metropolitan Area, 30 June 1969." Unpublished, 1969.

144. ——. "Military and Civilian Personnel by Washington, D.C. Metropolitan and Other Areas in the States of Maryland and Virginia, as of 30 June 1969." Unpublished, 1969.

145. ——. Directorate for Statistical Services. *Military Prime Contract Awards by Region and State, Fiscal Years 1966, 1967, 1968.* Washington, D.C.: 1968.

146. ——. *Military Prime Contract Awards by Service Category and Federal Supply Classification, Fiscal Years 1965, 1966, 1967, and 1968.* Washington, D.C.: 1968.

147. U.S. Department of Health, Education, and Welfare. National Center for Educational Statistics. *Projections of Educational Statistics to 1978–79.* GPO, 1970.

148. ——. *Statistics of Non-public Elementary and Secondary Schools, 1965–66.* GPO, 1968.

149. U.S. Department of Health, Education, and Welfare. Social Security Administration. Bureau of Federal Credit Unions. *Annual Report of the Bureau of Federal Credit Unions,* 1968. Washington, D.C.: 1969.

150. ——. *State-Chartered Credit Unions, 1968.* Washington, D.C.: 1969.

151. U.S. Department of Health, Education, and Welfare. Social Security Administration. Office of Research and Statistics. *Social Security Household Worker Statistics, 1964. Household Workers and Their Employers Under Old-Age, Survivors, Disability, and Health Insurance.* Washington, D.C.: 1968.

152. U.S. Department of the Interior. Bonneville Power Administration. "Construction Data by State." Unpublished worksheets.

153. U.S. Department of the Interior. Bureau of Mines. *Minerals Yearbook, 1967.* Vols. I–III. GPO, 1968.

154. U.S. Department of the Interior. Bureau of Reclamation. "Construction Data by State." Unpublished worksheets.

155. U.S. Department of Labor. Bureau of Labor Statistics. "Consumer Expenditures and Income, Urban Places in the Southern Region, 1960–61." Supplement 3- Part A to BLS Report 237–36, *Survey of Consumer Expenditures, 1960–61.* Washington, D.C.: 1964.

156. ——. Division of Economic Growth. "Final Demand by IO Sector for Selected Years and Projected 1980 (Millions of 1958 Dollars at Producers' Values)." Unpublished worksheets, 1970.

157. U.S. Department of Labor. Bureau of Labor Statistics. "Final Demand: Major Components and Total by IO Sector, 3% Basic Model (in Millions of 1958 Dollars at Producers' Prices) 1970 and 1980." Unpublished worksheets, 1969.

158. ——. *Patterns of U.S. Economic Growth.* BLS Bulletin No. 1672. GPO, 1970.

159. ——. "Projection Data for 1970 and 1980 State and Local Government Expenditures." Unpublished worksheets.

160. ——. *Projections 1970: Interindustry Relationships, Potential Demand, Employment.* BLS Bulletin No. 1536. GPO, 1966.

161. ——. "Projections for 1970 and 1980." Unpublished worksheets.

162. ——. *Projections of the Post-Vietnam Economy, 1975.* BLS Bulletin No. 1733. GPO, 1972.

163. ——. "Residential Construction for 1980, 4% Basic Model." Unpublished, 1969.

164. ——. "State and Local Government Purchases of Goods and Services, 3% Basic Model (in Millions of 1958 Dollars) 1970 and 1980, by Function and by Object Classification." Unpublished worksheets, 1969.

165. ——. "State and Local Government Purchases by IO Sector and Major Functions for 1970 in Constant Dollars at Producers' Value, 4% Basic Model." Unpublished worksheets, 1969.

166. U.S. Department of Transportation. Federal Highway Administration. "Highway Receipts and Disbursements, 1967–1970." News release, December 7, 1969.

167. ——. Bureau of Public Roads. *Highway Statistics, 1967.* GPO, 1968.

168. Wakefield, Joseph C. "Expanding Functions of State and Local Governments, 1965–1970." *Monthly Labor Review,* 90, no. 7 (July 1967): 9–14. 9–14

About the Author

Raymond C. Scheppach, Jr. is a senior economist at Jack Faucett Associates, a private research firm in Chevy Chase, Maryland. He received the B.A. in 1962 from the University of Maine and the M.A. and Ph.D. from the University of Connecticut in 1965 and 1970. In addition to supervising research projects at Jack Faucett Associates, Dr. Scheppach is a part-time instructor at Montgomery College, Rockville, Maryland. He is also an active member of the American Economic Association.